THE FUTURE

OF

VIOLENCE

THE FUTURE

OF

VIOLENCE

ROBOTS AND GERMS, HACKERS AND DRONES

Confronting A New Age of Threat

BENJAMIN WITTES

&

GABRIELLA BLUM

BASIC BOOKS

A Member of the Perseus Books Group

New York

Published by Basic Books,
A Member of the Perseus Books Group

Book design by Cynthia Young

Library of Congress Cataloging-in-Publication Data

Wittes, Benjamin.
  The future of violence : robots and germs, hackers and drones—confronting a new age
  of threat / Benjamin Wittes & Gabriella Blum.
       pages cm.
    Includes bibliographical references and index.
    ISBN 978-0-465-08974-1 (hardback) — ISBN 978-0-465-05670-5 (e-book)   1. National
  security.   2. Security, International.   3. Internal security.   4. Technology—Moral and
  ethical aspects.   5. Information technology—Moral and ethical aspects.   6. Civil rights.
  7. Violence—Prevention.   8. Crime prevention.   I. Blum, Gabriella.   II. Title.
  UA10.5.W57 2015
  303.601'12—dc23
                                                                    2014035741

10 9 8 7 6 5 4 3 2 1

For Ruth Kartun-Blum,
Janet Wittes, and Robert Wittes

CONTENTS

INTRODUCTION

IMAGINE FOR A MOMENT that we changed one fact about the 2001 anthrax attacks, which killed five people and sickened seventeen others in the wake of September 11, 2001. The FBI's suspect in the case, Dr. Bruce Ivins—or whoever else may have been responsible for the attacks—was clearly not attempting to kill as many people as he possibly could. The anthrax-laced letters all either specifically identified their packages as carrying the bacteria or warned recipients to "TAKE PENACILIN [*sic*] NOW"—which is kind of like putting a big sign on a bomb and cartoonishly labeling it "BOMB." Moreover, using the US Postal Service to distribute the packages kept the anthrax spores in relatively contained spaces: postal-system buildings, the buildings of targeted entities, and the channels of postal distribution. Nevertheless, spore leakage caused illness and even death among some people outside the postal system.[1]

Now imagine that the objective of the attack had been to maximize casualties and that the attacker acted accordingly. Instead of mailing labeled packages to specific targets, suppose he had created a delivery system aimed at reaching the public at large. Using a real website called DIY Drones, which describes itself as the "largest community for amateur unmanned aerial vehicles [UAVs]," let us say that the attacker built a robotic distribution system to spread the spores over densely packed groups of people. DIY Drones is not a site for the high-tech weekend warrior. The do-it-yourselfers it serves are hobbyists, as the site's policies make clear. "This site is just about amateur and civilian use," DIY Drones declares, warning that it tolerates "no discussion of military applications of UAVs" and will report to authorities "any discussion of UAV use that we feel is potentially illegal or intended to do harm." Still, it is not hard to imagine that our bloodthirsty anthrax attacker would find irresistible a site devoted to helping individuals build devices "capable of both remotely controlled flight . . . and fully-autonomous flight, controlled by sensors, GPS, and onboard computers performing the functions of an autopilot." Without too much trouble or expense, much less a pilot's license, he could build himself a drone capable of flying over a crowded stadium and spraying spores invisibly into the air.[2]

If this sounds far-fetched, it should not. The technology in reality is not that complicated. In fact, our hypothetical attacker may well have overinvested in automation. He could probably obtain the same effect by releasing spores from the back of a truck in a crowded downtown area or by hand at the stadium. Nor is the idea of using small drones for domestic terrorism limited to the realm of speculation. In September 2011, the FBI arrested a US citizen named Rezwan Ferdaus, as the Justice Department put it, "in connection with his plot to damage or destroy the Pentagon and U.S. Capitol, using large, remote controlled aircraft filled with C-4 plastic explosives."[3]

Had the anthrax attacks played out in one of these counterfactual fashions, no one reading this book today would doubt the proposition that it is possible for an individual to have his own personal weapons-of-mass-destruction program. Nor would anyone doubt that destructive power once reserved to states is now the potential province of individuals. Nobody today would doubt that the range of actors that states—and individuals—must consider as potential strategic threats has broadened dramatically.

To demonstrate this, let us change one fact in the already terrifying case of Luis Mijangos, an illegal immigrant in Orange County, California, who in 2011 pleaded guilty to computer hacking and wiretapping and was sentenced to six years in prison. Mijangos tricked scores of women and teenage girls into downloading malware onto their computers. In addition to using the private financial information that he stole from their computers for garden-variety credit card fraud, Mijangos, according to court documents, "read victims' emails and [instant messages], watched them through their webcams, and listened to them through the microphones on their computers." He also used the webcams to take surreptitious images of his victims. Moreover, "he used [those] intimate images or videos of female victims he stole or captured to 'sextort' those victims, threatening to post those images/videos on the Internet unless the victims provided more to defendant; in at least one instance he followed through on his threat and publicly posted nude photos of a victim. He also tricked victims into creating pornographic images/videos by assuming the online identity of victims' boyfriends."[4] Mijangos also used the computers he controlled to spread his malware further, sending to people in his victims' address books instant messages that appeared to come from friends and inducing new victims to download his malware. FBI computer forensics specialists identified more than one hundred computers infected by Mijangos, used by roughly 230 individuals, at least 44 of them underage. Prosecutors conceded that a great many other victims probably remain unidentified.[5]

Mijangos represents the democratization of *1984* and the power to track, probe, and invade the privacy of others. These days, Little Brother can do it too. And Little Brother may well operate outside Oceania. Bad as the Mijangos case was, if we simply change Mijangos's location, it gets dramatically worse. Imagine for a moment that he had operated out of not California but Nigeria, home to a great deal of spamming and online fraud activity. In the real story, Mijangos could ultimately be stopped because FBI agents were able to visit his house, interview him, seize his computers, and mine their contents—and ultimately because they had jurisdiction to arrest him.[6] A great many countries in the world, however, have neither the will nor the means to monitor cybercrime, prosecute offenders, or extradite suspects to the United States. Had Mijangos been in one of these countries, his case would today illustrate not merely the extreme vulnerability of individuals in a modern networked world, but also the impunity with which we can be attacked from just about anywhere on the planet and by just about anyone. Ironically, while we tend to think of government investigative powers in the networked world as Big Brother–like threats to our privacy, the Mijangos tale also suggests how important the role of government authority can be in protecting values such as privacy in a world where lots of Little Brothers menace us from both within and outside the states in which we live.

Now, more futuristically, let us change one fact about the famous assassination of Alexander Litvinenko, a former officer of the Russian Federal Security Service, successor to the KGB. Litvinenko wrote two books in which he accused the Russian secret services of bombing Russian apartment buildings and engaging in other acts of terrorism in order to facilitate Vladimir Putin's ascent to power. Facing prosecution in Russia, he fled and received political asylum in the United Kingdom. On November 1, 2006, Litvinenko suddenly fell ill and was hospitalized. He died three weeks later. When the cause of death was confirmed to be polonium-210 poisoning, one doctor wrote in a medical journal that "for the medical community, Litvinenko's murder represents an ominous landmark: the beginning of an era of nuclear terrorism." Following the trail of polonium in and out of London, British officials identified as their main suspect a former officer of the Russian Federal Protective Service, Andrey Lugovoy, but failed to get him extradited from Russia. Lugovoy, who denied involvement, was later elected to the Duma, Russia's parliament, whose members enjoy immunity from prosecution.[7]

But let us imagine that instead of arriving in London with the polonium—and thus risking both handling the poison and leaving traces behind—Lugovoy, or whoever else may have wished Litvinenko dead, simply sent a spider-shaped miniature drone with lethal capabilities to target him. Insect-size drones are already in development in many robotics labs around the world, and like a great many other technological developments, they are likely to become more widely available, cheaper, smaller, easier to handle, and more capable. A few years from now, future assassins might sit comfortably in armchairs in Moscow, directing mini-drones to monitor the movements of future Litvinenkos and target them at opportune moments in London or Shanghai or Addis Ababa.

Governments, including the US government, already target their enemies abroad with lethal force using robots—mostly drones—that enable them not to risk their own forces. But what happens when individuals and small groups can do this too? How do you govern a world in which no one legal system—based, as legal systems are, on things like national borders, jurisdictional boundaries, and citizenship—can regulate interstate deployments of force by unaccountable actors?

Finally, imagine we changed one fact about the 2010 British Petroleum (BP) Gulf oil spill. Instead of the spill's having taken place as a consequence of an accidental explosion, let us pretend that it was the result of a premeditated attack. Perhaps a terrorist group hit the *Deepwater Horizon* drilling rig. In this scenario, the damage would be the same, with the oil flowing in the same volume. The only difference between this dark fantasy and the reality that unfolded in the summer of 2010 is volition: in the fantasy, someone meant to do it, transforming the oil spill from a mere disaster into the worst assault on the United States since September 11, 2001.

One thing that stands out in this counterfactual scenario is the US government's incapacity, despite its ability to project police force anywhere in the country and military force anywhere in the world, to defend effectively and swiftly against this particular attack, which took place against private infrastructure. During the BP spill, the federal government acted largely to coordinate a private-sector response. It had no capabilities of its own to stanch the flow of oil or to plug the well. Such capabilities, instead, lay in the hands of a private corporation, one of a select group of corporations that have proven enormously innovative in offshore oil drilling. These corporations have proven so inventive, in fact, that only they, and not the US federal government, have the technological and logistical capability to deal with the national security threats—accidental or malicious—that their very innovations can now bring about.

Place the lessons of all these changed scenarios alongside one another:

- Modern technology enables individuals to wield the destructive power of states.

- Individuals, including you personally, can potentially be attacked with impunity from anywhere in the world.

- Technology makes less relevant many of the traditional concepts around which our laws and political organization for security have evolved. National borders, jurisdictional boundaries, citizenship, and the distinctions between national and international, between act of war and crime, and between state and private action all offer divides less sharp than they used to.

- Our nation—and every nation—can face attack through channels controlled and operated not by governments but by the private sector and by means against which governments lack the ability to defend, making private actors pivotal to defense.

Strung together, these lessons succinctly describe the security future with which citizens and governments must now grapple.

Much of what we think we know about privacy, liberty, security, and threat is no longer true. Much of what we have been taught about what threatens us, about what protects us, and about the risks and benefits of state power versus individual empowerment is obsolete. In the conventional understanding, international security is a state-to-state affair; the relationships between privacy, liberty, and domestic order are matters between individuals and their governments; and civilian technologies in the hands of individuals have relatively little to do with the way we order either governance at home or international security. We built the state to mediate disputes among citizens and to protect them from outside attack. We gave it power to contend with other states and to ensure it could govern effectively. Because we feared that power, we imposed constraints on it. And we imagined its power and the security it was meant to provide as being in tension with the liberty we expected it to respect. We built walls around our countries with legal concepts such as jurisdiction. And for the most part, these intellectual, conceptual, and legal constructions have held up pretty well. Yes, we had to adjust in response to Al-Qaeda and other transnational nonstate actors. And yes, globalization has complicated the discussion. But the way we think about security—what it means, where it comes from, what threatens it, what protects it, and the relationship between individual and collective societal security—has remained remarkably stable.

In what follows, we mean to persuade you that this way of thinking is now out of date. Indeed, we argue that our debate about the fabric of security and its governance is based on dated assumptions about a technological world that no longer exists. In our new world, you can pose a threat to the security of every state and person on the planet—and each can also threaten you. In our new world, individuals, companies, and small groups have remarkable capabilities either to protect others or to make them more vulnerable. In our new world, not only do privacy and security not generally conflict, but they are often largely the same thing. And in our new world, state power represents a critical line of defense for individual freedom and privacy, even as the state itself may be losing its ability to serve its purpose as the ultimate guarantor of security to its citizens.

Driving this new environment is a mix of technological developments. There is the radical proliferation of both data about individuals and technologies of mass empowerment available to individuals. Notwithstanding Edward Snowden's spectacular revelations about the National Security Agency (NSA), the state's comparative advantage in collecting data, manipulating it, and exposing individuals to risks or protecting them from threats is actually eroding, as ever bigger companies occupying ever more powerful market positions take on data collection and analytics as their business cores. The miniaturization and automation of weapons further weakens national boundaries—as well as the front door to your house—as effective lines of defense. Biological research and biotechnology are progressing at an unprecedented pace, bringing great promise—and great danger—to human security all around the globe.

Our new environment of highly distributed threats and defenses has already changed our lives, and it will change them more in the years to come. It will change our sense of privacy, of safety, and of danger. It will change our relationships with corporations, governments, and individuals whom we have never met. It will change the way we govern our collective security and how we manage our personal safety. And it may lead us to ask questions about how we organize ourselves politically at the local, national, and international levels.

Today, each person needs to fear an exponentially higher number of people and entities than only a decade ago. The threats to your personal security now include not merely governments and corporations but also other individuals around the world: stalkers, identity thieves, scammers, spammers, frauds, competitors, and rivals—everyone and everything from the government of China to the NSA to Luis Mijangos. You can be attacked from anywhere—and by nearly anyone.

And so can countries. All countries now face a similar array of threats—a much vaster array than in only the very recent past. The inevitable greater reliance by the modern state on computerized systems for all important societal functions—ranging from national defense to electricity delivery and water distribution to transportation, banking, and just about everything else—makes the state and its inhabitants increasingly vulnerable to exploitation and attack. Edward Snowden and WikiLeaks can more broadly disseminate closely held government information, which is also far easier to steal; a much wider range of actors can hack into networked systems and exploit or damage the information they contain or the functions they control.

This point is not simply about cybersecurity. Technologies that put destructive power traditionally confined to states in the hands of small groups and individuals have proliferated remarkably far, as a general matter. That proliferation is accelerating at an awe-inspiring clip across a number of technological platforms—in particular, networked computers and biotechnology and, in the not-too-distant future, robotics and nanotechnology as well. The technologies in question, unlike the technologies associated with nuclear warfare, were developed not in a classified setting but in the public domain. And they are not simple technologies either. They are platform technologies—that is, technologies that facilitate generative creativity in their users to build and invent new things, new weapons, and new modes of attack. As these technologies become cheaper, more and more people have the ability to give expression to what resides in their hearts in the digital world, in the physical world, and in the microscopic coding of life itself. And as these technologies get cheaper, we become, as a global community, ever more dependent on them for our health, agriculture, communications, jobs, economic growth and development, and even our culture.

These dependencies make states enormously vulnerable. Just as you are more vulnerable today to attacks from an ever widening array of actors, so are the United States and every other country in the world. Whereas once only rival states could contemplate killing huge numbers of civilians with a drug-resistant illness or taking down another country's power grids, now governments must contemplate the possibility of ever smaller groupings of people undertaking what are traditionally understood as acts of war. The past few decades have seen an augmenting ability among relatively small, nonstate groups to wage asymmetric conflicts against even powerful states. The groups in question have been growing smaller, more diffuse, and more loosely knit, and technology is both facilitating that development and increasing these groups' ultimate lethality. The trend seems likely to continue and probably even to accelerate. It ultimately threatens to give every individual with a modest education and a certain level of technical proficiency the power to wreak potentially catastrophic damage. As a thought experiment, imagine a world composed of billions of people walking around with nuclear weapons in their pockets.

This problem is not entirely new—at least not conceptually. The mad scientist mwuh-huh-huhing to himself as he swirls a flask and promises, "Then I shall destroy the world!" is the stuff of old movies and cartoons. In literature, versions of the scientist creating disaster date back at least to Mary Shelley in the early nineteenth century. In some sense, it just reflects the old literary fear of people playing gods—Daedalus and Icarus and the Tower of Babel—recast for a more modern, scientific world. Along with literary works set in technologically sophisticated dystopias, the character of the technologically empowered madman represents one of the ways in which our society expresses its fears of rapidly evolving technology.

The fantasy's sudden plausibility, however, is new. Across a variety of technological platforms, individuals and small groups are now playing enhanced roles in the affairs of countries and regions—and those roles will only grow more strategically significant as technologies of mass empowerment develop further and penetrate more deeply.

At the same time, the very forces that are causing threats to multiply are also distributing defensive capacity and responsibility. Only recently, governments alone bore responsibility for protecting nations. Today it is possible to attack a country without ever confronting a government-owned or government-controlled facility. The data pipes into the United States, for example, are largely in private hands—so that the government no longer controls the very channels through which this country might face attack. This means that private actors—and not just BP—are uniquely positioned to defend against attacks and that private actors must now bear responsibility for some aspects of security. The more technology proliferates, the less exclusive the government's security capabilities—and therefore its security responsibilities—become.

Our new world, in short, is one of many-to-many threats and many-to-many defenses. While it is not yet literally the case, every individual, every group, every company, and every state will soon have the potential to threaten the security of—and have his, her, or its security threatened by—every other individual, group, company, and state. We are thus in a moment unlike any other in the history of the world, one in which distance does not protect you and in which you are at once a figure of great power and great vulnerability. It is a moment that challenges cherished ideas at the core of our political identities, that requires us to face new realities at once exciting and terrifying. The world of many-to-many threats and defenses is radically populist, a place in which the relative power of the state to that of the citizenry is reduced and in which we are unleashing the enormous creative potential associated with giving people the power to do great things. It threatens, however, to be Hobbesian as well—an environment of unaccountable freedom to do great harm, in which the very lack of accountability for the harms we do may spur some of us to do them. And it raises a giant question of governance: How does a state provide for its security in such a world? How does it organize its relationship with both the individual subject to its jurisdiction and the individual beyond its jurisdiction who nonetheless threatens its citizens or, indeed, the state itself? And how does a state negotiate its relationship with other states, all with equal claim to independence and sovereignty, as well as with those other states' citizens? We mean to address these questions in this book.

A CENTURY AGO, IN 1914, in the wake of the assassination of Austro-Hungarian archduke Franz Ferdinand, foreign affairs writer F. Cun-liffe-Owen looked for the bright side. While "it is only natural that one should be stricken with horror at the brutal and shocking assassination," he wrote in the *New York Sun*, "it is impossible to deny that [the archduke's] disappearance from the scene is calculated to diminish the tenseness of the [general European] situation and to make peace both within and without the dual Empire." The archduke was so universally regarded as a "disturbing factor and as committed to forceful and aggressive policies, that the news of his death is almost calculated to create a feeling of universal relief."[8]

For anyone presuming to speculate about the future of global security, this article by poor Cunliffe-Owen—and the many hundreds of others like it that, across time and subject matter, have gotten big questions spectacularly wrong—is a cautionary tale with a loud moral: predicting the future offers many more opportunities to look stupid than to look prescient. Even with a horizon of just a few weeks, Cunliffe-Owen managed to misinterpret the triggering event for World War I as one of those moments of sudden relaxation that lets us all breathe a little easier. He was not an idiot; he appears to have been a well-respected foreign policy analyst. And he was not the only one. In 1913, David Starr Jordan, then president of Stanford University, scoffed, "What shall we say of the Great War of Europe, ever threatening, ever impending, and which never comes? We shall say that it never will come." If people like these could fail to anticipate the coming few months within 180 degrees of accuracy, one should probably approach anticipating the broad security trends of the coming decades with a certain humility.[9]

So let us start by making clear that our aim in these pages is not to sound the alarm about inevitable catastrophic attacks using advanced technologies. Such events, to be sure, may well happen; indeed, they may prove a recurrent feature of the world we describe. But many people have long predicted the proliferation of catastrophic terrorist attacks employing widely available variations of weapons of mass destruction and harming thousands or millions of people—and thankfully, these attacks have not yet happened. We are not synthetic biologists, computer scientists, or robotics engineers, and we are not aiming to assess the inevitability or likely frequency of malicious exploitations of modern technology. Our concern, rather, is the general problem of how to govern so as to effectively ensure security in an environment of simultaneous individual empowerment and individual vulnerability.

As such, we advance a single very general prediction: that modern society has not yet exhausted the implications for security and liberty of the dissemination around the world of technologies that empower individuals and of information about individuals. We believe both that this proliferation trend will continue to accelerate across a growing number of technological platforms and that it will do so in a fashion that will further complicate the task of governance in the interests of security. As it does so, it will profoundly challenge the manner in which we currently think about issues of surveillance, civil liberties, security, threat, and governmental responsibility, power, and accountability.

It follows necessarily that a great deal of the United States' current discussion of the laws and policies that govern privacy, liberty, security, and safety both within our shores and across borders is out of date—or fast becoming so. And perhaps more importantly—and more tectonically—it follows as well that the liberal political theory that gave rise to our vision of the role of the state in providing security requires reconsideration, if only to ensure that the state can meet the challenges of our new technological environment.

An enormous literature has developed in the post-9/11 world on the effects of the rising power of nonstate actors on traditional dichotomies in our law and governance: between the public and the private, between war and crime, and between the domestic and the international. Much of this literature has emphasized the role of technology in the breakdown of these dichotomies. As the President's Review Group on Intelligence and Communications Technologies wrote in 2013 in response to the Snowden controversies, "The traditional distinction between foreign and domestic has become less clear. The distinction between military and civilian has also become less clear, now that the same communications devices, software, and networks are used both in war zones such as Iraq and Afghanistan and in the rest of the world. Similarly, the distinction between war and non-war is less clear, as the United States stays vigilant against daily cyber security attacks as well as other threats from abroad."[10] Some of this literature, particularly the work of Philip Bobbitt, author of two major works on the history of warfare, and John Robb, a theoretician of asymmetric conflict, has taken on directly the challenge to the modern state that our new security environment poses. We draw on all of these prior insights but add what we think are a few important twists.[11]

For starters, we are not narrowly concerned with the admittedly serious problem of terrorism. Rather, we focus on what we believe to be the somewhat broader essence of the security challenge that modern states and individuals alike now face: that the new world of many-to-many threats and defenses puts enormous power—for good and evil alike— in the hands of an unprecedented array of actors, making us all at once more powerful and more vulnerable. That power increasingly includes the power to attack—for whatever reason and by whatever type of actor—at great distance and with diminished accountability.

An honest focus on the world of many-to-many threats demands a look back at some basic premises of liberal society. In a world in which everyone plays a role in everyone else's equation of threats and defenses and national and individual security are hopelessly intertwined, old governance questions demand new answers. We have not yet, as a society, figured out how to redesign the relationships between citizens and their governments, among governments internationally, or among people themselves for the provision of basic security and freedom in a technologically changing environment. We have not yet given adequate thought to how afraid we are of the countless Little Brothers and Medium-Sized Brothers our technology is creating—and whether fear of all these lesser brethren ought to imply some role for their biggest sibling in keeping them all in check. It is time to start doing so, and in these pages we take a preliminary stab at suggesting how one might go about it.

In doing so, we also attempt to integrate several debates that seem to take place largely in stovepiped abstraction from one another, despite their being, in our judgment, flip sides of the same coin—or, more precisely, multiple sides of the same die. America today has a cybersecurity debate. It has a smaller biosecurity debate. A heated debate surrounds the use of drones in the war on terrorism and, to a lesser extent, in the civilian sector domestically. We have a rich debate over privacy and civil liberties. Yet there is far less overlap among these debates than there ought to be. Cybersecurity experts will talk about the novelty of their security arena and mention the facts that attacks can be hard to attribute, capacity to launch attacks has proliferated very far, and the costs of computing power keep falling. Go to a conference on biosecurity and you will hear all of the same themes—discussed with an equal sense of menace and novelty—but with reference to an entirely different set of technologies.[12] Debates about drones and targeted killings tend also to be constrained, often ignoring the impending proliferation of drones and other types of lethal robots far beyond the US government—or any government—and for uses far beyond counterterrorism. The contemporary American debate contrives to define privacy values as existing in tension with cybersecurity goals rather than seeing good security and strong government enforcement as essential protections for privacy. We aim here to discuss these issues at a high altitude and to explore how these many issues flow from the same underlying fact: that technologies of radical empowerment are spreading in fashions that render us all both radically strong and radically threatened.

This is a book about the distribution of power when everything is recorded, everyone is watchable, and nearly everyone both poses a threat and requires protection. It is a book about the reshuffling of past eras' allocation of powers and responsibilities, domestic and international. It is a book that takes a disruptive look at surveillance and privacy, security and liberty. It is a book about technology and the shift it is bringing about in our collective sense of who protects us and who threatens us. It is a book about options for governance and political organization.

We begin by laying the factual groundwork for the discussion, describing how the proliferation of technologies of mass empowerment renders all of us, at once, naked, vulnerable, menacing, and essential to security. We detail the array of threats that states, corporations, and individuals alike now pose to each other, as well as the simultaneous vulnerabilities they incur as technology distributes capacity for attack. We show how defensive capabilities are devolving from the state to individuals and groups, making each of us key to our own defense, as well as to the defense of others. All of this, we explain, makes up a profoundly different security environment than any the world has seen before.

We then turn to the conceptual challenges that this new security environment poses—how it disrupts the traditional social contract described by the Enlightenment political theorists, how it forces us to rethink notions of privacy and the relationship between liberty and security within the liberal state, and how it defies the traditional allocation of powers among states over their territories and citizens. If anyone can attack anyone else from anywhere and our world is consequently becoming more Hobbesian, can the modern state keep us from the state of nature? And how should we think about its powers and its limits? How should we think about the relationship between liberty and security when we both rely on governments to protect us from radically empowered fellow citizens around the globe and also fear the power those same technologies give to governments? In a world in which borders represent less meaningful divisions than they once did, is the existing international order that delimits states' jurisdiction along territorial boundaries sustainable? Or is effective governance of security in a world of many-to-many threats and defenses necessarily international in character?

Finally, we attempt to glean some lessons for domestic and international governance. The purpose here is not to develop a laundry list of policy proposals but rather to develop an intellectual framework for policy making and, indeed, for citizens at large across a wide range of areas. Our aim is to help readers think through—using the very old technology of the printed word—the implications of new technologies for their personal and collective security and for the old and venerable political theories on which modern societies are organized.

PART I

THE DISTRIBUTION OF OFFENSIVE CAPABILITY

Using gene-splicing equipment available online and other common laboratory equipment and materials, a disgruntled molecular biology graduate student undertakes a secret project to recreate the smallpox virus. Not content merely to bring back an extinct virus to which the general population has no immunity, he uses public-source material to enhance the virus's lethality. His activities raise no eyebrows at his university lab, where synthesizing and modifying complex genomes is commonplace. Although time-consuming, the task is not especially difficult. He buys short pieces of the genome and strings them together—taking care not to order sequences long enough to alert the gene-synthesis companies from which he purchases, all of which screen orders for dangerous gene combinations. He synthesizes most of the virus himself to avoid detection. When he finishes, he infects himself and, just as symptoms begin to emerge, goes to an airport and has close contact with as many people as he can in a short time. He then kills himself before becoming ill and is buried by his grieving family; neither they nor the authorities have any idea of his infection.

The outbreak begins just shy of two weeks later and seems to come from everywhere at once. Because of the virus's long incubation period, it has spread far by the time the disease first manifests itself. Initial efforts to immunize swaths of the population prove of limited effectiveness because of the perpetrator's manipulations of the viral genome. Efforts to identify the perpetrator, once it becomes clear that the outbreak is not an accident, require many months of forensic work. In the meantime, authorities have no idea whether the country—and quickly the world—has just suffered an attack by a rogue state, a terrorist group, or a lone individual. Dozens of groups around the world claim responsibility for the attack, several of them plausibly.

Fantastic as this scenario sounds, there is nothing especially improbable or futuristic about it. The materials required to pull it off are already inexpensive, and the price of DNA synthesis continues to fall rapidly. People have already constructed viruses with long genetic sequences and have also modified existing organisms to enhance their propensity to kill. Although making these sequences behave like viruses still poses technical challenges, those challenges are fading quickly. As the National Science Advisory Board for Biosecurity bluntly put it in 2006, it is "possible to construct infectious agents from synthetic or naturally derived DNA. The technology for synthesizing DNA is readily accessible, straightforward and a fundamental tool used in current biological research. In contrast, the science of constructing and expressing viruses in the laboratory is more complex and somewhat of an art."[1] The number of people who could pull off this nightmare scenario today is not huge, but it is growing fast. Today's art will quickly become, like DNA synthesis itself, routine science, then just routine. Meanwhile, the number of people capable of less sophisticated biosecurity mischiefs, including some that could have devastating effects on significant quantities of people, is already large and far-flung geographically.

What is more, biotechnology is only one arena in which ever smaller groupings of people can leverage technology to attack ever larger entities— up to and including corporations, states, and societies at large. Cyberspace is another arena. The number of people capable of mounting a meaningful cyberattack has grown alongside the proliferation of globally networked computer systems. The opportunities for such attacks are themselves proliferating, becoming cheaper, and involving an increasingly diverse array of technologies.

The empowerment activities that these technologies enable run the gamut of morality—from welcome social and political innovations to attempted crimes against humanity. Indeed, how we feel about them— whether we view them as attacks or as an attractive form of people power—depends on who is employing them and for what ends. When Arab dissidents used social-networking platforms to organize, inform, and empower protesters at the expense of autocratic governments during the Arab Spring, we celebrated. When, beginning in 2008, the hacker collective known as Anonymous launched cyberattacks against corporations and entities offensive to its members, we responded with mixed feelings—with approbation for the honorable place of civil disobedience, on the one hand, and concerns about unaccountable mob rule, on the other. When Julian Assange, founder of WikiLeaks, created a computer system to distribute leaked material and individuals then used that system to expose US government secrets, we saw a lively debate between those who regard this as an attractive form of distributed journalism and those who regard it more dimly. When someone in 2001 milled and engineered anthrax spores for public dissemination, we responded with horror, as we did when, in 1993, the Aum Shinrikyo terrorist cult attempted biological attacks and then in 1995 successfully dispersed sarin gas on the Tokyo subway system.

The fact that technology can serve both useful and destructive purposes is as much a feature of fire, rocks, and spears as of any newfangled invention. In our modern age, however, new technologies are able to generate and channel mass empowerment, allowing small groups and individuals to challenge states and other institutions of traditional authority in ways that used to be the province only of other states. They are growing increasingly cheap and available. They defy distance and other physical obstacles. And, ultimately, they create the world of many-to-many threats, a world in which every individual, group, or state has to regard every other individual, group, or state as at least a potential security threat.

Modern technologies of mass empowerment have certain common features that warrant a close look: their rapid pace of growth and proliferation, their diffusion of power into individual hands, and their general trajectories of development. We focus here on three distinct technological spheres that exist today in different phases of development: networked computers, biotechnology, and robotics. An additional sphere, nanotechnology, is still in a more incipient phase, yet will likely affect all three other technological spheres in the foreseeable future. Other technologies of mass empowerment will surely develop in the years to come, but we focus on these three particular examples as illustrative of the class in an attempt to flesh out the sorts of threats this type of technological empowerment engenders. Rapid technological progress brings with it vast and definite advantages for huge numbers of people. But these technologies also have certain common features that, alongside the great good people can do with them, create a unique threat environment.

Modern Technologies of Mass Empowerment

Violence does not require fancy weapons. Seung-Hui Cho used widely available firearms to kill thirty-two people and wound twenty-five others at Virginia Tech in April 2007. It took only machetes to massacre most of the eight hundred thousand Tutsis and moderate Hutus during the hundred days' genocide in Rwanda in 1994. From Columbine to the Congo, individuals have conducted all manner of attacks, as lone wolves or in organized groups. According to some estimates, there are about 90 guns for every hundred people in the United States, and more than 650 million civilian firearms worldwide. Between eight and ten thousand people were killed annually in gun-related homicides in the United States between 2008 and 2012, and those account for only two-thirds of all murder cases. When people want to kill other people, they can.[2]

But while technology is no kind of prerequisite for violence, it does facilitate a range of violent behaviors. The technologies that cause the greatest concern for security these days are, perhaps unsurprisingly, the same ones that offer the greatest promise to humanity. The concern and the promise emanate from the same source: the double-edged nature of technological advancement. As defense policy analyst Andrew Krepinevich observes, "All the military revolutions of the last two centuries are in a real sense spinoffs from the Industrial and Scientific Revolutions that have been central, defining processes of modern Western history." There are, in effect, no walls separating the violent and the mundane. The iron forge used to cast church bells was instrumental in the development of the cannon in the fourteenth century. The telegraph and railroads were both driving forces in subsequent military revolutions. In the other direction, duct tape, the microwave, the Global Positioning System (GPS), and indeed computers were all originally developed, at least in part, for military use, only to find their way into everyday civilian life.[3]

By delivering dramatic new capabilities to humanity in general—and to individual humans in particular—technological development creates the certainty that some of those individuals will use those capabilities to do evil. When our ancestors lived in caves, most Australopithecines found the rock useful to crush berries, but a few used it to crush skulls; some honed the rock into a tool for hunting woolly mammoths, but a few turned that tool on each other. Most people now will use new biotechnologies to prevent disease; a few will use them to cause it. As businessman and former Microsoft technology chief Nathan Myhrvold put it,

"Technology contains no inherent moral directive—it empowers people, whatever their intent, good or evil."[4]

Because most people do not seek to harm others, the net impact of technological development is, in all probability, hugely positive for humanity. Socialization has always been essential to survival. Consequently, the Internet, media, telecommunications, travel, and commerce have greatly enhanced human well-being by making the world smaller and strengthening global interconnectedness and interdependence. They have toppled the barriers that, heretofore, had impeded global social development. In his majestic book on the history of violence, *The Better Angels of Our Nature*, Harvard psychologist Steven Pinker argues that our present international society is the least violent in recorded history, in part because technology, trade, and globalization have made us more reasoned and, in turn, more averse to violence. Fewer people in the modern world want to do bad things to others. Pinker's thesis, powerful and persuasive as it is, only captures one side of the coin, however. The very same technologies that help account for our society's relative peace now threaten to enable people to cause each other infinitely greater harm than ever before.[5]

In one sense, this is merely a feature of globalization. Although Pinker credits globalization with taming violence, legal scholar Philip Bobbitt and defense writer John Robb, in their respective books on globalization and terrorism, both link global communications, networking, and travel to a new era of terrorism and confrontation between the state and non-state actors. And both make clear that technology and its proliferation are key features of this development.[6] Similarly, in his paean to globalization, *The World Is Flat*, *New York Times* columnist Thomas Friedman pauses only a few times in his glee over what he terms the "flattening" of the world—that is, the geographical and social leveling associated with the proliferation of trade and technology around the globe and the accompanying distribution of capability. During one such pause, he briefly considers the security implications of the trend he otherwise celebrates: "Contemplating the flat world also left me filled with dread, professional and personal. My personal dread derived from the obvious fact that it's not only the software writers and computer geeks who get empowered to collaborate on work in a flat world. It's also al-Qaeda and other terrorist networks. The playing field is not being leveled only in ways that draw in and superempower a whole new group of innovators. It's being leveled in a way that draws in and superempowers a whole new group of angry, frustrated, and humiliated men and women."[7] But there's more going on here than simple globalization, and Friedman—in his description of the superempowerment of the world's real or perceived underdogs—is actually conflating distinct phenomena. Globalization is fundamentally about connectivity and travel worldwide, the ability to move people, goods, and particularly information at a speed and cost sufficiently low to make the world a smaller place. The true superempowerment of individuals, however, involves an additional element: cheap, widely available, and destructive technologies of attack.

Modern technologies of mass empowerment are not fundamentally weapons systems, but they do take to their logical conclusions certain trends in weaponry: those toward increased lethality at greater distance and toward giving more individuals the power do ever greater harm. Specifically, technologies of mass empowerment put more power, potentially a lot more power, in the hands of more people, potentially a lot more people. They thus push toward an extreme in which we have to fear ever more remote and ever more lethal attacks from an ever wider array of ever less accountable people wielding what legal scholar and theorist of technology and law Lawrence Lessig has called "insanely destructive devices."[8]

NETWORKED COMPUTERS

The most developed technology of mass empowerment is the planet's networked computer infrastructure. Access to the Internet is ubiquitous in much of the world: according to some statistics, 40 percent of households globally are connected, reflecting explosive growth over a decade ago. An immense and ever growing number of people are capable of manipulating computers connected to the network. As a result, the expertise to launch cyberattacks and cyberexploitations is widely, though certainly not evenly, distributed, and the subject of cybersecurity has spawned an enormous literature. For our purposes, the most relevant points are that cyberintrusions—whether aimed at military systems, intended to disrupt social and economic activity, or used simply to steal information, data, or money—take place constantly. They come from governments of rival nations, from members of criminal gangs, from politically motivated hacker groups, or simply from disaffected individuals. Identifying perpetrators involves time, money, and significant doubt. The anonymity and accessibility of the Internet, together with the sheer volume of cyberattacks, makes deterrence and attribution of intrusions particularly difficult.[9]

The objectives behind cyberintrusions can vary as widely as the societal functions that now depend on computerized networks. Most involve garden-variety attempts at fraud and theft. Some, like Luis Mijangos's crimes, involve more intrusive assaults on people's personal dignity— something closer to online rape. In others, as in the case of Mona Jaud Awana, a Palestinian woman, who lured an Israeli teenager via Internet chat to meet with her and then killed him, cyberspace only serves to facilitate traditional criminal or terrorist activity. Cyberintrusions also involve espionage, as attackers regularly steal huge volumes of information from companies and governments alike.[10]

Some intrusions seek not merely to exploit information technology systems but to damage them or alter their functioning. So-called denial-of-service attacks against a variety of governmental and corporate targets have become common in recent years. More sophisticated attacks that exploit software vulnerabilities and human weakness have become prevalent as well, threatening military systems, vital infrastructure, and other crucial, network-dependent installations.

Although hard to assess, the probability of a truly catastrophic cyberattack, like a meltdown of the world's financial system or a broad-based attack on the electric grid, is certainly not negligible. An attack of this magnitude will likely remain the province of professional intelligence services for some time to come. But a number of high-profile incidents in recent years have underscored the fact that such an attack cannot be ruled out. In 2007, the Department of Homeland Security conducted a test in which it hacked into a model power plant control system and destroyed a generator by changing its operating cycle. The nations of Georgia and Estonia found their government computers and Internet connectivity subject to systematic attack when they had political and military confrontations with Russia. And, of course, the possibility of cyberwarfare involving nuclear power plants was vividly on display in the case of the so-called Stuxnet worm, revealed in 2010 to have attacked the Iranian uranium-enrichment program by speeding up specific centrifuge models, and in other attacks of a similar nature dubbed "Olympic Games," both reportedly launched by the United States and Israel.[11]

While the highest-profile cybersecurity incidents of recent years have generally been state-to-state affairs, the power to conduct low- to medium-grade attacks and exploitations on a wide scale has clearly migrated to actors far below the level of sovereign states. The most famous example is the hacker group known as Anonymous, whose diffuse and largely uncoordinated membership has launched attacks on a range of targets—from Sony, to companies that refused to host WikiLeaks, to government websites, to the Church of Scientology. But it is not the only example. Consider the following, all of which took place in August 2013 alone: A hacker collective calling itself the Syrian Electronic Army launched successful attacks against Twitter, the *New York Times*, and the *Washington Post*, taking one newspaper off the Internet for the better part of a day and redirecting traffic from the other to its own site. Someone launched a denial-of-service attack on the entire Chinese Internet, slowing or stopping traffic for more than six hours (it was unclear whether the attack was the work of a nation-state). The press revealed "deep cyberattacks" against three banks over the previous three months, costing those institutions millions of dollars as hackers gained control of their wire-payments applications. A Pakistani hacker claimed credit for a series of hacks that affected 650 Israeli websites associated with the government, corporations, and individuals. A group of Afghan hackers, meanwhile, attacked Pakistani websites. One can compile a similar list for any month of any recent year.[12]

Of course, nonstate intrusions lie along a continuum, from entirely legitimate cyberactivism—which can often serve to erode government power in salutary ways—to cyberharassment and "hacktivism," all the way to full-on attacks. What all have in common is the use of widely distributed networked computers and telecommunications to allow individuals—for good or ill, on their own or in formal or informal arrangements with one another—to engage in conflict against governments or other large entities that have traditionally wielded great power.

GENETIC ENGINEERING, SYNTHETIC BIOLOGY, AND BIOTECHNOLOGY

The life sciences present a somewhat less developed case of this sort of technological leveling. The technology tools and expertise associated with genetic engineering have penetrated society less deeply than have networked computers and computer-programming skills. Still, the number of people trained in genetics and synthetic biology is large and growing quickly. Education itself is becoming more globalized, with both domestic and foreign students benefitting from the most advanced institutions and laboratories. Even more than the ubiquity of networked computing, the growing availability of genetic-engineering technologies threatens to put the power to launch a weapon-of-mass-destruction (WMD) attack in the hands of a great many people around the world with relatively inexpensive equipment and basic training.

Biological weapons are unique among WMDs. Like nuclear weapons, they have the capacity to do truly catastrophic damage. And like chemical weapons they are comparatively inexpensive and easy to produce. But only biological weapons can produce destruction far beyond the point of first impact by dispersing contagious pathogens that spread through the human network. As Myhrvold has bracingly put it,

> Modern biotechnology will soon be capable, if it is not already, of bringing about the demise of the human race—or at least of killing a sufficient number of people to end high-tech civilization and set humanity back 1,000 years or more. That terrorist groups could achieve this level of technological sophistication may seem far-fetched, but keep in mind that it takes only a handful of individuals to accomplish these tasks. Never has lethal power of this potency been accessible to so few, so easily. Even more dramatically than nuclear proliferation, modern biological science has frighteningly undermined the correlation between the lethality of a weapon and its cost, a fundamentally stabilizing mechanism throughout history.[13]

The long incubation periods for many pathogens mean that an infected individual, like the one we imagined at the beginning of this chapter, can travel and infect others before contamination becomes apparent, making it difficult to limit the impact of an attack. Moreover, illnesses caused by biological weapons are often hard to distinguish from naturally occurring outbreaks. It took investigators a year to realize that an outbreak of salmonella in Oregon in 1984 was the result of an attack by followers of Bagwan Shree Rajneesh. The converse risk also applies: authorities may wrongly attribute a natural outbreak to an act of terrorism. Although investigators eventually concluded that the outbreak of West Nile encephalitis in New York in 1999 stemmed from natural causes, the response by public health authorities had a lot in common with the response to a bioterrorism event because the natural outbreak presented similarly to one. The disease had never before occurred in the Western Hemisphere, and an Iraqi defector had claimed just months before the outbreak that Saddam Hussein was weaponizing the West Nile virus. The potential for mistakes can generate unwarranted conflict and undermine a government's credibility.[14]

The technology required to produce biological weapons is generally the same as that used in legitimate life sciences research; indeed, it is the bread and butter of the biotechnology revolution. Precisely because modern biotechnology holds so much promise and offers so many benefits for so many walks of life, the materials and skills required to develop these weapons are not rare. So, while it is extremely difficult for even a highly trained individual to build his own nuclear weapon, someone with relatively modest expertise and resources could potentially obtain or develop a biological weapon—with global consequences. As costs for resources and research continue to fall, the number of people whom governments around the world have to regard as capable, at least in theory, of developing their own personal WMD program grows commensurately.[15]

This is happening fast. Bioterrorism expert Christopher Chyba has likened the proliferation of gene-synthesis capability to the exponential growth in computer technology as predicted by Moore's law, named for Intel founder Gordon Moore, who observed in 1965 that the number of transistors on an integrated circuit, which is to say, the "power" of computers themselves, doubled every two years—a trend that has remained true ever since. Chyba states, "Just as Moore's law led to a transition in computing from extremely expensive industrial-scale machines to laptops, iPods, and microprocessors in toys, cars, and home appliances, so is biotechnological innovation moving us to a world where manipulations or synthesis of DNA will be increasingly available to small groups of the technically competent or even individual users, should they choose to make use of it."[16] Chyba notes that the cost of synthesizing a human genome has plummeted and will continue to fall and that as cost decreases, the efficiency of biotechnology continues to increase. According to one calculation, the speed of DNA synthesis increased five hundred times from 1990 to 2000. Another expert calculated that by 2010, an individual working alone would be able to synthesize genetic materials one hundred times faster than he could in 2003, and the increase has indeed been dramatic. To give a sense of what this means for the ability to build a personal WMD arsenal, it took researchers at the State University of New York three years to synthesize the complete poliovirus in 2002, but the following year, a different group of researchers synthesized a viral genome of comparative length in only two weeks.[17]

What is more, deadly pathogens are not that hard to come by. Many of the most notable and terrifying pathogens even occur naturally: anthrax, bubonic plague, the Ebola and Marburg viruses, tularemia, and

Venezuelan equine encephalitis can all be collected in the natural environment. That fact was not lost on the notorious Japanese cult Aum Shinrikyo, which attempted to obtain Ebola strains in Africa, though it did not successfully sicken anyone with them. In addition, many pathogens are stockpiled by commercial companies for legitimate purposes, even as governmental controls on these stockpiles have tightened in recent years. Moreover, even pathogens like smallpox and the 1918 flu virus, which have been wiped out in the wild, can now be re-created, as in the nightmare scenario described at the outset of this chapter. The literature available in the public domain describing—even routinizing—genetic-engineering projects involving the creation, modification, and enhancement of deadly pathogens should be at least as terrifying to policy makers around the world as box cutters or guns on airplanes. Viral genomes are relatively short. Many have already been mapped, and the materials required to synthesize or adapt them using related pathogens are commercially available.

Scientists have repeatedly demonstrated that where states, terrorists, or individual bad guys have the will, science has a way. The following are only a few examples. In 2001, Australian researchers published the results of a study in which they used gene-splicing technology to create a mousepox virus resistant to vaccination. (Mousepox, although not dangerous to humans, is a sufficiently close variant of human smallpox that the experiment demonstrates the likelihood that similar manipulation of the smallpox virus is possible.) The same year, a team of virologists in Germany and France constructed Ebola virus from three strands of complementary DNA. A year later, researchers from the State University of New York, Stony Brook, published studies of de novo DNA synthesis of the poliovirus, constructed using nucleotide fragments purchased from a mail-order biotechnology company. In similar experiments, scientists have successfully synthesized the encephalomyocarditis virus and the 1918 Spanish influenza virus—which infected an estimated one-third of the global population and killed between 50 and 100 million people worldwide.[18]

To be sure, technological obstacles still confront terrorist groups or individuals interested in launching a global pandemic, but they are growing increasingly surmountable. As technology continues to advance, the synthetic creation or adaptation of larger, more complex pathogens—including, potentially, the smallpox virus—will become cheaper and easier for a wider array of potential bad actors.[19]

If recent history is any guide, that is an ominous possibility. For while no terrorist group has successfully launched a mass-casualty biological attack, a range of cases demonstrate that there is no dearth of people who would like to do so. Aum Shinrikyo, which succeeded with chemical weapons where it failed with biological weapons, is not the only example. In another chilling indication of an individual's potential bioterrorism capabilities from 1995, Larry Wayne Harris, a former member of the Aryan Nations, faked stationery from a fictitious laboratory and easily obtained the bacterial agent of the bubonic plague from a private company. After the company shipped the bacterial cultures to Harris, an employee became concerned and contacted the Centers for Disease Control and Prevention. Thus alerted, authorities obtained a search warrant and discovered biological pathogens, as well as explosives, in Harris's car and home. Harris explained that he was stockpiling weapons in preparation for an imminent Armageddon. He pled guilty to one count of wire fraud. As noted earlier, the threat of bioterrorism became a reality with the anthrax attacks in October 2001. Illustrating the difficulty of ascribing responsibility for this sort of event, it took investigators seven years to develop an indictable case against a single individual, whose death made ultimate, adjudicated attribution impossible.[20]

If a terrorist were to overcome the challenges inherent in turning a naturally occurring pathogen into a deployable weapon, the consequences could be devastating. The US Office of Technology Assessment estimated, for example, that an airplane flying over a densely populated area such as Washington, DC, could kill as many as 3 million people by dispensing one hundred kilograms of properly aerosolized anthrax. A contagious virus specifically engineered for lethality against a relatively unimmunized population could, at least theoretically, kill many more. In the world of low-probability, high-impact events, this type of attack stands out for its relative plausibility. Indeed, the more one studies biothreats, the more one worries that the world's escape to date from major biosecurity disaster owes as much to good luck and to a failure of imagination and competence on the part of the bad guys as it does to the difficulty of the undertaking.[21]

THE EMERGING WORLD OF ROBOTICS

Robotics presents a more nascent field that is starting to exhibit key characteristics of mass-empowerment technologies. Robots have only begun to penetrate the mass consumer market. Most people still do not use them, let alone know how to design or deploy them for specialized missions or applications. At the same time, commercial industry is growing so reliant on robots that some predict they will forever transform the labor market; robots are already employed in assembly lines, hospitals, and distribution centers in much of the Western world. On the everyday consumer side, there are robotic vacuum cleaners, swimming pool cleaners, toys, and gadgets available from the Hammacher Schlemmer catalog. But for most individuals, robotics remains a field in its infancy, still more a matter for hobbyists than a vehicle for mass empowerment.[22]

On its face, the field does not present a technology quite so obviously mass empowering as do programmable networked computers or biotechnology. After all, most robots available to the consumer are off-the-shelf technologies programmed to perform a set of fixed tasks. But that will almost surely change. As Bill Gates has said with respect to robotics, society is today roughly in the same condition as it was with respect to personal computers back in the early 1980s. "As I look at the trends that are now starting to converge, I can envision a future in which robotic devices will become a nearly ubiquitous part of our day-to-day lives," Gates wrote. "We may be on the verge of a new era, when the PC will get up off the desktop and allow us to see, hear, touch, and manipulate objects in places where we are not physically present."[23]

This era is probably not that far off. Prices are falling fast. Power and capability are growing as computing power continues to develop. Knowledge of the core technologies in the unclassified sector is increasing quickly too, and the potential for individual tailoring of robotic machines is keeping pace. For a few hundred dollars, parents and schools can buy children Lego Mindstorms robotics kits, a kind of high-tech Erector Set that allows them to design and program complex robots with multiple different functionalities and sensors. Many schools now have robotics clubs that compete in national and international meets. Robotic gladiators have long fought to the death on television shows. Teams from around the country compete to design robots capable of the longest travel in the most difficult urban and off-road conditions. One of the present authors organized a "Drone Smackdown" in which teams modified a commercially available quadrotor (a flying robot with four helicopter propellers) and conducted dogfights with them. A generation is growing up with robotics as a part of its engineering DNA. It is only a matter of time before that generation shocks us with what it can do—and how cheaply.[24]

Robots are already remarkably good at watching people—and killing them. Indeed, military applications of robotic technologies have, to a significant extent, driven the ongoing revolution in robotics that society is now experiencing. The rise of drone warfare has changed the face of American counterterrorism efforts; what began as a surveillance tool that could occasionally deliver lethal force has evolved in a short time into a principal means of following enemy forces into territories in which the United States is reluctant to put its own forces on the ground.

But military robotics are not just the Predator drone and its newer, more powerful cousin, the Reaper. Robotics are playing an ever growing role in military operations more generally, doing everything from scouting terrain to checking for and disarming improvised explosive devices. Numerous new unmanned systems for operations on the ground, in the air, and at sea are in development or have already been deployed. These robots include ground vehicles, infantry substitutes, surveillance devices, supply and guidance systems, evacuation technologies, and, of course, dedicated weapons systems.[25] Consider two examples. In October 2011, it became public that the military had acquired a tiny kamikaze drone called the Switchblade, which *Wired* magazine's *Danger Room* blog described as follows:

> Instead of carrying a missile, the drone *is* the missile. Unfolded from a size small enough to fit in a soldier's rucksack—like a Switchblade; get it?—and launched from a tube, the spy cameras on board the drone scout an enemy position before the soldier controlling it sends it barreling into the target. It's a strictly one-way mission.
>
> . . .
>
> Soon, the Switchblade won't be the only Kamikaze drone out there. The spinning circles of death known as the Quadrocopter Microdrone is a homebrew combining tiny guns, laser targeting systems and an Xbox Kinect-style camera to hunt prey, with an optional iPad hookup for remote control.[26]

Ground-level systems are developing quickly as well. Military analyst Peter Singer, in *Wired for War*, describes a number of new weapons technologies that companies have already attached to robots. This is only one: "Metal Storm, originally invented by an Australian grocery store worker, is a gun that uses electricity rather than gunpowder to shoot out stacks of bullets. The switch from chemical to electric power allows it to fire far faster, as many as a million rounds per minute. Thus, instead of shooting at one target with one bullet, Metal Storm can do such things as deconstruct a target, by shredding it apart bullet by bullet, or put up an actual wall of bullets in the air to protect against incoming missiles."[27] The company that makes Metal Storm described the viability of this gun on robotic platforms as follows: "Small robotic platforms can carry single or multi-barrel Metal Storm weapons that can be attached to existing structures (such as a robotic arm or wing), or can be integrated with specialised mounts that can target independently of the movement and direction of travel of the robotic platform." Metal Storm has already conducted live firings from several robotic platforms, including the Dragonfly rotary wing unmanned aerial vehicle (UAV) and the iRobot Warrior and Talon unmanned ground vehicles.[28]

These technologies will obviously not remain exclusive to the United States. At least forty-five countries have robots in their military arsenals (almost all for nonlethal purposes for now), and nonstate actors are acquiring them as well. The Lebanese armed group Hezbollah reportedly obtained Iranian-designed drones and flew several Mirsad (Arabic for "ambush") drones into Israel, each capable of carrying explosives. Singer notes that the use of drones is not limited to large, nonstate armed groups such as Hezbollah and that more obscure groups are increasingly able to use or develop such technology. During the 2014 Israeli-Palestinian war in Gaza, Israeli authorities reported that they had shot down a Palestinian drone.[29]

These technologies will not stay forever in the military or paramilitary sector or in the domestic law enforcement sector, where they have similarly been growing in prevalence and use. Drones, as we noted earlier, have already found their way into the world of hobbyists. Just as civilian firearms moved beyond muskets as military weaponry advanced to include modern rifles and assault weapons, the civilian sector will not remain limited to Roomba vacuum cleaners while the military develops ever more powerful weapons. The organizers of the DIY Drones website earnestly describe themselves as only interested in civilian uses of UAV technologies, but they cannot prevent other actors—good and bad alike—from piggybacking weapons on top of the technologies the enthusiasts lovingly pioneer and refine.

Indeed, some of the most sophisticated technologies not only migrate to the civilian sector but also emerge from it. There exists a kind of continuum from remotely piloted model aircraft, to semiautonomously operated drones, to drones armed for combat. If weapons are common in a society and robots are common and gaining in power per unit cost, robotic weapons will follow as an almost inevitable economic consequence in the civilian sector. Why should a bank hire a security guard, who may fall asleep or get scared during a robbery, when a sentry robot like the ones designed for the Demilitarized Zone in Korea will cost less, stay cool in a crisis, shoot more accurately, and will not demand health insurance or vacation time? For that matter, why should a bank robber take the risk of getting arrested or shot when he can send in a robot capable of relaying his demands, carrying out the loot, and menacing the tellers with a Metal Storm grenade launcher? The right to keep and bear arms may pretty soon mean, in practice, the right to keep and bear robots.

Two other major trends in robotics make the field particularly worth watching as an area of mass empowerment. The first is toward increased autonomy in robots. Robots that provide, in essence, elaborate armed platforms for humans to control remotely are one thing; robots capable of making autonomous decisions, including firing decisions, are something else. Autonomy is not a binary feature—that is, one that either exists or does not. Robots can act autonomously or not along many axes, and the same robot can perform some functions on its own and reserve others for human control. For example, a robot might navigate, avoid enemy fire, and feed surveillance video back to humans all on its own but rely on humans for targeting and firing instructions. At least for now, people seem committed to keeping humans "in the loop" when it comes to the use of lethal force. That said, increased robot autonomy seems inevitable. Having one person control one robot is just too inefficient; as technology improves, robots will be able to accomplish some functions better without human involvement; and communications between people and devices will sometimes break down, necessitating that robots make their own decisions. As Singer writes, "Despite what one article called 'all the lip service paid to keeping a human in the loop,' autonomous armed robots are coming to war. They simply make too much sense to the people that matter." Indeed, some observers see increased robot autonomy—and the ever growing artificial intelligence research that underlies it—as inherently threatening in and of itself. Not all of these observers are technophobes. The cofounder of the artificial intelligence company DeepMind, which Google acquired in 2014 for roughly $400 million, said in an interview back in 2011 that the "number one risk for this century" was his own field. "Eventually," said Shane Legg, "I think human extinction will probably occur, and technology will likely play a part in this." He added, "If a superintelligent machine (or any kind of superintelligent agent) decided to get rid of us . . . I think it would do so pretty efficiently."[30]

The second trend worth watching involves size and cost, both of which are rapidly shrinking. Drones are becoming more insect-, bird-, fish-, and worm-like—more able to blend in with surroundings. Ever shrinking battery sizes—the most novel ones are thinner than a human hair—are allowing drones to become smaller and nimbler. Over the past few years, Harvard scientists have been building robotic bugs that can move with the same agility and speed as real-life insects, with the goal of creating "high-performance aerial and ambulatory microrobots" that can help in search-and-rescue operations, agriculture, environmental monitoring, and exploration of dangerous places. One of these bugs is the size of a penny. A short animated concept video by the Air Force Research Laboratory and General Dynamics on "micro aerial vehicles" shows a futuristic bee-size drone flying though an open window and taking out an enemy sniper with a miniature explosive payload. Since it was posted in 2009, it has been viewed more than two hundred thousand times and reposted all over the Internet.[31]

The individual is most unlikely to develop his own Reaper. But it is not too hard to imagine someone weaponizing something the size of the Nano Hummingbird, a tiny bird-size drone developed by AeroVironment with Pentagon support; the even smaller Black Hornet, developed by the Norwegian company Prox Dynamics; or the six-inch, twenty-five-gram Dragonfly developed by TechJect and available on Indiegogo, a crowd-funding website for raising money for various artistic or business ventures. If the individual cannot get his hands on these, he need only copy the effort made by scientists at Cornell University, who developed a hand-size drone that uses flapping wings to hover. The Cornell drone is special in that its wing components were made with a 3D printer.[32]

Three-dimensional printing—also called additive manufacturing—is a form of robotics that is also an empowerment technology of its own. In a manner similar to the way an inkjet printer uses layers of ink to create words or images on a page, a 3D printer receives input from a digital file and uses preloaded materials (like plastic or polyurethane or metal) to make a shape in a similar layer-by-layer process. Although 3D printing has been around for decades, its uses have largely been limited to commercial manufacturers. As the cost of 3D printing has declined, however, this technology has found more widespread and mainstream uses in homes, among hobbyists, in education centers, in medical care, and even in the fashion industry. In his 2013 State of the Union address, President Barack Obama acknowledged the promise of 3D printing "to revolutionize the way we make almost everything." But like other technologies discussed here, these benefits do not come without a downside. Gun aficionados have become increasingly adept at fashioning on home printers weapons that actually fire bullets. In late 2012, one group of gun enthusiasts designed an AR-15 that was capable of firing live rounds but would snap apart after firing only six bullets. Within a few months, the group had tweaked its design and has since printed an AR-15 capable of firing over six hundred rounds.[33]

The December 2012 tragedy at Sandy Hook Elementary School in Newtown, Connecticut, where a lone gunman fatally shot twenty children and six adult staff members, brought about calls for greater gun control in the United States. Some gun enthusiasts responded by turning to 3D printing as a means of accessing weapons they feared that new laws might ban. Cody Wilson, a law student at the University of Texas at the time and a self-described defender of the Second Amendment, uploaded to his website (defcad.org) files and designs for 3D-printing guns and magazines so that others could download them and print their own weapons at home. Within three months of the launch of Wilson's website, more than 250,000 weapons files for 3D printing had been downloaded, including files for printing a "Liberator" handgun, which had its first successful test firing in May 2013.[34]

Given today's possibilities, one has to imagine that in the not-too-distant future, a person at home might simply download the design for a robot, print key component parts, assemble them, and build a fully functioning insect-size surveillance drone. Arming it would be just one more step.

All of this means that ever smaller, less conspicuous, and more autonomous armed robots are coming to the civilian sector, as is the ability to make these robots on one's own. As robots grow more powerful and more capable of acting both independently and at greater removes, someone will use one to spy on and murder her cheating husband from a deniable distance. Someone else will use one to attack a mosque or synagogue or federal building in another city. The Luis Mijangoses of the world will send out insect drones to take surreptitious videos of women. And others will dream up ways to disrupt collective and individual security that we cannot even imagine today.

Nanotechnology: An Incipient Technology of Mass Empowerment?

Nanotechnology cannot yet be called a technology of mass empowerment. It is still in an incipient stage of development. It is currently the province of a great deal of basic research and an enormous amount of speculation. Yet it shows glimmers of the same features that the cyber-, bio-, and robotics realms are, to different degrees, manifesting now. It remains an open question how far down the road to the promise and peril of the true technology of mass empowerment nanotechnology will travel. The question is open because the true power of the technology remains at this stage disputed and because its availability to the masses remains altogether undemonstrated.

Nanotechnology is a materials science involving the manipulation of particles small enough to be measured in nanometers—that is to say, one-billionth of a meter. At that size—the scale of individual molecules and small groups of molecules—matter behaves differently than it does at the bulk scale, chiefly for two reasons: the ratio of an object's surface area to volume is radically greater, and the object's behavior is influenced by quantum mechanics as well as by Newtonian physics. As a consequence, the ability to manipulate material and create machines at the nanoscale allows the cultivation of properties that bulk-scale matter generally will not exhibit. This could mean simply better materials, or it could mean something much more dramatic. As one recent nanotechnology text puts it, "Nanobots could venture to places previously unthinkable for machines, such as into the bloodstream or into cells. They could be used on rescue missions, searching in places that are too dangerous or too small for larger robotics or humans to venture."[35]

Indeed, the technology for manufacturing microscopic robots has been around for a few years, but recent research has advanced to the point where microscopic robots can now assemble themselves and even perform basic tasks. The robotics industry, both governmental and private, is also making great efforts to enhance the autonomous capabilities of very small robots and nanobots. Human testing for tiny robots that can be injected into the eye to perform certain surgical tasks is now on the horizon. Indeed, one of the big promises of nanotechnology lies in the field of medicine, where it might permit attacks on viruses or cancer cells while leaving healthy tissue untouched.[36]

Nanotechnology thus has potentially broad implications for the development of all sorts of products. And like all such basic technological innovations, it can reasonably be expected to have implications for technologies of attack and defense as well.

It is not entirely clear at this stage what implications nanotechnology may have for the field of security, on either the personal or the broader military level. One obvious implication of nanotechnology is in the area of privacy; for example, it opens up the possibility of placing on—or even in—people tiny tracking devices that contain a huge amount of data about them. At the more macrosecurity level, much current military research and development related to nanotechnology seems to be defensive in nature. For example, the MIT Institute for Soldier Nanotechnologies describes its mission as improving the chances for soldiers' survival using nanotechnology by "decreasing the weight that soldiers carry [and] also improving blast and ballistic protection, creating new methods of detecting and detoxifying chemical and biological threats, and providing physiological monitoring and automated medical intervention." The "ultimate goal" is a "twenty-first-century battlesuit" that both protects the soldier better and is lightweight and comfortable.

Still, it requires great naïveté to imagine that governments and nongovernmental entities will not also explore the offensive possibilities of nanotechnology. For example, nanotechnology's ability to attack cancers without harming healthy tissues could theoretically be turned around to permit highly targeted attacks on healthy tissues. The air force is currently working to create sprays of nanoparticles, dispersible from drones, that tag vehicles and people and allow them to be tracked. As one nanotechnology text warns, nanoscale materials might plausibly be used to intensify lasers to make weapons, to create "self-guided antipersonnel bullets," or to make chemical or biological agents more difficult to detect and more lethal. The text goes on to forecast that "targeted strikes on buildings can become even more precise. The possibility of unleashing a 'swarm' of nanoscale robots programmed only to disrupt the electrical and chemical systems in a building is a far more militarily desirable solution than bombing the entire building."[37]

If a nanobot swarm sounds hopelessly futuristic, consider a research program at the National Aeronautics and Space Administration (NASA) called the Autonomous Nanotechnology Swarm (ANTS), which involves the development of "miniaturized, autonomous, self-similar, reconfigurable, addressable components forming structures"—in plain English, a group of tiny bots that act together for some larger purpose. According to NASA, this swarm behavior "is inspired by the success of social insect colonies" where "within their specialties, individual specialists generally outperform generalists" and "with sufficiently efficient social interaction and coordination, the group of specialists generally outperforms the group of generalists."

ANTS is being developed for purposes of space exploration, not war, and despite its title, the bots the program is developing are much larger than nanoscale. But it is hard to imagine that the ability to deploy lots of tiny robots—whether nano- or bulk scale—to swarm over a target area all pursuing the same objective in coordination with one another would not make Pentagon commanders salivate, at least until the enemy also figured out how to do it. Indeed, the ANTS project highlights the close relationship between civilian and military applications of this sort of technology. One of the most interesting applications of the swarm concept—a tetrahedral walking device designed to navigate extremely difficult terrain for purposes of space exploration—quickly gave rise to a related concept known as the TET warfighter, which also treks over tough terrain, only for military purposes.[38]

We are seeing here the same pattern as displayed in the cyber- and biotech arenas, though at a far earlier stage. The essential insights involve nonclassified breakthroughs. The materials in question are abundant, not scarce. The skills, rarified now, will become commonplace. To the extent that the technology ends up having potent applications for attack, it is unrealistic to expect those applications to remain in the hands of militaries.

THREAT FEATURES OF TECHNOLOGIES
OF MASS EMPOWERMENT

As even this cursory survey shows, technologies of mass empowerment differ enormously from one another—in terms of their availability to the public, the frequency of their use as technologies of attack, and the amount of damage different actors can currently hope to inflict using them. Still, all have certain features in common that bind them together and make this class of technologies uniquely challenging from a security point of view.

One shared feature of these technologies is that they are widely disseminated, accessible to the public, and require readily available training and materials. Unlike nuclear technologies, they do not require scarce resources that are difficult to extract and costly to manage. They were not developed principally in classified settings at government-run labs with the government solely in control of access to core materials and know-how. Rather, they emerged and grew in public, relying on widely available resources and open dialogue with national and international experts, thereby involving a great many interested actors in the venture.

Relatedly, unlike nuclear technologies, the technologies of mass empowerment were not developed with military purposes in mind. Scientists did not discover the double helix or sequence the human genome in order to figure out how to design viruses to kill people. Nor did engineers build the Internet so that terrorists or foreign governments could seize control of the Hoover Dam—or even so that our intelligence agencies could seize control of some other country's dams. Whatever research-and-development programs existed within national defense establishments to develop drones, private industry was also developing unmanned aerial systems in parallel. The civilian uses of these technologies allow many more actors to have access to their development, design, acquisition, and use than does the closed-loop development of dedicated weapons systems.

Increasing this access further is the rapidly falling cost of these technologies, enabling their nearly universal penetration into the marketplace. A technology available in theory to everyone but affordable in practice only for a very wealthy few—like, say, private aviation—might still raise some of the risks that concern us here, but the limited number of people with access to the technology limits the danger. Only when prices fall to the point where large segments of the public have access to a technology does it become a true source of mass empowerment. The essentially universal access to networked computers in advanced industrial societies is the most radical example of this phenomenon. A typical professional in the United States now has access to multiple connected devices—from desktop computers and laptops, to tablets, to smartphones. The price of entry for getting involved with robotics and biotechnology is collapsing. Drones the size of a cereal box and equipped with cameras are already widely available for less than $300 and can be controlled by an untrained user with a smartphone. Finally, and less visibly, a movement has sprung up to make synthetic biology available to all: the BioBricks Foundation is devoted to the development and sharing of "freely available standardized biological parts" and to "ensuring that the fundamental building blocks of synthetic biology are freely available for open innovation."[39]

More subtly, technologies of mass empowerment do not merely increase the power and capability of every individual or group with access to them, as all technologies do. They also increase what we might call metacreativity—that is, they do not merely increase the power to do things; they increase the power to increase the power to do things. We are talking about something even more tectonic than the development of technologies as significant as the cotton gin. Technologies of mass empowerment are not individual devices but, rather, whole technological fields—a series of breakthroughs in basic science and engineering, opening up new forums for human creativity and invention that build on themselves in a generative fashion. Whereas a hammer increases one's ability to build things, the closer analog to these technologies is the forge, which precipitated the development of metal tools in general. In other words, these are platform technologies, that is, technologies characterized by the development of new environments in which people can build and create things. A person can use a 3D printer to manufacture something entirely new, for example, or perhaps to print out the components of another 3D printer.

Moreover, technologies of mass empowerment tend to allow attacks from great distances. For as long as people have created weapons, they have sought to diminish the utility of distance as a defense and to create ever more remote opportunities for ever more lethal attacks. The first Australopithecus to pick up a rock to strike one of his fellows realized that he did not have to use his hand. The spear gave one of his descendants the ability to impale from whatever distance he could throw. The bow and arrow extended that distance still further—and also increased the attacker's accuracy and thus his safety. The gun, the artillery shell, the air strike, the cruise missile, and the Predator drone all follow this basic pattern of increasing one's capacity to attack from ever more remote and secure positions. The more distant and secure the attacker, the more difficult it is to hold him accountable or even to attribute the attack to him. As every student in a biological laboratory and every individual on his home computer becomes a possible threat to national or personal security, traditional techniques of surveillance, deterrence, and nonproliferation become increasingly ill-suited to detecting and preventing dangerous activities.

Finally, an important corollary of the ability to attack at great distance is a blurring of the distinction between foreign and domestic and between criminal and national security threats. States have different legal and policy tools at their disposal for meeting different kinds of security challenges. Law enforcement is different from warfare; domestic powers are different from international ones. The differences between these systems derive from profound differences in a state's ability to control activity on its own territory, where it has police power and governing institutions, versus abroad, where it does not. They also derive from different strategic considerations in dealing with various states and different sources of political accountability and legal authorities for acting domestically and abroad. Yet with the erosion of distance as a limit on attacks and the challenges of identifying their source or determining an attacker's motivations, it becomes increasingly difficult to know whether one is dealing with a domestic or international criminal matter or an act of war by a foreign state or group. It is hard to respond to a Chinese cyberattack if one is either not certain or is unable to prove that the attack is really foreign or whether, if it is foreign, it is really the work of the Chinese state rather than of patriotic hackers or entirely independent actors pretending to be the Chinese government. The anthrax attacks, which attempted to mimic a foreign terrorist attack, conversely had to be demonstrated to be domestic and thus not to warrant a response abroad. The more technology renders the attacker unaccountable and allows him to operate internationally, the more it diminishes differences between law enforcement and warfare, between foreign policy and domestic security, and between police work and covert military operations or diplomacy.

Integrated Fields, Integrated Threats

Even the brief overview we offer here of the new mass-empowerment technologies hints at an important aspect of their development: the lines between these technologies are porous. The technologies are quickly merging with one another. Modern robots are controlled by networked computers. They are, as we have seen, acquiring traits influenced by biology; indeed, engineers are already experimenting with the creation of actual cyborg insects whose flight can be controlled remotely. Drones, meanwhile, spread nanoparticles. Some of the scariest aspects of biotechnology, at this time, involve possible nanotechnological refinements to pathogens. A committee of the National Research Council back in 2006 convened to study "technologies convergent with the life sciences enterprise from other disciplines, such as materials science and nanotechnology, that may enable the development of a new generation of biological threats over the next five to ten years." And, of course, increased computing power is driving a great deal of innovation in nanotechnology and biotechnology as well.

We have treated these platforms separately because they involve different features and are at different stages of developments, but it is important to remember that technology in practice does not generally progress in the stovepiped manner in which we have described these fields and in which they are often discussed. Rather, it integrates insights across barriers. Just as the cavemen figured out that the rock they had sharpened worked even better as a weapon when mounted on wood they had whittled, modern people too are integrating their technologies to heighten their ability to do things, including attack one another. In reality, this society does not face just a biosecurity and a cybersecurity problem and harbor incipient security concerns about robotics and nanotechnology. It faces a broader problem of how people will make use of the incredible power these technologies—individually and in integration with one another—will give them.[40]

We do not purport to know where all of this is leading—whether the pace of technological change will continue to accelerate or will slow and let us catch our collective breath and adjust to the changes we have already wrought. Some reputable futurists—including, most famously, inventor Ray Kurzweil—have posited the former: that technological change will result soon in an effective merger of man and machine, a merger some have dubbed the "Singularity." Others, to be sure, take a more measured view, believing that the world cannot continue to observe Moore's law forever and that the pace of exponential growth will thus necessarily ebb over time.[41]

Whichever side of this debate proves correct, it seems clear that a period of rapid, transformative technological change still lies before us. Consequently, we have likely not exhausted the number of technologies that will magnify the power of states, companies, and individuals—both for great good and for great evil. There will be other technologies of mass empowerment because those already developed will spawn new ones. There will be others because the pace of technological change will lead to entirely new discoveries and because new discoveries will merge with old ones. Stanford political scientist James Fearon noted,

A friend of mine, a journalist, quips that we seem to be heading in the direction of a world in which every individual has the capacity to blow up the entire planet by pushing a button on his or her cell phone. . . . How long do you think the world would last if five billion individuals each had the capacity to blow the whole thing up? No one could plausibly defend an answer of anything more than a second. Expected life span would hardly be longer if only one million people had these cell-phones, and even if there were 10,000 you'd have to think that an eventual global holocaust would be pretty likely. Ten thousand is only two millionths of five billion.[42]

The world now has 7 billion human inhabitants.

"Cover her face," orders the Duke in John Webster's *The Duchess of Malfi* after he has killed his sister. In an era in which we can kill enemies we do not even have to see, our eyes are already largely covered. Physical distance creates a mental distance between attacker and attacked—one that may prove highly significant. The YouTube films of targeted killings by the United States, available for public information and entertainment, have attracted tens of thousands of viewers. And many commentators have worried that state access to lethal drones will lessen inhibitions about resorting to the use of force. Others have speculated that in an environment of control panels and onscreen moving targets, drone pilots—however seriously their activities are regulated or monitored—will acquire a "PlayStation mentality."[43]

Whether or not these concerns prove justified—and they are contested—some lessening of inhibitions may also occur when the motive for violence is personal: although sane nonsadists rarely have an interest in killing random people, having a zone of protected, forensic remoteness from victims—far greater remoteness than a simple handgun can provide—may, for some people, reduce inhibitions that derive, at least in part, from seeing, hearing, and feeling their victims.

One can doubt the attraction of such a free pass for the ordinary person. In *The Republic*, Plato tells of Gyges of Lydia, a shepherd in the service of King Candaules, who finds a golden ring that enables its wearer to become invisible. Arriving at the palace, Gyges uses his new power of invisibility to seduce the queen, murder the king, and take his place on the throne. If we believe, as Plato did, that the possibility of undetectability makes us more likely to commit murder, then the prospect of technologies of mass empowerment has to induce at least a little concern. Fearon's description of a future in which everyone carries around a button on his phone to destroy the world—we might call it today a "killer app"—is a crude metaphor, but it may be a crudely accurate one. And the concern is not limited to individuals with malicious intent. As the British Petroleum oil-spill crisis illustrates, it is also about accidents, the consequences of which technology will magnify as well as mitigate. If the genetically engineered virus gets released into the public, the fact that tragic error, not a terrorist attack, caused the release will be of cold comfort.

In a world that generates such a ferocious capacity for small groups to launch attacks, individuals and groups at all levels of society—and societies and states themselves—will face enormous vulnerability as a daily fact of life.

2

THE DISTRIBUTION OF VULNERABILITY

You walk into your shower and find a spider. You are not an arachnologist. You do, however, know that the tiny crawling octopod could be, at a minimum, one of four things. The spider could be real and harmless. It could be real and venomous. It could, conversely, be a personal surveillance spider, purchased from "Drones 'R' Us" for $49.95 and set loose by your next-door neighbor, who dislikes your noisy dog and is monitoring the spider on her iPhone from a sports bar downtown. The pictures of you undressed, taken by the spider, are now being relayed on several screens during a break in an NFL game at a local bar for the neighborhood's amusement.

You also harbor some small, perhaps paranoid concern about a more menacing possibility: your business competitor may have just sent a drone attack spider, purchased from a bankrupt military contractor, to take you out. There has been a rash of these killings in recent years, by organized crime and even by some ruthless elements of the business world. Upon spotting you with its sensors, before you have time to weigh your options, the spider—if it is, indeed, an attack spider—shoots an infinitesimally thin needle into your left leg and takes a blood sample. As you beat a retreat out of the shower, your competitor tests the sample on his smartphone for a DNA match to ascertain your identity. He compares the blood sample against a DNA profile of you that is already on file at EVER.com (Everything about Everybody), an international DNA database (with access available for $179.99). Once the match is confirmed (a matter of seconds), the spider will follow you into your bedroom, pausing only long enough to dart another needle, this time containing a lethal dose of a synthetically produced poison. Your assassin, who is on a summer vacation in Provence, will then direct his spider under the crack of your bedroom door and out of the house and initiate its self-destruct function. No trace of the spider will ever be found by law enforcement authorities.

This is the future—or, in the words of *The Terminator*'s Kyle Reese, "one possible future." As we have seen, we are well down the road toward insect-size drones. And while these drones will begin as surveillance devices, we can reasonably expect some to become capable of acting with lethal effect—and probably more quickly, more cheaply, and with greater availability to more people than we expect.

Now let us consider the flip side of this new distribution of offensive capacity—the concomitant distribution of vulnerability that offensive capacity engenders for us all. The same forces that operate to put the power of attack in everyone's hands also make everyone more vulnerable to that attack. To some extent, the new distribution of vulnerability is nothing more than a byproduct of the distribution of the power to attack; if every person has enhanced offensive capability, after all, it follows that every person must also be more vulnerable to attack. But the distribution of vulnerability also has features of its own. That is, it is not simply a function of the greater offensive power technologies of mass empowerment placed in the hands of individuals; it is also an independent function of the greater exposure technologies of mass empowerment created for individuals—exposure such as that engendered by EVER.com, the fictional database in our spider nightmare. These technologies create this exposure because they tend to induce ever increasing human dependency upon technology, and this dependency enhances our vulnerability too.

What Makes Us Vulnerable?

To better see the future, let us start with the present. Your life and that of every other person in an advanced industrialized country produces a mosaic of digital information stored on public and private computer servers around the world. Most of the tiles of your personal mosaic do not reside in your hands. They consist of the electronic fingerprints you leave with increasing frequency over the course of your day-to-day existence on computers controlled by third parties: they are the websites you visit, the toll booths you pass through, the purchases you make online or with credit cards, the prescriptions you fill, the phone numbers you dial, the e-mails you send, the library books you check out, the specific pages you have read on your Kindle, the restaurants at which you make online reservations, the steps you take as measured by your Fitbit, the photos you post on Facebook, and the photos that others post of you.

Very often, your mosaic works for your protection—to keep your credit cards safe from identity thieves, for example. More often still, it works for your convenience—to give you discounts, to match you with products you want to buy, to connect you with people you want to talk to and let you keep away from those you would like to avoid. But your mosaic is also an open diary that, in other hands, exposes you to many forms of vulnerability. Your enemies, the government, foreign governments, fraudsters, identity thieves, information jockeys, and legitimate businesses can all learn more about you by diving into your mosaic—legally or illegally, benignly or maliciously, to protect or to attack—than by rifling through your desk or bedroom. It is easier. Your mosaic is actually a richer source of information about you. And just as some day someone might send a spider to watch or attack you, today your mosaic presents an inviting and fruitful source for exploitation or attack by people who do not have your best interests at heart.

And here is the rub: your individual mosaic—composed, as it is, of the transactions and data that make up your life—is itself only a single tile in the much larger mosaic that records modern technological society and its behavior. That larger metamosaic too is being stored, retained, and constantly processed by governments, companies, and individuals. Along the way, each of these tiles is potentially rendering vulnerable those same governments, companies, and individuals the metamosaic also empowers. How much data is in our data-driven society? The best estimate is that, in 2013, there were twelve hundred exabytes of stored information on Earth, 98 percent of it digital. For reference, a one-exabyte file is sufficient to contain 1 billion full-length, high-definition feature films. This is what people mean by "Big Data."[1]

The mosaic and the spider represent different facets of our new vulnerability. The latter represents an extreme, possibly fanciful case of our vulnerability to physical attack and harm that results from technological innovation. The former represents our willing assumption of vulnerability in exchange for convenience and capability. That is, with our embrace of information technologies, we have opened the door to other people's actions. The mosaic and the spider together embody a kind of law of technological development: technologies that distribute power and capability will also tend to distribute dependency, exposure, and vulnerability.

In cataloging the ways that technologies of mass empowerment distribute and enhance vulnerability, it is important to remember that the same technologies, somewhat paradoxically, also distribute greater security. The benefits to society in security, health, and welfare from technological progress are enormous, and technological development thus functions in general as a huge net plus for human well-being. The biotech industry, for example, offers enormous promise for improved human health, and the number of people who wish to use biotechnology to spread disease is presumably no greater than a rounding error on the number of people whom biotechnology enables to improve vaccines and therapies. People today live longer and more healthily than ever before, in large part due to these technologies. Even if we factor in the possible accidental release or mutation of certain dangerous bioagents, the average person can usually assume that advances in biotechnology in the aggregate will help him. Similarly, while storing data in the cloud makes it part of your mosaic, it also protects that data from house fires and robberies and, more commonly, from hard disk crashes. High-tech societies in general promise more, not less, human security than do more technologically primitive societies.

But, as it turns out, it is possible to spread vulnerability even in the course of distributing security and well-being. A world in which 99 percent of people are using technologies to enhance security and 1 percent uses them to grotesquely magnify their capacity to inflict mass harm is one of concurrent increases in security and vulnerability. The closer we get to the nuclear-bomb-in-the-pocket scenario, the less we can plausibly describe new technologies only in terms of the benefits—even the security benefits—they promise and the more we have to think about outlying cases. The more biotechnology makes it possible to design global pandemics that are sufficiently aggressive in their spread to amount to a global catastrophe, the more we have to think about heightened vulnerability in the context of an atmosphere of heightened well-being. Some forecasters predict that given growing levels of production, consumption, and population, even without any further technological progress, we are already turning Earth into an uninhabitable place. If that is really the case, the benefits of technological progress could prove to be nothing more than an ironic footnote in the larger tale of the human race's ultimate self-destruction—the means by which we the frogs have made our pot of water more comfortable as it comes to a boil.

Even if the ultimate reality is nowhere near that dire, technology distributes vulnerability by increasing the number of different means by which we might plausibly be subject to attack. The caveman was subject to very few possible assaults; you are subject to a great many more—and have to defend against each of them to be secure. When we say that technologies of mass empowerment tend to distribute vulnerability, we mean that they increase the number of different channels of vulnerability through which the average person, corporation, group, or state might realistically face attack. Whether in the aggregate these technologies increase or decrease vulnerability is a function of how many people wish to attack you through the channels they open, how damaging such an attack would be, and how capably you can defend against it.

This new distribution of vulnerability spares nobody and crosses technological platforms. Governments and corporations also have mosaics, after all, and they too face the same potential exposures as individuals do. The surveillance spider from "Drones 'R' Us" might be after trade or government secrets, not your naked form in the shower. In a world of insect drones, the Secret Service would necessarily have to think differently about the occasional annoying fly that landed on the president's forehead. By and large, government officials have no better means of protecting themselves against harmful biological agents than you do. And privacy, which we call secrecy when it comes to government, is eroding for everyone. As former counterintelligence official Joel Brenner puts it, "Your difficulties with electronic privacy, the electronic theft of America's cutting-edge technology, and the government's loss of state secrets are a lot more alike than you know." The "cruel irony," Brenner writes, is that "if you want to shield yourself against information theft or hide your own identity as you go about your business, it is extremely difficult. But if you want to hide your identity in order to attack a person or an institution, it's unnervingly easy." That is true even if you want to attack a government. Just ask Edward Snowden, who did far more damage to the National Security Agency—while keeping his own head down—than any comparable figure could have done before the agency, like all agencies, began storing its information centrally in readily copied, digital form.[2]

We have a certain societal awareness of the distribution of vulnerability, but even after Snowden, WikiLeaks, Stuxnet, and endless discussions of the way Google and Facebook handle our data or how Target and Neiman Marcus handle our payment information, we do not tend to talk about distributed vulnerability as such. Public discussion tends to neglect the link between the vulnerability of big institutions and state actors and that of individuals, and with respect to individuals, we tend to think about the issue of the metamosaic largely in terms of the erosion of personal privacy. This formulation of the problem couches it in a familiar, comfortable vocabulary, but it also tends to focus on only one single dimension of what is really a multidimensional matrix of concerns. Invading someone's privacy is only one way of exploiting his or her technologically induced vulnerability, after all. Focusing on privacy may be a useful way to think about the surveillance spider, but it tends to crowd the attack spider out of the conversation. Using a more contemporary, less hypothetical example, we limit ourselves if we think, chiefly in terms of privacy, about the activity of Luis Mijangos—the sextortionist we discussed in the introduction—or, less dramatically, about those who would steal others' identities in order to raid their bank accounts. Yes, such people create privacy problems, but their victims lose much more than privacy.

Thinking about the distribution of vulnerability in terms of privacy also obscures the important conceptual common ground such intrusions share with, say, the anthrax attacks or—moral differences aside—with the activities of hacktivist groups like Anonymous and WikiLeaks. Indeed, focusing on privacy obscures the similarity to other instances in which people are leveraging technology to exploit vulnerabilities that other people's technological dependencies have created. It also, as Brenner points out, obscures the fact that individuals are only one class of actors for whom technologies of mass empowerment distribute vulnerability. Governments, corporations, and nongovernmental organizations do not have privacy, but they do have secrets to keep, secrets upon which our personal security often depends.

As a society and as individuals, we have several choices as to how to handle our new technologically induced vulnerability. We can accept it and simply live with more risk. We can use technology to advance social norms that would inhibit attacks and exploitations. We can develop defensive technologies to manage vulnerability, sometimes quite effectively. We can even learn to enjoy the vulnerability—as, for example, when we turn the sharing of previously private information into giant social-networking platforms, which we then use as a means of mass entertainment and socialization.

We cannot, however, eliminate our new vulnerability, and some of it will have significant harmful consequences. Once the first caveman learned that a rock could crush a skull as well as berries, his fellow cavemen were instantly less safe—and because they soon learned this too, his marginal power did not persist. He too was less safe.

Vulnerability Features of New Technologies

We earlier described several common features that characterize technologies of mass empowerment. The corresponding mass vulnerability has distinct features that warrant similar consideration.

The vulnerability features of technologies of mass empowerment include, of course, the mirror images of features related to the power to attack. There is much greater distribution of vulnerability to biological attacks in a world where we distribute widely the ability to conduct them than in one where such capacity is tightly contained. More prosaically, a world with widely distributed firearms of great firepower is one with enhanced vulnerability to school shootings. A world in which we make fertilizer widely available is one of abundant food—and occasional truck bombs in front of government buildings. Vulnerability flows ineluctably from the empowerment of those who would—or might—harm us. And the more power we give such people, the more vulnerable we are. A psychopath with a rock threatens more injury to more people than one with only his bare hands. If that psychopath has a spear, a musket, or a gun, the vulnerability of others around him grows commensurately. If he has an automatic weapon, he can render vulnerable an entire university campus, movie theater, or youth political movement in Norway. We see the same effect with surveillance. A Peeping Tom—or government—relying merely on sight and sound for data collection is less capable than someone—or some entity—empowered with lenses, microphones, satellites, and GPS tracking devices.

But the distribution of vulnerability also includes features related less to the inherent qualities of the technologies and the power they disseminate and more to the social impact of those technologies and the predicaments they create for individuals and institutions. The first of these social impacts is a sense of nakedness, a feature particularly pronounced in cyberspace. It is a cliché of the privacy literature that we all live in an electronic fishbowl, a modern Panopticon. The popular metaphors for privacy loss are remarkably consistent in their suggestion of people being stripped and exposed to unwanted, leering attention. *The Transparent Society*, *The Naked Crowd*, *No Place to Hide*, *The Unwanted Gaze*—these are only some of the titles on the subject published in recent years suggestive of looking through things: windows, curtains, clothes, souls, even people themselves. The metaphor captures something real, a sense that the mosaic gives countless public and private actors comprehensive insight into who we are, where we are, what we think, and how we behave. One relatively harmless but striking example of the undressing power of the mosaic, as told by the *New York Times*, occurred when a man in Minnesota berated the manager of his local Target after his teenage daughter received a store mailing with coupons for baby clothes. Using data from millions of annual purchases, Target's marketing division had apparently developed an algorithm that found that pregnant women tend to buy large amounts of unscented lotion at the end of the first trimester and a few weeks later to purchase mineral supplements. A few days after the father visited the store, he called the manager to apologize: Target had picked up—before he had—that his daughter was pregnant.[3]

Before the mosaic, government and corporations too stand naked. Their mosaics include countless pages of public record material that, but for its digitized availability, nobody would ever read. Like your mosaics, institutional and governmental mosaics also contain sensitive materials that those institutions cannot fully protect or keep from leaking to the outside world. Espionage and counterespionage have been part of international political life from its very beginning. But technology strips off many covers, allowing interested parties to collect more information from greater distances, with greater speed, leaving few fingerprints. In the old days, to protect valuable information, we had a safe. Corporations and large organizations, including the government, had storage facilities protected by locks and guards and alarm systems. These days, it would take a city-size storage facility to keep physical records that major institutions wish to protect. The storage facilities, the records, and the locks and guards are mostly virtual, and the thief need not physically enter a room to steal from it. In fact, much of the time, the storage keeper does not even know that a theft has occurred. The US government only learned that hundreds of thousands of secret diplomatic cables and other documents had left its classified network when WikiLeaks began making them public, and it only learned of Edward Snowden's leaks when the *Guardian* began making National Security Agency (NSA) documents public. Similarly, it took the Israeli government more than two years to learn that an enlisted soldier had copied two thousand documents, some highly classified, onto a CD and taken them with her upon her discharge from the army. With no physical evidence of a break-in and no documents physically missing, the theft became known only when an Israeli reporter admitted to relying on classified materials, received from the soldier, in his reporting.[4]

What is more, the mosaic sometimes renders espionage irrelevant, since much information that used to be highly classified and expensive—satellite imagery, for example—is now freely available from services like Google Earth. Governments and corporations too now operate in an increasingly transparent environment, with no place to hide from the unwanted gaze.

The problem is not limited to cyberspace; nor is the inability to shield oneself limited to information exposure. Technologies of mass empowerment have a way of going through things—that is, through the walls behind which we attempt to hide. During the anthrax attacks, biological agents easily made their way into people's homes and workplaces. Luis Mijangos managed to penetrate the homes of his victims using their webcams; more recently, the Federal Trade Commission took enforcement action against a manufacturer of Internet-enabled cameras whose lax security practices allowed hackers to harvest live video of babies sleeping in their cribs. Miniaturized robots are so eerie because we fear their ability to penetrate our defenses while blending into our environment—to look through and under things, to rifle through our private possessions, to watch us while we cannot see them, possibly to attack us.[5]

Another feature of distributed vulnerability derives from our growing dependence on mass-empowering technologies. Once technologies develop, we forget how we ever lived without them and find ourselves surprisingly unequipped to get on as we used to. A hundred years ago, a lengthy power outage in the northeastern United States would have been a real inconvenience, perhaps even life threatening for some people. But it would not have been a catastrophic event. Back then we knew how to function reasonably well without electricity or even running water, and nothing in our lives depended on computers. Take down the electrical grid today, keep it down for a protracted period, and you would have a mass-casualty scenario: no climate control, hospitals and other essential services on limited power using backup generators, traffic lights out of service, underground transportation systems paralyzed, no elevators, no cell phones or computers to communicate with, no gas pumping and transportation thus brought to a halt, and a shutdown of all production, commerce, and the stock market. Authorities would be reduced to functioning at the bare minimum, law and order would become difficult to maintain, market activity would grind to a halt for many corporations, and individuals would be largely helpless. There would be no one to get you out of the elevator stuck on the twenty-third floor.

In most of the world, people are no longer hunter-gatherers—we have largely lost the skills to survive that way. We are no longer even the creatures of the Industrial Revolution; that too is an evolutionary period now behind us. Rather, modern society sits atop many interlocking technological layers and is continuously dependent on their vitality and resilience for its day-to-day functioning and also, to no lesser degree, on its own confidence that the layers will work and interlock. We are daily adding to these layers of technological dependency in all aspects of society. Each layer gives rise to new dependencies—and thus to new vulnerabilities. An everyday glance at any modern city finds people not looking around to navigate—as the hunter-gatherer or even the earlier urban dweller would do—but gazing at iPhone screens. The new urban creature prefers to trust a simulacrum as a guide to reality. It is anyone's guess what effect this development will have on the human brain. Many young people swear they now find it difficult to write by hand and no longer find it necessary to memorize mathematical formulas all students used to know. The coming generation will grow up without the ability to sense naturally the right direction to walk or drive in. On the other hand, people the age of the present authors have a comfort with computers and multiple electronic devices that an older generation would find bewildering. And even today's young adults will surely find themselves bewildered by what future generations learn to do with the tiny objects that at once scare us, empower us, and induce our dependency. When someone tampers with technology that we rely on, we are more helpless than we used to be. The reason this is a major theme of science fiction is that it speaks to something deep and true and frightening.

Stewart Baker, former policy chief at the US Department of Homeland Security, elegantly describes cycles in which technological innovation leads to social excitement about new technology and then dependency upon it. These cycles, he argues, take place with inadequate appreciation for the degree of vulnerability that all this dependency generates. For example, we build airplanes and fly them all over the world. We dramatically lower the price of commercial flights until long-distance travel is a norm in people's lives. Once this happens, however, hardly anyone spends much time considering the possibility that someone smart and creative might make missiles out of our commercial jets using nothing but box cutters and ruthlessness. "Technology—cheap commercial jet travel—made the [9/11] attacks possible. In fact, it made attacks like September 11 more or less inevitable," Baker writes. The question is, what attacks on ourselves are we now similarly making inevitable with the additional layers of dependency we incur daily? In the not-too-distant future, for instance, when driverless, semiautonomous cars take over our roads, people will be far more vulnerable to manipulations of the systems controlling these cars. Could we be inviting terrorism through mass traffic accidents?[6]

This is not a Luddite argument against technological development and adoption—merely a recognition that innovation that creates dependency also creates exposure. This effect operates largely independently of the earlier-noted reality that technologies that expand the power to attack necessarily expand vulnerability to attack.

The relationship between dependency and vulnerability is as inevitable as it is scary. Consider, for a moment, the smallpox vaccine. Smallpox, an often-fatal disease under any circumstances, is particularly devastating to a population previously unexposed to it; both its propensity to spread and its lethality are dramatically higher. That is why smallpox killed so many Native Americans, who had not previously confronted the virus, following the colonization of the New World. In the twentieth century, however, vaccination worldwide led to the virus's extinction in the wild, with the result that vaccination stopped, and today's world population almost entirely lacks immunity to the disease, should it ever reappear as a result of human manipulation or reintroduction. In other words, we are now almost entirely dependent on the success of our earlier public health efforts—and hugely vulnerable should those efforts ever fail or be undermined. In a similar vein, consider our reliance on antibiotics, which, over less than half a century, went from nonexistence to ubiquity for the most minor ailments. This development has saved an extraordinary number of lives, but the overuse of antibiotics for trivial matters also creates public health problems, encouraging the development of drug-resistant strains of bacteria.

The world of robotics, too, exhibits the close correlation between dependency and vulnerability. Consider the US government's growing reliance on drones and other robotic systems. On the traditional battlefield, for an army to seize an enemy's tank, troops had to capture it physically or else destroy it from the air—then destroy another and another. Robotic systems are often cheaper than tanks, easier to maintain, and lifesaving for our own troops—all reasons for their growing prevalence in advanced militaries. However, their effective operation depends on computers that enable command, control, and communication to guide and operate them, a dependency that generates vulnerability to malfunctions or tampering, possibly affecting an entire fleet of robots that operate on the same system. A military that relies on robots reaps great benefits but also faces the new vulnerabilities typical of these systems. And this new type of exposure is not unique to militaries or other armed groups; it is relevant to any corporation, institution, manufacturing plant, or medical center that relies on robots in its operation.

This point applies to all the technologies we use and not only in catastrophic, life-threatening cases. We are told to be careful about what we post on Facebook, what we write in e-mails, and how we use our credit cards online. Yet the advice, though sound, misses a big part of the point. Yes, we can avoid sending that snide e-mail about a colleague. And if we cannot help ourselves, we can at least take care not to hit "reply all." But electronic communications have become so endemic in modern life that we cannot realistically avoid storing large quantities of information in media over which we do not have ultimate control. We can only hope that there will never be a police investigation to which our transactions and communications are relevant and that the information technology departments in our workplaces are taking reasonable precautions to protect our information—and not themselves spying on us aggressively. We must also trust that our coworkers do not have the will or capacity to abuse or exceed whatever access they may have to our data. And we have not even started to worry about China, Russia, and other aggressive foreign state security services—or whether our communications might get swept up by the NSA.

Corporations and governments face similar dilemmas. They are well aware that economic espionage abounds and that competitor corporations, as well as other governments, invest considerable resources in spying on them. According to former counterintelligence official Joel Brenner, China, Russia, France, and Israel all engage in economic espionage against US companies, and private enterprises in these and other countries profit considerably from information they obtain. Yet corporations have no choice but to use computerized systems for everything from research and development to accounting, marketing, distribution, and communications. Indeed, technological innovation is the very business of the most vibrant American corporations. Although companies do make considerable efforts to protect themselves from cyberattacks and exploitations, weaknesses are inherent in the dependency.[7]

Governments, too, rely on computers to store and analyze gigantic volumes of information. Once stored, however, this information is vulnerable to exploitation and manipulation. Like everyone else, therefore, governments have to invest mounting resources in protecting everything from private data on citizens to military planning to espionage against foreign states. The more secrets the government collects, the greater the effort it must exert to protect them. But real protection is either extremely expensive or exists only when one isolates a computer from the network—thus severely limiting its utility. Connecting data streams is crucial for effective government functions. Think only of the 9/11 Commission's insistence on better sharing of information among relevant government security agencies. Yet better information sharing also erodes information security. The wide sharing of highly classified materials allowed Private First Class Bradley (now Chelsea) Manning to download hundreds of thousands of State Department cables from an army intelligence computer terminal near Baghdad onto one CD and share them with WikiLeaks. And the wider sharing of information allowed Edward Snowden to access so much of it. Sharing information means greater vulnerability. So does not sharing information.

In short, a society that stakes its future on the Internet, as today's society has done, makes itself enormously vulnerable to those with the will and the capacity to use its communications architecture to disrupt, say, its banking or military operations. Individuals, governments, and corporations relying on information technology to manage their lives and affairs necessarily distribute vulnerability to themselves in doing so.

This brings us to another feature of the distribution of vulnerability, one to which we have already alluded and that we might term the "Brenner effect." We are referring to Joel Brenner's Thomas Friedman–esque idea of a flattening of power relationships in the world, such that the vulnerabilities confronted by individuals are not so different from those confronted by states and governments: "The difficulties of protecting your privacy and mine and the difficulties of keeping secrets in an intelligence agency or corporate office are remarkably alike. Secrecy is to companies and governments as privacy is to individuals. Both rise or fall on the same technologies and cultural proclivities, and at the moment, both are falling precipitously."[8] The Brenner effect is key to understanding the new distribution of vulnerability, because it is the feature that brings about distribution rather than simply an increase in exposure. The privacy literature almost entirely ignores the Brenner effect, treating the problem of vulnerability as one of heightened individual exposure—always to governments, often to corporations, and sometimes even to other individuals. Most commentators, however, do not address the fact that those same governments and corporations are also themselves naked before individuals, before the press, and before one another. Consider the fact that according to one estimate, 95 percent of the US military's information transfers occur on civilian networks, rendering military communications as vulnerable as their civilian counterparts.[9]

In other words, even as technology generates a leveling in the attack function, it also generates a reciprocal leveling in vulnerability—exposing states to strategic threats from actors whom they used to regard merely as citizens or subjects or, indeed, aliens. To put it bluntly, we are all in the same boat now, one in which we are vulnerable to surveillance, theft, harassment, and even physical attack from a variety of actors capable of pursuing us with diminished accountability for their actions. It is a predicament that Thomas Hobbes never contemplated but that became very apparent after the 9/11 attacks: the weakest and the farthest away now have strength enough to attack even the Leviathan—even as the Leviathan can deliver a Hellfire missile anywhere in the world with pinpoint accuracy.

This raises another feature of the new vulnerability: it knows no geographic boundaries. Just as you cannot hide behind the lock on your front door, national borders do not offer an effective barrier against the spread of viruses, whether biological or electronic, or against information exploitation or remotely operated weapons. The Leviathan now has to protect itself against all potential enemies anywhere in the world, and it must also offer some degree of protection to its citizens from all potential enemies they may have anywhere, too.

Finally, the distribution of vulnerability involves the acceptance of some degree of metaexposure. That is, we live in a fishbowl even as we exploit the fact that others live in a fishbowl too. Luis Mijangos's spying on and extortion of women and girls were ultimately traceable by the FBI. Brenner offers a lengthy account of the successful effort, presumably Israeli, to kill a Hamas leader in Dubai, in which the activities of the secret agents were all captured on hotel cameras and other surveillance devices. "A few years ago," Brenner writes, "the assassins and surveillance teams would have vanished without a trace, but not this time. This was the first political assassination in history where most of the operation—all but the actual killing—was recorded on 648 hours of video, supplemented by electronic passport, travel, and key-card entry records." The FBI caught up with alleged anthrax terrorist Bruce Ivins in part because of e-mail and telephone records, GPS tracking of his car, and detailed forensic examination of the anthrax that he allegedly sent. Although technologies of mass empowerment make it easier to attack with impunity, impunity does not last forever. The same mosaic that documents every aspect of our lives also exposes us when we attack—so that, ironically, attacking also makes us vulnerable.[10]

PATTERNS OF DISTRIBUTED VULNERABILITY

Let us consider some concrete examples of the distribution of vulnerability in practice. While the spider scenario offers one possible example of our future vulnerability, our current situation offers no dearth of examples of risk, incurred every day and in every stratum of society, that we simply did not have to think about even as recently as a few years ago.

As with offensive capability, the distribution of vulnerability is most visible in the cyberarena—for the simple reason that technologies of connectivity have achieved nearly universal penetration, and society's dependence upon them is total. In this arena, we can also see repeated examples of metavulnerability—that is, of people's exposure to attack and surveillance even in the course of exploiting other people's exposure to attack and surveillance.

Judging from their behavior, most people do not feel especially unsafe online, and good data on the actual prevalence of cybercrime are notoriously difficult to come by. The reason for the latter is that a lot of cybercrime, particularly against companies, goes unreported because it tends to embarrass the companies in question, and we have little definitional consensus regarding what counts as cybercrime to begin with. Is a garden-variety fraud scheme that happens to take place online cybercrime, or do we mean to limit the concept to crimes that require networked computers? People use the term to mean many different things, and how one measures the severity of the problem partly depends on what crimes one considers it as encompassing. What is more, some analysts believe that the industry that has grown up around cybersecurity has significantly hyped cybercrime data in order to generate markets for its products. Wherever the truth lies, the cyberplatform clearly offers both individuals and larger entities many new modalities of attack, some with direct parallels to earlier forms of victimization, some that seem more novel. And the costs of defending against many types of cybercrime are generally huge in comparison to the direct costs of the attacks themselves.[11]

The most obvious channel of attack that the cyberworld opens up involves new modalities of theft—most notably theft of individuals' money, corporations' intellectual property, and governments' secrets. Simple cyberrobbery seems pretty common. One US Bureau of Justice Statistics study, for example, found that 7 percent of Americans aged sixteen or older—16.6 million people—had fallen victim to identity theft in 2012 alone. Most of these cases concerned credit card or bank account fraud, but other accounts were involved as well. An earlier study found that 5 percent of Americans above the age of sixteen had experienced identity theft over a two-year period, suggesting that the problem may be on the rise. While financial institutions absorbed most of the losses and individuals generally spent little time repairing the damage, some cases proved more difficult to handle. Victims of 3 percent of those cases were still dealing with the fallout of the identity theft six months later; 20 percent of victims described the episode as "severely distressing."[12]

Not all identity theft takes place online, of course, but its prevalence in recent years surely reflects the increased online presence of the average individual, as well as the availability and insecurity of mosaic data, people's susceptibility to phishing attacks, and the ability, once one has access to someone's account information, to exploit it quickly. Notably, statistics show that personal theft (including pickpocketing and purse snatching) and property theft in the United States have generally been on the decline in recent years. Considered against an overall decline in physical crime, the prevalence—and likely increase—of cybercrime, while unsurprising, warrants special attention.[13]

But cyberrobbery and cyberfraud are not the only new channels of vulnerability opened by the cyberarena. Online sexual assault, which does not always have a clear analog in the nondigital world, is another. Besides that of Mijangos, several horrifying sextortion cases have taken place over a relatively short period, each allowing an attacker to effectively invade the homes of relatively large numbers of victims by turning their own technology against them. In the spring of 2012, the owner of an Indiana Internet service provider was indicted on federal charges for extorting sexually explicit webcam videos from young boys by threatening to expose their prior uploads to friends and family. The FBI has estimated that he may have harmed hundreds of underage victims. Around the same time, a Florida man was charged with sextortion offenses with respect to eleven underage girls around the country, extorting from them images and videos in "various states of undress, naked, and engaging in sexually explicit conduct." Even if the sextortionist is in the United States, he can reach far-away computers, as in the case of one nineteen-year-old computer science student from California convicted of sextorting several young girls and women in the United States, Canada, and Ireland. Nor is cybersextortion a solely American phenomenon. In 2013 an Israeli man was convicted of extortion, sexual harassment, and the publication of obscene material after posing as a female soldier and tricking young girls into communicating with him. Under pressure, the communications became sexually explicit and exploitative. In denying the man's appeal against the two-year prison sentence imposed on him, the Israeli Supreme Court stated, "The thought that children are unsafe in their own home is a difficult one, and it turns out that there, in their own room in their house under the watchful eye of their parents, the appellant managed to trick them, hurt them, and cause them unimaginable harm."[14]

Cyberblackmail need not be about sex; it may just be about money—and may sometimes blur the line between shakedown and fraud. Another phenomenon on the rise has been the intentional infection of computers with malware by companies that then quickly solicit infected consumers with an offer for computer cleanup software.[15]

The cyberworld also opens new opportunities for school bullies. In the past, kids could harass a vulnerable classmate at or on the way to and from school; they could even post humiliating pictures or notes on school walls. It takes nothing away from the viciousness of such behavior to note that, however defenseless the victim might be in school, he or she had avenues of escape. Home could serve as refuge, as could transferring to a different school. Both acts physically removed the victim from the scene. Today, however, bullies can reach their victims wherever they are, and the humiliating pictures go on social-networking sites, where they are far harder to take down. They also reach a much bigger audience and continue to haunt victims even when they have taken reasonable steps to remove themselves from the presence of their tormentors. A 2013 Bureau of Justice Statistics report showed that about 9 percent of students aged twelve to eighteen reported having been bullied online. A wave of suicides by teen victims of cyberbullying over the past several years has sparked a great deal of attention, along with legislative proposals for harsher penalties and prosecutions under computer crime laws that were clearly not written with these types of acts in mind.[16]

Again, our point is not that cyberspace has made crime more prevalent or even necessarily worse than in the physical world—or that people are less secure because of it. We mean only that it has increased the number of ways we can face attack and rendered our traditional means of self-protection—separating ourselves from threats with walls, state lines, and even oceans—less relevant.

Notably, not only individuals face increased vulnerability. The cyber environment for corporations, while hotly disputed, is clearly bad too. The National Computer Security Survey documents the nature, prevalence, and impact of cyberintrusions against businesses in the United States. In 2005, it found that among close to eight thousand businesses examined, 67 percent detected at least one cybercrime (crimes in which the computer system is the target), and nearly 60 percent detected one or more types of cyberattack (including computer viruses, denial-of-service attacks, and electronic vandalism or sabotage). In a 2013 survey of 1,402 businesses, the British Department for Business Innovation and Skills found that 93 percent of large businesses (over 250 employees) and 87 percent of small businesses had suffered some sort of security breach, with 78 and 63 percent, respectively, being attacked by an outsider and 39 and 23 percent, respectively, experiencing distributed denial-of-service attacks.[17]

This phenomenon exists not only in America but throughout the cyberconnected world. To cite one example chosen almost at random, in 2010, leading Russian real estate websites were threatened with denial-of-service attacks if they did not pay a monthly sum of money to an online source. Those who refused to satisfy the ransomware demands quickly discovered that the blackmailers meant business. Those that did pay, on the other hand, were offered a further service: the ability to shut down their competitors' websites. Another example comes from India, which has recently overtaken the United States as the top global creator of junk e-mail messages. Beyond flooding inboxes, its flourishing community of spammers, hackers, and cybercriminals has inflicted serious harm on Indian consumers and businesses. According to research and accounting firm Ernst & Young, data or information theft was the most commonly committed form of fraud in India in 2011, costing companies targeted by cybercriminals as much as 5 percent of their profits. The Indian government actually has more serious concerns regarding what goes on in cyberspace than junk e-mail and cybertheft: according to the minister of state for communications and information technology, hackers attacked more than one hundred Indian government websites in the first quarter of 2012, generating grave concerns about national security vulnerabilities to terrorism and other threats.[18]

We could go on and on and on, for there are countless examples of new forms of vulnerabilities affecting governments, companies, and people who now have to scramble to secure channels of potential attack that did not exist a few years ago. Importantly, however, the vulnerabilities confront not only would-be victims but would-be attackers as well.

Indeed, the Brenner effect extends vulnerability even to those who would exploit the vulnerability of others. In the Indiana sextortion case, investigators were able to trace the Internet protocol (IP) address of the computer being used for the sextortion back to a man named Richard Leon Finkbiner, on whose computer they found thousands of video files involving underage victims engaged in explicit activity. In other words, Finkbiner's own mosaic gave him away, even as he allegedly preyed on the technologically induced vulnerability of teens. In early January 2013, Finkbiner pled guilty to "child exploitation, extortion, and possession of child pornography in exchange for a recommended sentence of 30 to 50 years in prison."[19]

This basic pattern plays out again and again on a great many levels: we are vulnerable to attack and surveillance, and so are our attackers. The Iranian government could not protect its nuclear program from an elaborate cyberattack by the United States and Israel, even by keeping the computers controlling its centrifuges disconnected from the Internet. The United States could not protect its intelligence from WikiLeaks or the *Guardian*, and Israel's Mossad was unable to protect its operatives from being filmed in Dubai. Cyberspies, presumably from China, in a single operation were able to infect at least 1,295 computers in more than one hundred countries with malware capable of taking full control of systems in order to spy on the Dalai Lama, news organizations, and the governments of numerous countries. But, as we will show in Chapter 3, these same cyberspies could not protect their operation from a group of Canadian researchers and security consultants who later issued a report about how they had seized control of the espionage network and "actively monitored [it] for two weeks [to] derive an extensive list of infected systems, and to also monitor the systems operator(s) as the operator(s) specifically target[ed] computers." The spies' control servers, the Canadian investigators reported, "were identified and geo-located from the captured traffic," and they could then be "probed" and identified, allowing investigators "to view and control the network." The mosaics of the Dalai Lama, governments, and news organizations gave them away to the presumably Chinese spies. But the spies had mosaics too—and those mosaics gave them away to a group of freelance Canadians.[20]

Or consider the hacktivist group Anonymous, an informal hacker collective that has launched cyberattacks and exploitations against such corporate and government powerhouses as the US Department of Justice, the FBI, Stratfor, the Universal Music Group, and many others. The group is a textbook example of the distribution of the attack function—a diffuse international network of like-minded, technically capable cyberprotesters whose prowess and loose-knit structure make its members resemble the wily mammals that once scampered between the lumbering feet of clumsy but powerful dinosaurs—in this case, dinosaurs of industry and sovereign power. And nothing quite demonstrates the new distribution of vulnerability like the havoc—some of it good-natured, some of it not—that the group has managed to wreak on these entities of great power and prestige.[21]

Yet Anonymous, too, has its mosaic. And Anonymous, too, is only as strong as its weakest link. In the summer of 2011, federal investigators homed in on a hacker named Hector Xavier Monsegur, a member of Anonymous and a leader of the related group LulzSec, who went online by the moniker "Sabu." Sabu's downfall, according to press reports, was the product of classic mosaic surveillance. According to one account, Sabu was always careful about masking his IP address, until he lapsed and entered an Internet chat room using no proxy server. That gave federal authorities his identity. They had been watching him for weeks until he briefly revealed himself, at which point they feared he would begin destroying evidence of his activities. So they moved in.[22]

Monsegur, a single foster father, quickly flipped, pled guilty, and for the next seven months actively helped the FBI build a case against other Anonymous members. The result, in March 2012, was a considerable set of charges against five other major hackers in the United States and abroad. Other indictments followed. Anonymous members found themselves as exposed to law enforcement as their own targets were to them. Prosecutors later credited Monsegur with helping to stop hundreds of cyberattacks. He also appears to have been involved in overseas cyberintelligence operations. He was eventually sentenced to time served and walked away a free man. In sentencing him, a federal judge said, "You have done as much as any human being can do in terms of helping the government to make up for your past wrongs and to avert other damage to probably millions of people."[23]

That same complex interaction of power and vulnerability exists on the biological front as well. Our knowledge of genetics has already delivered dramatic new approaches to disease control and therapies for all sorts of conditions. It has sparked innovation in agriculture and brought food to more people. It has even generated new cosmetic treatments. Biotechnology thus promises—indeed, has already delivered—great progress in human security, that is, in lessening vulnerability. Yet, again, in the hands of the wrong people, medical knowledge can become a way of generating danger. Sometimes, even in the right hands, medicine, microbiology, accidents, and menace can become hopelessly entangled.

Consider, for example, the controversy that erupted in 2011 over the publication of flu research by two groups of entirely reputable scientists. In December of that year, the US government, for the first time in its history, asked two scientific journals, *Science* and *Nature*, to withhold certain details of biomedical experiments they were about to publish. These details concerned ways of modifying the bird flu to make it more capable of spreading among human beings. Upon realizing that in the wrong hands this data could be used by terrorists, deranged individuals, or rogue states to launch a flu pandemic, the National Science Advisory Board for Biosecurity (NSABB), a panel overseen by the National Institutes of Health, approached the journals' editors with a request to withhold some of the methodological details of the study.[24]

Later, however, the board shifted gears. Following what it described as the presentation of "additional nonpublic data" and "key clarifications" by the authors, as well as subsequent revisions to the manuscripts, the NSABB met again. Its members came to a unanimous judgment that one of the papers, by Dr. Yorshihiro Kawaoka, could safely be published in full. The members, however, split over the manuscript by Dr. Ron Fouchier: a majority of twelve members recommended publishing it, with certain clarifications and the withholding of certain information, concluding that it was not "immediately enabling" and "may benefit public health and surveillance efforts." In other words, on balance they concluded that publication of the research would reduce human vulnerability. A minority of six members, however, saw the matter in diametrically opposite fashion. In their view, the data in the manuscript were "immediately and directly enabling." Even as revised, they argued, it "provide[d] information that would enable the near-term misuse of the research in ways that would endanger public health or national security." The mutations described in the paper, they contended, constituted flu viruses "transmissible between ferrets by respiratory route" and as dangerous as the original strain, which causes illness in people.[25] In other words, the dissenting voices thought that the publication of the data, on balance, would enhance vulnerability, making an attack or accident in the form of a flu pandemic more likely.

In the end, the research was published in full in the June 21, 2012, issue of *Science*. In response to the controversy, many flu virologists put a voluntary moratorium on research into the pathological potential of bird flu. The moratorium ended in January 2013, after more than a year, when the forty researchers who had agreed to the moratorium decided to start work again. As Dr. Ron Fouchier, author of the controversial *Science* piece, put it, "That means that 40 of the world's leading experts in influenza research seem to think that the benefits outweigh the risks." Another researcher elaborated, "The risk exists in nature already, and not doing the research is really putting us in danger." Those researchers decided, among themselves, that foregoing research was riskier than performing it. Everyone here had the same goal: to protect people from disease, expand treatment options, and control the spread of infectious agents. Yet there was a lack of consensus as to whether fateful steps like publication would advance or undermine that goal.[26]

The Brenner effect yields similar patterns with respect to robotic weaponry, which both spreads and accrues vulnerability. As a great many terrorist operatives in Somalia, Yemen, and the tribal areas of Pakistan have learned, it is hard to hide from a Predator drone. Yet, true to the rule that a predator will always be preyed upon (and that an advantage is also always a disadvantage), robotic instruments themselves turn out to be vulnerable to viruses and hacks—just like any other device that depends on code and networking. And the hackers need not be states or even sophisticated technology companies. In December 2009, the *Wall Street Journal* reported that insurgents in Iraq had used a $26 piece of off-the-shelf software to capture live video feeds from Predators. Later, *Wired* magazine's *Danger Room* blog reported that the control computers driving the US drone fleet had been hit with a virus that proved resistant to efforts to remove it from both classified and unclassified computers at the air force base in Nevada from which the drones are controlled. "We keep wiping it off, and it keeps coming back," one person familiar with the problem told *Wired*. "We think it's benign. But we just don't know." A military that increasingly depends on highly sophisticated and highly connected technology inherently incurs vulnerability even as that technology renders it an ever more effective and menacing means of distributing vulnerability to others.[27]

SYMMETRIES AND ASYMMETRIES

Although, in key respects, we are all in the same boat, the distribution of vulnerability remains unequal. To note a leveling trend in which vulnerability tends to spread is not to say that the spread is total or even. To say that we all stand naked before our mosaics is not to say that all of our mosaics are equally well developed, ripe for exploitation, or interesting. Indeed, some people's nakedness excites a great deal more fascination than other people's. And some is more easily seen. The US government has a far more developed mosaic than, for example, you do and represents a dramatically more attractive target as well. You, in turn, have a dramatically better-developed cybermosaic than does a poor person in Mali—who likely does not have one at all—and you also present a more appealing target. But the US government, for all its attractiveness as a target, also has vast defensive resources unavailable to you—let alone to the poor person in Mali, whose only defense lies in having too few resources to have incurred much mosaic exposure to begin with. Enormous asymmetries thus remain in the degree and quality of vulnerability and the capacity of different actors to protect themselves. To say that we are all in the same boat, in short, is not to say that we are all in the same cabin class. To note a leveling trend is not to say that the world of vulnerability is flat.

The spread of technologies of mass empowerment has not, so far, returned us to a worldwide Hobbesian state of nature in which all are constantly attacking all—and fearing attack from all. In well-functioning societies, after all, not many aspire to be school shooters, and few set out in the morning to spy on each other in detail. Statistically, you are unlikely to face an online sexual assault or even, more prosaically, a serious identity theft. The costs you incur by storing your life in the mosaic will probably not exceed the benefits of the many conveniences the mosaic affords. You will, it is to be sincerely hoped, not fall victim to the pandemic spread of a disease caused intentionally or accidentally by human interference with a viral or bacterial genome. Rather, you will continue to reap the benefits of the biotechnology revolution while the dangers remain hypothetical, the stuff of science fiction and alarmist, fearmongering futurists. You do not have to fear that the spider in your shower is more than a spider—at least not yet. For now, the distribution of vulnerability in this area is a trend, not an endpoint. Technology may strip us naked, but it still protects us in other ways.

The trouble is that there may be a tipping point beyond which this general rule ceases to be true or the exposure grows intolerable or oppressive on its own terms. It could be the nuclear weapon in the pocket, the global pandemic, or another form of catastrophic event. Or it could be that the number of channels of vulnerability—and the number of people with access to those channels—becomes so great that the net effects of technological development cease to be salutary. A perfect distribution of vulnerability—the ungoverned terror of the state of nature—is precisely the condition that liberal political theory conceived of government as re-mediating. For now, however, we see a trend. The question, therefore, is how far the current trend will progress, what forces will push against it, and whether we will develop defensive systems and governance approaches that limit the vulnerability of actors of different sorts at all levels of society.

We turn now to these defensive capacities.

3

THE DISTRIBUTION OF DEFENSE

WHEN THE DALAI LAMA and the Tibetan government-in-exile found themselves under a sustained campaign of cyber intrusions in 2008, they did not turn to their host government—the government of India—for protection. Nor was the investigation that uncovered the so-called Ghost-Net attacks conducted by the intelligence service of either a friendly nation or one of the many other governments and international organizations that GhostNet turned out also to be targeting—a list that included Bangladesh, Cyprus, Germany, Indonesia, Iran, Latvia, Malta, Pakistan, Portugal, Romania, Taiwan, and Thailand, as well as the North Atlantic Treaty Organization and the Association of Southeast Asian Nations Secretariat. In a strange inversion of the way security is usually handled, in which governments investigate attacks on individuals and organizations, a group called the Information Warfare Monitor investigated GhostNet and revealed its many attacks on governments. The Information Warfare Monitor describes itself as "a public-private venture between two Canadian institutions: the SecDev Group, an operational think tank based in Ottawa (Canada), and the Citizen Lab at the Munk Centre for International Studies, University of Toronto." Rather than a police organization or an intelligence agency, it is basically a collection of private and university researchers who decided to play in the big leagues against a major cyberespionage network targeting governments and likely run by China. At least in this instance, a small nonstate group uncovered something big and directed at states.

Seen from one vantage, the GhostNet case may not appear all that unusual. After all, these investigators did something like national security journalism: a private outfit investigated an espionage network and broke a big story. Viewed this way, the incident feels familiar enough. But there is another way to look at the Information Warfare Monitor's GhostNet study, one that makes it seem a little less familiar. From this vantage, we see traditional players in foreign policy and espionage turning to private outsiders for technical and investigative help and protection, and the spread of technologies of mass empowerment gives these outsiders the ability to engage as players in the cyberdomain against an active intelligence operation. The authors of the GhostNet report note that "cyberspace has empowered individuals and small groups of non-state actors to do many things, including executing sophisticated computer network operations that were previously only the domain of state intelligence agencies. We have entered the era of *do-it-yourself* (DIY) signals intelligence."[1] What the authors do not say, but which the existence of their report testifies to loudly, is that we have also entered the era of DIY signals counterintelligence.

We have seen how new technologies of mass empowerment distribute threats and thus also distribute vulnerabilities among various actors. As a consequence and in parallel, the defense function is distributing too. Technologies of mass empowerment, after all, are not exclusively technologies of attack. They also empower many more actors to participate in defense. The proliferation of biotechnology, for example, allows any number of people and organizations to work on vaccines—just as it allows people to experiment with building their own viruses. The proliferation of networked computers enables the proliferation of cyberattack capability, but it also generates a cybersecurity industry. A necessary corollary of the distribution of the capacity for attack and the distribution of vulnerability, therefore, is a parallel distribution of the ability to defend.

Indeed, the GhostNet incident is far from the only case in which technologies of mass empowerment have put into private hands the robust defensive capacities we typically associate with governments or in which governments have thus come to rely on private expertise for key security functions. And it is not just governments like Latvia, Malta, and Cyprus that are seeing this migration of security responsibilities to private actors. Which US government agency in February 2013 uncovered the Chinese People's Liberation Army cyberespionage group known as Unit 61398, tracked its operations, outed some of its operatives, and identified the location of its home base? None, actually. The report, which served as a harbinger of a major federal indictment against Chinese military officers in May 2014, was the work of a private computer security company then known as Mandiant. Mandiant took DIY signals counterintelligence to a whole new level with its concerted effort over time to reveal what it described as a recurrent "advanced persistent threat" responsible for "security breaches at hundreds of organizations around the world." Months after Mandiant's report, the Pentagon, for the first time, declared in its annual report on China that the Chinese military was engaged in persistent cyberespionage against the US government. As cybersecurity policy specialist Paul Rosenzweig wrote in response, the sequence "leaves me wondering (quite seriously) if there is something wrong with the picture that this declaration follows the action of a private sector company (Mandiant) instead of preceding it."[2] There have been other similar cases since.

The trend of the private sector's playing a major role in defense is not in any sense limited to cybersecurity. Consider an American company called Palantir Technologies, whose website describes its product as "software that reveals intelligence hidden within hairy complex systems," designed "for integrating, visualizing and analyzing the world's information." Since September 11, 2001, the intelligence community has been looking for better ways to "connect the dots"—the tiny items of intelligence that are insignificant on their own, mere needles in the giant haystacks of information available to authorities, which, properly analyzed, offer the actionable leads needed to identify and counter threats. In the wake of 9/11, the government famously tried to produce a massive data-mining system to do this, but as Shane Harris, author of *The Watchers*, writes, "It failed." On the other hand, Palantir has not failed. As Harris notes in a magazine article, Palantir's software represents a real breakthrough in the problem of "how to organize and catalog intimidating amounts of data and then find meaningful insights that humans alone usually can't." As a result, government agencies are lining up to patronize this Silicon Valley start-up:

> Palantir has sold its software to the CIA, the military's Special Command, and the Marine Corps, which use it to help track down terrorists. The FBI, the Defense Intelligence Agency, the National Counterterrorism Center, and the Department of Homeland Security are customers. The director of the National Security Agency (NSA) has said Palantir's software could help the agency "see" into cyberspace to defend against hackers and spies attempting to breach government computer networks. The board that's set up to oversee federal stimulus spending uses the software to spot fraud. The Los Angeles Police Department uses Palantir. So does the New York Police

Department, whose intelligence-and-counterterrorism unit rivals the sophistication of the FBI and CIA.[3]

Or consider another example from an entirely different context: a company called ShotSpotter, which deploys audio sensors around high-crime neighborhoods in cities. Whenever a gun is fired, ShotSpotter's systems triangulate the sound of the gunshot to a precise location, identify the sound as a gunshot (as opposed to, say, a firecracker or a truck backfiring), and notify local police of the spot where the gun discharged. From its nerve center in Mountain View, California, ShotSpotter serves police clients nearly instantaneously in around seventy cities all over the country. It allows police to respond to gunshots that may not provoke 9-1-1 calls and to do so far more quickly and with far greater geographical precision than if the cops were to rely on locals to call in the shots.[4]

The role of the private sector in security is, of course, far from new. Defense contractors have long operated as private-sector arms of the state for purposes ranging from logistical support to transportation, communications, and the development and manufacture of weapons systems. Indeed, in recent years, especially in Iraq and Afghanistan, private contractors have become key players in vital aspects of government security work. A great many technologies with security implications and applications have been developed in the private sector or by private companies, often under government contracts. And the intelligence community has long turned to private partners for analytical help.[5]

In one sense, the distribution of defensive capacity is a blessing for those worried about the distribution of offensive capacity. It is a counterweight and a force multiplier for governments that suddenly have to police a proliferation of ultracapable attackers. It offers individuals and companies a potential alternative to government as an address for protection. It is a deep comfort that just as the advent of technologies of mass empowerment has given enormous numbers of people the capacity to do great harm, it has also given enormous numbers of people and organizations the capacity to prevent that harm. Indeed, the proliferation of defensive capability is—at least in theory—exponentially greater than the proliferation of offensive capability because the good guys vastly outnumber the bad guys.

But the distribution of defense also raises big questions about the role and primacy of the state in matters of both national and individual security.

The exploding development of technologies that, though not intended for security purposes in the first instance, nevertheless have potential application to security problems necessarily makes the age-old government reliance on private technical capacity loom larger. More fundamentally, the law of security itself has begun adapting—slowly, incrementally, and in a fashion that largely escapes the public debate—to the fact that private actors are taking on security responsibilities. Even in the fabric of the law, we are knitting the private sector into the security functions of the state. The result is a relationship between the private sector and the state that looks a lot less like the traditional relationship between government and the defense contractor entrusted with security-related tasks and a lot more like the relationship between government and the private sector in general-purpose health and safety regulation. In that latter relationship, the private sector does not assume any official security role on behalf of the state; nor does it act in lieu of state agents. Instead, private entities are mandated by law with the responsibility to ensure that ordinary commercial or recreational activities are conducted in a fashion that is safe and healthy for everyone. As the lines separating security-related products and activities from those that are not become increasingly blurry, so defense from harm becomes less a primary governmental function and more a collective responsibility that harnesses the private sector.

THE MIGRATION OF DEFENSIVE RESPONSIBILITIES

Watching the scandal unfold in the summer of 2013 over surveillance by the National Security Agency, you might not have guessed that a migration of security responsibilities to private actors was under way at all. The spree of leaks by former NSA contractor Edward Snowden revealed an agency of awesome collection power—one with mind-boggling capacity to target global Internet and telephone communications, one that was breaking strong encryption systems and systematically gobbling up records of telephone calls placed domestically and scooping up large volumes of e-mails and other electronic communications all over the world. It is a collection capacity unrivaled in the history of the world. And at least at first glance, it is the government that has it.[6]

Yet, look again and the picture gets fuzzier. Yes, the scope of government collection activities is awesome. And yes, it is growing, if largely as a function of the ever increasing volume of mosaic data available for collection. But consider the specific information Snowden released and what it really reveals. It shows the government seeking court orders against Verizon—and presumably other telecommunications carriers—under a federal statute for access to domestic data about who is calling whom. It shows the government dependent on Google and Facebook and other Internet companies for access to those Internet communications it is so busily sweeping in. It shows, in short, that the government's power here is actually derivative; it depends on the law to demand help from private actors, without whom government would be lost. In short, those awesome collection powers are not just technical capacities; they are also legal powers to compel private assistance in collection.[7]

Indeed, while government's defensive powers may be growing as technology and innovation give it more capacity, its defensive powers are simultaneously growing less organic and more dependent. To meet the new distributed threat environment, even the most powerful governments are turning to forms of distributed defense, using law, money, and other inducements to recruit the private sector to tasks it cannot perform on its own. The Food and Drug Administration (FDA) cannot make your food and drugs safe; the Nuclear Regulatory Commission does not directly operate nuclear power plants. These agencies oversee regulatory processes by which the companies that make food and drugs or operate nuclear plants perform those activities in a safe manner. Increasingly, security is coming to work the same way.

There are visible and invisible forms of this migration. The most visible is the increased reliance on contractors, of which Snowden himself represents—at least for the government—an ill-fated example. At another level, the CIA started In-Q-Tel, a not-for-profit venture capital firm that invests in software, infrastructure, and material—including in Palantir—for the CIA and other US intelligence agencies. It is a public-private partnership, which, as then CIA director General David Petraeus observed, is essential for the intelligence community's modern challenges: "It used to be acceptable to take years to build a new capability. Now we're lucky if we have months between identifying a need and deploying a solution. Sometimes the deadline we're facing is only weeks—or even days. Industry's ability to rapidly prototype new products and get them to market—especially our market—is a skill that government simply cannot match. And so, in many cases, we rely on the private sector for the developmental speed that intelligence work requires."[8]

The US intelligence community is not the only official body seeking the assistance of the private sector. Kaspersky Lab is a Russian multinational computer security company and the world's largest privately held vendor of software security products. With regional offices all over the world, Kaspersky boasts that its products and technologies provide protection for more than 300 million users and more than 250,000 corporate clients worldwide. (Many observers also believe the group has ties to Russian intelligence agencies.) In May 2012, Kaspersky Lab announced that in investigating a virus that had infected Iranian Oil Ministry computers, it had identified the malware Flame, which it described as potentially "the most sophisticated cyber weapon yet unleashed." Kaspersky claimed that its investigation was originally commissioned by the United Nations International Telecommunication Union (ITU). Although the ITU denied this, it acknowledged Kaspersky as a "key partner" in its cybersecurity initiatives, which involve cooperation with industry and public-private partnerships. Other entities that have partnered with the ITU include Symantec, the United Nations Office on Drugs and Crime, Microsoft, and others.[9]

In both of these cases, we see very public recruitment of industry in one form or another to assist public authorities in performing their own security functions. Indeed, so pervasive is the understanding that the private sector has a key role to play in cybersecurity that the term "public-private partnership" has become a cliché in the cybersecurity world. Unlike traditional contractors, who merely stand in for government actors in performing a security function, this type of public-private partnership is driven not by efficiency or cost-cutting concerns but rather by the realization that private industry today has capacities that, particularly when aggregated, governments cannot replicate on their own. Just as the FDA alone cannot protect the food supply, the NSA all by itself—even with all its capacity—cannot actually conduct its signals intelligence mission.

A subtler trend than the reliance on private actors for their expertise has been legal reliance on them for their special position within the architecture of threats and vulnerabilities. That is, certain companies provide privately owned channels through which one can now attack the United States, and the law is adapting to make those who own and operate these channels take responsibility for their security.

In 1994, Congress passed the Communications Assistance for Law Enforcement Act (CALEA) "to make clear a telecommunications carrier's duty to cooperate in the interception of communications for law enforcement purposes." The passage of CALEA, which requires that telecommunications companies maintain the technical capacity to facilitate lawful wiretaps as technology progresses, generated an intense controversy between law enforcement and civil liberties activists, who decried a proposal they saw as making wiretapping easier. Today people who remember the CALEA fight at all remember it as an early skirmish in what became a long-running standoff between those who want a more and those who want a less libertarian Internet. In retrospect, however, and for the present purposes, CALEA carried a different significance.[10]

CALEA represented a congressional acknowledgment that technology was outstripping the government's security function, that absent a deliberate intervention by private parties—specifically, by the telecommunications companies—the government would lose its ability to conduct wiretaps, even with appropriate court warrants. Congress thus recognized formally in law that certain industries, by the nature of their businesses, had capabilities that government lacked and that the failure to deploy these capabilities would impair the government's capacity to perform some of its most basic functions. It recognized further that only a tight relationship between government and these industries could ensure the deployment of these capabilities. And it thus demanded that the telecommunications companies build this relationship into the very technical architecture of their systems. Whereas in the past telecommunications companies ran wires that the government was free—with a warrant—to tap using its own agents and alligator clips, modern digital telecommunications infrastructure threatened to make this authority irrelevant by mingling zillions of communications together in a giant digital bit stream. So under CALEA, the law required that "a telecommunications carrier shall ensure that its equipment, facilities, or services . . . are capable of . . . expeditiously isolating and enabling the government, pursuant to a court order or other lawful authorization, to intercept, to the exclusion of any other communications, all wire and electronic communications carried by the carrier." And it authorized the Justice Department to pay the companies to upgrade their systems to facilitate this capability—a provision that functioned at the outset as way of paying off the telecommunications companies so that they would not oppose the bill.[11]

Under CALEA, the telecommunications companies—corporations whose business is not delivering security products to the government but providing consumer services to the general public—became legally integrated with the nation's law enforcement and intelligence apparatus. This happened not because of some changing conception of civil liberties or because of a government power grab but because technological development had made the government's security function, as we had come to under-stand it, unachievable absent pervasive private-sector involvement. If the companies did not build the network to be watchable, it would not be.

CALEA is an early example of one way in which we can reasonably expect the law of security to adapt to the distribution of defensive capacity brought about by technologies of mass empowerment. It is by no means the only example. CALEA itself has grown in scope over the years and is now understood to cover not only traditional telephone communications but also Internet traffic and voice-over-IP transmissions. The FBI, as of this writing, is pushing for further expansion of the law.[12]

In the same period that Congress passed CALEA, the government sought to persuade manufacturers of telecommunication devices to adopt an encryption standard known as the Clipper Chip, which had built into it a back-door decryption method that the government could use with a warrant. The measure failed because of a combination of civil libertarian and industry opposition, but it has a similar intellectual trajectory to CALEA: technological development gave individuals—including individual bad guys—the ability to encrypt their communi-cations, and the government, fearful of losing ground in its ability to protect security, asked industry to bake its ability to intercept into the fundamental architecture of products. While the Clipper Chip was ac-tually an NSA-designed system, not a private innovation, the episode nevertheless represents an example of government urging private actors to design their systems so as to enable, rather than impede, government security functions. Interestingly, one of Snowden's disclosures revealed that after the Clipper Chip initiative failed, the NSA secretly pushed many companies to create just such a back door in their encrypted prod-ucts. In the fall of 2014, the FBI began publicly pushing companies to retain the ability to decrypt smartphone data.[13]

This trend of legally requiring that security concerns be addressed architecturally has continued into the present. In 2008, Congress passed the Foreign Intelligence Surveillance Act Amendments Act of 1978 (FAA), which, along with its temporary predecessor law, created a statutory basis for parts of the George W. Bush administration's earlier warrantless wire-tapping program. Like CALEA, the FAA, which was renewed in 2012, responded to the awesome proliferation of communications technology by binding the telecommunications companies more tightly to the na-tion's intelligence apparatus. Recognizing that espionage was impossible without the pervasive cooperation of these companies, the law gave the government the ability—with a kind of basket warrant—to demand and receive the assistance of the telecommunications companies in programs of overseas collection. Under the terms of the law and the orders the government could seek from the Foreign Intelligence Surveillance Court pursuant to its provisions, the telecommunications carriers would turn over not merely an individual's communications but giant streams of content over time, so long as the targets were "reasonably believed" to be overseas. It was this law, in part, whose operations Snowden compromised.[14]

Espionage used to involve theft and the surreptitious tapping of wires. Now it involves statutes that obligate major companies, under court orders, to share whole feeds of data with the government, to clear corporate personnel to participate in highly classified activity, and to participate in an integrated way with covert programs. The reason is clear: The lines into and out of the country are owned and operated by private parties. The data streams are broken into bits, transmitted, and reassembled at the other end by these private parties. The government quite simply lacks sufficient access to and control over these data streams to conduct surveillance of them without the cooperation of these private parties. So the law, to the extent the country still seeks to engage in espionage, simply has to compel the parties with actual capabilities to use them to facilitate the espionage we wish to engage in.

The legal obligations reflected in laws like the FAA and CALEA draw on threads in the relationship between the intelligence community and the telecommunications carriers that go back a long way. The Church Committee, a US Senate select committee established in the aftermath of the Watergate scandal to study intelligence activities, reported in 1976 on Operation Shamrock, under which the NSA received from RCA Global and ITT World Communications copies of millions of international telegrams sent to or from Americans:

> The SHAMROCK program began in August 1945, when representatives of the Army Signals Security Agency approached the commercial telegraph companies to seek post-war access to foreign governmental traffic passing over the facilities of the companies. Despite advice from their attorneys that the contemplated intercept operation would be illegal in peacetime, the companies agreed to participate, provided they received the personal assurance of the Attorney General of the United States that he would protect them from suit, and that efforts be immediately undertaken to legalize the intercept operation. Apparently

these assurances were forthcoming, because the intercept program began shortly thereafter.[15]

Operation Shamrock is not a happy precedent; it was one of the gross civil liberties abuses by the government uncovered in the Watergate era. But it turns out that Shamrock so disquieted the American civil libertarian sensibility not because the government was relying on the cooperation of private actors in surreptitious covert programs but because it was doing so extralegally. Relying on those same actors under an act of Congress and with ongoing judicial review rubs people in a very different way. And one can see in the movement from Shamrock to CALEA and the FAA the enhanced comfort that both statutory schemes and ongoing review can provide for controversial relationships between government and the private sector. In 1976, Congress saw the close cooperative relationship between the NSA and the telegraph companies as disreputable—and stopped it. By 1994, by contrast, Congress had come to see preserving some such close relationship between the NSA and industry on telephony as essential. And in 2007 and 2008, it mandated—admittedly with all sorts of legal limitations designed to prevent the sort of spying on Americans that had characterized the early postwar period—a very tight operating relationship between the government and the carriers, one in which the industry lives under a constant obligation to facilitate the flow of data to government.

This trend toward compelling industry participation in government security programs is visible not just in telecommunications. Consider the requirements on banks to report suspicious wire transfer activity to the Financial Crimes Enforcement Network (FinCEN), a federal agency that tracks money laundering and other misbehavior involving money. Financial institutions have long been required by law to report any wire transfers of $10,000 or more, and it is a crime to structure a series of financial transactions so as to evade those reporting requirements. But the law, since passage of the USA Patriot Act in 2001, has also required banks to report various categories of suspicious activity. Indeed, the catagories on the forms that FinCEN uses for reporting suspicious activity include everything from money laundering to bribery to computer intrusions to terrorist financing. Any transactions the banks consider fishy have to be reported to FinCEN, and these are then mined by the agency for relevance to a range of investigations. But notice who does the initial screening. The identification of the transactions has to be conducted not by the government but by the financial institutions themselves, which have had to adjust their accounting systems to build in algorithms to identify reportable suspicious activity. Government does not control the channels of an immense swath of economic activity. For authorities to know who is giving what money to whom, the private actors who operate the banking system have to provide the front line of surveillance. And under these regulations, they do it on a routine basis.[16]

Not all examples of the migration of security responsibility to private actors have yet made it into law. The government had to stand back and watch as British Petroleum (BP) tried to plug the hole it had made at the bottom of the Gulf of Mexico—that is, as a foreign corporation took the lead in defending America's coastline against devastation. The Oil Pollution Act of 1990 made BP the "responsible party" in financial terms for the cleanup. But BP was effectively the responsible party in practical terms as well; that is, it was the party responsible for conducting the actual operation necessary for the defense of the country's interest in the wake of the disaster. The reason is the same as for why the law makes banks the frontline surveillance gatekeeper for suspicious financial activity: BP had capability, essential to a successful resolution of the problem it had created, that the government lacked. This actually is a conventional health and safety regulation, which normally allocates responsibility to the party best situated to prevent the harm (most commonly, producers or manufacturers); yet we can see it here playing a national security role.[17]

For a less visible example, consider the relationship that has developed between the Secret Service and manufacturers of color laser printers, which are a potential dream come true for currency counterfeiters. The widely dispersed, cheap ability to make high-quality, detailed color images might—without some kind of intervention—have serious implications for the integrity of the currency. So quietly, without legal compulsion, printer manufacturers began to build their systems so as to embed identifying information onto every page that the printers spew out. Color laser printers now produce a barely visible pattern of tiny dots on each page, a pattern that allows the Secret Service to trace those pages back to the specific printer that produced the image.[18]

Take all of these examples together—and there are many more—and the trend is clear. It runs deeper than just routine cooperation between government and the private sector on security matters. It is, at some level, a migration in law, practice, and custom of important security functions—surveillance, analysis, interception, and even protection of the coastline—from government to private actors. This migration is taking place not because of any philosophical or ideological shift toward a belief in privatization. Nor is it taking place because of some loss of faith in government capacity or even because of the inherent limits of government capacity. Rather, it is taking place because of an underlying shift in actual control over the architecture through which attacks and other security threats take place and through which vulnerability to attacks expresses itself. It used to be that to attack America, one had to land troops on her shores or fly airplanes over her territories. If one could invade the United States by landing troops on privately controlled beaches and traveling only on privately owned roads and streets, the owners of those beaches, roads, and streets might take on certain legal and practical responsibilities for securing the use of their property.

Something similar is starting to happen on many physical and virtual frontiers: one can attack America—or any other country—in a variety of ways while interacting only with architecture owned and operated by private parties of various sorts: by using color printers or telecommunications infrastructure; by transferring money through private banks; by purchasing genetic sequences from private companies or using machines built by other private companies to construct one's own genetic sequences or modify existing ones; or by printing and assembling devices that in turn injure or kill people. This inevitably invests in the operations of these intermediary parties some aspect of the security function.

This is, we suspect, the thin edge of a very significant wedge.

THE PERILS OF DISTRIBUTED DEFENSE

The idea that private parties have citizenship obligations to cooperate with and participate in various aspects of the government's security functions has been around a long time. To cite an elemental example, the principle that the grand jury is entitled to every man's evidence—that every person has some obligation to help investigative efforts surrounding crimes—has lain beneath the entire criminal justice system since the dawn of the republic. No less elemental is military conscription, which is still the norm in many countries, remains a specifically enumerated congressional power in the US Constitution, and is considered the prerogative of the state vis-à-vis its citizens. The government has long had a bewildering array of legal authorities under a variety of statutes to collect information held in the hands of private parties pursuant to criminal, civil, and national security investigations—and these laws have sometimes included affirmative reporting obligations on the part of those private parties. When threat levels rise, governments frequently secure the voluntary cooperation of private parties with relevant information and expertise. As legal scholar Jon D. Michaels writes in an informative article evocatively titled "Deputizing Homeland Security," when "the demand for intelligence and intelligence operatives spiked after 9/11, the wide-scale solicitation of private assistance suddenly reemerged as a respectable and perhaps even necessary practice." Government programs sprang up—many of them voluntary, some not—under which "corporations representing all of the major retail and service industries—including telecommunications, finance, and commercial travel—are routinely turning over reams of information to the government. And it's not just corporate data dumps; it's also doormen, pilots, truck drivers, retail clerks, repairmen, and parcel couriers, who have been enlisted by government, their employers, and even their own unions to detect and report suspicious activities on the ground."[19] Even the notion that certain companies, by dint of the nature of their businesses, acquire special security responsibilities has precursors. The nuclear energy industry, for example, necessarily has to take responsibility for securing and accounting for radioactive materials that would otherwise proliferate. And the government has long had the authority under the Invention Secrecy Act to effectively gag inventors by preventing private parties submitting patent applications for technologies with national security significance from talking publicly about their innovations, essentially binding these private parties to the government, whether they want to be so bound or not. What is new here is the rise of nongovernmental actors capable—either on their own or in concert with governments—of defending the platforms they operate or engage with and the centrality of those platforms to the lives of individuals and nations.

This distribution of defensive capacity may sound like good news, and in many ways it is. But it is not entirely good news. This idea of a distributed defensive function is a disquieting one—all the more disquieting the more one contemplates it. The notion that the government has a monopoly over security policy is old and venerable. Erode it, and you erode a part of the conceptual basis for modern government itself.[20]

The government's monopoly over security policy is deeply embedded in the American constitutional fabric, at least as that fabric developed over the country's history. As an original matter, this point was contested. The Constitution contains a few important textual exceptions to the proposition that national security is a federal responsibility. One of these exceptions, the Second Amendment, embodies the Framers' reverence for state militias, both as a means of fending off native attacks and as a means of preventing federal encroachments on state prerogatives. The other, the Letters of Marque and Reprisal Clause of Article I, contemplates a limited role for the private sector in military engagements under congressional supervision. The basic idea was that privateers—government-backed pirates, essentially—might receive congressional sanction to attack and seize enemy shipping. But the broader presumptions in the document were that Congress would make the rules of security and that the president would lead the armed forces and the larger executive apparatus in a military or other crisis. And these presumptions have proven more lasting. Indeed, they have dominated in the country's subsequent development with respect to the governance of security. Conversely, the exceptional institutions envisioned in the Constitution—privateers and militias—have long since lapsed into disuse. Centralized command authority and strong executive leadership in times of crisis have become mainstays of the American political system.[21]

Strong central government and, within that government, a strong executive, were designed to yield a democratically accountable government that could actually do things. And not coincidentally, some of the concerns that led to the creation of a strong central government and a strong executive were, among others, security related. Alexander Hamilton, father of the American conception of the strong executive, himself minced no words on this point, justifying the power of the presidency as necessary for defense and security. In fact, enhancing security was one of his principal arguments in favor of the centralizing features of the Constitution more generally. First on Hamilton's list in Federalist 23 of "the principal purposes to be answered by union are these—the common defense of the members [and] the preservation of the public peace, as well against internal convulsions as external attacks."[22]

History has treated Hamilton kindly on this point. There is, at this stage, huge historical weight behind centralization as a governance principle for the optimization of defense. There is a reason that militaries organize themselves hierarchically—that they have vertical command structures. There is a reason that nations facing significant security threats tend to have strong central governments with strong executive leaderships. The reason is that, as Hamilton famously put it, "energy in the executive is . . . essential to the protection of the community against foreign attacks." Yet the distribution of defensive capacity tends to push against this notion—now so embedded in the American fabric—of a strong state being the organ of our protection. If government does not control the channels through which attacks will take place, government alone cannot meaningfully protect those channels. If every person can play with and design robots, including robots that print the component parts of other robots, governments alone cannot protect us from robots. If a virus—or a vaccine—can emerge from any of thousands of private labs, the private sector will necessarily play a crucial role in biosecurity.[23]

The fact that the defense function, as a consequence of technology proliferation, grows ever more distributed thus involves a bit of a paradox: government potentially has a great deal of help, but the mechanism of that help cuts against centuries of developed understanding of how societies most effectively organize themselves against external and internal threats. They do not generally do it by diffusing power through a multiplicity of actors—much less a multiplicity of private actors, accountable to an even greater multiplicity of shareholders (including foreign shareholders). They do it, generally speaking, by creating a small, centralized, and empowered hierarchy of officials responsible for security. Countries that tolerate private armies and highly diffused military power—Afghanistan, Somalia, and Yemen, for example—do not fare well in the modern world. The emergence of technologies of mass empowerment thus stands to touch the very structural arrangements of power in American life—and life in most other states as well.

Think about it this way. During the Cold War, almost nobody wanted to see a nuclear war. And there was a fair bit of talk about and public training for civil defense and public involvement in preparedness. Yet the individual role in preventing the Soviet Union from launching a nuclear attack against the United States or starting a conventional war against the West—or vice versa—was, in actual fact, vanishingly close to zero. Today, similarly, almost nobody wants to see a devastating biological attack or a crippling cyberattack. But unlike during the Cold War, individual scientists and engineers and groupings of them play enormous roles in biosecurity and cybersecurity: driving the innovations that can wipe out infectious diseases, developing security applications that will make the bad guys' jobs harder, spotting the security implications of new research, identifying security flaws in commercial software before the bad guys do, reporting on colleagues engaged in suspicious activities out of sight of authorities. The companies and universities that employ these people play a huge role too. And somehow, policy has to incentivize all these disparate actors to play the roles they could usefully play.

None of this looks very much like the way we normally think about national security. It looks far more like the way we think about protecting health and safety, which routinely involves distributing obligations to a diverse array of actors who do not think of themselves as in the business of protecting health and safety. Carmakers would describe themselves as in the transportation business, but the law in countless ways requires that they be in the safe transportation business. Candy manufacturers think of themselves as producing chocolates, but the law imposes on them the responsibility to make sure those chocolates are safe to consume. Bars think of themselves as places to get a drink, but local governments impose all kinds of obligations on them to protect health and safety, including not overserving those who have had one too many. In all these cases, the responsibility for safety is allocated to the private actor best situated to ensure it. We are seeing in the security space the adoption of this same model, which rejects reliance on a unitary government power.[24]

THE DISTRIBUTION OF DEFENSE—
PAST AND FUTURE

The United States has some historical experience with the problem of distributed defense. As we noted, there was a time in this country's early history when its central government was too weak to take sole responsibility for defending the nation. The national army was nascent, and the government therefore relied on state militias. The navy was in its infancy; yet the ocean was vast, and the coast was long—far too vast and much too long for the early US government to hope to patrol it all. So the states leveraged the private sector as a kind of force multiplier.

Privateering was a form of business, not of soldiering. Privateers funded their own operations and made money by keeping the "prizes" they seized. Precisely because of this decentralization, privateering became a tool for mustering private capital, private energy, and private risk in the service of public military objectives. Privateers played a significant role in the Revolutionary War, and the Framers were generally enthusiastic about them as a means of crowdsourcing the conflict. John Adams reportedly called the Massachusetts privateering law "one of the most important documents of the Revolution." And Thomas Jefferson wrote that "every possible encouragement should be given to privateering in time of war. . . .

Our national ships are too few . . . to . . . retaliate the acts of the enemy. But by licensing private armed vessels, the whole naval force of the nation is truly brought to bear on the foe." This sort of enthusiasm for the role privateers played in the American Revolution led the Framers to write into the Constitution—immediately next to the congressional power to declare war—the authority to "grant Letters of Marque and Reprisal."[25]

Indeed, as Stephen Budiansky writes in his naval history of the War of 1812, by the time that war broke out, "privateers had been enveloped in a mist of romanticism; the Republicans lauded them as 'the militia of the sea' and 'our cheapest & best Navy.' And with the way they seemed to roll republican virtue, American entrepreneurialism, and authorized swashbuckling into one, they offered a story no newspaper editor could improve upon." During that conflict, Congress upped the ante and passed a law known as the Torpedo Act, which put on all British warships a bounty worth half their value to any civilian who managed to destroy one. Budiansky writes that "inspired by that incentive, a number of inventors and daredevils began hatching schemes"—schemes that "especially outraged" the more conventionally minded British naval officers.[26]

Yet, by the war's end, privateering was on the decline. One of the war's great legacies was the consensus that developed in its wake in favor of greater military preparedness—and, more particularly, greater professional military preparedness. The United States, despite its Constitution, has issued no letters of marque and reprisal since the War of 1812, and an international convention banned privateering in the mid-nineteenth century in any case. As the country grew and the federal government consolidated its role, both the militia and the privateer faded away—and with them faded any sense of national defense as a distributed function.[27]

Nobody today should argue for any kind of simple revival of state-sanctioned privateering—though proposals of this sort have materialized in the context of counterterrorism policy. There are plenty of good reasons to concentrate the power of enforcement in the hands of the government, especially where such enforcement involves a violent action against another actor. But the problem we face in thinking about security more generally is not altogether unlike the problem of a nascent country with a lengthy coastline along a hopelessly vast ocean filled with dangers. Thus, the grand theory behind privateering—that policy can incentivize large numbers of private actors to deploy their own resources toward common security objectives—does have contemporary appeal. And some such policy making is already happening, either in law or in the voluntary cooperation of private actors. This is only likely to grow in scope and magnitude in the years to come.[28]

Take, for example, the commercial trade in zero-day vulnerabilities, which bears an eerie similarity to the relationship between privateers, pirates, and government. Zero-day vulnerabilities are software coding or design errors that can be accessed and exploited by an attacker, yet are unknown to the vendor of the software, to antivirus firms, or to the general public. They can be used to deliver malicious payloads, such as spyware or viruses, or even to take control of a target computer. Being unknown, they cannot be specifically defended against. Stuxnet, for instance, reportedly exploited five zero-day attacks at once. Operation Aurora, a famous Chinese hack of Google, used a zero-day vulnerability in Internet Explorer, and the same group is believed to have used up to eight zero-day flaws in other attacks on major corporations. Those who look for and discover zero-day flaws can thus function as outlaws (if they mean to exploit them for criminal purposes), as a crucial line of defense (if they mean to help software vendors secure them before an attack), or as a component of aggressive state or nonstate offense (if they mean to help attack someone else). Just like an eighteenth-century ship captain, the hacker who discovers a zero-day vulnerability might be a privateer or a pirate, depending largely on who is paying him and what cause he aligns with.[29]

Given the high stakes involved, it should come as no surprise that in recent years a thriving market has developed around zero-day flaws, with governments, vendors, and end users all willing to pay considerable sums to find these vulnerabilities, either to exploit them or to defend against them before they are exploited. The US government has a deep interest in both the offensive and the defensive application of zero-day vulnerabilities—which has sometimes gotten it in trouble. Some boutique firms specialize in unearthing zero-days and then use brokers to sell them to the highest bidder. As with privateering, one wants policy to incentivize the right sort of people to look for zero-day flaws and use the information for the right sort of purpose—and to punish the wrong sort of people for doing the same thing for less savory reasons.[30]

Creating this kind of incentive structure in the context of modern technologies of mass empowerment faces considerable challenges. Chief among these is the fact that one does not want nongovernmental actors ever performing certain functions. It is bad enough that anyone possesses the power to use lethal force, for example, or to deprive people of their liberty, or to fight wars. Allowing governments to do these things is justifiable only because of necessity. To treat them as less than the strict province of democratically accountable actors invites the privatization of coercive power. The distribution of defensive capacity, depending on how it takes place, can have troubling implications for civil liberties. It raises the question of who we want our mercenaries to be and what powers we do and do not want them to have.

Moreover, when nongovernmental actors are empowered to play a defensive role, it is difficult to ensure that they will play that role only where we want them to. The vendors and brokers of zero-day flaws may sell them to the US government, allowing the government to defend against these previously unknown vulnerabilities; they might also sell them to parties whose computers the United States wishes to attack—say, the Iranians. Having private captains with armed ships is a dangerous business, the line between privateering and piracy being thin indeed.

All of this is to say that the migration of security responsibility from the executive branch and its diffusion among a range of other actors is not necessarily something to be celebrated in a "power to the people" sort of way. Some of this diffusion will prove to be an attractive form of high-tech neighborhood watch. But some will end up looking more like high-tech vigilantism. The distribution of defense is a phenomenon whose gravity we should appreciate and whose reality will often warrant concern. It raises profound questions about how one organizes large numbers of actors interested in other goods to act on behalf of a collective security that may benefit them or their shareholders in only indirect ways and may actually encumber their more immediate interests along the way.

Still, given the degree to which offense is currently outpacing defense, one does not have to embrace distributed defense with any sort of populist enthusiasm to appreciate its necessity and value. The disparity between offense and defense right now might seem puzzling. In principle, it seems that the distribution of defensive capability should extend at least as far as the distribution of the ability to attack—defenders being so much more numerous than attackers. Just as the ancient privateer could outfit his own ship, the modern person or company wishing to secure platforms has the same access to technology as those wishing to use them for attack—and presumably the financial incentive to do so. If so, defense should meet attack on its own distributed terms. In practice, however, defensive capability has lagged behind offense. To some degree, this simply reflects an asymmetry in the respective roles of attacker and defender: attacking is easier. The defender must prevent all possible attacks from all possible sources and secure all possible targets. The attacker has to find but one point of vulnerability.

What is more, new technological advances will often favor offense over defense. It takes a while after the invention of a new offensive technology to figure out how to defend against it. We have a cybersecurity problem because the network—and our collective dependence on it—has grown far faster than our collective ability to defend it. We have a biosecurity problem because viral genomes are relatively simple compared to human biology, and our collective, distributed knowledge of how to defend the network that consists of our own bodies in interaction with one another pales in comparison to the ease of attacking this network. One suspects that offensive uses of robotics will wildly outpace defensive uses for at least some time to come. The terrorists in Pakistan are not flying drones to defend themselves against our drones, and the technology for 3D printing of guns is progressing far faster than either the capacity to regulate who builds those guns or the technology to 3D-print body armor. So the distribution of defense faces not only huge organizational difficulties, incentive problems, and leadership questions but also a structural imbalance: defending complicated technological platforms is really hard, and large numbers of invisible and anonymous attackers have a huge built-in advantage.

In short, distributed defense is both a reality and a necessity—albeit a very difficult reality and necessity—of our current security environment. And while the challenges of distributing defense are enormous, collectivized individual defense arrangements have long historical precedents. We see them in neighborhood expectations that people will put locks on their doors and keep an eye out for suspicious loiterers. We see them further in the private companies that offer burglar alarms, security cameras, and monitoring devices. These are all part of noncoordinated distributed security applications for residential neighborhoods and businesses. Such arrangements sometimes do and sometimes do not have elements of state sponsorship and leadership—as did the militias and the privateers. Now that security is again becoming a more distributed function, we need, more than ever before, to learn to think about mechanisms for delivering and governing it.

At least to some degree, these mechanisms will involve more use of the wisdom—and vigilance—of crowds. In the software world, programs that do not sit upon any single computer but run across networks of computers are called distributed applications. Peer-to-peer file sharing is a classic example. A single person running a file-sharing system is a lonely fellow—and the system in question lacks any power. Give him ten thousand other users running the same software, however, and the system becomes a powerful engine of creativity or, depending on the users, intellectual property piracy. Some sources of network instability—particularly so-called distributed denial-of-service attacks—involve similar creations of large, highly distributed networks. The hacktivist group Anonymous is, at its core, all about distributing the attack function among like-minded, technically capable hackers. The very name of WikiLeaks embraces the concept of distributed functionality, with "wiki" referring, of course, not to the distribution of computing power itself but to the crowdsourcing of content creation or, in the case of WikiLeaks, the crowdsourcing of leaks and sharing of leaked materials.

The world has seen amazing demonstrations of what large groups of people can do when they pool expertise—even with very limited coordination. The most famous example is Wikipedia, but this is far from the only one. Anyone who has used WordPress—an open-source blogging platform that has become the leading product of its type in the world—knows that it does not take a major software company to produce a major piece of software. It is an interesting fact—highly salient for our purposes here—that open-source software tends to be more stable and secure than proprietary code. Although this point has its dissenters, the open-source software movement's famous statement that "given enough eyeballs, all bugs are shallow" may have real application not just to computer bugs but to viral ones as well and, indeed, to security in the modern era more generally.[31]

These kinds of arrangements fade to irrelevance in the face of unitary state threats. They take on great importance, by contrast, when the threats grow smaller and more numerous and when government—even highly powerful government—is less capable of contending with them. A grizzly bear is well positioned to take on another grizzly bear; it is badly positioned to take on a hive of bees. And if one is concerned about beehives, one does not delude oneself that the answer is grizzly bears—however powerful they might be.

Whether or not the distribution of defense is ultimately a welcome development, it is a reality whose three central features are now upon us and will become more pronounced as technology marches forward. We can state these three features simply enough: First, government's power to defend architecture essential to individual and collective security is eroding in relative terms, not because government's own power is decreasing but because the power of others is increasing faster than is government's power. Second, the same radical empowerment of individuals that distributes the power to attack also gives individuals unprecedented defensive capacity. Third, as a result, the entities that build, maintain, and use this architecture are, as a consequence of their involvement, developing some degree of defensive capacity in government's place.

This means that the provision of security will increasingly involve interrelated actions and behaviors by everyone and everything from individuals to governments. And the level of security we enjoy will be influenced ever more in relative terms by the behavior of nongovernmental actors and ever less by the behavior of governments.

In the world of many-to-many threats and many-to-many defenses, security will not ultimately hinge on how big and strong a grizzly bear one can deploy—though that may still matter too. It will hinge instead on whether one can incentivize one's own swarm of bees. Who are our privateers in this new environment? And what do our letters of marque and reprisal look like? That is, what is the instrument or set of instruments by which policy makers can make it attractive for private actors to apply their energies, funds, and imaginations to securing the platforms they operate?

The key question, ultimately, as many of the security functions of the state continue migrating to private parties, is what effect this migration— and, more generally, a world of many-to-many threats and defenses—will ultimately have on the state itself. The state's most fundamental raison d'être is the provision of security from both domestic and external threats. Yet what happens as the new technological environment begins to impact our most basic assumptions about the role of the state in providing security and about the relationships between citizens and governments and between governments and one another? These are the questions to which we now turn.

PART II

4

TECHNOLOGY, STATES,
AND THE SOCIAL ORDER

THE 2012 JAMES BOND FILM *Skyfall* features 007 fighting a former agent turned all-powerful hacker who is out for revenge against "M," the head of MI6. A subplot has M, played by Judy Dench, facing a commission of inquiry for operational failures on her watch, while the hacker launches an armed attack on the hearing at which she is testifying. As the scene mounts toward the confrontation—with music raising the dramatic tension and with the hacker and his armed minions blasting their way to the hearing room—M, the head of a major nation's intelligence service, gives a short speech in response to her critics, contemptuously schooling her inquisitors about the state of the world she confronts:

> Today I've repeatedly heard how irrelevant my department has become. Why do we need agents? The Double 0 section is now rather quaint. Well, I suppose I see a different world than you do. And the truth is that what I see frightens me. I'm frightened because our enemies are no longer known to us. They do not exist on a map. They are not nations. They are individuals. Look around you. Whom do you fear? Can you see a face, a uniform, a flag? No. Our world is not more transparent now. It's more opaque. It's in the shadows. That's where we must do battle. So before you declare us irrelevant, ask yourselves, how safe do you feel?[1]

A Bond movie is admittedly a strange place to find a deep, forward-looking question of political theory. Yet, beneath its purple prose, M's speech—and in some caricatured ways, the movie more broadly—captures features of the modern world that tend to erode the viability of today's nation-state. It captures the empowered individual actor capable of wreaking havoc; the opacity of a world in which attribution of responsibility for acts of violence is difficult; the invisibility of threats in such a world and the terror that such a world engenders. Most importantly, the movie as a whole captures both the apparent weakening of the state and the state's continuing importance. M herself, near the end of her career and—spoiler alert—her life, represents a gravely weakened Leviathan. Yet, at the end of the day, she—through Bond—is still the one who protects us, as she sneeringly reminds those who would question her. And that is still the source of her authority.

As if to reinforce this point, M's speech ends with Dench quoting Alfred Lord Tennyson's "Ulysses":

> We are not now that strength which in old days
> Moved earth and heaven, that which we are, we are;
> One equal temper of heroic hearts,
> Made weak by time and fate, but strong in will
> To strive, to seek, to find, and not to yield.[2]

As she finishes, a gun battle erupts between the hacker's hired army and the remains of the Leviathan. M's authority lasts only as long as she can make us feel safe—a project toward which, in the movie's final scene, Bond recommits himself with her successor, as he puts it, "with pleasure."

The environment we have described in the first part of this book, and which M beseeches her listeners to recognize, forces us to think about some basic first principles of our current political organization. Most fundamentally, it makes us think about the essence of the relationship between states and their citizens, the relationship between states and one another, and indeed, the very question of why we have organized ourselves within state structures for the past several centuries in the first place. With respect to all of these questions, security—both of individuals and communities—plays a central role, and new technologies of mass empowerment are challenging precisely the state's ability to protect security. So let us take a closer look at how the changing security environment might affect the nature of the state, the traditional and future roles that we want the state to play, and why we empower people like M in the first place.

THE STATE'S MONOPOLY OVER VIOLENCE

Back in 1919, people got their political theory from more august sources than Bond films. During the German revolution that led to the ill-fated Weimar Republic, sociologist and economist Max Weber gave a speech at the University of Munich, later published as an essay titled "On the Vocation and the Profession of Politics." In this lecture, Weber coined his famous definition of the modern state as "that human community which (successfully) lays claim to the *monopoly of legitimate physical violence* within a certain territory, this 'territory' being another of the defining characteristics of the state." While "violence is, of course, not the normal or the sole means used by the state," he argued, "it is the means *specific* to the state." Weber was speaking of a world in which heads of intelligence services did not need to explain their continued relevance or the threats they needed to avert, a world in which the state still moved the earth and could claim legitimate violence as its specific province—a world in which, for the most part, an enemy still had a uniform, a clearly defined army, and a visible plan of attack.

The historical origins of the state, Weber argued, lay in the consolidation by political leaders of the means of governance. In its full embodiment, the state, complete with its bureaucracy, emerged as the political organization that preempted other entities from claiming comparable or greater authority to wield power in the name of the public good. The consolidation of power was particularly important in the sphere of security. The quintessential modern state exists when a government controls a bounded territory with nearly exclusive security and policing powers. Its continued existence depends on the tacit acceptance of its power by the people, who have a shared interest in subjecting themselves to its authority. The organized rule of the state through its rational authority and bureaucracy requires, in Weber's formulation, "command [over] the material resources necessary to exercise physical force if circumstances should demand it." Should the use of violence as a means disappear, he argued, the very concept of the state would likely lose its claim to legitimacy and vanish along with it.[3]

As Weber observed, the association of the state with a monopoly over violence was not always the case in practice, even if it was meant to be in principle. In fact, only toward the twentieth century did the project of consolidating legitimate power in the hands of a centralized governmental authority really take off, with the emergence of what some have termed "the national state." For the first three hundred or so years of the state's existence, its power was far from consolidated. Nonstate actors, including privateers (such as those employed by the United States in its wars against Britain), mercenaries (who made up much of the armies of European countries), and mercantile companies (such as the East India Company, which had its own private army), all functioned as authorized warriors, alongside a range of pirates and other rogue forces. As economies expanded, authorized nonstate violence produced an array of unintended and adverse consequences for sovereigns. These included incidents in which mercenaries drew their home states into conflicts or the mercantile companies fought each other, fought states with which their home states were at peace, or even fought their home states themselves. They also included a sapping of men from official militaries and a tendency of private fighters to ransom enemy ships and soldiers rather than to destroy or kill them. Consequently, states began a process of consolidating national power, abolishing privateering, relying on national standing armies rather than on soldiers of fortune, and revoking the licensing of mercantile companies' private forces.[4]

Today, the modern state appears to be losing its monopoly over violence, if not in principle at least in practice—returning us to a pre-Weberian understanding of the exclusivity of the state as the legitimate purveyor of violence. Employees of private military companies constitute a revival of sorts of the medieval mercenary, and the patriotic hackers and sellers of zero-day attacks bear some analogs to the premodern privateers. Meanwhile, large and small corporations distribute technologies of mass empowerment across the globe, enabling individuals to spy on and attack one another. And these are just the nonstate actors whose activities are sanctioned by the state. An abundance of others operate outside, even in defiance of, any state authority. The developed state clearly now faces many more potential enemies than ever before—from the other states it has always had to contend with to the superempowered citizens, foreigners, and nonstate groups wishing to do the state or its citizens harm.

At the same time, and complicating matters immeasurably, technology may ultimately empower no actor more than it empowers the developed state itself. Technological development allows the Leviathan to better organize its bureaucracy, enforce law and order, provide essential services, and protect itself from harm. It provides authorities with more and better information and record keeping about people, goods, and activities, which in turn allows for better monitoring and control of mass populations and for more and better defenses against threats, both natural and man-made.

Predicting how technological shifts—whose direction, speed, and completeness remain highly uncertain—will eventually impact the state's ability to govern effectively is a tenuous, perhaps impossible, exercise. At this point, it remains unclear whether the state will maintain, increase, or decrease its relative power over other actors, and this equation might work out differently for different states and with regard to different types of enemies. Still, at a minimum, it is clear that states will face a wider array of potential hostile actors in the context of more distributed defense. And we think it reasonable to assume that the pace of mass empowerment will outstrip, in the long run, the pace of Leviathan empowerment. That is, while the Leviathan's power may increase in absolute terms, the empowerment of the many will take place faster; therefore, the Leviathan's power relative to other actors will decrease.

As a conceptual matter, if new technologies across multiple different platforms are indeed democratizing power and distributing more widely the ability to engage in significant violence, Weber's definition of the viable state, however idealized, becomes somewhat of a problem. If individuals and small groups can acquire unprecedented power to attack other individuals, groups, and indeed states—over great distances and without detection or accountability—does it matter whether the state still has a formal claim to a monopoly over legitimate violence? Most acutely, if nonstate actors can routinely challenge the authority of even strong states from within their territories, as well as from outside their territories, can the state still effectively serve a primary security function? And if not, is our modern notion of the state at risk? Or is it already largely obsolete? Do we not need some form of world government if we are effectively to police a globe in which anyone anywhere can attack anyone else anywhere else?

To be clear, we do not envision the demise of the state in the foreseeable future; nor do we foresee the emergence of any kind of world government. Yet, to fully capture the challenges of governance in the world of many-to-many threats, it is worthwhile, at least as a thought experiment, to imagine the extreme cases of the processes we describe. To begin this thought experiment, let us first examine the theoretical underpinnings of the state's monopoly over violence and the medley of interests that led us, the citizens, to submit to state power in the first place. With these foundations in mind, we can then turn to imagining what might happen if the state were to lose that monopoly, either entirely or partially.

The Modern State and the Domestic Social Contract

The nation-state as we know it is a recent historical phenomenon, only around four to five hundred years old. It has superseded many other political forms, and it exists today, as in the past, alongside still other forms. Some, like tribal or familial forms of governance, are as old as human history. Others, such as transnational linguistic or ethnic communities, have become prevalent in more recent times. One could, and perhaps should, imagine the modern state as a transient phenomenon on the world's stage, destined to be replaced by other forms, just as the ancient Greek polis was succeeded in time by early empires or as feudal European kingdoms and principalities eventually merged to make the modern nation-state.

Although it is not impossible that the advent and dissemination of technologies of mass empowerment will herald the state's ultimate demise and replacement with different structures of human governance, the state has so far proven remarkably resilient, withstanding all previous rumors of its impending death. Karl Marx believed that the mass technologies he was witnessing in the nineteenth century (such as the high-pressure steam engine and the telegraph) would precipitate a proletarian revolution that would eventually dissolve the bourgeois state based on private property—which is to say virtually all liberal states. Twentieth-century globalization engendered speculation about a borderless world and the end of the nation-state as we know it, speculation that intensified during the early years of the Internet. The advent of the European Union (EU) ushered in enormous excitement about transnational superstructures that would reduce the significance of the state. Yet, ironically, amid all the talk of borderlessness, the state has flourished. Today there are 193 member states in the United Nations, up from 51 when the organization was established in 1945, with yet more entities vying for independence and recognition as states. Euromania has faded; the EU, today, is something of a mess, a model as much of overambition as of successful transnational governance. For the moment, and for the foreseeable future, the modern state represents our political reality.[5]

By and large, this is a good thing. While techno-anarchists tend to cheer the erosions of state power triggered by new technologies, the state actually has much to recommend it. Most importantly for present purposes, the emergence of states has had a profound impact on the human experience of violence, which—even taking into account the mass violence perpetrated by states themselves—has declined substantially in the era of state-based governance as compared with earlier times. As Steven Pinker concluded in his account of the historical decline of violence, the state's monopoly on force, when used to protect its citizens, "may be the most consistent violence-reducer that we have encountered." Citizens of functioning states look to their authorities to provide them with security, and citizens of failed states suffer the brutal consequences of the absence of effective authority. Indeed, as much as state power—like all power—is susceptible to abuse, it has also proven essential in protecting individual rights and freedoms. The institutions of the state, Pinker notes, are "necessary for the reduction of chronic violence, which is a prerequisite to every other social good."[6]

Most people today have largely accepted the idea that it is in their interest to live in a territory governed by a state that enjoys a monopoly on the legitimate use of violence and can protect their rights and freedoms from encroachment by others—that is, to live in a state that guarantees reasonable levels of safety (of course, none guarantees a life free of risk) and is not itself a tyranny or at imminent risk of becoming one. Alternative visions of religious empires or global anarchy are most commonly seen as threatening not only to the idea of a state-based world but also, ultimately, to our individual safety and security, as well as to our everyday rights and liberties.

Undoubtedly, states serve many valuable functions other than the provision of security in the narrow sense: they supply public goods such as transportation, education, and health care; they engage in the redistribution of resources to assist those in greater need; and they provide the laws and institutions that set the stage for many of our private interactions. Even if one believed it was possible to provide all these functions through private contracting or voluntary cooperation, one thing seems clear: without the basic provision of a reasonable level of security, none of these other civic, economic, or everyday interactions could take place. In this sense, the state's foremost function is the provision of internal and external security.

The justification of the nation-state as provider of security is closely associated with the branch of the larger liberal tradition commonly known as social contract theory. Social contract theory is by no means the only useful framework for thinking about questions of governance or the political structure of the state and indeed has long been subject to serious criticism. Yet its centrality to that part of modern political theory devoted to the security function of the state and the freedoms it guarantees makes it a compelling starting point for considering the potential effects of a world of many-to-many threats and defenses on our existing governance structures.

Social contract theory has antecedents in the biblical idea of the divine covenant, in Greek and Stoic philosophy, and in Roman and canon law. One such account was offered by Plato to explain citizens' duty to obey the laws of the Greek city-state. In the dialogue "Crito," Socrates, sentenced to death by an Athenian jury for corrupting the city's youth, rejects the pleas of his students to escape prison and death by going into exile in another city. The justification Socrates offers for submitting to his sentence rests on what he frames as an implicit contract between the citizen and the city. Every adult citizen, he argues, has had the opportunity to assess the city's laws and how the city conducts itself. He has been able to choose whether to leave or stay. If he wishes to leave, he can take his property with him and find another home. In choosing to stay, he enjoys the benefits of the city's laws. But staying also implies an agreement to abide by those laws and to accept the punishments they prescribe—including the death penalty.[7]

Modern notions of the social contract emerged at the cusp of the European Enlightenment, around the mid-seventeenth century, not long after the nation-state was making its first appearance on the world stage. In its modern formulation by Hugo Grotius, Thomas Hobbes, John Locke, and their successors, the contract took a twist from the one imagined in the *Crito*: rather than representing a pact concluded between the individual citizen and the existing sovereign, to whom the citizen owed gratitude and loyalty, the modern social contract was understood as an agreement negotiated among the citizens themselves, with the state being an outcome of—rather than a party to—the bargain. The modern theorists sought to explain not why citizens were required to obey their sovereign but why the sovereign was entitled to sovereignty in the first place.

The effort, in other words, was to legitimize the idea of sovereignty as the authority of the ruler over his subjects, including the desired—although for a long time thereafter unattainable—consolidation of power in the hands of the ruler. The preoccupation with sovereignty was born out of the emergence of the modern state, which sought to replace the medieval dreams of a universal empire and a universal church.

These earlier forms of European governance had been largely based on feudalism and manorialism, in which a narrow stratum of monarchs and nobility financed groups of knights, through whom they controlled their lands, extracted goods from peasants, and fought constantly for the protection of their rights and honor. Feuding and armed self-help were legitimate under the law of the time, and the freedom to declare and wage private wars was considered an inalienable birthright. Historians have shown that the default occupation of adult upper-class males of the time was warrior and that males spent much of their lives training for or participating in physical combat.[8]

The introduction of gunpowder and the ensuing professionalization of military power (including the introduction of the uniform, the construction of barracks, and improvements in logistics) all contributed to a crisis in late medieval warrior practice. As the technology of warfare evolved, feudalism backed by constant battle became unsustainable. As large contingents of infantry and archers replaced heavy cavalry as the dominant form of military force, sovereigns no longer had to rely on lesser lords for knights, and the relative power of those lords declined, leading to greater centralized authority. Similarly, the spread of gunpowder added to the dominance of central authorities, which could afford firearms and the large armies it took to maneuver and deploy them. The kingdoms and principalities that constituted the landscape of early modern Europe were forced to raise larger, more expensive, and more capable militaries in order to survive. Larger armies required control over larger territories and larger populations from which to extract resources, collect taxes, and conscript soldiers. The process of creating military power, explains social scientist Charles Tilly, tended "to promote territorial consolidation, centralization, differentiation of the instruments of government and monopolization of the means of coercion, all the fundamental state-making processes. War made the state, and the state made war."[9]

By the mid-seventeenth century, Europe was experiencing an upheaval of wars and revolutions, divided between the large monarchies of Austria, France, England, and Spain and the remaining locally governed principalities, free cities, duchies, and feudal kingdoms. The Protestant Reformation shattered the earlier religious unity under the Roman Catholic

Church, leading to the Thirty Years' War in which much of Europe took part. The 1648 Peace of Westphalia that ended the war marked the beginning of the modern state-based international order. Redrawing borders, the agreements that made up the Peace of Westphalia also established the modern principle of sovereignty, according to which independent political units were free to govern themselves with few limitations, just as they were forbidden from intervening in each other's domestic affairs.

Respect for sovereignty was thought essential for keeping Europe peaceful and consolidating the power of rulers over restless subjects. But once kinship, religious, and even tribal ties no longer sufficed to ensure obedience to secular rule, European states required an alternative justification for their sovereignty, existence, right to protect their rule by force, and entitlement to the obedience of their subjects. With the era's turn to secular enlightenment, the early theoreticians of the modern state searched for this justification in science and reason. Just as Galileo and Isaac Newton were laying the foundations for modern physics, the Enlightenment political theorists were grounding the first efforts to justify the authority of modern states in the idea of a social contract.

It was no accident that the early theorists—the Dutch Grotius and the English Hobbes—developed their social contract models against a political background of turmoil and upheaval. Both based the primary justification for sovereignty in the state's provision of security and ability to protect the freedoms of its inhabitants. Grotius, having been imprisoned during a violent dispute between orthodox Calvinists and reformers, held that the citizens of every state had come together and chosen the form of government they considered most suitable for themselves. Having made that choice, they thereby irrevocably transferred the right of government to a ruler, in the process forfeiting the right to control or punish him, no matter how tyrannical or corrupt he became. Grotius's account is thus, in some limited, primordial sense, a liberal one in that it recognizes individuals' rights and freedoms in the first instance, but it also results in the potential renunciation of these rights in exchange for order and security.[10]

Hobbes, the most famous of the Enlightenment social contract theorists, was undoubtedly influenced by Grotius, and he came by his grim view of humanity and his belief in an absolutist government honestly—partly through his own experience of the English Civil War (1642–1651), which pitted the king and his monarchist supporters against the parliamentarians, who demanded more power for the quasi-democratic Parliament. The ensuing violence, along with the breakdown or splintering of institutional forces that had contributed to social cohesion and offered personal security—including religion, tribe, and custom—drove Hobbes, hiding in France for fear of his life, to conclude, with Grotius, that political power must be held by an absolute ruler.

Unlike Grotius, however, Hobbes treated the social contract not as a fact of human history but rather as an imagined social process. His introduction of the idea of the social contract begins with his famed "state of nature"—the bleak condition in which humans, driven by their passions, would find themselves if they were to exist outside any state authority: "During the time men live without a common Power to keep them all in awe they are in that condition which is called Warre; and such a warre, as is of every man against every man." In this condition, he famously wrote, "there is no place for Industry; because the fruit thereof is uncertain: and consequently no Culture of the Earth; no Navigation, nor use of the commodities that may be imported by Sea; no commodius Building; no Instruments of moving, and removing such things as require much force; no Knowledge of the face of the Earth; no account of Time; no Arts; no Letters; no Society; and which is worst of all, continuall feare, and danger of violent death; And the life of man, solitary, poore, nasty, brutish, and short."[11] People, argued Hobbes, could only avoid this condition by agreeing among themselves, out of self-interest, to subject themselves to a higher authority that would maintain law and order and offer defense and security to those under its rule.[12]

Although Hobbes's state of nature and social contract were imagined conditions, he argued that they contained vital themes from, and therefore lessons for, the real world. Within any society, he believed, there will always be ambitious men who seek to gain power for themselves by force, deception, and other nefarious means. The inevitable consequences of these efforts will be social and political strife and violence—a condition not far removed from the state of nature. The rational thing to do, he argued, is what his imagined occupants of the state of nature would do: create a Leviathan—an all but absolute ruler—who would constrain their passions by means of institutions of authority and the enforcement of rules.

Individuals, per Hobbes, do enjoy certain natural rights and freedoms, which the sovereign ought to respect. The social contract itself is an expression of these rights and freedoms, whereby individuals have agreed to empower the sovereign in order to promote their welfare and protect themselves from harm. Once empowered, however, Hobbes's sovereign has the right to enforce the laws against everyone and by whatever means he considers necessary for the state's preservation, even if such enforcement violates individual rights and freedoms. The sovereign is answerable to no other man and is entitled to exercise power and eliminate any source of political and social unrest. Indeed, any disobedience to the sovereign's edicts is, in effect, an act of "warre" that warrants punishment.[13]

Importantly, however, there is one qualification to the absolutist tenor of Hobbes's social contract. No man, he posited, can relinquish his right to protect himself from violence, even violence at the hands of the sovereign: "For the right men have by Nature to protect themselves, when none else can protect them, can by no Covenant be relinquished." From this qualification derives the one case recognized by Hobbes as relieving citizens of their duty to obey the sovereign, namely, the case in which the sovereign proves himself incapable of protecting them. When this situation arises, the sovereign has violated the social contract, and citizens are effectively thrown back into the state of nature. Having lost its justification for ruling, the Leviathan loses its authority over its citizens: "The Obligation of Subjects to the Sovereign, is understood to last as long, and no longer, than the power lasteth, by which he is able to protect them."[14]

Less than forty years after Hobbes's *Leviathan*, John Locke published his own variation on social contract theory. Following Hobbes, Locke began from a hypothetical and precarious state of nature and the resulting necessity of establishing—through a social contract—a state to protect citizens. But unlike in Hobbes's imagined world, this protection comes not from a simple "common power" but rather from an impartial authority that promulgates and enforces rules of right and wrong—particularly rules enjoining citizens from mistreating one another—sets the terms of punishment, and adjudicates disputes involving injury and property. Once such impartial authorities are in place, Locke argued, each person should surrender any right to judge for himself between right and wrong and to determine who owns what. Like Hobbes, Locke thought it crucial that the government be secure from violent challenge so long as it is able to enforce the law. Like Hobbes, too, he believed that once the government is no longer able to enforce the law, it loses its raison d'être.[15]

Locke's conception of government, however, was fundamentally different from the authoritarian models of Grotius and Hobbes. Unlike his predecessors, Locke recognized that the threat to citizens' safety and security may arise not only from fellow citizens but also from the government itself. For both Hobbes and Locke, the sovereign offers protection of rights and freedoms; yet Locke's recognition that the sovereign himself may also pose a threat to these rights and freedoms drove him to demand greater limits on the power of the sovereign. If Hobbes's sovereign enjoys nearly absolute power and owes few duties to his subjects (even if, ideally, he is bound by some moral principles under the laws of nature), for Locke, citizens enjoy God-given freedom that they are not authorized to cede to the sovereign. The sovereign may legitimately exercise his powers only so long as he uses those powers for the purposes for which they have been delegated to him by nature—in other words, to protect the citizens' rights and well-being.

In Locke's famous phrase, government derives its authority to govern from the consent of the governed. Tyrannical rule thus breaches the social contract—representing an improper use of the sovereign's delegated powers and hence a declaration of war against the sovereign's subjects. A government therefore loses its right to rule not only if it becomes incapable of enforcing the law and protecting its subjects but also if it becomes tyrannical—at which point the social contract dissolves and the government may be justifiably resisted, by force if necessary. Locke's determined view of a limited, law-bound government, coupled with his treatment of the executive and legislature as two separate powers (as opposed to Hobbes's indivisible sovereign), had a strong influence on both the American and French revolutions and the constitutions adopted thereafter. Again, security plays a key role in Locke's vision of the social contract, but his conception of security is more sophisticated and comprehensive than Hobbes's. It includes both the security the government provides to the citizen from threats from others and that guaranteed to the citizen from the government itself.

A half-century after Locke, Jean-Jacques Rousseau outlined still another variant on social contract theory, one preoccupied with reconciling the seeming tension between individual liberties and freedoms and subjection to sovereign power. Rousseau was far less concerned than Hobbes and Locke with security and the role of the state in providing it. He had a far kinder vision than his predecessors of human nature, one in which "Man is born good," and this may have reduced his fear of undergovernance. Man's nature leads him to desire only to be treated fairly, to share in equality, not to prey on others. The state of nature against which a government must guard is thus not necessarily a Hobbesian state of war; it is uncertainty. Without rules or order, "man's relative existence in the state of nature depends on a thousand other constantly changing relations, he can never make sure of being the same for two instants of his life; peace and happiness are for him but a flash; nothing is permanent but the misery that results from all these vicissitudes." The purpose of government is thus not fundamentally the provision of security in some narrow sense but rather the articulation and enforcement of rules that make it possible for citizens to enjoy rights and freedoms within a society. To be fully compatible with the liberal ideal of individual rights and freedoms, the sovereignty of government must itself be an expression of these rights and freedoms, a reflection of the general will of those governed—however this general will is to be deduced.[16]

The tradition of social contract theory has tended to follow Rousseau away from the security-oriented fixations of Grotius, Hobbes, and Locke. In modern times, prominent theorists such as John Rawls and Robert Nozick have carried very different banners of social contract theory. Much like their predecessors, each of the modern theorists offers his own view of human nature, the state of nature, and what the social contract can and therefore should offer the citizens of every state. But contemporary scholars have built on the tradition of Rousseau—as well as Immanuel Kant—to imagine what the social contract model could offer not only in terms of the optimal design of government but also in order to afford citizens the fullest degree of social and economic justice. For contemporary theorists, main points of contention include such questions as the degree to which states should facilitate a redistribution of wealth, manage industries, or provide certain social services.[17]

Yet the security function, even when left undiscussed, is still there. The traditional security function of the state, in its narrow sense, is taken as obvious, as requiring no further justification or elaboration. Even Nozick, a staunch advocate of limited government, holds that the state should continue to play a narrow protective role, even as all other governance functions are to be channeled to the private market and to actual—rather than imagined—contracting.[18]

Modern times have seen many diverse forms of government—monarchy, fascism, national socialism, communism, military and civilian dictatorship, theocracy, and liberal democracy—that vividly express competing versions of social contract theory. Regimes leaning toward totalitarianism go beyond even the bleakest visions of Grotius and Hobbes of an absolute government virtually unconstrained in its power, equating the security of the state with the rule of the sovereign and eliminating any domestic or international challenges. On the more liberal side of the spectrum, following the tradition of Locke and Rousseau, domestic constitutions emphasize the constraints on the Leviathan, promising civic rights and freedoms as, among other things, a positive expression of citizens' liberty and security. Different states also display different visions of social and economic policies that constitute yet a broader notion of human security. While Hobbes's famously autocratic prescription will attract few citizens of any liberal state today, his broader point remains an essential insight: we need the protection of a strong state as a precondition for the meaningful exercise of liberty. For this reason, the one common feature of all these different contractarian visions is the promise, however insincere, of the state to provide security, however defined, in exchange for the right to rule.

Technologies of mass empowerment threaten to undermine precisely this promise. Indeed, it is hard to contemplate a world in which anyone can attack anyone from anywhere, in which we have greatly distributed both the power and the vulnerability to attack, without thinking of Hobbes's state of nature, or what he called "warre," the situation from which the Leviathan state was meant to extricate us. The more we think about the development of technology, the more we see how technology can undo almost any contract a state may be founded upon. A world in which public and private actors, both domestic and foreign, can access our mosaics with minimal governmental controls may require a very different social contract from the one we grew up with. In a world where those same actors can send a spider drone into our showers, the idea of contracting to establish a government that will protect us may be obsolete; or at least, we may have to return the state's promise of security from its peripheral, assumed place to its Hobbesian centrality to any social contract that gives to others the right to rule.

Can the state endure once it is unable to prevent the electrical grid from being shut down, the lethal spider drone from attacking you in the shower, or new or manipulated biological agents produced in garages anywhere in the world from threatening your health? And if the state cannot meet these challenges, is there any other entity—smaller or bigger—that can?

THE INTERNATIONAL SOCIAL CONTRACT

It has become a cliché that our world had grown smaller. The first pictures of Earth from outer space, the Internet and other technologies of connectivity, international air travel, and the media have all shrunk the significance of oceans and continents so that we can imagine the world as a contiguous unit sharing a single horizon, approachable and reachable from wherever one happens to be. Yet, ironically, even as we have grown closer together, governments have proliferated. We have evolved into transnational communities yet seldom ask ourselves why we have no transnational government. Perhaps it is just a little too much to swallow. The fact that the world was once organized under empires that ruled vast territories and populations through centralized command seems too anachronistic to matter to our present-day international order of sovereign nation-states, divided and protected by inviolable territorial boundaries.

Yet, when we consider safety and security in the modern age, the current system seems at least theoretically vulnerable. No sovereign state has the capacity to fully protect itself and its people, and at least some sovereign states will fall woefully short of adequately protecting their citizens from domestic and transnational harms. If we apply the logic of Hobbes, who argued for the creation of a government powerful enough to protect us, should we not begin imagining some international social contract grand enough to do so—one that would inevitably involve sovereign states coming together to create some sort of transnational Leviathan? If we take the thinking that led to domestic governance and the nation-state to its logical conclusion, can, ought we not now imagine a more international government, one with courts and police forces, to protect us, citizens and states, from ourselves?

The prospect of a world government has long tantalized humanity. For centuries, it posed as a tempting means of deliverance from a perpetual state of conflict and war both inside and outside states. The concept has been especially attractive to "grand architects" as varied as Dante, Kant, and Lenin, who all investigated the concept or even, in some cases, worked on the assumption of its being the likely end result of the development of human governance. Mostly, though, unlike the domestic social contract, the idea of a universal government has been treated as a utopian fantasy, not a political phenomenon worthy of vigorous inquiry.

There is a good reason why the idea has never developed the same sort of traction as the social contract has at the domestic level; the international social contract presents us with an underlying empirical problem. Whereas modern political theory has busied itself with supplying a justification for a familiar structure, the nation-state, the international system has remained sovereignless, making any international social contract an ideal to be imagined rather than a reality to be explained. It is telling that when Hobbes imagined the state of nature, he likened the relationship among the hapless individuals in that condition to the relationship among sovereign states. Locke, too, supposed that "all princes and rulers of independent governments are in a state of nature" with respect to one another. And while all states may face the problem of a world of many-to-many threats, they still have profoundly different interests, identities, and values. And none is eager to cede its power to rule to global systems that might bind it, yet operate beyond its control.[19]

Early visions of world government took the form not of some proto–UN Charter or Universal Declaration of Human Rights but of universal empire. In Dante's imagination, humanity could only be rescued from being "a many-headed beast" if "the whole earth and all that humans can possess be a monarchy, that is, one government under one ruler. Because he possesses everything, the ruler would not desire to possess anything further, and thus, he would hold kings contentedly within the borders of their kingdoms, and keep peace among them." Like Hobbes some 350 years later, Dante was an exile from his home—in his case war-torn Florence—during a period of decline in the Holy Roman Empire. Unlike Hobbes, he saw the solution to war not in a strong domestic Leviathan but in a return of the empire to earlier days of glory, which in his eyes were "a part of God's providential plan for humanity."[20]

By the mid-seventeenth century, however, as the Peace of Westphalia entrenched a system of sovereign states, the notion of a world empire had lost much of its appeal. The ideal of sovereignty was at once a derivative and a construction of an anarchic international system. Anarchy between nations required sovereignty to be understood as a state's nearly absolute authority over its own territory and a nearly absolute prohibition on the exercise of authority over another state's territory. Also, to keep the peace, it was necessary to have strong states, able to police their territories effectively and prevent revolutions and upheavals from destabilizing other states. The imagined international social contract of the time thus had to depart from the vision of an empire and instead took the form of a federation of states. Such a federation could only come together on the basis of explicit, actual consent of the sovereign units comprising it, rather than through an imagined bargain, like the domestic social contract.

In this spirit, Charles Castel (Abbé de Saint-Pierre), who found Hobbes's argument for a national state highly relevant for the international system, believed that an interest in self-preservation should lead the princes of Europe to contract to form a federation of states, as he argued in his *Project for Making Peace Perpetual in Europe*. That contract, he imagined, might include a permanent congress that could adjudicate all conflicts between the contracting parties, and it would have states acting in concert against any member who broke the contract or disregarded the decision of the congress. Kant, too, suggested a federal union of free and independent states that would agree to surrender themselves to an authoritative adjudicatory body that would apply international law—those rules that bind even sovereign states. For Kant, a federation was not the ideal but rather a sensible compromise between the utopia of "an international state (*civitas gentium*)—which would necessarily continue to grow until it embraced all the peoples of the earth" and the observation that the world's states, in practice, wanted nothing to do with this idea. The Kantian vision resembled in some respects the coming together of what became the United States or, more recently, the European Union.[21]

The nineteenth and twentieth centuries saw revivals of proposals for world government, as technology made the world more interconnected through travel and communication and made wars so very much more devastating. The atomic bombings of Hiroshima and Nagasaki drove Albert Einstein to assert, "A world government must be created which is able to solve conflicts between nations by judicial decision. This government must be based on a clear-cut constitution which is approved by the governments and nations and which gives it the sole disposition of offensive weapons." A number of international nongovernmental organizations were established in the West, with many voices calling for the transformation of the United Nations into a universal federation of states with powers to control armaments. President Harry S. Truman, who gave the order to use the atomic bombs, had an Einstein-like belief in the possibilities of international governance too. He, after all, oversaw the establishment of the United Nations and was said to have kept in his wallet these lines from Tennyson's poem "Locksley Hall":

> *For I dipt into the future, far as human eye could see,*
> *Saw the Vision of the world, and all the wonders that would be;*

> . . .

> *Till the war-drum throbb'd no longer, and the battle-flags were furl'd*
> *In the Parliament of man, the Federation of the world.*
> *There the common sense of most shall hold a fretful realm in awe,*
> *And the kindly earth shall slumber, lapt in universal law.*[22]

M, it seems, is not the only one for whom Tennyson struck a chord, but then again, Truman was only in small part a utopian. Like M, he represented a Leviathan too.

Indeed, the years immediately following World War II—before the Cold War brought virtually all global cooperation to a halt—saw the heyday of the idea of world federalism. *One World*, in which Wendell Willkie, a lawyer and the Republican Party's nominee for president in 1940, gave an account of his global travels and discussed the possibility of a world government, sold over 2 million copies. Writer and publisher Emery Reves's *The Anatomy of Peace* called on the nations of the world to replace the United Nations with a federal world government and became the guiding spirit of the rising world federalist movement.[23]

Just as different political philosophers had their own visions of the domestic social contract, competing ideologies imagined different roles and functions for a world government. On their side of the Iron Curtain, for instance, the Soviets viewed Western proposals for world government as nothing but an exercise in American capitalist imperialism. The communist social order had its own attendant vision of an international social contract, under which, as Lenin put it, the "proletarian state will begin to wither away immediately after its victory because the state is unnecessary and cannot exist in a society in which there are no class antagonisms."[24]

The end of the Cold War allowed, for the first time in history, some experiments with transnational institutions that, though far from constituting a world government, were nonetheless a novelty in a world of sovereign states. In 1992, the Maastricht Treaty established the three pillars of what is now termed the "European Union," creating an unprecedented transnational structure to which sovereign states ceded power. In 1998, the Rome Statute set in motion the first ever International Criminal Court with direct power over citizens, even citizens of states that had not consented to its authority. For proponents of greater world government, these were only the first steps toward a desired consolidation of international power in the hands of global authorities. Such consolidation of power, they argued, was inevitable if the world was to meet its greatest challenges—from climate change, to transnational crime, to poverty, to pandemic disease.[25]

Despite its appeal to diverse ideologies, the concept of world government, whether in the guise of an empire or a federation, has always met with aversion and skepticism—and it has tended to end in tears. Some critics have found themselves unable to square the idea with the disparities in size and power of states or with the nationalist attitudes of citizenries. Moreover, they point out, different countries have exhibited entirely different degrees of respect—or lack thereof—for international agreements and the rule of law. Other skeptics have feared not the outcome so much as the process, the cost of such a revolution. Others still have doubted the ideal itself, arguing that a world government would merely aggregate power in the hands of a few; that it would eliminate cultural, linguistic, and social differences; that it would never be democratic but was bound to prove either tyrannical or ineffectual—or both. Clearly, there is no guarantee that a world Leviathan would be more like the globalized version of an effective and stable liberal democracy rather than an overblown Somalia. Rather than a world government, skeptics have argued, the answer to wars, environmental degradation, and other global problems lies in better-governed states working with one another through noncoercive, decentralized structures of cooperation—not in global government but in global governance.

The term "global governance" aptly describes the current international system—or, at least, its tendencies over the past several decades. The Westphalian system of sovereign states today looks very different from the 1648 prototype. True, the international system remains, if not quite anarchic, then certainly a self-help-based system. There is no international military or police force, and when, after the UN Charter was signed, an attempt was made to design an international force, the Cold War quickly rendered it a pipe dream. The United Nations Security Council, which the Charter entrusted with maintaining world peace and security, has proven itself more consistently deadlocked by the conflicting interests of its permanent members than effective in fulfilling this task. There still exists no comprehensive mandatory adjudication process in the international system, and the few international courts that do exist are, for the most part, limited in their jurisdiction or otherwise dependent on state consent to their adjudication; their rulings, in practice, are often ignored.[26]

Yet it is also true that the "state of nature" among nations today differs considerably from that of any earlier time. It is certainly different from Hobbes's description of sovereign states in the mid-seventeenth century as perpetually locked "in the state and posture of Gladiators; having their weapons pointing, and their eyes fixed on one another; that is, their Forts, Garrisons, and Guns upon the Frontiers of their Kingdoms; and continuall Spyes upon their neighbors, which is a posture of war."[27] Today, a plethora of international laws and regulations governs almost every sphere of state conduct: how wars should be prosecuted, which endangered species must be saved, how to protect human rights, how to immunize children, whether to mine the deep seabed for natural resources, and how air travel and communications must be conducted. The international system has also given rise to hundreds of international and regional organizations, including the World Trade Organization, the World Bank and the International Monetary Fund, and the World Health Organization. These interstate organizations exist alongside numerous nongovernmental international institutions, such as the International Committee of the Red Cross, the International Standardization Organization, and the Internet Corporation on Assigned Names and Numbers. Though not constituting a "government" in any traditional sense, these organizations further promulgate rules, whether binding or not, in their areas of responsibility (for example, the safety features of refrigerators or the handling of financial instruments) and execute their own policies.

These rules and institutions penetrate so deeply into the province of the state, into sovereignty in fact, that the modern concept of sovereignty, though still very much a feature of statehood, no longer means that a state can be entirely independent of other states; nor is it as free to conduct itself entirely as it sees fit—at least not without huge consequences. Countries that insist on the freest of free reins—like Iran and North Korea—become international pariahs. Although the international system is still rife with disputes and conflicts, the growing web of international interactions, economic interdependence, and benefits from interstate cooperation constantly generates inducements for states to comply with their international obligations and with tribunals' decisions and to avoid inflicting short-term self-serving harm on the interests of other states.

This is, in short, what global governance means today. And one can argue that this international political structure of sovereign states, loosely bound to one another through webs of explicit contracts and continuous interactions, provides an adequate basis for the management of the great problems of the world, even if the solutions it generates often fall far short of the ideal. Certainly, one could take the significant decline in the incidence of interstate wars since the end of World War II to mean that even without an international Leviathan, the interstate state of nature is now a relatively tame one. Moreover, even if global governance falls short of the ideal of a world government, perhaps it is the best we can do: indeed, if the advent of nuclear weapons did not prove sufficient impetus to heed Einstein's call for a world government, why should the spider drone or the mosaic offer states any kind of further inducement to surrender themselves to some supranational authority?

This skepticism may well prove correct, yet one counterargument is at least worth considering: the nuclear bomb empowered states to attack one another; the spider and the mosaic imagine people attacking one another without regard for states or their borders. It is a serious mistake, in other words, when measuring the degree of violence in the world, to focus solely on interstate violence. The decline in interstate wars over the past several decades has to be weighed against a sharp increase in nonstate violence, which technology is likely to exacerbate. So the world of many-to-many threats and defenses may demand greater international governance not because of threats emanating from other states but because of threats emanating from a wide range of nonstate actors, domestic and international.

We have traditionally thought of international governance largely in terms of the preservation of peace and the resolution of disputes between nations—and, to a lesser extent, in terms of the joint pursuit among states of common objectives that require collective action. But if we take seriously the idea that one person or group of people might anonymously attack another person or group of people from across international borders, we must also take seriously the reality that whatever happens in any country's territory may now affect concretely the security of any other country. Consider the absence of any laws prohibiting cybercrime in some countries, the complete lack of control over biological or chemical agents in others, and the entire collapse of domestic law and order in still others. This reality may embolden proponents of radically enhanced global governance, which they might see as necessary not only to protect the world from nuclear self-annihilation but also from more mundane, and more ubiquitous, transnational forms of violence and attack. The growing necessity of more global governance might just drive the nations of the world to embrace it.

To put this another way, the world of many-to-many threats blurs the line between the domestic social contract, which liberal governance theory has largely embraced, and the international social contract, which it has largely eschewed. If we take this threat environment seriously, we may have to ask whether it is possible to have a viable domestic social contract if we do not also have some measure of international social contract. In *Skyfall*, the hacker who ends up attacking Parliament while M is testifying begins his operations overseas. The domestic social contract means little if someone overseas can export the state of nature back into the Leviathan's domain. Nor is the Leviathan really the Leviathan if all of the other Leviathans fail to govern effectively and the littler fish hold none of them in awe.

Reshaping the Social Contract amid the Democratization of Violence

Science and technology have long played a critical role in driving political change. They have played a crucial role in drawing and redrawing the maps of the world, in determining who conquered and who was conquered, and in growing and expanding empires even while rendering them vulnerable to challengers and competitors. From the spear to the crossbow, the chariot to the cannon, the airplane to the nuclear bomb, those in possession of the most powerful weapons have usually overpowered those who are not. Means of transportation, communication, and logistical support, all dependent on technology, have given a decisive advantage to those better able to deploy them. There was nothing natural or preordained about the boundaries of empires, cities, principalities, or modern states; all were drawn through blood and steel, beneficial marriages, peaceful surrenders, moral and religious ideas, economic development, and political compromises—often in the shadow of technological power.

In large part, technology and advances in science have promoted globalization and allowed the modern state to reach untold, imperial proportions—and to take on imperial problems. All states today struggle with problems that transcend their borders: Belgium must tackle transnational pedophile rings that end up harming Belgian children; Iceland's economy was severely hit by the Wall Street crisis; and small island states face an existential threat from rising ocean levels caused by global warming resulting from greenhouse emissions from major industrial economies. Large or small, the modern state is a Leviathan that faces international governance challenges that none of the original social contract theorists could have imagined.

The prospect of an erosion of state authority will, of course, alarm and excite people to different degrees depending on their views of human nature and on the value they place—positive or negative—on the authority of the state itself. Attitudes may also vary depending on the degree to which people believe that individuals are prone to violence if they are free from, or can bypass, constraints on their power—a question on which the original social contract theorists differed and about which contemporary experts on neuroscience, developmental psychology, criminology, and social studies are still in disagreement.

The truth is that different states will perform differently in this new environment. Technology may distribute power, but it does so unevenly. Variations will inevitably develop within any single country and across countries, privileging those with greater access to advanced technology and the knowledge of how to use it. Some states will acquire enormous powers with which they will be able to threaten others, as well as their own citizens. Some states will not. And here again, there is no guarantee that in the long run states—certainly not all states—will win this race. Already, HSBC Holdings and JP Morgan Chase & Co. have assets greater than the gross domestic product of a great many countries around the world, and some nonstate armed groups—such as Hezbollah in Lebanon, Hamas in Gaza, and the Revolutionary Armed Forces of Colombia (FARC)—have larger groups of armed fighters and arsenals than do the governments of Costa Rica and some small island nations, even though these governments represent UN member states. In June 2014, the Islamic State of Iraq and Syria, an offshoot of Al-Qaeda that swept through Iraq and seized territory previously held by the government, was reported to have assets worth more than $2 billion.[28]

In other words, some Leviathans will outperform others, and some will do more poorly than nonstate entities. States that are failed, fragile, or not technologically savvy will face greater dangers. And because of their inability to effectively police their territories, they will also, however indirectly, pose greater risks to others, states and nonstates alike, as perpetrators of violence use them as launching grounds for their attacks.

Within each state, too, new technologies will redistribute power. And how this happens will largely depend on how much technology empowers individuals relative to its concurrent empowerment of the Leviathan in each state. In some states, technology may empower some oppressed populations vis-à-vis their tyrants, which may be a boon to a liberal vision. But technology will also, in all likelihood, empower organized criminal groups, terrorists, and lone crazies against liberal democracies, resulting in an erosion of the power of democratic communities to govern themselves. In fact, compared with effective totalitarian regimes, liberal democracies may prove more vulnerable to attacks because they generally encourage technological proliferation and are less coercive in their control of it.

If the outlying, extreme case really comes to pass—if technologies of mass empowerment enable many isolated individuals or diverse non-state actors to injure or violate other individuals on a mass scale anywhere around the globe with substantially reduced fear of detection and punishment—we are in big trouble. Much of civil and political life as we know it will likely come to an end. At the very least, the state under these circumstances will face profound changes, as will individuals in going about their daily lives and associating with others. Spreading a sense of anarchy has long been a strategy of revolutionary movements. It does not take millions fighting other millions to shake our sense of personal security or our confidence in existing institutions. Simply put, it is not easy to find ungoverned, unprotected populations that nonetheless behave well. The closer our new environment comes to approaching that scenario, the more we will have to rewrite the terms of the social contract to compensate for the reduced vitality of our age-old bargain with power.

That said, as noted at the outset, we have no reason to assume that the outlying case is imminent, or even likely, or that the state per se is in extremis just yet. The jury is still out on how technology affects the relative power balance between offense and defense in general and between the empowerment of the state and the empowerment of the governed specifically. Although offensive power is currently outpacing defense, that may not persist forever. Defensive power tends to grow naturally alongside offensive power, even if it lags behind; zero-day attacks make software engineers more cognizant of potential future problems, and every new biological virus sparks new research into treatment and prevention. Moreover, it is possible that the state may survive, even flourish, because it makes the most effective use of new offensive powers, because it employs its regulatory and enforcement mechanisms to block attacks against it and its people, or because it develops more potent countermeasures than any of its likely alternatives.

It is possible, yet we suspect unlikely. Although we do not expect the state to fade away or become irrelevant, it is hard to avoid the conclusion that the world of many-to-many threats and defenses is likely to weaken it. And while reduced state power makes totalitarianism less sustainable, it also demands an adaptation of the extent and means of the Leviathan's promises of security, liberty, and freedom. With these general observations in mind, it is possible to sketch at least a few of the contours of the adaptation that both states and citizens would have to make to the social contract to refit it for the world of many-to-many threats.

For one thing, as threats materialize beyond imagined scenarios, we will grow ever more tolerant of enhanced state capacity—including in formerly unthinkable areas—to the extent that such capacity is necessary for the state to keep ahead of individual empowerment in the technology race. To some degree, this is already happening. We see it in laws like the Communications Assistance for Law Enforcement Act and the Foreign Intelligence Surveillance Act of 1978 Amendments Act, which try to preserve the Leviathan's power to govern by preserving its relative capacities to monitor private and commercial communications. Recall that both these laws order private communication carriers to cooperate with and facilitate the government's monitoring of citizens' communications. Our traditional liberal social contract would never have allowed government to grab giant swaths of private communications were it not for a technological environment that made that governmental capacity necessary for ensuring security, at least in the estimation of Congress and with the apparent tolerance of the public.

The positions of neither Congress nor the public remain fixed. In the aftermath of Edward Snowden's revelations, we are currently witnessing a heated debate over massive government collection and data-mining operations, which are being justified as necessary to keep government ahead of the titanic flood of data in the mosaic and the many menaces hiding in the bit stream. Not everyone believes these operations in their current scope are actually necessary, and many would like to see more checks and balances to keep such operations appropriately constrained.

As with other instances of governmental response to security threats, public opinion varies with threat perception. The more the world of many-to-many threats and defenses develops, and the more the public perceives itself as endangered, the greater will be the demand to calibrate the Leviathan's capacities to give it, if not—in Weber's formulation—a monopoly on violence, certainly a qualitative edge in the use of violence.

As part of its adaptation, the new social contract will not rely exclusively on government or its agents as providers of security. The more we come to rely on private parties for our security, the more these parties become, in some sense, organic to our social contract: not simply as citizens subject to government rule in exchange for the security they receive but as actors privileged and indeed obligated by the security benefits that they can provide. Just as we purchase our burglar alarms from private vendors and hire private security guards to protect our businesses from shoplifters, so we will look to the private market to augment the defensive capabilities of the state. Already, Norton or McAfee, not the government, protects our personal computers from malware—albeit not all that effectively. Already private industry is developing countersurveillance, detection, and defensive shields, including vaccinations and treatments for emerging pandemics.

Consequently, the state is no longer the sole party occupying the privileged position that society accords to those who defend it. As we have noted, in some ways this is not so much a new phenomenon as a revival of the pre-twentieth-century state, which did not fully monopolize either the means or authority to engage in violence but relied on hired guns like privateers and mercenaries. Yet, against the backdrop of more than a century of state-centralized security, the new privatization of security might invite new challenges to the very idea of a sovereign to which one owes at least a measure of allegiance. If the state as such is no longer the main provider of security, civic duties, from tax payment to fidelity to the law, may become open to challenge, unless a strong case can be made that privatization is still managed by, and operated in the shadow of, the state's power rather than in defiance of or in parallel with it.

Indeed, the new social contract will increasingly require that companies play the roles enabled by their capabilities. The state still demands a right to rule in exchange for the provision of security, but it now also demands by law and custom a more active participation in defense from those actors with unique or essential capacities. These obligations of citizen and corporate service—which we might analogize to jury service, tax paying, and the obligation to respond to compulsory judicial process—will become more common in the law as security becomes impossible without private collaboration. We see this not merely in our laws that require corporate assistance to government in monitoring individuals electronically but also in current congressional discussions of imposing legal requirements on companies that maintain critical infrastructure to ensure cybersecurity. In other words, we will increasingly weave into our social contract both our dependency on private industry and a positive requirement that industry and private actors play in full the security roles of which they are capable.

Legal scholar Philip Bobbitt has argued persuasively that, rather than dissolving, the state is adapting itself to the forces of globalization by shifting from the nation-state to what he terms the "market state." The market state, he claims, seeks to maximize its citizens' welfare by deregulating and transferring more of its traditional economic functions to the private sector, which is arguably more efficient, inclusive, and pluralistic. A similar process, he adds, is taking place in the context of war making. Rather than fight with large conscripted armies, states will increasingly fight future wars using a multitude of partner organizations.[29] These may include private military companies, corporations, and nonprofits, ranging from companies like the private security service provider Blackwater (now known as Academi) to the International Committee of the Red Cross.

Technology, we agree, will drive this process further. National and international policies, labor and economics, health and consumption will all shape and be reshaped by the spread of information technology, robotics, and the development of biotechnology. There will undoubtedly be a greater need to employ and partner with the private sector to meet all the challenges that new technology introduces and to realize all the potential it offers. In addition to Bobbitt's focus on deregulation in some areas, however, we suspect that we will also see more expansive regulation of these private parties in other spheres: a greater concentration of government power may become part of the new social contract that emerges. With threats emanating from more dispersed and less easily detectable sources, and with technological platforms being perpetually susceptible to abuse, government will likely come under pressure to impose stricter oversight and regulatory constraints on those with access to such platforms. This reactive concentration of regulatory power may have adverse effects on free markets and will require serious thought about its implications for individual privacy and liberty.

Perhaps most challengingly, the social contract is likely to grow more international. The question of what is considered a matter of security for any one country, or indeed for any one of us, is growing far more complex. If ISIS is assuming control of parts of Iraq and Syria, is that a matter of security for the United States? Or for any American citizen? How about the genocide in Darfur? Is the publication by WikiLeaks of thousands of classified cables, some embarrassing to foreign governments, a security threat to those foreign governments? And what about biomedical research at an insecure facility in South Asia? The original Leviathan was meant to protect citizens from their own destructive passions, as well as from external threats to their security. Those external threats were considered a fact of life, much like earthquakes or pandemics. But the Leviathan did not need to reach halfway around the globe to find and destroy an enemy of the state; it did not have to monitor a distant state ravaged by civil war and competing rebel groups to know when a threat was beginning to form. Nor did it perceive itself as having humanitarian obligations toward fragile, menaced populations other than its own.

Yet, as states become ever more threatened by both foreign states and nonstate sources, their interest in what happens beyond their borders grows in tandem. And their ability to protect their own citizens, to fulfill the most fundamental aspects of their own domestic social contracts, will increasingly hinge on what transpires in the domains of other Leviathans: on the domestic regulatory and enforcement regimes that govern access to and use of technology, on the motivations and actions of individuals and groups in those countries, and on the international flow of information, materials, and goods. The policies of every government, powerful governments in particular, now influence more than ever before the welfare and security of people everywhere, including people who are not citizens of the state and who thus would never have been considered parties to the original social contract.

The future of the social contract, in other words, cannot be framed simply in terms of what governments owe their own citizens and what they offer them in return, or even in terms of what states owe one another as part of their bilateral relationships. If the essence of the social contract is a simple trade—the authority to govern in exchange for the protection of individual security—and if any country's conduct now affects the safety of citizens of other countries and vice versa, we must also begin to ask what states owe and demand from other states, as well as other states' citizens, and what those citizens may in turn demand and expect from states other than their own. We can see this process happening in foreign reactions to Snowden's leaks about the National Security Agency. People in Germany and Brazil are outraged that the US government spied on them, and they are not mollified by the protections guaranteed in US law to prevent spying domestically or on US citizens or residents. They seem to believe that US law and policy owes them something. And the president of the United States seems to agree: in a January 2014 speech, Barack Obama announced that the United States recognized the privacy rights of foreigners abroad in conducting its espionage operations.[30]

In the absence of an international Leviathan, it necessarily falls to the member states of the international community to negotiate their mutual obligations in the new threat environment and to design agreed-on governance structures to enforce them. And this reality creates a paradoxical dynamic of its own in which unilateral actions, generally by the most powerful states, will tend to determine the rules of the game for much of the rest of the world—and begin defining a new social contract along the way. Not unlike the domestic adaptation, this process will test the international community's commitment to the human rights of individuals and the degree to which this commitment can withstand global threats to security.

M is the embodiment of the modern state's promised trade of security in return for authority. And she is still necessary. She may, in fact, be more necessary than ever before, for all the reasons she states. Technology makes her stronger, but it probably makes other people stronger even faster. And she is thus falling behind. The further behind she falls, the less good her case to Parliament is—and the less able she is to work with all the other Ms in the world and all the other parliaments. The further behind M falls—the more she is "made weak by time and fate"—the less it matters if she is "strong in will."

As M simultaneously acquires new strengths and falls further behind, the basic relationship between the state and its citizens changes. Our notions of liberty and security shift too, as do our notions of privacy and surveillance, to which we turn next.

5

RETHINKING PRIVACY, LIBERTY, AND SECURITY

"THOSE WHO WOULD GIVE UP essential Liberty, to purchase a little temporary Safety, deserve neither Liberty nor Safety." Benjamin Franklin penned these words, perhaps the most famous ever written about the relationship between liberty and security. A version of them appears on a plaque in the Statue of Liberty. They are quoted endlessly by those who assert that these two values coexist in a precarious, ever shifting balance that security concerns constantly threaten to upset. Every student of American history knows them. And for more than two centuries, lovers of liberty have pondered them, knowing that they speak to a great truth about the constitution of civilized governments: that when we empower government to protect us, we risk making a devil's bargain from which we might lose in the long run.

Very few people who quote these words, however, have any idea where they come from or what Franklin was actually referring to when he wrote them. They appeared originally in a 1755 letter to the colonial governor that Franklin is believed to have drafted on behalf of the Pennsylvania Assembly. Written in the midst of the French and Indian War, the letter was a salvo in a power struggle between the governor and the assembly over funding for security on the frontier. The assembly wished to tax the lands of the Penn family, which ruled Pennsylvania from afar, in order to raise money for defense against French and Indian attacks. But the governor, acting at the behest of the family—which had appointed him—kept vetoing the assembly's efforts to tax the Penn lands.

The "essential liberty" to which Franklin referred was not what we would think of today as civil liberties. Franklin, rather, was defending the right of a local legislature to pass laws and govern in the interests of collective security. And the "purchase [of] a little temporary safety" of which Franklin complained was not the ceding of power by the people to some government Leviathan in exchange for a promise of protection from external threat. Indeed, in Franklin's letter, the word "purchase" does not appear to have been a metaphor. He meant it quite literally. The Penn family was offering to pay cash for defense of the frontier—if the assembly backed down on its claimed power to tax the family's lands. And the governor was criticizing the assembly, meanwhile, for insisting on including the lands in its taxes and thus forcing his veto and leaving frontier defense unfunded. Franklin was thus complaining of the unenviable choice facing the legislature between making funds available for defense and maintaining its right of self-government. And he was criticizing the governor for suggesting that the assembly should be willing to give up one to ensure the other.[1]

In short, Franklin was not describing some tension between governmental power and individual liberty. He was describing, rather, effective self-government in the service of security as the very liberty it would be contemptible to trade. Notwithstanding the way the quotation has come down to us, Franklin saw the liberty and security interests of Pennsylvanians in this instance as aligned. The difference between what Franklin meant and what we moderns now hear in his words perfectly encapsulates the modern tendency to mangle intellectually the true relationship between liberty and security—a relationship we must understand better if we mean to maximize both freedom and safety in the coming generation.

In practical terms, this means thinking hard about privacy and what it really means in a world in which everything gets recorded. A great many debates over the liberty-security relationship in practice boil down to debates over privacy and surveillance—particularly over the handling of our mosaic data and who gets to do what with it. We have a tendency to frame such questions in terms of balance, and we hear in Franklin's words the prototypical statement of balancing and zero-sum trade-offs. But particularly in a world of unlimited data and many-to-many threats and defenses, this tendency is wrong. Framing the relationship between liberty, privacy, and security so simply leads us astray.

Franklin's quotation shows up as the epigraph to a dissent by Judge Stephen Reinhardt of the Ninth Circuit Court of Appeals in a 2004 case called *United States v. Kincade*. Thomas Kincade, a decorated seaman, robbed a bank in 1993, spent a number of years in prison, and became eligible for supervised release in 2000. In 2002, his probation officer asked him to submit a blood sample under the federal DNA Act, which required collection and retention of DNA profiles of people convicted of federal felonies. Kincade refused. Challenges to state and federal DNA databases were nothing new. All of the federal circuit courts of appeals had seen them, and all had upheld DNA databases, which match the DNA in physical evidence collected at crime scenes with the DNA profiles of large collections of individuals convicted of crimes. The majority of the Ninth Circuit also upheld the law, although it split as to the basis for doing so. The plurality of the court saw "substantially diminished expectations of privacy" on the part of convicts, only a "minimal intrusion occasioned by blood sampling," and "overwhelming societal interests so clearly furthered by the collecting of DNA information from convicted offenders." It therefore saw no problem under the Fourth Amendment with requiring Kincade's cooperation—and blood. Another judge concurred on different grounds, arguing that the collection was a so-called special-needs search, justifying an intrusion on liberty. All saw, in other words, a price in liberty worth paying for law enforcement.

Reinhardt and several of his colleagues, by contrast, saw the price in liberty as unacceptable—a positive nightmare with "catastrophic potential." Reinhardt began by quoting Franklin's warning; he then went on to invoke J. Edgar Hoover's surveillance of civil rights leaders, the harassment of communists in the postwar era, and the internment of Japanese Americans during World War II—all of which, he noted darkly, depended on the centralized collection and storage of information about people. Under the majority's theories, he warned, "all Americans will be at risk, sooner rather than later, of having our DNA samples permanently placed on file in federal cyberspace, and perhaps even worse, of being subjected to various other governmental programs providing for suspicionless searches conducted for law enforcement purposes." He concluded,

> Kincade, by the terms of the DNA Act, will effectively be compelled to provide evidence with respect to any and all crimes of which he may be accused for the rest of his life. Every time new evidence is discovered from a crime scene, the government will search Kincade's genetic code to determine whether he has committed the crime—just as the government might search his house for evidence linking him to the crime scene—despite the fact that the government may never have cause to suspect him again. Moreover, the maintenance of his

DNA will permit a myriad of other known and unknown uses of the samples, by governmental authorities, as technology evolves, in violation of his full future expectation of privacy.[2]

Lost in the debate between Reinhardt and his colleagues was the fact that it is far from obvious that Kincade's privacy, on the whole, is harmed by his presence in the federal DNA database.

Framing the problem as one of trade-offs between Kincade's liberty and privacy and aggregated public safety misses the privacy benefits that accrue to him as a result of being included in the database. Indeed, as Judge Guido Calabresi of the Second Circuit Court of Appeals wrote in a different case, "the systematic collection of probationers' DNA samples under the Act has the potential to provide a net gain in privacy for the individuals who are required to provide samples. Having DNA on file may very well help to exculpate such individuals by avoiding misidentification and, thus, preventing much more serious invasions of their privacy in the future."[3]

The ultimate net effects on privacy, either for Kincade or for any one of us, of having our DNA profiles stored in a mass database is a complicated equation. But considering only the costs to privacy without also considering the possible benefits is stacking the deck in evaluating it. Indeed, nowhere in the Ninth Circuit debate do either the majority judges or the dissenters mention that every time police collect a piece of evidence from a crime scene and run it through the system, that system will now exclude Kincade as a suspect to the extent the DNA evidence does not match his profile. This will spare him scrutiny by police, scrutiny that is inevitably more intrusive than either the one-time drawing of blood or the trivial—and altogether theoretical—privacy intrusion of having (along with millions of others) one's DNA electronically compared to samples run through the system. Particularly for the former convict, who will tend to attract police attention when crimes take place in his vicinity, routine automatic exclusion can have significant—if entirely invisible—privacy benefits. Being in the database may well spare a suspect the possibility of a search warrant being executed against his house. It may even spare him the possibility of being wrongly prosecuted.[4]

The notion that privacy is under siege is a cliché of the digital era, but the truth of the matter is far more complex. In some ways, the very idea of privacy is eroding. With countless details of our lives recorded constantly, even the word "privacy" no longer captures the true values we wish to protect in conjunction with the data in our mosaics. "Threats to privacy" end up covering dangers of very different magnitudes and for which we should expect entirely different levels and forms of protection. We describe as privacy violations everything from the icky feeling of being watched when advertisers target us based on our behavior to victimization by identity thieves to surveillance by active government agents. Yet, in other ways, the same forces that erode privacy also enable it; we can look up our sensitive medical conditions without leaving our homes, and we can buy all sorts of things in secret. It is not always clear whether privacy is ebbing or flowing, and the perceived trade-offs we make with our liberty do not always erode liberty in practice either.

THE PROBLEM OF BALANCE

The metaphor of balance—in which some added bit of liberty or privacy weighs down the scales and disrupts the security side or some new security measure necessarily forces the liberty tray upward—is pervasive in our rhetoric. It lives in our case law. It lives in our academic discourse. It lives in our efforts to describe our reality. It lives in our imagination. It lives in the calls to shift the balance in perilous times by giving up liberty in the name of security, and it lives as well in the calls to restore the balance by abandoning security measures said to injure freedom. The image of balance arises especially vividly in the context of surveillance, where every augmentation of government power is said to come at some cost to liberty and privacy. Proponents of more aggressive surveillance justify such steps as valuable and as imposing only allowable costs in light of some compelling governmental or societal security need—as the Ninth Circuit majority did in *Kincade*. Opponents criticize those steps as excessive enhancements of governmental power taken at the expense of freedom or privacy. We seldom stop to ask whether and when our surveillance programs are really coming at the expense of liberty at all, or whether the relationship might be more complicated than that.

The notion of a balance between liberty and security has a claim on our imaginations because it captures with a simple image a tension between two key objectives of enlightened government. At times arising acutely, this tension presents itself in several different forms, though these forms overlap, and some expressions of the balance thesis reflect more than one of them. At its most basic, the balance thesis is an analytical point— an observation that liberty and security exist in tension with one another and that enhancing one will often threaten to detract from the other. A corollary of this observation is the notion that the balance in question shifts during crises. As former chief justice William Rehnquist put it in his book about civil liberties during wartime, "In wartime, reason and history both suggest that this balance shifts to some degree in favor of order—in favor of the government's ability to deal with conditions that threaten the national well-being."[5]

A second version of the balance thesis presents an argument that there should be a balance, often accompanied by the concern that we have failed to achieve that balance or that things, in practice, have slipped away from the balance we ought to strike. Commentators vary in their opinions of the direction in which we have strayed from balance, but the idea of balance as the goal recurs throughout the writings of lawyers, commentators, and policy makers.

However framed, the balance thesis has two truths at its core. First, public safety measures often have implications for liberties. The powers to imprison criminal suspects and to conduct certain types of surveillance, for example, do entail liberty and privacy costs and, moreover, are ripe for abuse and require vigilant checking and oversight. This much is uncontroversial. Second, civil liberties tend to diminish during wartime in the name of public safety.

It is also the case, however, that taxes tend to go up during wartime, and some public health measures can also negatively impact people's liberty. (Think of compulsory vaccinations, say, or requiring people to purchase health insurance.) Yet it is far less common in our vocabulary to describe a general tension between security and fiscal responsibility or between public health and liberty. And similarly, the fact that some security measures will negatively affect civil liberties does not mean that security and liberty are generally in tension with one another or that increases in one will generally come at the other's expense. The notion of such a crude set of trade-offs is not merely simplistic. It is, most of the time and with respect to most exercises of government power, just wrong—even absent a many-to-many-threats-and-defenses environment.

The more sophisticated articulations of the balance thesis actually acknowledge this. For example, legal scholars Eric Posner and Adrian Vermeule restrict their apparently dramatic claim of a "straightforward tradeoff between liberty and security" to policy making "at the security-liberty frontier," thus acknowledging that in circumstances short of the frontier, balancing should not apply. Stated this way, their formulation of the thesis is unobjectionable. At some point, after all, any two goods will conflict. One might just as well speak, to use our earlier example, of a public health–liberty frontier, that spectrum of situations in which one has exhausted all of the policy options to enhance public health that do not encumber freedom. Plotting two values against one another is only useful if one imagines that the frontier lies sufficiently close to the zone of actual policy making that measures to maximize one good will, in general, negatively impact the other.[6] But if Posner and Vermeule's formulation of the balance thesis resolves the conceptual problems with its cruder articulations, it raises an important empirical question. Do liberal democracies really live on the liberty-security frontier?

Posner and Vermeule clearly believe that they do—that, as they put it, "advanced liberal democracies rarely overlook . . . opportunities [to enhance both values]. Only a very dysfunctional government would decline to adopt policies that draw support from both proponents of increased security and proponents of increased liberty." If one accepts this proposition, their thesis becomes hard to distinguish in practice from the more conventional version of the balance thesis.[7]

The trouble is that it is just not the case that functional democracies necessarily optimize the blending of security and liberty. Different functional democracies, for one thing, choose different blends, and many of them review and revisit their blends from time to time. Unless all choices made by liberal democracies by definition place them along the frontier (assuming we had the capacity to identify and chart the frontier in the first place), Posner and Vermeule overstate the extent to which democracies never miss opportunities—even significant ones—to enhance both liberty and security.

To take one concrete example from the world of counterterrorism, President Barack Obama considers the closure of the Guantánamo Bay detention facility and the consequent release of a number of its inmates as serving the aggregate national security needs of the United States. Such a release would undoubtedly also realize the liberty interests of the detainees in question. Yet, Congress, by encumbering such detainee transfers over several years, has effectively impeded the executive branch from veering closer to its view of the optimal liberty-security frontier.[8]

To illustrate more vividly that simple balance is the wrong metaphor to describe the general relationship between these values, consider a point so obvious that it tends to get overlooked: the least free countries are not the most secure, and the freest countries are not the least secure. One could demonstrate this with social-scientific data showing the comparative likelihood of violent death in free and totalitarian societies, but a simple, impressionistic gut check will suffice for present purposes. Freedom House lists among the freest nations in the world Australia, Austria, the tiny island nations of Kiribati and Palau, New Zealand, the United States, the Scandinavian countries, the Bahamas, and Uruguay. By contrast, in its least free category are, among others, North Korea, Somalia, Sudan, and Uzbekistan. In which group of countries would you feel safer? The question answers itself. In truth, the relationship between the aggregate levels of liberty and security in a society is dramatically closer to a direct relationship than to an inverse one. This fact alone suggests a profound defect in any metaphor that assumes some generalized trade-off between the two goods.[9]

This general observation about the contemporary world meshes nicely with the observations of Enlightenment political theorists, who figured out early that the optimal amount of government power to maximize meaningful liberty was not zero. We have seen Hobbesian worlds—places where the total absence of government authority creates anarchy. They exist today in Somalia, parts of Yemen, Afghanistan, and Pakistan; we see them also in Iraq. They are not free in any sense that a rational person would understand the word. They are some of the most terrifying places in the world. Without what Thomas Hobbes called "a Common Power, to keep [the people] in awe, and to direct their actions to the Common Benefit," there is no way to enforce agreements, resolve disputes, or force people to live peaceably. Only through the ceding of some measure of individual liberty to state power, as Hobbes argued, can one's residual liberty be made worth anything.[10]

Hobbes's diagnosis of absolute liberty as breeding violence and danger has stood the test of time better than his famously autocratic prescription. But other Enlightenment philosophers figured out that just as liberty required security to have value, so too did security require liberty to be real—and that it was thus important to individual security to limit sovereign power and apply law not only to people but also to government. Charles de Montesquieu defined "political liberty in a citizen [as] that tranquility of spirit which comes from the opinion each one has of his security, and in order for him to have this liberty the government must be such that one citizen cannot fear another citizen." This is impossible, he wrote, when legislative and executive powers are fused, "because one can fear that the same monarch or senate that makes tyrannical laws will execute them tyrannically." Similarly, if "the power of judging" is combined with either legislative or executive power, liberty is impossible. "All would be lost if the same man or the same body of principal men, either of nobles, or of the people, exercised these three powers"—and liberty would be lost precisely because the concentrated power would deprive those beneath the sovereign of security from him.[11]

John Locke made the same point in his *Second Treatise of Government* when he wrote, "For he being supposed to have all, both legislative and executive power in himself alone, there is no judge to be found, no appeal lies open to anyone who may fairly and indifferently, and with authority, decide, and from whose decision relief and redress may be expected of any injury or inconveniency that may be suffered from the prince or by his order."[12] In other words, our modern notion of separation of powers flows from a sense of liberty and security as bound up in one another—indeed, as defined in terms of one another.

In more recent literature, the lack of individual security is part of the very definition of what it means to lack freedom. This theme runs, for example, throughout *1984* and other dystopian visions of totalitarianism. George Orwell in several places explicitly links the absence of physical security with the absence of freedom:

> He began thinking of the things that would happen to him after the Thought Police took him away. It would not matter if they killed you at once. To be killed was what you expected. But before death (nobody spoke of such things, yet everybody knew of them) there was the routine of confession that had to be gone through: the groveling on the floor and screaming for mercy, the crack of broken bones, the smashed teeth, and bloody clots of hair. Why did you have to endure it, since the end was always the same? Why was it not possible to cut a few days or weeks out of your life? Nobody ever escaped detection, and nobody ever failed to confess. When once you had succumbed to thoughtcrime it was certain that by a given date you would be dead. Why then did that horror, which altered nothing, have to lie embedded in future time?[13]

The close link in the writings of both Orwell and the Enlightenment theorists between the extreme physical insecurity of the individual—who faces certain torture and death—and his lack of liberty dovetails perfectly with the Freedom House list of countries that are not free. Just as we have seen

Hobbesian lands and noticed that they are not free in any meaningful sense, we have also seen Orwellian lands—and we notice that the North Korean individual is not secure.

The Framers of the Constitution, like the Enlightenment theorists, had no doubt that the dominant relationship between meaningful liberty and security was one not of tension but of mutual dependency and congruence. The Constitution's preamble envisions that it will at once "insure domestic Tranquility, provide for the common defense, . . . and secure the Blessings of Liberty"—linking the security and freedom values as a package, not setting them off against each other. And this interrelation and interdependence pervades *The Federalist Papers* too. Alexander Hamilton in Federalist 1 warns his readers not to forget that "the vigor of government is essential to the security of liberty; that, in the contemplation of a sound and well-informed judgment, their interest can never be separated; and that a dangerous ambition more often lurks behind the specious mask of zeal for the rights of the people than under the forbidden appearance of zeal for the firmness and efficiency of government." Similarly, Hamilton's famous warning in Federalist 8 that war "will compel nations the most attached to liberty, to resort for repose and security to institutions which have a tendency to destroy their civil and political rights" comes in the context of an argument for greater, not lesser, government power. Hamilton's point is that absent a strong central government, there is a greater likelihood of war among the states—war that would then produce terrible erosions of liberty. In the absence of a central government powerful enough to ensure peace, he argues, "we should, in a little time, see established in every part of this country the same engines of despotism which have been the scourge of the Old World."[14]

Similarly, in Federalist 51, James Madison—clearly channeling Hobbes and Locke—argues that a government can only guarantee liberty to the extent that it "guards one part of society against the injustice of the other part." In a country, he writes,

> under the forms of which the stronger faction can readily unite and oppress the weaker, anarchy may as truly be said to reign as in a state of nature, where the weaker individual is not secured against the violence of the stronger; and as, in the latter state, even the stronger individuals are prompted, by the uncertainty of their condition, to submit to a government which may protect the weak as well as themselves; so, in the former state, will the more powerful factions or parties be

gradually induced, by a like motive, to wish for a government which will protect all parties, the weaker as well as the more powerful.[15]

Madison sought to create a government that was divided enough structurally not to become an oppressor itself and that ruled over a people with a sufficient diversity of interests that no majority could gang up on the few. Yet he did not lose sight of the fact that the government needed to be powerful enough to restrain the "violence of the stronger." In Federalist 70, Hamilton goes so far as to argue for a strong executive in the name of liberty. "Energy in the executive is a leading character in the definition of good government," he writes. "It is essential . . . to the protection of property against those irregular and high-handed combinations which sometimes interrupt the ordinary course of justice; to the security of liberty against the enterprises and assaults of ambition, of faction, and of anarchy." One strains to find any semblance in *The Federalist Papers* of the crude version of the balance thesis that is now so common.[16]

The idea of balance, in other words, described reality badly even centuries before technologies of mass empowerment began lessening the governability of individuals worldwide. There are certainly times when exertions of government power can and will erode liberty—say, when government seeks to arrest or spy on political dissidents—and restraint from such exertions will augment liberty. But there are also times when exertions of government power will enhance liberty—say, when government seeks to identify and arrest serial killers—and restraint from such exertions will erode it. Similarly, there are times when, as the balance thesis would suggest, augmenting privacy or liberty will erode security—as when, for example, one disallows valuable surveillance activity conducted with strict oversight under the rule of law. But there are also times when augmenting privacy will enhance security—as, for example, when one better protects individuals' online data from falling into the hands of identity thieves or when one restrains government surveillance from running amok.

While the balance metaphor is misleading under the best of circumstances, it is particularly so as applied to technologies of mass empowerment in an environment in which threats and defenses are widely distributed. In that context, it is incomplete to the point of inducing a deep cognitive error. In our coming security environment, after all, we might at times harbor more fear of many Little Brothers than we do of any one Big Brother. Indeed, securing ourselves against a great many Little Brothers may sometimes require a Leviathan capable of robust

enforcement actions. Similarly, leaving important domains of human activity unpatrolled in the name of restricting government power may sometimes undermine, rather than promote, freedom. There will be situations
in which the essential forces eroding human freedom will not be governments and in which we might therefore choose to strengthen government
precisely in order to protect liberty better. None of this looks much like a
balance scale or, as legal scholar Philip Bobbitt derisively puts it, "a needle
oscillating between two poles."[17]

The development of technologies of mass empowerment, as we have
seen, creates vast new arenas for human activity. One does not necessarily
maximize freedom in such circumstances by minimizing governance and
governmental power. Moreover, if one believes—as we have suggested—
that private actors are going to play an increasingly large role in the provision of security in the future, this fact, perhaps paradoxically, at once
erodes government's monopoly on security and at the same time requires
strong government. After all, someone needs to coordinate, direct, and
create incentives to encourage the complex set of private actions that will
cumulatively protect us while also ensuring the accountability of private
actors to society at large. That necessarily implies a role for government
power in the protection of secure freedom.

The Problem of Privacy

The idea of privacy has deep roots in American democratic thought and
provides a convenient vocabulary for all sorts of issues implicating personal autonomy, seclusion, reputation, and the ability to control information about oneself. But as a distinct legal concept, privacy is an idea
of surprisingly recent vintage. It developed in American law and political
culture only in the nineteenth century and only in response to the development of surveillance technologies that outmoded earlier ways of thinking about keeping government and outsiders out of one's business. In their
now legendary 1890 *Harvard Law Review* article, Louis Brandeis and Samuel Warren introduced the right to privacy, claiming that "instantaneous
photographs and newspaper enterprise have invaded the sacred precincts
of private and domestic life, and numerous mechanical devices threaten
to make good the prediction that 'what is whispered in the closet shall be
proclaimed from the house-tops.'" Indeed, the concept of privacy was not
originally separate from the concept of property in law. It emerged as a
legal concept of its own only as technologies and organizational structures

rendered property rights inadequate to protect people from publicity and surveillance they regarded as offensive. To put it simply, we created privacy because we had reached a technological tipping point that required a conceptual breakthrough.[18]

We tend to discuss policy issues concerning control over our mosaics of data using the language of privacy for the simple reason that we do not yet have a word for the value we instinctively wish to protect, and privacy represents the closest value to it that liberalism has yet articulated. There is no doubt an intuitive logic at work in our invocation of privacy here. If one imagines, for example, the malicious deployment of all the government's authorities to collect the components of a person's mosaic and then the use of those components against that person, one is imagining a police state no less than if one imagines an unrestricted power to raid people's homes. If one imagines unrestricted commerce in personal information about people's habits, tastes, and behaviors—innocent and deviant alike— one is imagining an invasion of personal space as destructive of a person's privacy as breaking into that person's home and then selling all the personal information one can pilfer there.

Yet privacy as traditionally understood no longer accurately or fully describes the threats from which we seek protection. The idea of privacy as a legal matter was not inevitable. It was, in fact, deliberately created in response to the obsolescence of previous legal concepts designed to shield individuals from government and one another. This obsolescence developed because breaches of people's solitude no longer required physically breaking into their homes or rummaging through their physical possessions.

Ironically, today technology is rendering privacy itself incapable of describing the violations and vulnerabilities people feel with respect to the mosaic—and it describes those violations less and less well as time goes on. Much of the material that makes up your mosaic, after all, involves records of events that take place in public, not in private: driving through a toll booth or shopping at a store, for example, are not exactly private acts. Most mosaic data, moreover, is sensitive only in aggregation; it is often trivial in and of itself—and we consequently think little of giving it, or the rights to use it, away. Indeed, mosaic data by its nature tends to be material we have disclosed to others, often in exchange for some benefit and often with the understanding, implicit or explicit, that it will be aggregated and mined for what it might say about us. It takes a certain intellectual jujitsu to attribute to an invasion of privacy the concern we feel about the management of amalgamations of public activities that we have transacted knowingly with strangers in exchange for benefits. What is more, we have tended to develop privacy protections piecemeal; we pass laws in response to the last incident that outraged us. A video store released the rental records of Robert Bork during his Supreme Court nomination fight, so the United States has a privacy law for video rental records—but not for book purchases or library records or iTunes or Kindle downloads—that is much tougher than its privacy law for educational or health records. There is no coherence to what we protect, how rigorously, or by what means. The reason is simply that we no longer know what value we are trying to shield or how that value interfaces with life in a modern society.

So, just as we once needed privacy because earlier ideas no longer described the stresses on our seclusion from the outside world, today privacy itself is being outstripped by technological development. We do not mean this in some crude sense: that privacy is dead, so we should stop protecting it or, as the phrase goes, you have zero privacy anyway, so get over it. We mean it in a different, deeper sense: that the concept of privacy badly describes the value we wish to protect in a culture in which we routinely conduct transactions using, as currency, data about ourselves. What is more, the various issues commonly grouped together under the rubric of privacy are by no means of comparable weight. Some involve little more than sentiment. Others involve most profound issues of personal security. In a world of many-to-many threats, we cannot afford to confuse the two; nor can we afford to fail to prioritize among different privacy threats. We need to understand that some forms of surveillance—to the extent that they secure platforms against privacy-threatening misuse—can actually enhance privacy. We need a sophisticated concept of privacy, or some more refined idea altogether, that describes better the challenges posed to individuals by having so much information about them stored in their mosaics.

Nearly forty years have passed since philosopher Judith Jarvis Thomson asserted that "perhaps the most striking thing about the right to privacy is that nobody seems to have any very clear idea what it is." This is certainly still the case, and in some sense, it must be, given the many different domains implicated by the term "privacy"—from national security to commerce to medical treatment to education. Consider for a moment the astonishing range of mosaic issues that we treat under the rubric of privacy. There is, for starters, what we might call privacy as sentiment— the way it makes us feel when information about us is available to strangers and the sense that, quite apart from any tangible damage a disclosure might do, our data is nobody else's business, particularly not government's. Privacy as sentiment is at the core of the conception of privacy embraced by many civil liberties and libertarian activists. It is also central to writers on the subject who bemoan privacy's erosions. Law professor and privacy expert Daniel Solove, for example, devotes an entire chapter of one of his books to the way that "digital dossiers" make us feel like characters in Franz Kafka's *The Trial*. It is a common complaint among such commentators that the fact of surveillance makes people behave differently, chilling deviant lawful behavior and encouraging conformity.[19]

Privacy as sentiment is central to contemporary discussions of the mosaic. A 2010 Federal Trade Commission (FTC) staff report on digital privacy, for example, notes that the commission's prior conception of privacy, based on harm prevention and ensuring consumer-informed consent for the use of data, was inadequate because "for some consumers, the actual range of privacy-related harms is much wider and includes . . . the fear of being monitored or simply having private information 'out there.' Consumers may feel harmed when their personal information—particularly sensitive health or financial information—is collected, used, or shared without their knowledge or consent or in a manner that is contrary to their expectations."[20] In this conception of privacy, we do not look to the specific tangible harm that a disclosure or collection does to a person. The disclosure or collection is itself the harm because of the way it makes the person feel—and because of the behavioral change it may induce.

A good example of privacy as sentiment in contemporary public policy is the long-running dispute between the European Union and the United States over the provision of airline passenger data to American law enforcement. Europeans have objected to this on privacy grounds. Yet, in the voluminous literature the subject has sparked, there is very little consideration of the specific harms to airline passengers of the government's receiving the same data that these passengers give to the airlines when they make reservations for international travel. The harm seems simply to lie in the fact of having one's data reported at all. It is perhaps psychological or maybe an autonomy-based argument—something along the lines of a person's right to control information that pertains to her own life and to decide to whom and in what way it can be distributed.[21]

A related conception of privacy sees in it some kind of right not to be the subject of targeted advertising and behavioral profiling—at least in its more aggressive forms. The FTC staff report is infused throughout with this vision, a sense that consumers should "be able to choose whether to allow the collection and use of data regarding their online searching and browsing activities." The report proposes "a more uniform and comprehensive consumer choice mechanism for online behavioral advertising, sometimes referred to as 'Do Not Track.' Such a universal mechanism could be accomplished by legislation or potentially through robust, enforceable self-regulation." This is another version of the desire to control our own data or, more aspirationally, to control data about us.[22]

Many commentators also see in privacy some right to control our reputations. In a lengthy *New York Times Magazine* article, for example, writer Jeffrey Rosen discussed "the costs of an age in which so much of what we say, and of what others say about us, goes into our permanent—and public—digital files. The fact that the Internet never seems to forget is threatening, at an almost existential level, our ability to control our identities; to preserve the option of reinventing ourselves and starting anew; to overcome our checkered past." Solove wrote an entire book, titled *The Future of Reputation*, about this problem, arguing, "We must . . . balance the protection of privacy against freedom of speech." The reputational components of privacy range enormously in severity. They can be a mere matter of an inability to purge the public record of one's youthful indiscretions—those pictures of you with a lampshade on your head that you would prefer to relegate to a past life. They can also include far more serious harms associated with the inability to stanch the flow of information that—legitimately or illegitimately—subjects one to public shaming or ongoing consequences. Sometimes this has the feel of justice—for example, when the hacker collective Anonymous threatened to out cyberbullies who had taunted a teenage girl toward suicide and effectively extorted their apologies. Sometimes, it seems deeply unjust—as when a twenty-five-year-old teacher-in-training in Pennsylvania posted a photo of herself on MySpace wearing a pirate hat and drinking a beer and was denied graduation as a result of her supposedly "unprofessional," though perfectly legal, conduct.[23]

Finally, at the higher end of the harms scale, privacy concerns morph into matters of personal security. Systems that do not adequately protect user privacy potentially give rise to identity theft, fraud, financial crimes, and stalking. A lack of privacy can also expose a person, under some circumstances, to unjustified arrest and prosecution and other adverse actions at the hands of government. A great many personal security issues associated with the mosaic ultimately boil down to questions of system integrity and identity verification—and these are matters impossible to sever from the privacy, for example, of passwords or of personal data not intended for disclosure. The security of your online bank accounts is not distinct from the privacy of those accounts and the records they contain.

This very brief and far from comprehensive overview of the work we are asking the concept of privacy to do for us gives a flavor of its breadth and diversity. We use the word to describe everything from a nonspecific set of anxieties quite divorced from any particular imagined harm to matters pertaining in a tangible and specific sense to most fundamental matters of personal security and safety. Moreover, it is clear from the foregoing that our concerns about privacy are by no means limited to what the government might do with our personal information—the potential oppression by Big Brother—and include what private vendors, colleagues, acquaintances, and other Little Brothers anywhere around the world might do with it. With all the weight we put on the concept, it is no wonder that we shield none of these interests very effectively.

In fact, privacy describes rather inaptly our real expectations with respect to third-party handling of mosaic data—at least to the extent that our behaviors in the marketplace reflect our expectations. Whatever political vocabulary we apply to mosaic issues, we do not seem to express an expectation of nondisclosure or confidentiality with our behavior. Indeed, when one stops and contemplates what genuinely upsets us in the marketplace, privacy as such does not describe it well at all. It is not just that we happily trade confidentiality and anonymity for convenience. It is that we seem to have no trouble with disclosures and uses of our data when they take place for our benefit. For example, we positively expect our credit card companies to keep an eye on our transactions to protect us against fraud. We do not experience a sense of violation when computers—and ultimately humans—mine our data for irregularities in those transactions and then call us to verify their legitimacy. We do not mind credit reporting when the details the agencies report are favorable, accurate, and enable us to obtain credit. Huge numbers of consumers happily let the contents of their e-mails guide the advertising they receive from their e-mail providers. We react with equanimity when companies use our purchase data to recommend further purchases or when they amalgamate data from multiple sources to provide us with the services we want. We do not punish companies that aggressively use our data for purposes of their own, so long as those uses do not cause us adverse consequences. Were we actually concerned with the idea that another person had knowledge of these transactions—what we might describe as "privacy per se"—we would react to these and many other routine online actions quite hostilely. We would not knowingly allow merchants to track our purchases in exchange for a small discount. We would not move aggressively away from the anonymity of cash transactions.

To put the matter simply, we react positively or negatively to the collection, storage, and use of our mosaic data in proportion not to whether that data is used in a fashion that protects our privacy or confidentiality but to whether it is used for our benefit or to our detriment and, critically, how seriously to our detriment. This is not quite privacy we are asking for. It is something else—something more like an expectation that our data will not rise up and attack us and that the custodians of our mosaic tiles will preserve our interests, even as they act in their own.

In other words, we speak in the language of a balance between liberty and security, though we do not really seek to balance these intertwined goods, and we speak in the language of privacy though we seek something more complicated and nuanced than simple, generic privacy.

THE HOSTILE SYMBIOSIS

But if not as balance, how should we think about the relationship between liberty and security in the world of many-to-many threats and defenses? And if not as privacy, how should we think about the security and secrecy of our personal data in a world in which someone might have to comb through it in order to protect us from someone else's abuse of it? How should we think about surveillance that at once threatens our privacy and promises to keep us safer in our uses of new technologies that allow others to threaten us too?

In 1929, evolutionary biologist Julian Huxley, science fiction writer H. G. Wells, and Wells's son, G. P. Wells, jointly authored a nine-book, three-volume treatise on the life sciences and evolution. Titled *The Science of Life*, the work is primarily of historical interest nowadays. It contains a ferocious defense of evolution, contending that it is a fact beyond reasonable argument. It reflects a skeptical attitude toward vogue racial attitudes of the time. It also contains an embarrassing enthusiasm for the eugenics movement. And buried in this lengthy tome is the following paragraph:

> The phrase "hostile symbiosis" has been used to describe the state of our own tissues—all of the same parentage, all thriving best when working for the common good, and yet each ready to take advantage

of the rest, should opportunity offer. There is a profound truth embodied in the phrase. Every symbiosis is in its degree underlain by hostility, and only by proper regulation and often elaborate adjustment, can the state of mutual benefit be maintained. Even in human affairs, partnerships for mutual benefit are not so easily kept up, in spite of men being endowed with intelligence and so being able to grasp the meaning of such a relation. But in lower organisms, there is no such comprehension to help keep the relationship going. Mutual partnerships are adaptations as blindly entered into and as unconsciously brought about as any others. They work by virtue of complicated physical and chemical adjustments between the two partners and between the whole partnership and its environment; alter that adjustment, and the partnership may dissolve, as blindly and automatically as it was entered into.[24]

This passage, in our view, captures the essence of the relationship between liberty, privacy, and security in an age in which any entity can theoretically attack or defend you. It is a relationship of profound mutual dependence yet, simultaneously, mutual danger and hostility. An adjustment to one actor in the symbiosis may aid the other actors, may harm one or more, or may advantage one with respect to the others. It may cause the relationship to adjust, to reformulate, or to dissolve. But like the symbiosis between the sea anemone and the clown fish, the relationship is never one of simple balance. Whatever hostility there may be, there is too much dependency for that.

In considering any action that may alter the equilibrium between the partners in the liberty-privacy-security symbiosis, one has to consider several questions we tend to blur together but that are actually distinct from one another. The first question is, whose liberty, privacy, and security stands to be affected by that action? Any given person's liberty and security interests will generally align rather precisely; that is, relatively few measures will make a person more secure but also make her less free. Such measures do exist; being in an isolated prison cell may keep you very secure by ensuring that you are very unfree. We can see such measures also in the detention of the mentally ill person who poses a serious threat to herself, in the protective custody of a person who faces a grave risk of violent harm, or when parents prohibit a teenager from going out and pursuing reckless behavior. Moreover, there is a sense in which many safety measures—including requirements to use seatbelts, wear hard hats, or maintain hygiene practices—increase people's safety at some cost to their liberty. Yet, at least up to a point, most measures that enhance the security of a given person will also enhance her liberty, and vice versa, for the simple reason that the person in question is generally freer to do as she pleases if she is more physically secure.

The same is true of privacy. Most people, most of the time, see a congruence between their privacy interests and their security interests. And while we can all think of examples, like airport security screening, which promise us each greater security in exchange for compromises of our privacy, these situations are actually not the norm. The far more typical situation is when the same step that makes you more secure also protects your privacy—indeed, it makes you more secure because it protects your privacy, and vice versa. The lock on your door does both, for example. In most cases, the values are not even severable.

The far more common clash between liberty and security is when the same measure that makes one person more secure and free comes at the expense of the liberty and security of another person. That is, we are not trading off any one individual's liberty against that same individual's security. We are trading one person's liberty, privacy, and security off against another's. By making person x less safe and less free, we hope to make person y more so. In other words, while we often talk about liberty, privacy, and security in general, this formulation is actually lazy and tends to skate over important choices concerning whose liberty and security we in fact care about and whose we are willing—even eager—to throw over the side of the boat.[25]

To cite an extreme example, let us say that person y is a serial rapist and person x is a potential rape victim. In this situation, each person's own liberty interests will align almost perfectly with his or her security interests. Person y will be both freer and more secure if he is not caught. Person x will be freer and more secure if y is caught and imprisoned. Their interests, however, are diametrically opposed. Society simply has to choose whose interests it will heed. Decent societies make the choice that person y's liberty and security is an evil insofar as it endangers the liberty and security of person x and all other persons like her. In such a case, the choice is easy.

That choice becomes far more difficult when we consider the same question without having positively identified person y as a serial rapist but, say, merely suspect him of being one. Then we are considering the liberty and security interests of, on the one hand, the universe of possible criminal suspects against the liberty and security interests of, on the other hand, the universe of possible rape victims. Here we face hard choices between the interests of different groups in society for whom we have genuine and competing concerns—the wrongly accused and the potential victims of the rightly accused. And this is indeed a project of balancing. But critically, it is not chiefly a project of balancing liberty against security. It is, again, a project of balancing one person's liberty and security against another's, and that balancing is hard not because liberty and security are in conflict but because our information is insufficient to enable confident decision making as to whom we want to protect more rigorously.

Trading off across different groups or individuals becomes a still trickier task once those whose liberty and security we contemplate sacrificing are aliens, perhaps halfway around the world—to whom, the traditional thinking goes, a government owes fewer protections. The extraterritorial reach of the Constitution has been the subject of heated academic and policy debates precisely because it implicates these questions. Does the liberty of those detained at Guantánamo Bay count in the equation? Does the privacy of Afghan tribal leaders matter? And what about Americans communicating abroad—not to mention German chancellor Angela Merkel or ordinary German citizens whose phones and e-mails the National Security Agency (NSA) might sweep up?

Complicating the discussion is the fact that while we often speak of liberty and security as simple quantities, both goods have a great many dimensions, and a plethora of different things can threaten either. To be precise when we speak of what a given measure is likely to do to the relationship, in other words, we need to identify what liberty is threatened and what sort of security we are attempting to augment. For example, street crime is commonly low in totalitarian countries as compared to those with other forms of government. The individual may thus face no security threat in the form of mugging or murder but a very great one in terms of being sent to a labor camp or tortured by the police. Conversely, in a society with weak government, a person may face no threat of political oppression, yet receive no protection against nonstate predatory forces like drug-trafficking gangs, religious extremists, or ordinary criminals. Meanwhile, a strong government that keeps order domestically and does not oppress its people may yet have inadequate military power to prevent foreign invasion and the conquest of its cities and thus may ultimately protect neither the liberty nor the security of its citizens all that well. It is therefore possible for a given measure to increase security in some respects while making people more vulnerable in others or to augment liberty in some ways while constricting it in others.

When we speak of either liberty or security, the level of granularity at which we look at the relationship also matters a great deal. The same security measure might legitimately be said to affect liberty positively or negatively depending on the focal length of the lens through which we view it. That is, are we concerned primarily with the liberty and security of individuals or with the aggregated liberty and security of society in general? Consider, for example, an aggressive enhancement of government surveillance powers—one that offers intelligence operatives significant new leads in pursuing terrorists but also necessarily results in a degree of snooping on innocent people, as well as a degree of uncertainty about what use the government might make of the information it collects. This is, for example, the case with several of the NSA programs Edward Snowden disclosed. One might respond to this program very differently—whether one is inclined to oppose or defend it—if one is primarily thinking about the privacy and liberty of individuals rather than of society at large. In the former case, one would tend to see the question in terms of a conflict between the liberty and privacy of the surveillance subjects, on the one hand, and the liberty and security of potential victims of terrorism, on the other. One might ask, is the imposition on the privacy of the former group worth the added protection it offers to the latter group? In the second case, by contrast, one would tend to look at broader questions of the scope of government power: Do we feel freer and safer, and is our privacy better protected in a society in which government does or does not have this power? Those are very different questions, and they may not produce the same answers.

Another way of thinking about the granularity with which we view the liberty-security relationship is that while we tend to evaluate the liberty of a society in terms of its protection of individual rights and, indeed, to conflate individual rights and aggregate liberty, these are not quite the same thing. The summary execution of the serial rapist would likely increase aggregate liberty and security in some meaningful sense by making women less fearful of sexual violence, but it is not the act of a society that respects individual rights. The law in liberal democracies generally concerns itself not with aggregate liberty—the ability of the public in general to do as it pleases—but with the specific rights of individuals. Underlying this approach is the belief that where individual rights are protected, society as a whole is better off. In American constitutional law, for example, free speech exists not as a general right of the public to communicate as much or as widely as it desires but rather as an individual right not to have government restrict one's speech. Similarly, the Fourth Amendment, which protects against unreasonable searches and seizures, does not protect privacy in the way that many Europeans think of the term. That is, it does not ensure some generalized right to have companies handle one's data as one might wish. Rather, it restricts government from engaging in certain conduct with respect to individuals. The result is that it is possible, common even, for a measure both to enhance the general liberty of a society and to conflict with the specific guaranteed rights that society promises to an individual; think, for example, of an approach to taking the serial rapist off the streets far less draconian than summary execution: using evidence seized from his apartment without a warrant. In such instances, it may be proper to talk about balancing, but, once again, we are not really balancing liberty against security; rather, we are balancing societal liberty and security against an individual's rights.

Debates over surveillance powers and programs tend inexorably to lapse into the language of balance. This perhaps reflects the Fourth Amendment itself, which, by asking questions of reasonableness, lends itself to judgment calls. Judges often handle these judgment calls by creating balancing tests in the law. The fundamental command of the Fourth Amendment that searches be reasonable creates a perhaps inevitable inclination to weigh liberty costs against security gains. Whether the issue is the NSA's collection of bulk metadata under the Patriot Act or airport security screening, we fall very quickly into a zero-sum discussion. And this framework, to be sure, certainly describes some surveillance disputes and some aspects of a great many more. But it does not describe all. And it will, in particular, obscure the impact on liberty, privacy, and security of a particular category of surveillance activity that will, we suspect, only grow in importance as technological development creates endless new venues for human creativity, commerce, and communications—and, along the way, for mayhem, crime, terrorism, and other security problems.

ANOTHER MISUNDERSTOOD QUOTATION

Having opened with a famed quotation on the liberty-security relationship that, in context, means something very different from what its many quoters assume, let us conclude this chapter with another: Justice Robert Jackson's warning that "there is danger that, if the [Supreme] Court does not temper its doctrinaire logic with a little practical wisdom, it will convert the constitutional Bill of Rights into a suicide pact."[26] Jackson's quotation is often cited as the flip side of Franklin's—with Franklin assumed to have been warning that one should not give up liberty in the name of security, and Jackson assumed to have been warning conversely that one protects liberty too strongly at great risk to security. The trouble is that just as Franklin was saying something else entirely, Jackson was not saying anything this crude either—which is probably why the rest of his remarkable passage tends to get left out of the quotation.

Jackson wrote this line in the last paragraph of his dissenting opinion in a free speech case called *Terminiello v. Chicago*, which the court decided in 1949, a few years after Jackson returned from his stint as chief prosecutor at the Nuremberg war crimes trials. The question of how civilized societies should deal with totalitarians was still very much on his mind when he confronted the case of a fascist-leaning priest who had given a vile, fire-breathing speech to a group of sympathizers at an event to which communists had turned up to protest. A riot nearly ensued, with the two mobs squared off against one another, and the priest was charged with disorderly conduct and fined $100. The Supreme Court overturned the judgment on free speech grounds, on the theory that all Arthur Terminiello had done was speak. Jackson saw things differently. "Underneath a little issue of Terminiello and his hundred-dollar fine lurk some of the most far-reaching constitutional questions that can confront a people who value both liberty and order," he wrote. "This court seems to regard these as enemies of each other, and to be of the view that we must forego order to achieve liberty. So it fixes its eyes on a conception of freedom of speech so rigid as to tolerate no concession to society's need for public order."

For Jackson, the issue was that two totalitarian movements that did not believe in liberty were squaring off against one another, and for liberty to exist, the police in a democratic culture simply had to have the authority to prevent things from spiraling out of control into mob violence. He quoted Joseph Goebbels concerning how the Nazis had made use of democratic freedoms and then "declared openly that [they] used democratic methods only in order to gain the power, and that, after assuming the power, [they] would deny to [their] adversaries without any consideration the means which were granted to [them] in the times of [their] opposition."[27] And Jackson insisted that confronted with such movements, "no liberty is made more secure by holding that its abuses are inseparable from its enjoyment." Free speech, in other words, will not be made stronger by protecting it so rigidly that

> the population can have no protection from the abuses which lead to violence. . . . We must not forget that it is the free democratic communities that ask us to trust them to maintain peace with liberty, and that the factions engaged in this battle are not interested permanently in either. What would it matter to Terminiello if the police batter up some communists or, on the other hand, if the communists batter up some policemen? Either result makes grist for his mill; either would help promote hysteria and the demand for strong-arm methods in dealing with his adversaries. And what, on the other hand, have the communist agitators to lose from a battle with the police?

Jackson then concluded with the following: "This Court has gone far toward accepting the doctrine that civil liberty means the removal of all restraints from these crowds, and that all local attempts to maintain order are impairments of the liberty of the citizen. The choice is not between order and liberty. It is between liberty with order and anarchy without either. There is danger that, if the Court does not temper its doctrinaire logic with a little practical wisdom, it will convert the constitutional Bill of Rights into a suicide pact."

In other words, like Franklin, Jackson was actually denying a stark balancing of liberty and security interests and asserting an essential congruence between them. He was, in fact, critiquing the court for assuming that allowing the government leeway would necessarily come at the expense of meaningful freedom. His criticism of the court was that by denying authorities the ability to maintain minimal conditions of order, it was empowering people who disbelieved in both freedom and order. The suicide pact to which he referred was the choice of anarchy with neither liberty nor security over a regime of ordered freedom. That's actually much more similar to, than different from, what Franklin was asking for two hundred years earlier. Both were, after all, arguing for the ability of local democratic communities to protect their security—and liberty—through reasonable self-government.

First Amendment law has long since passed by Jackson's specific point about what sort of utterances should and should not trigger liability for their propensity to cause violence. But his larger point stands. In the hostile symbiosis between liberty and security, one does not maximize one partner at the other's expense. They are locked together—embracing, choking, supporting, and endangering each other. Often, the values will entirely align with one another. Yet the doctrinaire embrace of one to the other's detriment will always ultimately disserve both.

Of course, even in the hostile symbiosis, the familiar problem of choosing among sometimes competing values—the problem that is the focus of the balancing paradigm—remains. Different approaches to privacy protection, for instance, would blend liberty and security in different measures, and the political duty of choosing among them does not go away. And just like with balancing, the crucial point is often who gets to choose: political choice largely depends on the polity that is invited to weigh in on the decision, and an American polity is likely to choose a blend that disfavors foreigners for the benefit of Americans.

This question of how states should engage with the liberty—and the power—of foreigners is another question technologies of mass empowerment put on the table, one to which we now turn.

6

RETHINKING LEGAL JURISDICTION AND THE BOUNDARIES OF SOVEREIGNTY

IN DECEMBER 2011, a hacker using the nom de guerre "OxOmar" gained access to tens of thousands of Israeli credit card accounts and disclosed information about thousands of them online. In comments he posted, he described himself as a Saudi national, "one of the strongest haters of Israel," and threatened Israelis: "You are not safe from me and Muslim hackers. We'll fight all of our lives against Israel, we'll harm you in any way we can. . . . [L]et's destroy Israel and have a free Palestine without enemies." A month later, OxOmar and his friends in a group known as Group-XP hacked the Israeli stock exchange and the El Al national airline, although trading and flights were not affected. The group called the act a "gift to the world for the New Year" designed to "hurt the Zionist pocket."[1]

At one point, Israeli bloggers suggested that they had identified OxOmar as a nineteen-year-old living in Mexico. OxOmar, for his part, denied living in Mexico. No publicly confirmable information definitely establishes either OxOmar's identity or his whereabouts, either at the time of the cyberattacks or now. Let us assume, however, that he was, in fact, a Saudi citizen and that he did carry out his attacks while in Mexico.[2]

OxOmar's attacks were somewhat distinctive for being politically motivated, for targeting Israelis as Israelis, and thus for raising national security concerns, but they are by no means exceptional for crossing borders. Examples abound of incidents that, while less ideologically pernicious, ultimately caused far more harm than did OxOmar in using the Internet to attack faraway targets. On May 5, 2000, a cyberworm was sent from a computer located outside Manila, the Philippines, moving westward through an attachment to e-mails bearing the enticing subject line "ILOVEYOU." Upon a user's opening the attachment, the virus would attempt to steal passwords and credit card information from the host computer and then transmit itself to all e-mail addresses in the recipient's address book. Because the e-mail and attachment seemed to arrive from familiar addresses, recipients trusted them, and the worm continued to spread throughout Hong Kong, Europe, and finally the United States. Within ten days, more than 50 million infections—an estimated 10 percent of Internet-connected computers in the world at the time—had been reported. Numerous corporations and government agencies—including the Pentagon, the CIA, and the British parliament—had paralyzed computer systems. By the time all was said and done, the "Love Bug" was estimated to have caused up to $10 billion in damage.[3]

The alleged author of the Love Bug virus, Onel de Guzman, was not an ideological cyberwarrior but a failed computer science student at the Amable Mendoza Aguiluz Computer College in the Philippines. Professors at the college noticed similarities between the Love Bug virus and de Guzman's rejected thesis proposal, and US and Philippine investigators quickly traced the virus back to a computer in de Guzman's apartment. Unlike in the case of OxOmar, who remained free from any legal action, the Philippine government initially did file charges against de Guzman. But prosecutors failed to obtain a conviction, largely because the Philippines had no specific laws against computer hacking at the time (the country did later pass the Electronic Commerce Act, outlawing computer crimes). And while the United States requested de Guzman's extradition, the Philippines denied it on the grounds that Philippine law demands, as a condition of extradition, that the allegations for which another country seeks a suspect amount to crimes in the Philippines too. De Guzman, like OxOmar, remained a free—and in some circles revered—man.[4]

Together, these two stories—and a great many others like them—demonstrate the inherent difficulties in attribution, regulation, and enforcement operations when individuals conduct attacks on targets hundreds or thousands of miles away. They also demonstrate how the crude lines separating acts of crime from acts of war are blurring, posing challenges—in scope, if not in concept—for state responses to such attacks. Consider the following questions: Which country's laws should determine whether OxOmar or de Guzman committed a crime? Which country has jurisdiction over the case: the one from which the acts were carried out, the one whose nationals were involved, or those countries that suffered the most harm? Does it matter where the attacked servers were physically located for purposes of jurisdiction? Does Mexico or Saudi Arabia or the Philippines bear any responsibility, as a state, for the actions of its private citizens? Where national security is presumably implicated, as in the case of OxOmar's attacks, should the perpetrator be considered a common criminal or, as some Israeli officials suggested, a terrorist, and would that distinction matter? Should a hacker's ideological motivations for the attack affect the legal response to his actions? If the scale and effect of a cyberattack are large enough, might a hacker be thought of as a belligerent engaged in a use of force? And what could Israel do even if it had managed to successfully track OxOmar down, for instance, in Mexico? Could it arrest him? Could it target him with lethal force? Or could it only request that Mexico extradite him or enforce its own law against him, as the United States had tried—and failed—to do in the case of de Guzman?

These questions all stem from the organizing principle of state sovereignty, which guides the current structure of our international legal system, as well as from the instincts with which we approach questions of legal jurisdiction. They reflect an understanding of the state as existing in a defined territory, with a government that maintains a monopoly on the legitimate use of force within it—that is, the state as social contract theorists such as Thomas Hobbes and John Locke understood it.

Recall that under the terms of the social contract, individuals generally surrender their right to use force to the government, which in turn undertakes to protect them from one another and from what would have been their fates in the state of nature. In addition, the government undertakes to protect its citizens from external threats, often by calling on them to participate in organized defense forces assembled to fend off threats from other states. A political state thus forms through a collective surrender and reallocation of individuals' power. The state is sovereign in the determination of its own internal affairs, the governance of its territory, and the policing of its citizens. But other states are equally sovereign, so no state has much of a say in how another state governs its affairs within its territory.

This idealized conception of how sovereign states relate to one another, in turn, has given rise to a particular, simplistic, and increasingly problematic way of thinking about law—one built, as legal scholar Philip Bobbitt has noted, around a set of stark, polar opposites, or "antinomies." In this view, particular actions are either *public* (acts of a public official such as a police officer) or *private* (undertaken by individuals or firms), *territorial* (taking place within a state's borders) or *extraterritorial* (taking place outside those borders). Individuals or firms whose activities are subject to regulation are either *citizens* of the state that seeks to regulate them or *aliens*. Laws that regulate conduct are either *domestic* (enacted by a state's legislature) or *international* (derived from a negotiated treaty or a binding custom). A violent act is either a *crime* (a violation of a state's laws against murder, assault, or some other action) or an *act of war* (a political act of collective violence).[5]

To be sure, these simplistic oppositions do not fully capture the complexities of interactions between states and their citizens and states and other states—and they never have. To take but one example from the early nineteenth century, the American and British governments bitterly disagreed over questions of citizenship and the legal authority of the Royal Navy to seize American sailors and press them into service. The failure to resolve this controversy was one cause of the War of 1812. What is more, both the categories and the juxtapositions have been eroding for some time, with globalization and interdependence among states, the emergence of powerful political, military, and economic nonstate actors, and the spread of international human rights norms all checking the exercise of sovereign power.[6]

These problems notwithstanding, questions of law, and particularly questions about law pertaining to security and violence, still tend to be framed with reference to sovereignty-driven juxtapositions. These juxtapositions still shape our thinking about who has the power to legislate, adjudicate, and enforce the law. They determine against whom states can apply their own regulations, and they set limits on the sort of conduct that a given state can regulate without antagonizing other states. They also determine what actions a state might take unilaterally and what actions require international cooperation or the consent of other states. In a world of many-to-many threats, in other words, long-established oppositional categories still purport to draw the legal boundaries of the power states can exercise in protecting themselves and their citizens from external threats or from threats whose origins they may not know.

Yet, as the OxOmar and de Guzman cases illustrate, the simplistic oppositions associated with the traditional picture of the sovereign state are today under greater strain than ever before. The emergence of the modern, globalized world—marked by unprecedented levels of cross-border activity, the presence of powerful nonstate actors, and notions of international human rights that imagine enforceable limits on the conduct of all states—has massively amplified the difficulties of using these categories to frame principles and practical solutions to contemporary problems. Geographical boundaries matter less for purposes of defense. Citizenship matters less in determining threats. War and crime are becoming harder to distinguish from one another. The difference between the impact that individuals and corporations can have on events and the impact of public officials is diminishing. Overall, sovereignty no longer holds quite the same moral or practical force it once did. All of this presents a major challenge for the future regulation of threats, vulnerabilities, and responses.

A SHORT HISTORY OF STATE SOVEREIGNTY AND ALLOCATION OF POWER

In 1926, a French steamer, the SS *Lotus*, collided with a Turkish steamer, the SS *Boz-Kourt*, as the two sailed on the Mediterranean Sea just north of Mytilene. The Turkish steamer sank, and eight Turkish sailors died. When the French steamer arrived in Constantinople, the Turks arrested, prosecuted, and imprisoned the French crewmember on watch at the time of the collision, one Monsieur Demons. France moved before the Permanent Court of International Justice (PCIJ), the predecessor to the present-day International Court of Justice, to challenge Turkey's right to prosecute a French citizen for acts originating from a French vessel, even if those acts ended up having effects on Turkish citizens. The PCIJ, however, rejected the French claim, finding that nothing under the international law of the time prevented Turkey from doing so: "The rules of law . . . emanate from [states'] own free will as expressed in conventions or by usages generally accepted as expressing principles of law. . . . Restrictions upon the independence of states cannot therefore be presumed." The PCIJ's ruling stood for the principle of "voluntarism": any limits on state power could stem only from a voluntary decision by the state to relinquish some of that power. Unless a state voluntarily ceded its authority to apply its law to a particular scenario, it had the power to exercise that authority at its discretion.[7]

Voluntarism was a direct manifestation of the broad conception of sovereignty embodied in the Westphalian system of independent states. In this vision, sovereignty denoted the nearly absolute power of a ruler to conduct the affairs of his or her state as he or she saw fit, so long as doing so did not interfere with a matter falling within the sovereignty of another state. Sovereignty was thus Janus-faced. Internally, it left the established government largely free to govern its citizens as it saw fit. Externally, it meant that no sovereign could intervene in the internal affairs of any other sovereign. Since all states were equally sovereign, domestic independence and immunity from external intervention were the inherent rights of all free states, regardless of differences in size, population, or power among them. And since all free states were, in principle, sovereign, any limits on their power, including the exercise of jurisdiction over foreign nationals for acts committed outside their territory, had to be found in some clear international rule and could not merely be presumed. As France could not point to such a rule, or so found the PCIJ, Turkey was free to exercise its judicial power over the unfortunate Monsieur Demons.

This broad conception of sovereignty and its derivative allocation of state power inevitably led to clashes among competing sovereigns. After all, the determination of which persons and events fell within the sovereignty of one state, rather than another, was often unclear: Why does Turkey's exercise of jurisdiction over a French national for acts that originated from a French vessel not encroach on France's sovereignty, France might ask? If the high seas do not belong to any state, how is the exercise of any country's jurisdiction over incidents taking place there not a violation of the principle of sovereign equality? Could the Janus-faced model of sovereignty—one that, barring some explicit prohibition, promised all sovereigns complete freedom to do as they wished but also prohibited them from intervening in each other's internal affairs—sustain itself in a world of growing interactions and interdependencies among those states? In the absence of some global policing power, could the inevitable competition over sovereignty mean anything other than perpetual disputes requiring accommodation, bargaining, deterrence, or conflict?

The need to resolve clashes of jurisdiction of the kind that emerged in the SS *Lotus* case grew in the decades that followed, as transportation and commerce developed rapidly and as an increasing number of activities and individuals moved between territories. And over time, the PCIJ's view of voluntarism proved, as a guiding principle, to invite anarchy and disorder. Most fundamentally, the extreme view of sovereignty it embodied posed a special challenge to international law's greatest ambition in the second half of the twentieth century: the minimization of the use of force between states. Indeed, the very Hobbesian nineteenth-century view of sovereignty went so far as to hold that sovereigns were free even to wage war with one another, as long as they complied with certain limits on how the war would be prosecuted. Without an explicit prohibition in international law on the use of force, after all, states could not be said to have voluntarily renounced the sovereign power to use warfare in their self-interest. This was still largely the case when the PCIJ rendered its *Lotus* decision. But as the world began aspiring to a more peaceful international order, the principle of voluntarism had to give way. If international law stood any chance of playing a pacifying role in international affairs, it had to adopt a more constrained view of what sovereignty meant and how voluntarist states could be toward international obligations.

Voluntarism did not disappear altogether; even today, states are usually entitled to pick and choose many of their international obligations. But the breadth and scope of international obligations and prohibitions have grown exponentially since 1926. And in parallel, the extreme embrace of residual freedom—to do what is not explicitly forbidden—has yielded to a more constrained view of state freedom of action, especially where the interests of other states are implicated. Accordingly, modern principles of extraterritorial jurisdiction have in effect reversed the SS *Lotus* decision: if Turkey, at the time, could exercise its adjudicatory and enforcement powers over a French citizen for actions he committed on a French vessel because nothing in international law at the time prohibited it, today Turkey would have to look to international law for an affirmative basis for the exercise of its jurisdiction.

This move away from residual freedom of action and toward requiring some affirmative legal authorization happened not overnight but through a gradual change in various international legal regimes. On the specific issue of collisions on the high seas, for instance, subsequent international treaties have rejected the PCIJ's *Lotus* decision and adopted the French position, according to which only the flag state can exercise jurisdiction over people and activities on its vessels. In the same vein, the right to engage in hot pursuit—in which the agents of a coastal state chase after a vessel that has violated the state's domestic law and escaped to the high seas—runs only up to the point at which the offending vessel has reached another state's territorial waters. Much more profoundly, the lessons of the two world wars prompted a change in the regulation of the use of force between states: the 1945 UN Charter codified many of the Westphalian principles, including sovereign equality, political independence, territorial integrity, and nonintervention in the internal affairs of any other state. And it thus codified the sanctity of national boundaries as setting a geographic limit on each state's legitimate exercise of unilateral power. The idea that a state's authority terminates at its borders has been one of the most widely accepted principles of our international system, giving rise to the now familiar image of the political dissident who seeks safety from oppression at the hands of her own government by crossing a geographic border and entering the territory of a welcoming state.

But the UN Charter also did away with the nineteenth-century vision of a sovereign prerogative to wage war by prohibiting all uses of force between states save in the immediate exercise of self-defense against armed attack. In its postwar rejection of extreme voluntarism and its embrace of territorial boundaries as denoting the limit of states' power, international law has thus become far less hospitable to any one state's efforts to reach beyond its shores and regulate people or activities outside its borders.

Limiting extraterritorial assertions of power also made sense given the original social contract's understanding of the relationship between citizens and governments. Governments are best situated to regulate the conduct and people within their own territories. A state's legislatures, judiciaries, and executives often do not have enough relevant information regarding foreign people and activities to govern well abroad. Nor does any state necessarily have the right motivations for good governance outside its own territory; it would be too easy for a foreign law enforcement official to breezily disregard the liberties of nationals of foreign countries when he or she has no obligation to account to the populations of those countries. Indeed, democratic legitimacy requires that the people who are governed have some control over those who govern them.

AN INTRODUCTION TO THE LAW OF JURISDICTION

The problem is that notwithstanding all the sound reasons for international law's modern reticence about allowing states to reach beyond their territory, the OxOmar and de Guzman cases show that states' interests in reaching across their borders are becoming more, not less, pronounced as technologies of mass empowerment enable terrorism, cyberattacks, and other harmful acts from faraway lands. Precisely at the time when international law looks with increasing disfavor on extraterritorial jurisdiction, there is ever more reason to believe that states will claim the authority to regulate and respond to conduct that threatens them, even when undertaken by foreign nationals or perpetrated outside their borders. This trend, in turn, will inevitably generate clashes with other states' conceptions of their own sovereignty. Once again, international law will have to respond and adapt to the emergence of new technologies and the geostrategic changes they bring about.

To understand the kinds of pressures on the current system that are likely to emerge or intensify given the new threat environment, it is worth describing how jurisdictional power today gets divided among states under existing international law. In a nutshell, jurisdiction—or the power to exercise legal control over a person or action—can take one of three forms: it can assert the power to regulate conduct, to adjudicate disputes, or to enforce legislation or judicial decisions through the state's policing agencies. Within its own territory, a government is free to legislate, adjudicate, and enforce laws without much consideration for the interests of other states, except insofar as the government has voluntarily relinquished its power to do so. So, for example, the most obvious country to exercise jurisdiction over OxOmar would be Mexico (provided, again, that OxOmar was in fact conducting his attacks while in that country), and the Philippines would be the obvious country to exercise authority over de Guzman. Once activities, goods, or people fall outside the state's territory, however, the exercise of any of the three forms of jurisdiction by that state must take into consideration the rights of other relevant states. That is, Israel cannot deal with OxOmar without confronting Mexico's territorial sovereignty by one means or another or without encroaching on Saudi Arabia's sovereignty over its nationals. This is true even though Israel's interests in responding to OxOmar's conduct seem much stronger than Mexico's. The same is true for the United States' dealings with de Guzman. Whereas territorial jurisdiction is absolute and requires no justification, extraterritorial jurisdiction must now be grounded in international legal permission to be legitimate.[8]

Of the three forms of extraterritorial jurisdiction, international law is most permissive with regard to the power of a government to legislate rules that pertain to people and activities outside the state's borders. This means that in many instances, conduct can be deemed a crime by more than one state, even if it originates within a single territory. So in theory, the Philippines, the United States, and any other country affected by the Love Bug might all, in slightly different ways, proscribe de Guzman's conduct—the Philippines by prohibiting cyberattacks originating from within its territory, the United States or any other affected country by prohibiting cyberattacks on its computers or transmitted through its computers or infrastructure.

By contrast, international law is least tolerant of extraterritorial enforcement powers—that is, of policing activities that take place in a foreign state's territory without the latter's consent. The reason is obvious: such activities as investigations, searches, and arrests are most closely associated with public power and therefore intrude most aggressively on the foreign territorial state's sovereignty. They are thus most likely to cause interstate friction. Israel would thus, under existing law, have a hard time claiming it had a right to send agents to Mexico or Saudi Arabia or any other foreign country to arrest OxOmar and bring him to trial in Israel without the other country's consent.

No extraterritorial power exists without limitations. To exercise jurisdiction of any kind beyond its shores, a state must demonstrate that it has a legitimate and recognizable interest in asserting power—whether through legislation or any other legal means—over people and activities beyond its borders. International law currently recognizes four guiding principles that establish such legitimate interests. The first three require some connection to the state invoking jurisdiction and might thus be understood as an extension of the state's domestic sovereignty. The fourth does not require such connection and by both name and reach is universal.

The first principle of extraterritorial jurisdiction—the "nationality principle"—evolved ultimately from the view of citizens as not only the "property" of the king but an extension of his person. This principle still recognizes the state's legitimate interest in some activities of its own nationals abroad. It shows up most commonly in areas such as taxation, military service, and certain criminal activity, and accords with the idea that citizens owe some allegiance to their country of citizenship, in exchange for the benefits they derive from their status as citizens. Accordingly, the Supreme Court ruled in 1932 that the United States had the authority to require a US citizen living in Paris to appear as a witness in a criminal trial in Washington, DC, and to punish him if he failed to do so. A great many countries have laws regulating the conduct of their citizens wherever they happen to be.[9]

A second principle, known as the "protective principle," recognizes that states' right to defend themselves extends, at least to some degree, to their property and nationals overseas. The protective principle allows states to address extraterritorial conduct that is threatening to the national security of the state—think of attacks on embassies or state officials abroad, hostage taking of citizens abroad, material support for terrorism, and even currency counterfeiting or drug trafficking. Just as the state has an inherent right to defend itself against external threats, it has a right to protect itself from those who would do it harm, even if they are nonnationals or outside its domain. In 1946, the House of Lords upheld the conviction for high treason of William Joyce, an American citizen who held a British passport and, as "Lord Haw-Haw," broadcasted messages from Germany during World War II seeking to persuade the Allies to surrender. "No principle of comity demands that a state should ignore the crime of treason committed against it outside its territory," wrote Lord Jowitt. "On the contrary a proper regard for its own security requires that all those who commit that crime, whether they commit it within or without the realm, should be amenable to its laws."[10]

The third recognized principle that permits extraterritorial jurisdiction allows a state to exercise its powers vis-à-vis conduct that, although taking place beyond its borders, results in injury to one of its citizens. Known as "passive personality," this form of jurisdiction is most commonly invoked in response to violent crimes or instances in which a victim is attacked because he is a citizen of the state; in this sense, it is close in spirit to the protective principle. Here, too, the principle evolved because of the special relationship that exists between a state and its citizen. Passive personality is a kind of mirror image of the principle of nationality: just as the citizen owes allegiance to her state, the state owes allegiance to its citizen and can demand justice on her behalf. This jurisdictional principle applies not in cases of accidents, like the Turkish and French steamers colliding, but rather in cases like that of Fawaz Yunis, a Lebanese citizen, whom US federal agents lured onto a fishing boat sailing out of Cyprus. Once in international waters, they arrested Yunis, transported him to the United States, and charged him for his role in a 1985 hijacking of a Royal Jordanian Airlines jet in Beirut. In a broad (and contentious) reading of the passive personality principle, the US District Court in Washington, DC, found that the fact that two of the passengers on the hijacked plane were American citizens justified trying Yunis in the United States, even though there was no indication that the hijackers targeted the plane because of those American citizens.

If we return to the tales of OxOmar and de Guzman, we can see how the nationality, protective, and passive personality principles might play out in practice. Israel would have a strong claim of jurisdiction over OxOmar on the basis of the protective principle, since the attacks were deliberately aimed against the state of Israel. For Saudi Arabia, a jurisdictional claim would have to be based on OxOmar's (presumed) Saudi nationality, though it is not at all clear that other states would recognize cybercrimes as among those crimes with which the citizenship state should concern itself. As for de Guzman, it is unclear that any of these principles would have given the United States a legitimate interest in prosecuting him, as he was not an American citizen, his attacks did not amount to a national security threat, and there was never any indication that he was intentionally targeting Americans—although, as we shall see, US authorities may still have had a jurisdictional claim over de Guzman on other grounds.

At the furthest reach from territorial sovereignty lies a fourth customary principle that grants extraterritorial jurisdiction: the "universality principle." Anchored in conventions and custom, this principle empowers states to prescribe and adjudicate crimes of a particularly heinous nature, including genocide, war crimes, and crimes against humanity, as well as other specific crimes, such as aircraft hijacking or hostage taking. Although originally designed to grant states jurisdiction over stateless pirates on the high seas, the universality principle came, after World War II, to stand for the idea that some offenses are so grave that they defy any boundary or nationality, giving the entire international community a stake in their regulation, prevention, and punishment. In some sense, therefore, rather than an attempt to resolve clashing claims of jurisdiction, the universality principle was actually meant to ensure accountability even when the most relevant countries for enforcing it had no interest in doing so.

As it currently stands, however, the universality principle has no application to either OxOmar or de Guzman for the simple reason that their alleged crimes were neither of the magnitude nor of the type with which the principle is concerned. In theory, nothing precludes the states of the world from agreeing in the future—for instance, through a negotiated treaty—to grant each other universal jurisdiction over cyberoffenses without the need to show a relevant state interest in the case. But this seems politically unlikely, at least for the foreseeable future, since states do not even agree on what cybercrime is.

Although all four principles of extraterritorial jurisdiction are accepted and recognized internationally and seem straightforward enough on paper, their application in specific cases often stirs up a great deal of controversy. Even what counts as "territorial" or "extraterritorial" is far from clear. What happens, for instance, in cases of drug trafficking, price fixing, or conspiracy to commit murder, all of which can take place (at least in part) outside a state's territory, yet end up having effects within that state anyway?

This problem is not new and by no means limited to the advent of technologies of mass empowerment either. In 1989, to cite a famous example, the United States invaded Panama, captured its leader, Manuel Noriega, and brought him to trial in US courts on ten counts of drug trafficking, racketeering, and money laundering. Although Noriega was a foreign national and his actions took place in Panama, the United States asserted territorial jurisdiction to adjudicate his case and enforce any punishment based on evidence that some of the drugs he trafficked had found their way into the United States. Similarly, under the 1890 Sherman Antitrust Act, US courts have held several foreign corporations liable for antitrust violations committed abroad because their practices had a substantial effect on the American market. Under a broad reading of the territorial principle, the United States could thus have claimed jurisdiction over de Guzman for harming American computers even though the harm originated from a foreign citizen in a foreign land.[11]

Not everyone agrees, however, that local effects in a given state are enough to confer territorial jurisdiction over an activity conducted outside that state's territory by noncitizens—particularly when the jurisdiction implies some limitation on another state's own jurisdiction. In reaction to the expansive American assertion of antitrust jurisdiction, Canada, the United Kingdom, Italy, Australia, the Netherlands, and France all enacted blocking legislation, effectively prohibiting cooperation with judicial or administrative proceedings in other countries. In adopting the first such blocking statute in 1947, the premier of Ontario, Canada, remarked, "I trust no citizen of the United States will forget that Canadians are just as proud of their own nationality and just as jealous of their own sovereignty as is any citizen of their own country."[12]

In a globalized world, numerous activities will generate numerous extraterritorial effects, whether in the sphere of the economy, the environment, safety and security, human rights, culture, or just about anything else. If each country is to assert jurisdiction over activities merely on the basis of effects within its territory, "extraterritorial" will simply become another word for "territorial"; the concept of national sovereignty as a matter of law will mean, at once, everything and nothing.

This problem will likely grow more acute as technology further empowers people to harm each other across national borders. How should a nation's government consider an organized criminal gang in another country that steals credit card numbers on a systematic basis from its own citizens? How should it consider biotech research on flu in a foreign country when the research procedures are sufficiently insecure as to make likely an accidental release of a highly contagious new strain that could spread to its own citizens? The territorial principle seems dated, if not obsolete, when it is as easy to chat with a person in Hong Kong as with the person sitting next to you—and all the more so when you can control the spider drone sitting next to that person in Hong Kong.

Even if we could agree about what activities count as extraterritorial, the application of the four principles that grant states jurisdiction over such activities is also subject to great controversy. Domestic courts in many countries will sometimes reject a government's assertion that it has the right to enforce its laws extraterritorially and will refuse to apply domestic law to foreign nationals or acts abroad. Conversely, state officials are sometimes lax in enforcing laws against their own citizens who harm others abroad. Jurisdictional clashes abound as regulatory regimes regarding finance, labor standards, environmental protection, safety, intellectual property, and other areas have departed from and conflicted with parallel regimes in other states. And these clashes have invited a range of responses—from efforts to harmonize domestic laws with foreign ones in particular fields to jurisdictional hijackings by the strongest states in the system.[13]

In this environment, jurisdictional boundaries will surely produce gaps of accountability, when those with the legal powers to exercise jurisdiction choose not to and those with the interest in exercising jurisdiction lack the legal power to do so. This is often, as both the OxOmar and de Guzman stories demonstrate, because even though an interested state has the power to proscribe the relevant activity, it cannot get its hands on the perpetrator—that is, to enforce its laws—without violating another state's sovereignty. At other times, the problem turns out to be the opposite: too many interested parties are vying to exercise jurisdictional powers over the same person or activity. The current international law framework seems ill-positioned to handle the questions presented and exacerbated by the emerging security environment we have described.

In some sense, as we have seen, the laws addressing security threats are no different in principle from food safety standards, antitrust rules, or norms of corporate governance. Just as the international system has found ways to address jurisdictional conflicts in all these other areas—or just to live with these conflicts—so too might we expect it to find ways to accommodate different states' interests in exercising jurisdiction over transnational threats. In another sense, however, security is different—and not because it is more important than environmental protection rules or health standards, though it may well be a prerequisite for all other public regulatory activity. Security is different, rather, because its control is more closely related to the historical rationale for the state itself. As we have seen, jurisdiction over threats to the state, its people, and their property is in some sense the very foundation of sovereignty.

States, in other words, generally value security more than other interests. M did not stand in front of Parliament and establish her right to rule by wagging her finger about antitrust issues, though the premier of Ontario did. Nor did James Bond run riot over the sovereignty of other countries in an effort to enforce labor standards.

It is therefore to be expected that the more diffuse transnational violence becomes, the greater the challenge it will pose to the existing allocation of territorial and extraterritorial exercises of power in a state system based on sovereign equality; the greater also will be the opportunities for perpetrators to evade accountability by exploiting jurisdictional differences among states; and the greater too will be both the need for and the difficulty of state cooperation in addressing security threats.

REGULATING VIOLENCE: CRIME AND WAR

Jurisdiction is not the only feature of sovereignty that an environment of many-to-many threats and defenses forces us to think about. No less fundamental is the traditional dichotomy between the two distinct systems under which we regulate violence, namely, criminal law and the laws of war. The blurring of lines between these two systems, to some extent, also blurs the boundaries between the internal and external facets of sovereignty.

In its pure form, criminal law deals with domestic crimes, those that take place between and among the citizens of the state. It is each Leviathan's province to protect individuals from the state of nature. It both empowers and constrains the sovereign in dealing with internal threats to orderly life. Because it is an internal matter, traditionally, criminal law has been subject to domestic formulation and enforcement. Some exceptions notwithstanding—for instance, with regard to internationally defined crimes—national legislatures decide what types of behavior to outlaw, how to prosecute transgressors, and what type of sanctions to authorize. Because it is a matter of internal sovereignty, moreover, different states often differ in their criminal law codes, in investigative and trial procedures, and in sentencing those found guilty. Recall that the United States and the Philippines at the relevant time had different computer fraud laws that they could bring to bear on de Guzman. Saudi Arabia, incidentally, has no written criminal code at all.

The laws of war, by contrast, are international in origin. They were designed to empower and constrain the sovereign in defending the Leviathan from external (and, later, also internal) threats to its public authority and control. Unlike under domestic criminal law, the primary addressees of the laws of war are not individuals but states and organized armed groups. Historically, the laws of war developed through reciprocal commitments between rival sovereigns and, from the mid-nineteenth century on, through multilateral agreements that all independent states were invited to join. In addition, a host of customary international norms evolved over centuries through consistent state practice and a sense of legal obligation, adding another layer of rules on warfare. The lion's share of the substantive laws of war—including rules concerning targeting, detention, the treatment of occupied populations, weapons, and other matters—purport to apply equally to all belligerents, even if some countries, including the United States, resist some of the more recent additions to these laws.[14]

These traditionally distinct modes of regulating violence, criminal law and the laws of war, both trace back to the Janus-faced understanding of sovereignty—one reflecting the ruler's traditional power to ensure domestic discipline as he sees fit, the other reflecting his power to use violence to defend his state against other powers, as well as to conclude deals with them to refrain from the rawer exercises of their respective powers. In practice, the two modes have not remained completely distinct domains, and they began merging long before technologies of mass empowerment. Although criminal law remains largely domestic, and the laws of war largely international, some material overlap has developed over time. One of the strongest driving forces behind this growing convergence has been the evolution of modern international human rights law, which, beginning in the second half of the twentieth century, sought to place individuals—rather than states—at the center of international law's concern.[15]

With the rising importance of individuals qua individuals, the nearly sanctified ideal of state sovereignty as granting absolute domestic powers and a perfect shield from external intervention has lost much of its appeal. In the modern political order, by contrast, the state, the sovereign, and the people are no longer quite such a unified entity—a single Leviathan. Rather, they constitute three distinct units, and the people enjoy rights and freedoms that all states must respect in all circumstances. Lockean limited government has thus prevailed over the less constrained Hobbesian ruler—at least as far as international law would have it. Consequently, the international system no longer conceives of domestic law and order as being whatever the sovereign wants it to be. Rather, a host of international human rights instruments, many of which have come to be viewed as expressing customary international obligations with universal reach, seeks to regulate aspects of substantive criminal law—for instance, demanding the criminalization of sexual violence or prohibiting the criminalization of the exercise of speech or religion, demanding due process in criminal trials, shielding defendants from self-incrimination, and restricting the types of punishments permissible for those convicted.[16]

At the same time, the international laws of war, originally designed to regulate interstate conflicts, increasingly apply in almost equal measure to cases of civil wars within the state. Internal conflict is no longer simply a domestic matter for the sovereign to deal with as he or she sees fit. Moreover, while the enforcement of the laws of war once depended on reciprocity between states, with individuals at the mercy of leaders' decisions to comply or not comply with the agreements they had signed, modern international law vests legal protections with the people, not with their governments to bargain over or around. Breaches of the laws of war are now a matter of international interest, giving every state around the world standing to demand compliance under universal jurisdiction and creating some independent enforcement mechanisms, such as the International Criminal Court in The Hague. The individual thus became the bearer of both rights and obligations under international law, alongside whatever rights and obligations attached to his or her state.

The bodies of criminal law, international human rights law, and international laws of war have thus grown more enmeshed than ever before. This process of integration sought to promote what international jurist Theodor Meron has called the "humanization of the law of war," as well as to universalize certain principles of human dignity as an enduring check on state power. Particularly in times of emergency, the synergy of these three legal fields, it is hoped, will serve to better safeguard the rights of individuals from the urge of armed rivals to sacrifice them on the altar of national security and state interest.[17] And still, the original understanding of these different bodies of law, their different motivations and rationales, means that their blending into a coherent set of rights, obligations, and protections cannot be an entirely smooth process. In fact, on occasion, the boundaries that each field draws around state sovereignty and power cross one another, forcing states uneasily to classify acts of violence and security threats into one of several ill-fitting categories.

Consider the different stances toward violence taken by criminal law and human rights law, on the one hand, and by the laws of war, on the other. Criminal law starts with the presumption that any violent act between private individuals, absent extraordinary circumstances or justifications, is forbidden and punishable. Only violence sanctioned by the state—mostly, for policing purposes—is lawful, and even then only under the strictest conditions. The laws of war, conversely, accept violence among combatants as lawful, with few limitations. Combatants' shooting at each other requires no explanation or justification other than the underlying condition of warfare; in fact, the captured soldier, absent evidence of war crimes, is immune from prosecution for acts of violence committed in conflict.

The different legal regimes for law enforcement and warfare also stem from opposite assumptions about the temporal and geographical dimensions of conflict and enforcement. Law enforcement belongs to the everyday, the commonplace. It is the normal state of affairs; all states experience some level of crime, and all thus need to engage in law enforcement. War, by contrast, is considered an extraordinary event, a departure from ordinary political—and indeed personal—life, and its extraordinary occurrence in time and space permits some departure from the ordinary conceptions of the right to life or liberty of those affected by it.

The convergence of these two modes of regulating violence has been driven not only by an ideological concern for the individual but, perhaps more strongly, by the disruption of the categories of violence. That is, the advent of modern forms of violence, especially terrorism but also some transnational crime, has further obfuscated the line between acts of crime and acts of war. The terrorist is not commonly associated with a state, at least not directly, in the sense that a soldier operates as a formal arm of a state; the terrorist either acts alone, as did Anders Behring Breivik of Norway, in which case he looks more like a criminal, or he acts as part of a group or network, like Al-Qaeda, in which case he looks more like a combatant, a member of an organized armed group. His motivations may be political, religious, or ideological, and his victims will tend to be anonymous, targeted for their association with a particular group, as in warfare. By contrast, the victims of most violent crimes are targeted for reasons related to their individual identity, not their group affiliations—though this is not always the case. Acts of terrorism often inflict few casualties, fewer than those of famous serial killers, but they also sometimes produce mass casualties, thus resembling more the effects of war. When both the attacker and his victims are citizens of the same state—as with the 1995 Oklahoma City bombing by Timothy McVeigh and the 2002 Beltway sniper killings by John Allen Muhammad and Lee Boyd Malvo—the threat to sovereignty remains internal, as with any common domestic crime. But once the terrorist is foreign, and particularly once he operates from a foreign location, the threat takes on a more external, warlike character in its challenge to the state. Some terrorist acts, such as that of Breivik or the Tsarnaev brothers' 2013 attack on the Boston Marathon, constitute singular, one-off events; others, such as the September 11, 2001, attack on the World Trade Center and Pentagon, are part of ongoing campaigns of terrorism that have no particular temporal boundaries. All these distinctions can make it difficult to classify acts of terrorism as criminal or belligerent in nature. Consider the shooting spree by Major Nidal Hasan at Fort Hood in 2009, which resulted in the deaths of thirteen people and injury to more than thirty others. While many in the media and politics have referred to the shooting as an act of terrorism, the Department of Defense determined that it was the "criminal act of a single individual."[18]

The ambiguity of what terrorism is or what it looks like has also led different states to deal with terrorism under different paradigms—as an act of war, a crime, or some mixture of both—depending on their national attitudes toward the use of force and human rights and the types of terrorism they have experienced. Most European countries, in which terrorism has primarily involved homegrown terrorist organizations, commonly perceive terrorism as a crime, a matter to be dealt with using ordinary law enforcement measures. For these countries, a murder is a murder, whether its perpetrator has financial, romantic, or ideological motivations. For the United States, Israel, and a growing number of countries in the Middle East and Africa facing both domestic and foreign terrorists—often on a larger scale than in Europe and often involving the projection of force from beyond the country's own borders—terrorism also has the features of war. It represents a defiance of state sovereignty with which the state cannot deal solely by means of traditional law enforcement. Instead, the state resorts to the use of armed force as should be governed by the laws of war, in a manner that no civilized society would ever tolerate in ordinary domestic policing.

Terrorism implicates not only the distinction between warfare and crime but also the jurisdictional questions of territorial and extraterritorial regulation that we considered earlier. When, after all, can a state capture a terrorist outside its own borders? When can it prosecute him? When, if at all, can it kill him? Does it require the consent of the territorial state for a law enforcement or belligerent act within that state's territory? Must the victim state defer to the territorial state with respect to the prosecution or incapacitation of a terrorist under such circumstances? And what happens when the laws of one country permit actions that another country's laws proscribe?

The debate over the correct classification of terrorism is not only about different legal paradigms. More fundamentally, the different legal paradigms stand for the scope of the state's sovereign right to defend itself against real or perceived threats, where such defense comes at the expense of either the rights of individuals or the sovereignty of other states.

A world of many-to-many threats and defenses magnifies all of these questions. And it turns out that terrorism is but one example of threats that break down the existing oppositional categories on which much of our domestic and international law rests. OxOmar offers another example and de Guzman yet another. But so might have Bruce Ivins, the alleged 2001 anthrax attacker, had he sent his letters internationally. One does not, after all, need an organized group to slip between the cracks of the binary divisions of foreign versus domestic, public versus private, or criminal versus belligerent. One needs only two abilities: to attack a state or a polity at a level of ferocity that exceeds the normal threshold of crime and to do so from a position of sufficient distance to defy the territorial jurisdiction of the country one is attacking. And technologies of mass empowerment are putting precisely these two things in the hands of nearly any creatively malevolent person who wants them.

DIVISION OF LABOR—STATE RESPONSIBILITY
FOR PRIVATE VIOLENCE

So maybe, some commentators have argued, the answer to gaps in and competition over jurisdictional power lies in state accountability for private individuals' acts of violence. If OxOmar, de Guzman, and other private actors—liable for their conduct under the domestic laws of the several states that fell victim to their actions—cannot be held to account under the laws of those states, perhaps Mexico and the Philippines should ultimately be regarded as the responsible parties. Might it be possible to attribute the acts of individual international criminals or terrorists to states as a way of overcoming the accountability gap? Would it be desirable to make more privately perpetrated harms into state-to-state matters?[19]

The anarchic nature of the international system does not mean that states owe no obligations to one another. Just as some social contract theorists have held that even in the state of nature, relationships among people ought to be governed by natural law—the basic moral tenets that can be easily deduced from reason alone—so do states' obligations toward each other exist, as a matter of international law, regardless of whether there is any global government to enforce them. These international obligations may be grounded in treaties, customary law, or merely general principles of the international system. When states breach these obligations, they incur the legal duty to make reparations, in the form of diplomatic gestures, monetary compensation, or required actions or inactions. Because there is often no mechanism to resolve disputes over violations or to enforce the obligation to make reparations, international law permits injured states to engage in countermeasures—reciprocal violations or other unilateral sanctions—as a means of self-help. Where the initial violation is of a particularly grave nature (such as genocide or some other international crime), the entire international community is instructed to use all lawful means at its disposal to stop the breach and bring the delinquent state into compliance.[20]

To think about state conduct, however, is an exercise in anthropomorphism. States do not act; humans do. Where humans serve in some official capacity—as political leaders, judges, military or police officers, local government personnel, or authorized contractors—their conduct is imputed to the state itself. Things become more complicated when individuals or groups that are neither part of the state apparatus nor have any contractual ties to it commit acts that implicate international law. Such cases include both criminals and armed groups whose violence impacts other states or foreign citizens; it also includes factories that pollute the environment or dump hazardous material in transboundary watercourses, as well as, these days, patriotic hackers who attack their country's enemies without the overt sanction of their government. Traditionally, such acts can be attributed to the state only if it can be shown that the state has exerted a significant enough degree of control over these nonstate actors and their conduct to incur responsibility for them. In other words, the liability of the state depends on the nonstate actor's acting as a de facto agent of the state. In all other cases, the state will not be held directly responsible for the acts of individuals, groups, or corporate entities, even if these actors have unlawfully harmed other states or actors within them. The state might bear some other types of responsibility—for instance, for not preventing the harm or not punishing those responsible for it—but not for the harmful act itself.[21]

To illustrate, if an American citizen kills a Belgian citizen anywhere around the globe, we do not say that the United States has committed a murder. Belgium has a right to put the American killer on trial if it captures him, and the United States may have a duty to do so. But we do not attribute the murder itself to the United States. In contrast, the United States held that Afghanistan was responsible for the September 11 attacks because the state and the organization were sufficiently linked, and the state had harbored the organization sufficiently to render the acts of the latter attributable to the former. This holding served as a justification for the United States in its subsequent invasion of Afghanistan. If a terrorist group based in Germany attacked a bus of American tourists, by contrast, the odds are that the United States would not view Germany as having committed the attack. At most, it would ask whether Germany had acted with all due diligence to prevent it. And even if it had not, this omission would not constitute the same type of injury as if Germany itself had carried out the attack. Along the same lines, the United States did not hold Germany responsible for the September 11 attacks, although the cell that executed them did much of its planning from Hamburg.

In recent years, there have been a number of proposals to attribute a greater number of private criminal acts to the states from which they are carried out as a way of overcoming the problem of attribution and the accountability gap. Focusing mainly on cybersecurity, proposals of this nature imagine holding any state from which a cyberattack has emanated presumptively responsible for the attack itself. Such proposals have generally taken one of two forms: the first would penalize states for failing to take appropriate steps to stop attacks that originate within or transit across their borders; the second would shift the burden of proof to states from within whose borders attacks had emanated to show that the states were not responsible for them.[22]

These proposals have the advantage of solving the attribution problem by treating most or all government and private cyberattacks as acts of the state itself. Perhaps fearing penalties, states might be more hesitant about engaging in cyberattacks themselves and might do more to prevent private actors from engaging in them from within their borders. The regime of territorial liability would likely further provide states with the incentives to strengthen cybersecurity in homes, universities, workplaces, and government facilities, to provide more funding for law enforcement, and to cooperate more fully with other nations in investigating attacks.[23]

Presumed state accountability also has considerable drawbacks, however. For one thing, the international system can only realize the benefits of a territorial liability regime if states are actually able to prevent and patrol cyberattacks from within their borders. Many states do not have the capacity to do this, and threatening these states with retribution for attacks they may have had nothing to do with and have little power to prevent is unlikely to make anyone any safer. Indeed, even the most powerful states do not have the ability to stop all harmful cyberactivity that occurs within their borders. The United States, for example, would likely incur a huge amount of international liability if it were held accountable for every cyberattack or exploitation ever carried out by MIT students, and even more so if it were held liable for attacks with roots abroad but using computers in its territory as proxies. As a result, the definition of what constitutes a cyberattack would, by necessity, be limited to the most serious attacks, and defining this set would prove difficult and contentious.[24]

In addition, to effectively patrol cyberspace, states would need to allow substantial intrusive governmental interference with the private network, which many in the United States and other democracies would find objectionable. At the same time, states bent on restricting freedom of expression could use the strict liability regime as a pretext for imposing draconian restrictions on Internet use. These same states, as legal scholar Jack Goldsmith points out, are likely to want the definition of a cyberattack to be expansive enough to include attacks by "hacktivists wielding anti-censorship weapons." No less pernicious is the possibility that actors who dislike a particular state will exploit the territorial liability regime to implicate that state by launching attacks from its territory, thereby antagonizing victim states and instigating interstate conflict.[25]

In short, the problems generated by the territorial liability proposals are at least as serious as the attribution and jurisdictional problems they are designed to solve. For this reason they are unlikely to be adopted internationally any time soon. This leaves intact the attribution problem and, with it, the jurisdictional gaps in accountability.

Problems of attribution and accountability may seem relatively unimportant while the stakes remain relatively low. In both the OxOmar and the Love Bug cases—and many others like them—the victim states and their citizens easily absorbed the costs and did not suffer long-term or significant harm. In other cases, the costs, while substantial, are largely invisible—a migration of wealth from rich countries to developing economies driven by stolen intellectual property. But what if, instead of crashing computers or disclosing, corrupting, or stealing data, an individual's cyber- or bioattack resulted in death or serious injury—and in large numbers? Could the victim state then reasonably hold the host state accountable? And short of that, could it assert the right to act unilaterally against the perpetrator, perhaps using force to capture—or even kill—him?

A few months after OxOmar and his fellows' attacks, various blogs claimed that OxOmar had died, reportedly of acute asthma. The blogosphere was quickly filled with speculations that the "acute asthma" had been nothing other than the devious workings of the Israeli Mossad. No source outside a few blogs confirmed OxOmar's death; nor do we have any reason to believe that the Mossad, even if it had been able to locate OxOmar, was sufficiently concerned about his operations to go to the trouble of plotting and carrying out his assassination. But that is not the point.[26]

The point, rather, is that we cannot dismiss out of hand the specter of a state's resorting to the use of lethal force where it cannot otherwise guarantee its own safety and the safety of its citizens. States do these things, after all—even if Israel did not in this case. It is a prospect grounded in precedent. The Israelis have a long-standing practice of killing terrorists around the globe, and other countries, including the United States, have likewise resorted to eliminating certain perceived enemies. The empowerment of individuals to inflict great harm from great distances, sometimes from locations that lack effective domestic policing, necessarily raises the question of how much more dangerous an OxOmar would have to be before a state might reasonably resort to inducing an acute asthma attack.

To summarize all this very simply, the distribution of threats around the globe is already exerting pressure upon the legal principles that have traditionally allocated legal powers among states, and this pressure will only grow over the coming years. It will challenge the specific rules that govern interstate relations, including those that have defined what any one state can do in reaction to violence against it, whether by private or public actors. At some point, if the trend continues unabated, the existing international legal regimes that delimit the boundaries of sovereignty will face a considerable challenge to their rationale and practicability.

The task then, to which we turn in greater detail later on, will be to find the right governance structures to allow states to defend themselves and their citizens against harm from others without turning much of the globe into the Wild West. Before turning to that most challenging of governance questions, however, let us look at the options available to states for domestic governance in terms of both surveillance and the use of a broader array of legal measures to control and regulate domestic conduct.

PART III

7

THE SECURITY OF
PLATFORMS AND THE FUTURE
OF SURVEILLANCE

THE ANCIENT ROMANS built roads—a network of more than eighty thousand kilometers of passable stone roads throughout the Italian peninsula, much of Europe, the Near East, Britain, and North Africa. One scholar notes that with the occasional public ferry across a river or strait, it was possible to do an astonishing 21,600-kilometer circuit around the ancient world—all on Roman roads: from Alexandria to Carthage to Cadiz to London, up to the border of Scotland, to Leiden, Strasbourg, and Milan, to Constantinople, Ancyra, and Antioch, and back to Alexandria again by way of Suez. The Roman roads even crossed the Alps. As this scholar writes, "Up to the eighteenth century the Alps were not again so accessible as they had been in the second."[1]

This incredible network was not just for emperors or used only by their armies—as Egyptian roads had been. Nor, like Persian roads, were they exclusively trade routes. Although built for military purposes, writes Estruscan studies professor Romolo Augusto Staccioli, the "Roman roads were open to everyone, without regard for privilege or exclusivity. Free of servitude and tolls, they served the cities as well as the countryside. Over their paving stones passed soldiers, magistrates, emperors, governors, administrators, functionaries, contractors, tax collectors, and postal couriers. But every other variety of humanity used them too."[2]

The Romans took their roads very seriously; the roads were durable enough that many of them still survive today. They allowed Rome to move troops around the empire quickly and thus to project power into the far reaches of her domain. They allowed commerce and human mobility.

They operated, in short, as a giant platform for Rome's expansion and the projection of her culture over a huge geographic area, a platform for growth, communication, and human interactivity. They were the closest thing to the Internet the ancient world had.[3]

But having built this remarkable platform and become dependent upon it, Rome also had to secure it. The security of Roman roads had more than one dimension. Rome had problems with banditry along stretches of road too long to patrol. Travel was dangerous, a matter of fear for many Romans; murders along the roads were common. Indeed, bandit attack is listed in one Roman legal discussion, alongside old age and sickness, as a common form of death. Travel along the roads scared people enough that wealthier individuals traveled with small armies of armed slaves. When Spartacus led his slave revolt, his army equipped itself by robbing travelers along the roads. A certain level of banditry was simply a cost of having the road network—and certainly a cost worth bearing.

Sometimes, however, the security situation got out of hand. In the first century BCE, for example, during a period of particular lawlessness following Julius Caesar's assassination, banditry spiked. As the ancient historian Suetonius records, "Gangs of robbers openly went about with swords by their sides, ostensibly to protect themselves, and travelers in the country, freemen and slaves alike, were seized and kept in confinement in the [prisons] of the landowners." In response, Octavian in 36 BCE appointed a man named Sabinus to repress banditry. Sabinus organized a campaign of executions, stationed guards along key roads, conducted searches of the estates, and restored order within a year. Historian Ray Laurence writes that Octavian became enormously popular in Italy as a result of Sabinus's road security program. Cities even began naming him among their gods. The Romans, Laurence writes, had a professional cadre of bandit hunters. And the punishment of bandits was a grisly feature of moving on the roads, along which bandits would be crucified both to mollify the families of those they had killed and as a warning to other potential bandits of what lay in store for them.[4]

This constant fight with bandits took place when Rome was still strong. As the empire waned, however, the roads that had facilitated its projection of force outward came to provide a platform for inward attacks by others. The roads Rome had built so that its own troops could menace its foes ultimately offered the Goths direct access to Rome itself. In 410 CE, the Visigoth king Alaric I sacked Rome, leading a large army over the very roads Rome itself had built. With the platform now undefended, there was virtually no opposition. As historians Sam Moorhead and David Stuttard put it, "Using the Flaminian Way, as if it were his own, [Alaric] marched south along the Adriatic coast, destroying various cities along the way, before following the ancient road across the Apennines to Rome."[5]

Over the course of the nineteenth century, the United States built its own platform for growing its landmass, power, and culture: railroads. The transcontinental railroads were pivotal in America's westward expansion. Like the Roman roads, the American railroads quickly formed a giant network enabling all sorts of what we now call connectivity. They enabled the country's massive industrialization and great movement of goods and people; entire cities came to life on their backs. They also played a huge role in America's developing national culture. Standardized time, for example, came into existence because railroads imposed it on local communities; before railroads, nobody cared if the time in one town was the same as in another a hundred miles away. Families began spreading out—yet could also remain close. Intercity sports leagues became possible. Traveling across the country—once a matter of months—became a matter of days.[6]

And just like Rome's roads, America's new platform immediately required security. The banditry of the Old West railroads remains the stuff of legend. But the men whose names today evoke a romanticized outlawry—Jesse and Frank James, Butch Cassidy and the Sundance Kid—once represented a real security problem with which the country had to contend. The Wild West's outlaws were, as often as not, train robbers. And just as bandits threatened the Roman roads, these robbers threatened to destabilize America's key platform for development and expansion. As William Pinkerton of the Pinkerton Detective Agency wrote in 1893, "Train robbing has been practiced pretty steadily in the South and West during the last twenty years, but during the last few months outrages of this character have increased at an alarming rate." Train robberies made it extremely costly to move money between cities. They made people fearful of using the rails. They eroded confidence in the platform.[7]

The response to the train robberies around the twentieth century included a series of measures that we would now call a public-private partnership. The railroads created teams of Rangers who relentlessly pursued the bandits until they caught or killed them. The Pinkertons, a form of nineteenth-century private security contractor, also hunted down robbers. And ultimately, states began creating official railroad police forces. Pennsylvania created the first transit police force in 1901. By 1910, at least nineteen other states had authorized police forces to patrol the railroads and use lethal force if necessary. What is more, the railroads themselves began hardening the cars, making them out of steel, and they also hardened the safes in which the trains carried the money. The express companies put armed guards on the trains. The Pinkertons recruited spies from among the railroad workers. And this multifaceted campaign of private action and public policy began to pay off. According to writer Richard Patterson, train robberies peaked in 1900, fell the following year, and after a brief blip upward in 1902, began falling for good.[8]

We were seeing then the same pattern—albeit in much slower motion—that we are witnessing now with new technologies of mass empowerment. New platforms unleash human creativity and provide bases on which to build new frontiers of power and culture. Yet, at the same time, they create new security issues that, left unaddressed, leave the platform unsafe for use and potentially threatening to the society that created it. For a platform to be healthy, it has to be at least minimally secure. And those responsible for governing it, whether public authorities or private owners or both, somehow have to give people adequate confidence in the security of a platform so that they will willingly use it.

PLATFORMS AND THEIR NATURE

The *Oxford English Dictionary* (*OED*) defines a "platform," first, as a "surface or area on which something may stand, *esp.* a raised level surface." It goes on to describe it as "a raised level surface on which people or things can stand, usually a discrete structure intended for a particular activity or operation." The word often conveys a forum for performance of some kind, such as a stage or a dais. It connotes a specialized flat space designed to support human activity. It is elevated. It does not itself perform or participate in the human activity in question, but its existence provides the activity a forum that, in turn, somehow promotes or permits it. A stage promotes performance of dance, drama, and music. A boardwalk promotes walking and shopping by the seashore. Platforms are flat surfaces on which we do things.

In the technology arena, the word has an escalating series of ever more metaphorical meanings. Engineers often describe as platforms robotic structures onto which one can attach more refined structures that, in turn, perform specialized tasks. The intelligence and military communities often emphasize that unmanned aerial systems are not just weapons but dramatically effective intelligence collection platforms. This usage is in one sense literal. Particularly in ground robotics, robotic platforms are sometimes raised mobile flat surfaces on which other robotic systems perform their tasks—just like the older level surfaces that, in another use of the word "platform," the *OED* tells us, were used for mounting artillery. But this usage also carries a more abstract element. Some robots are vehicles that serve as mobile bases for other robotic activity and look nothing like platforms in the literal sense of the word.[9]

In a somewhat similar vein, the automobile industry uses the term "platform" to refer to a standardized set of vehicle production and design elements, upon which a manufacturer might build a number of very different seeming car models, thus simplifying manufacturing and greatly reducing production costs. Again, the term conveys something literal—a standardized set of attributes related to wheelbase, chassis, and floor plan that cumulatively form a flat physical structure on top of which the rest of the car gets placed. Yet it also has a metaphorical component—that is, the term conveys a common set of protocols and elements that together provide a foundation for further creativity and development.[10]

With respect to technology, the word "platform" has taken on this latter meaning, which is less physical than a gunnery or some common chassis for disparate vehicles made by a common manufacturer. When we speak of a "computing platform," we refer to a group of compatible hardware and software specifications, the use of which enables people to develop and launch applications. For example, the Windows computing environment, the Macintosh operating system, and the iOS environment all provide combinations of hardware and software similar enough in essential performance and specifications that, like a physical platform, they provide a forum in which humans can build and run programs. A similar usage has developed in the biotech world, where we speak of "vaccine platforms"—that is, manufacturing methodologies for vaccines based on common specifications and systems—and "molecular diagnostic platforms," which involve combinations of devices designed to analyze cell or bacterial specimens for characteristics of interest. More generally, we speak of a "platform technology" as one that supports the development of other technologies.[11]

For present purposes, consider a platform to be any facility or common set of procedures or specifications that enable human activity. The house is a platform for human habitation, for example, and the banking system is a platform for financial transactions. The network of airports and their associated infrastructures, organizations, procedures, and regulations cumulatively create a platform for intercity commercial air travel. More metaphorically, a platform can be merely a set of ideas: the limited liability corporation, for example, provided a platform on which to build a great deal of modern capitalism and finance.

Developed platforms tend to encourage networking. Be it the ancient Roman road, the nineteenth-century American rail system, the telephone, the Windows operating system, or the Internet, a platform links the people who use it to one another. The reason is simple: platforms become more developed because people use them. Use of the same technology tends to bring large numbers of people together; one meets other actors on a stage, after all. Conversely, if one builds a stage and nobody performs on it, the stage has not served as an especially useful platform. The history of technology is full of potential platform technologies that did not become major platforms because people did not adopt them; railroads beat out canals for moving freight, and in the United States, anyway, both interstate highways and intercity air travel ultimately beat out railroads for moving people. The technology itself, in other words, is insufficient. For a platform to be vibrant, to develop, it needs a network of people standing upon it. And this network, once created, has a way of expanding so as to push the platform itself toward expansion as well. These two effects reinforce one another, creating a deep developmental nexus between a platform and the network that uses it.

Technologies of mass empowerment, in particular, tend to create or reveal platforms. They do not, to be sure, lie at the root of all platforms. But it is not an accident either that the word "platform" shows up—in strikingly similar usage—with respect to networked computing, biotechnology, and robotics. Technologies of mass empowerment, after all, create common systems and protocols under which growing networks of people can do things in interaction with one another. The Internet offers the most developed example of this phenomenon. In that sense, it is very much like a city—a large manufactured platform for human activity that has, within it, any number of subsidiary platforms. A city has apartment and office buildings, neighborhoods, and commercial districts, each functioning as a subplatform for a subset of activity. The Internet, similarly, has any number of smaller, interior networks. These include regional and private networks connected to the larger Internet, as well as communications protocols that piggyback on top of the larger architecture for specific applications (like Skype, for example); the interior networks also include content from around the globe that is interlinked thematically, creating subject-area subnetworks that operate nonregionally.

Sometimes, however, the platform is not built by humans but merely exposed by developing human knowledge. With biotechnology, for example, the fundamental platform is not technological but natural, and advances in human knowledge have served more to reveal what was already there than to develop it as an original matter. Biotechnology, after all, is that body of knowledge, skills, and techniques that can be applied through the platform of human or other forms of life. In biotechnology, the network and the platform are quite literally us. And the platform's development lies less in its creation than in understanding the way it operates and how we can manipulate it or alter its operations.

That said, some aspects of the bioplatform are manufactured. Consider, for example, the BioBricks Foundation, which describes itself, as we noted earlier, as working toward "a world in which scientists and engineers work together using freely available standardized biological parts that are safe, ethical, cost effective and publicly accessible to create solutions to the problems facing humanity." By "freely available standardized biological parts," the foundation is referring to genetic sequences that perform in known ways and that can be incorporated into bioengineered projects, much the way software engineers use standardized computer functions in the code they write. Or consider the International Genetically Engineered Machine (iGEM) Foundation, which "fosters scientific research and education by establishing and operating the Registry of Standard Biological Parts, a community collection of biological components." Such "development of well-specified, standard, and interchangeable biological parts is a critical step towards the design and construction of integrated biological systems," iGEM explains. These projects describe the development of something like a manufactured platform in synthetic biology.[12]

Platforms are similarly developing in consumer and hobbyist robotics. The DIY Drones community, for example, uses a series of unmanned systems based on the Arduino robotic operating system, whose developers describe it as an "open-source electronics prototyping platform." The ArduCopter, ArduPlane, and ArduRover all build off of Arduino. Whatever the modality of their development—whether built, exposed, or some combination of the two—the underlying effect seems similar across platforms: there is an important relationship not merely between platforms and networking but between technologies of mass empowerment and both.[13]

For present purposes, let us consider only the public platform—that is, the platform that is open to public use—and specifically, only to the public networked platform: the publically accessible playground, the network of airports, the postal service, the Internet, or the human genome. The technology to make up a public platform can be crude or sophisticated, manufactured or natural. The defining feature is simply that some organization, private or governmental, or some set of circumstances is making available some infrastructure for activity on which the public can exercise freedom.

Focusing on platforms can actually be a good way to think about security measures. In some respects, we do this instinctively. We think about the security of air travel, not of individual airplanes. We think about the security of cyberspace, less about the security of individual transmissions. If you want to know how secure you are, looking to the security of the environment in which you operate only makes sense. Security in a world of many-to-many threats and defenses is, at bottom, a project in securing to the greatest extent possible our developmental platforms—just as the Romans had to secure the roads and the United States had to secure the rails.

Indeed, people will not trust or use platforms that are insecure, at least not for things they care about or when they can avoid it. The unpatrolled playground in a crime-ridden neighborhood goes unused by children and ultimately becomes a platform for other activities—drug dealing, for example. As we have seen, the insecurity of railroads in the American West significantly inhibited the flow of money between cities, and the insecurity of roads in ancient Rome inhibited people's willingness to travel. In more modern times, restoring public confidence in airline security after September 11 was a great challenge for a number of governments. Fear of identity theft and the insecurity of information still threaten to erode confidence in some aspects of life on the Internet. And the US Postal Service experienced a significant drop-off in usage during the 2001 anthrax attacks. Platforms, whether in private or public hands, operate socially very much like streets. They require a measure of patrolling if we want people to feel safe enough to use them. And as with making a city safe, that patrolling involves a complex interaction of public policy, government enforcement and regulatory action, corporate behavior, and individual behavioral norms.[14]

This is not to say that people will avoid a platform entirely if it is not secured. Americans rode the rails despite the chances of confronting the James brothers, and the Romans used their roads despite the dangers—just like the residents of bad, inner-city neighborhoods today walk their streets. We constantly leave digital records of all aspects of our lives—the tiles of our mosaics—on computers around the world, even knowing that we are making ourselves vulnerable by doing do. Some people are irrational about risk; some activity is so essential that it is perfectly rational to absorb risk to engage in it. But it does not take an economist to see that reduced security on a platform will inhibit people's use of it to some degree, and the more safely people can use a platform, the more freely they will do so.

THE ROLE OF SURVEILLANCE

Patrolling a platform can be one way of ensuring its security. That patrolling may be intrusive; it can also be mild to the point of insignificance. The key point is that when we value the freedom that these platforms enable—to create, to communicate, to build, and to travel—surveillance of them is not a simple loss to liberty. It can, rather, add to liberty, even to privacy, insofar as it enables us to use those platforms safely.

Surveillance has a bad name because it is a tool of repressive governments, and its reputation has grown worse after Edward Snowden's disclosures and the ensuing nearly daily revelations about the surveillance activities of the United States and other Western powers. But it is a grave, if common, mistake to treat aggressive surveillance as presumptively a tool of repression to be eyed suspiciously by liberty-loving people. It can often be key to keeping platforms free for public use. Indeed, the security of platforms offers perhaps the paradigmatic case where surveillance methods can enhance liberty in ways we do not always recognize. Like the guards stationed along the Roman roads who made travel safer and freer by patrolling the platform, measures—even some relatively intrusive measures—that build confidence in platforms and enable their use can be net plusses for liberty. Consider, for example, the modern equivalent of those guards stationed along the roads: airport security screening. Passengers willingly subject themselves to quite invasive searches of their bags, patdowns of their persons, and what amounts to electronic strip-searching by backscatter machines. In other contexts, this very same behavior would legitimately give rise to criminal prosecution for sexual assault or lawsuits for harassment or invasion of privacy. Yet we subject ourselves to it because we value the liberty that such surveillance enables—the freedom to travel—more than we resent the intrusions. And critically, we value the freedom to travel safely, without which the freedom to travel is somewhat an illusion, more than we value the freedom to travel free of surveillance.

One mechanism by which we tend to avoid intellectually confronting the liberty-enhancing quality of certain types of surveillance is a linguistic trick: we often avoid calling it surveillance. When we station a police officer to patrol an inner-city playground, we call it "community-oriented policing." When we scan letters for anthrax spores, which the US Postal Service began doing after the anthrax attacks, we call it "screening," a word we also use to describe airport security measures. The trick is comforting but mindless. Platform surveillance is no less surveillance than is wiretapping. But in the hostile symbiosis between liberty, privacy, and security, it triggers a different sort of interaction between the three partners than wiretapping does. And we thus often react to platform surveillance very differently than we do to surveillance directed at particular individuals. Communities will sometimes demand greater police presence in public spaces like playgrounds. They do so because they have made choices both about the relative costs and benefits to liberty of having those spaces patrolled and about whose liberty they care about on these platforms. Unsurprisingly, to cite an obvious example, they decide that they care more about the liberty of their children to play securely than they do about the liberty of the drug dealers who have taken these spaces over in the absence of police presence and turned them into open-air markets. They also prefer the tangible well-being of their children to any amorphous privacy concerns, including of those innocent bystanders who may have an inherent aversion to government surveillance in principle. There are countless examples of communities and society as a whole making similar choices—often requiring sustained, serious surveillance—in the interests of liberty as they perceive it.

Privacy concerns and attitudes toward surveillance vary culturally, and they also evolve over time. In Britain, public authorities and private actors operate millions of closed-circuit television cameras. Although the mass installation of video cameras across the country met with some resistance, the residents of Britain have acquiesced. As noted by the *New York Times* in 2007, "Video surveillance is widely accepted in Britain, viewed as a fact of life rather than an Orwellian intrusion." Attitudes toward video surveillance are changing in the United States as well. Law enforcement officials used a security camera at a nearby department store to identify the suspects in the Boston Marathon bombing in April 2013. In the bombing's aftermath, one survey revealed that Americans overwhelmingly favored following the United Kingdom's example of installing omnipresent closed-circuit television cameras in public places. In Washington, DC, Police Chief Cathy Lanier has described a palpable change in public sentiment regarding security cameras. A few years ago, city residents were overwhelmingly opposed to the pervasive installation of security cameras in public areas, citing privacy concerns, she reports. But today, she says, DC residents welcome, even demand, additional cameras in public spaces in their neighborhoods.[15]

Washington, DC, is certainly not alone in investing heavily in platform surveillance. In Oakland, California, city officials used a $7 million federal grant, originally intended for counterterrorism efforts, to build a big-data crime-prevention system, using cameras, license-plate readers, and gunshot sensors stationed around the city. Federal funding also supported the New York Police Department's big-data system, which links three thousand surveillance cameras with license-plate readers, radiation sensors, criminal databases, and terror-suspect lists. Meanwhile, police in Texas have bought a drone with Homeland Security money, something that Alameda County, which Oakland is part of, also tried to do but shelved after public protest.[16]

Libby Schaaf, an Oakland City Council member, gave the city's high crime rate as the justification for the city's big-data system: "It's our responsibility," she said, "to take advantage of new tools that become available." She added, though, that the program would be able to "paint a pretty detailed picture of someone's personal life, someone who may be innocent," a concern that drove the American Civil Liberties Union of Northern California to describe the program as "warrantless surveillance" and to warn that "the city would be able to collect and stockpile comprehensive information about Oakland residents who have engaged in no wrongdoing."[17]

At least for now, in the battle between cameras and anxiety about them, cameras are winning. These skirmishes over surveillance of public spaces take place in the context of a certain level of social acceptance of such patrolling—combined with significant levels of apathy and ignorance, which also yield toleration of it.

PLATFORMS AND THE LAW

Our surveillance law—indeed, our law in general—does not think in terms of platforms and their security. It is deeply rooted, as a general matter, in legal approaches conditioned by the Fourth Amendment, which approaches surveillance in terms of the rights of individuals and the reasonableness of searches and seizures directed against them. The amendment guarantees the right of the people to be "secure in their persons, houses, papers, and effects against unreasonable searches." The mechanism for protecting this right is, generally speaking, to require that searches be approved in advance by judges, who issue warrants only if there is "probable cause" to justify the search. "As new technologies emerged—and offered new sources of information about citizens," writes former Department of Homeland Security policy chief Stewart Baker, "privacy advocates sought to squeeze law enforcement access to the new information into this standard 'search' model." The result, says Baker, is that most privacy laws "offer some kind of watered-down Fourth Amendment protection," in which the government gets access to information if it "can obtain some kind of legal process (e.g., a subpoena or court order) based on some kind of predicate set of facts (e.g., the data is 'relevant to an ongoing investigation')."[18]

The Fourth Amendment surveillance model, in which the government gets permission to conduct surveillance against a person after having made some requisite showing to a court, is not inevitable; it is certainly possible to design surveillance rules differently, as many countries do. But it is the way our law tends to approach the problem, focusing on protecting individuals and their rights, not on the physical or metaphorical spaces that we need to protect. The result is that we have an oddly schizophrenic attitude toward platform surveillance. Often, we simply define it as not involving a search at all, thus placing surveillance entirely outside constitutional scrutiny. This is the case, for instance, when a security guard monitors people at a shopping mall or a police officer patrols the streets. On the other hand, some platform surveillance may receive undue scrutiny given its minimal level of intrusiveness. For example, surveillance may technically constitute a search because of either the ownership of a platform by private parties or the specific manner in which government conducts the surveillance, particularly in the context of electronic surveillance of communications.[19]

The general rule of thumb that the law does not think in terms of platforms has exceptions—doctrines and ideas that approach surveillance questions with concern for platform security. The so-called special-needs search doctrine, which permits certain warrantless surveillance and searches that are "beyond the normal need for law enforcement" and for which the "probable-cause requirement [is thus] impracticable," has provided a basis for upholding certain practices that represent species of platform surveillance. But the special-needs doctrine is not limited to the security of platforms. Nor, as we noted before, does platform surveillance necessarily involve what we would consider a search under modern Fourth Amendment law at all. The law, in short, has a limited vocabulary for this sort of surveillance.[20]

Moreover, the special-needs doctrine by its nature does not attempt to identify when a given platform security measure will enhance or erode freedom. The doctrine assumes, rather, that freedom will be—to one degree or another—lost because of surveillance measures, and it asks courts to weigh this loss against some putative security gain. This supposed balancing between liberty and privacy on the one hand and security on the other will sometimes be real. But the presumption of a trade-off of one value for another, as we have argued, is not always correct. The more highly networked public platforms develop globally, the more we are going to have to think about when that premise is right and when it is wrong. And more broadly, we are going to have to think about principles for surveillance that allow for aggressive patrolling of those platforms so as to keep the Leviathan at least slightly ahead of the littler fish.

The law's failure to think in terms of platforms takes place against a much larger background of irrationality in surveillance law. Indeed, American surveillance law, which governs access to communications and data about what people are doing, is, in general, an incoherent mess. The rules that govern the shielding of data about us from government, in particular, do not reflect any consistent set of policy or philosophical judgments. This is unsurprising given that our very conception of privacy itself is also an incoherent mess. Considered as a whole—and government collection authorities very seldom are considered as a whole—these laws espouse few analytically recognizable principles at all. They are rather a haphazard patchwork of authorities and restrictions pieced together over time with different concerns paramount during different periods and with little consideration of the interaction of disparate rules with one another. The degree of protection afforded to any given class of information may or may not have anything to do with how sensitive that information is. In some instances, relatively sensitive data receives irrationally little protection; in other instances, relatively trivial data receives dramatically enhanced protection. What is more, the law often allows the government to obtain the same materials under numerous duplicative authorities using completely different instruments. The standards under which officials may obtain information using these different rules may be similar to one another or may vary a great deal, depending on the authority in question and the type of investigation. In other words, we have no coherent approach to regulating the government's collection and processing of mosaic data at all.

To cite one of countless examples, if the government wants access to your e-mails, and those e-mails are stored on your computer, the government needs a search warrant. On the other hand, if it wants to force a telecommunications or Internet company to turn over your e-mails stored in the cloud, the legal standard varies depending on whether the e-mail has been opened and on the e-mail's age. To be specific, the government needs a search warrant if the e-mail is recent and unopened; it merely needs a subpoena if the e-mail is stored in the cloud and either has been opened by the user or is more than 180 days old.[21]

If that does not make any more intuitive sense than the idea that records of your video rentals, but not of your Amazon or iTunes purchases of goods or music, should be accessible only with a showing of probable cause, you are not missing some secret unified field theory that binds it all together. It simply does not make much sense. The law often suggests a degree of protection utterly disconnected from the protection it affords to comparable data and which it cannot and therefore does not in practice deliver. It thereby marries obscurity with inconsistency. The principles supposedly guiding this area conflict with one another, and we do not follow them anyway. The reason is that we are really not sure what value we are trying to protect—which makes that value difficult to weigh against competing goods and values.

The Supreme Court has done no better than Congress in regulating government surveillance in the modern era. In one of the court's recent forays into the problems of the mosaic, the justices handed down their decision in the 2012 case of *United States v. Jones*, which challenged on Fourth Amendment grounds the planting on a suspect's car of a GPS tracking device and its subsequent monthlong monitoring. The easy part for the justices was determining that this required a warrant. The reason it required a warrant, however, produced three separate opinions that represent three entirely different visions of how we should think about surveillance in a digital age. Five justices, in an opinion by Antonin Scalia, held that the physical planting of the GPS device on the car constituted a search because it amounted to a trespass on the suspect's property. Four justices, in a concurrence by Samuel Alito, derided this understanding as an anachronistic application of eighteenth-century tort law that held law enforcement to account for "conduct that might have provided grounds in 1791 for a suit for trespass to chattels." These justices, in the absence of better guidance from Congress, focused on the nature of the surveillance, not on the trespass that enabled it. And they held that "relatively short-term monitoring of a person's movements on public streets accords with expectations of privacy that our society has recognized as reasonable." Conversely, "the use of longer term GPS monitoring in investigations of most offenses impinges on expectations of privacy." Justice Sonia Sotomayor, meanwhile, while joining Justice Scalia's opinion, wrote separately to urge the court to reopen the doctrine under which material voluntarily disclosed to third parties goes unprotected by the Fourth Amendment. This doctrine, she argued, "is ill suited to the digital age, in which people reveal a great deal of information about themselves to third parties in the course of carrying out mundane tasks." The mosaic, she contended, "can attain constitutionally protected status only if our Fourth Amendment jurisprudence ceases to treat secrecy as a prerequisite for privacy."[22] Many observers hoped that *Jones* would shed light on how the Supreme Court will think about geolocation data in the future. It tells very little—unless a police officer's hand physically touches a car.

One might reasonably argue that society cannot realistically define the circumstances in which it can tolerate platform surveillance until it has more successfully defined the parameters of legitimate individual surveillance. In our view, however, this may precisely invert the truth. The questions associated with platform surveillance may actually be easier than those in which government targets and collects data on individuals. And a look at what American law in practice tolerates and under what circumstances suggests a series of principles that ought to have broader application to the problem of platform security. To wit, while platform surveillance is far from an anything-goes zone, American law does seem to tolerate rather a lot of it, at least under certain specialized circumstances.

And this, in turn, raises an important question: How precisely can we identify those circumstances? When do we regard our liberty, privacy, and security interests in platform surveillance as symbiotic, and when do we regard them as hostile? There are surely forms of platform surveillance we would not tolerate, after all. The challenge here is to identify the conditions in which we perceive such surveillance as enhancing freedom and those in which we will not tolerate surveillance measures, even in the name of making platforms safe for public enjoyment and use.

WHEN WE TOLERATE PLATFORM SURVEILLANCE

Although there are no simple answers to these questions, there are discernible patterns in our practice from which we might derive guiding principles. Our tolerance of platform security measures, in reality, often hinges on several interrelated but distinct conditions. The more of them a given measure satisfies, the more likely we are to regard the surveillance as legitimate.

The most important of these conditions is that the surveillance should not target any particular individual. The cop on the playground is watching everyone. The anthrax mail-screening system does not look specifically at whether your mail is giving off spores; it looks at whether mail in general is exuding spores and only then identifies the offending packages. Everyone goes through a minimum level of airport screening. The surveillance, in other words, is, programmatically speaking, surveillance of the platform and its use, not surveillance of any particular person who may be using it. While surveillance of the platform may come to focus on individuals and may involve significant invasions of their privacy, the individual per se is not really its concern.[23]

Relatedly, platform surveillance is concerned not with investigation but with deterring and preempting activity that threatens safe public use of the platform. The cop does not patrol the playground in order to investigate a crime. She does it to establish presence and to make the playground an unattractive site for criminal activity. Airport security screeners are not investigating any particular plot; they are preventing people from bringing dangerous materials onto airplanes. Again, platform surveillance may result in investigations. If, for example, the cop on the beat or the security officer at the airport has with her a dog trained to sniff for explosives or drugs and that dog gets excited about a particular person, this might justify a search, which might in turn lead to an arrest. But the purpose of the surveillance is not to build a criminal case against anyone. Indeed, where the courts have found the purpose of surveillance to be investigative, rather than securing the platform, surveillance has often been struck down. For example, while the Supreme Court has upheld drunk-driving checkpoints, it has struck down checkpoints for drug trafficking. The difference, the court wrote, was that the narcotics checkpoint lacked the "vehicle-bound threat to life and limb that the sobriety checkpoint . . . was designed to eliminate."[24]

Moreover, platform surveillance has to be conducted in a nondiscriminatory manner. It loses legitimacy when it is abused or comes to focus on one group or another; airport security officials are constantly fending off allegations that Muslims or people from particular countries get a tougher look, and police forces get pressured when they give disproportionate attention to those "driving while black." New York City's stop-and-frisk policy ultimately foundered precisely on the perception that it was not applied evenhandedly. Platform surveillance only gets accepted when it is perceived to focus in a nondiscriminatory fashion on all platform users, not on specific categories of them—particularly not when those categories are suggestive of invidious discrimination or are not reasonably tailored to individuals who pose some high risk to the platform. Indeed, one perpetual challenge of platform surveillance is to keep a policy that appears neutral on its face from becoming discriminatory in practice.[25]

Oversight also matters. That is, we are far more comfortable with platform surveillance measures when we believe that someone is watching the watchers than when we believe the surveillance takes place without adequate accountability. One can see this point acutely in the Snowden-era controversies. Critics of the National Security Agency's (NSA) surveillance saw the agency's activities as lacking adequate oversight. Defenders of it stressed the judicial, congressional, and executive branch checks on the bulk data collection the agency conducted. An enormous amount of the political fight over the surveillance measures took the form of a fight over the integrity of the oversight mechanisms that supervise them. Is the secret court constituted under the Foreign Intelligence Surveillance Act a rubber stamp? Does it have an adequately adversarial process? Is NSA's compliance program good enough? It matters who is watching—and how carefully—those who are spying on us.

Finally, the type and level of intrusion on the individual has to be reasonably calibrated to the type and magnitude of threat to the platform and no more than necessary to secure it. Where surveillance involves a minimal intrusion, we tolerate it even in the face of a very low-probability threat: even though the number of biothreats being sent by mail is trivial, for example, postal service screening for anthrax raises relatively few objections because an effective screening system does not require opening or reading correspondence, making any cost to privacy minimal. If, however, the threat to the platform does not justify the intrusion, people will not feel as though the liberty, privacy, and security they have given up to government by subjecting themselves to the surveillance facilitates some greater liberty and security in their use of the platform. This is why people who believe that the threat to air travel is mostly hype tend to be more offended by airport security measures than are people who believe the threat is real. And people understandably take still greater offense when surveillance they regard as unnecessary is intrusive—for example, where full body imaging, or what the American Civil Liberties Union has termed a "virtual strip search," is used as a surveillance measure. Similarly, a policeman patrolling a playground in a crimeless neighborhood will not seem nearly as protective of freedom as that same policeman in a high-crime neighborhood; he may even seem like an oppressive presence put there to discourage lawful behavior (like teenagers kissing) or to keep minorities out of the neighborhood. In other words, for platform surveillance to have legitimacy, the public has to believe that it is necessary.[26]

When platform surveillance meets these conditions, when authorities monitor the use of the platform for noninvestigative purposes in a nondiscriminatory fashion that is not targeted at individuals or groups, when surveillance is subject to rigorous oversight, and when people believe surveillance is necessary for the platform's safe use, we often find a social comfort level with surveillance that we might otherwise find troubling under the Fourth Amendment or other privacy norms. And critically, it engenders this social comfort level precisely because we do not perceive our liberty, privacy, and security interests as clashing with one another. Rather, we perceive ourselves as having all agreed to give up a little of each in order to garner some greater measure of all: the ability to use the platform securely for purposes of our own.

As applied to some platforms, like the streets or the playground, this comfort level is sufficient that we sometimes do not even think of the patrolling as surveillance at all. As applied to some others, however, even a basic level of patrolling under highly controlled circumstances still generates intense controversy. Consider the dispute over cybersecurity and whether the government might reasonably install sensors to screen Internet traffic—including private traffic transiting over private networks—for malware and attack agents. Such a system, which would look for malicious code but not examine the contents of communications beyond what is necessary to verify the presence or absence of malware, is in many ways more similar to than different from the anthrax scanning of physical mail—though there are certainly some significant divergences. Yet, for a variety of reasons, such ideas are treated with grave discomfort by many in the business and civil liberties communities, who regard this sort of surveillance as per se threatening to privacy. The relative comfort level we have developed with the physical surveillance of public spaces has not transferred to virtual spaces—at least not yet.[27]

SOME GOVERNANCE PRINCIPLES

The larger disputes over the handling of mosaic data—and even the narrower corner of those disputes that involve government access to mosaic data in the hands of third parties—could fill a book of their own. Here we want to advance a single high-altitude conceptual approach to thinking about the security of platforms: that is, to suggest that the surveillance of platforms is a critical feature of governance in a world of many-to-many threats and defenses. And we want to urge an overt doctrinal tolerance of programmatic surveillance of public, networked platforms where the conditions described above exist. The law, in our view, should move to embrace, even encourage, such surveillance and should do so not as a compromise of liberty but in its name.

The distinction between the platform with a physical presence and one without does not warrant the huge difference in attitude it seems to generate. The distinction between patrolling city streets or the National Mall and patrolling cyberspace for malware is not chiefly one of principle. If we accept that we are unsafe flying unless the Leviathan monitors human access to airplanes, we should at least be willing to ask whether we are similarly unsafe without some authority's monitoring people's access to and tinkering with the human genome—and viral and bacterial genomes, for that matter.

Importantly, this principle does not mean that people have no privacy rights in connection with their use of public, networked platforms. Just because you are out on the public roadways does not mean you subject yourself to all manner of search; a cop, even out in the open, for example, cannot search you without a reasonable suspicion of some misconduct. Similarly, just because you use the mail and thus subject yourself to anthrax screening, you do not forfeit all Fourth Amendment protection in your correspondence. Absent cause, inspectors still may not open and read your letters. Privacy rights and surveillance coexist all the time and in complicated ways. The major point is that the use of a public, networked platform involves entering a zone in which activity of some sorts is presumptively subject to generalized monitoring, that one has limited privacy rights in the act of engaging the platform itself. You may still be entitled to private communications, but you should not expect privacy in the sending of blocks of data that threaten the integrity of the platform—and you should not expect zero electronic screening of your e-mails to verify that the data packets you send are, in fact, benign.[28]

This basic idea—that we should tolerate certain programmatic surveillance to protect public, networked platforms and regard this surveillance as fundamentally liberty enhancing—will not always result in aggressive surveillance programs. The platforms themselves differ so greatly from one another that the practical opportunities for effective surveillance activity will necessarily differ greatly as well. In some areas, promising avenues of platform surveillance may not materialize at all. Our point here is simply that where it is promising, we should not regard platform surveillance as presumptively liberty eroding, as it obviously would be if we knew to a high degree of certainty that there were no serious threats to the platform and that these threats did not themselves pose serious dangers to our liberty and privacy. When contemplating a given surveillance measure, in other words, we should not begin with the operative assumption that it will cost us freedom. We should begin, rather, by asking whether in the hostile symbiosis between liberty, privacy, and security, this new program or activity will tend to enhance all, diminish all, or enhance some at the expense of the others. We should not assume that it will bring out the hostility in the symbiosis, though we should certainly be aware of—and vigilant against—that possibility.

Consider two examples involving two different platforms. The first example, to which we alluded above, was posed by legal scholar Jack Goldsmith, who hypothesizes that existing government intrusion-detection systems devoted to protecting government networks from cyberattack and exploitation might be expanded in the coming years to protect the larger privately owned components of the network as well. Goldsmith imagines that a mandatory intrusion-prevention system "might place sensors at the point of entry for all communications coming into the United States, as well as at each Internet exchange point among internet backbone providers and between the backbone and major cloud service providers and the large private firms associated with critical infrastructure." The government would play a role both in identifying the malware signatures that such systems would identify as threatening and in responding to any intrusions detected. But it would work hand in glove with the telecommunication carriers, which operate the Internet's backbone. In Goldsmith's hypothetical, the NSA would inevitably play an important role—as it already does in existing intrusion-protection systems. It is, after all, the agency with the relevant expertise to conduct this sort of mission. As he rightly notes, this scenario "is a nightmare for many civil libertarians: the dreaded all-powerful, privacy-destroying, DoD-affiliated, generals-run NSA cut loose to use its giant computing and analytical powers in the homeland, in conjunction with private firms, to suck up and monitor the content of private Internet communications; store those communications, temporarily; trace the source of malicious agents in these communications all over the globe, including inside the United States; and take active steps to thwart malicious communications, even when they originate in or use computers in the United States."[29] Goldsmith's hypothetical is not all that hypothetical—though it is not yet a reality either. The government already has such a system in place for its own information systems. And the NSA has reportedly been contemplating the sort of expansion Goldsmith describes, though the controversies engulfing NSA since the Snowden leaks have at least temporarily complicated plans for enhancing NSA cybersecurity powers.[30]

If we consider this scenario in the terms outlined above, it looks a lot less obviously like a civil liberties nightmare. Although looking at it through the lens of platform security would not resolve anxieties about the NSA's involvement in domestic matters, it would suggest a series of questions that might separate versions of the program that pose real dangers from versions that might enhance liberty. For example, we might probe as to whether the system would focus on any individual or group. We would want to know whether the system was really operating to protect the network, not as part of specific investigations. We would want to know whether the system discriminated against users or treated everyone's traffic the same way. We would surely ask questions about the chances and consequences of false positives. We would ask whether the surveillance was reasonably calibrated to counter genuine threats to the platform. We would ask whether and how the system might be prone to abuse and whether the protections against abuses include adequate oversight and remedies. We would want to know whether and under what circumstances information collected for one purpose might be diverted to other purposes, worthy or less worthy, creating a kind of mission creep that makes all information available for all purposes.

Perhaps most importantly, we would also ask questions about the nature of the screening of the data packets, which, unlike the screening of physical mail for anthrax, inevitably involves some measure of examination of their content. Does the system merely compare transiting packets against known malware signatures, or does it do any kind of deeper examination of those packets? Does it store them beyond the time it takes to screen them—and how long is that exactly? Do humans ever see the contents and, if so, under what circumstances? And does the system evaluate in any way the substantive content of the communications, beyond establishing whether the packets include malware signatures? These latter questions would be pivotal to understanding whether the program really has no investigative component or is really aimed at examining the contents of communications that we believe should, absent individualized suspicion, remain private.

How we evaluate this program, how we decide whether it alters the hostile symbiosis between liberty, privacy, and security, should depend enormously on the answers to these questions. If, for example, we were to find that content examination in fact took place beyond the simple comparison of packets to signatures, that the system did not treat all communications similarly, or that humans looked at the substantive content of communications without individualized suspicion of the senders, we might rightly see the program as a serious threat to liberty and privacy. On the other hand, if we were to satisfy ourselves that the answers to these questions were reasonable, we might conversely view this system as fundamentally enhancing our liberty and privacy by—without making our communications materially more available to government agents—allowing us to send and receive those communications with diminished threat from malicious actors. We might then see it less as a nightmare for civil liberties than as a protective umbrella that makes us freer—one that does not empower Big Brother but does empower the Leviathan to restrain a great many Little Brothers.

Similarly, it is possible to imagine technological means of frustrating to some degree the use of gene-synthesis equipment for illicit or unauthorized creation of pathogens. The major gene-synthesis companies in the United States—which sell gene sequences by mail, phone, and the Internet—screen orders for sequences associated with certain dangerous agents and refuse to sell such sequences to those who are not registered to work with them. At least in theory, this should prevent a bad actor from buying, say, the smallpox virus genome or sizable segments of it and then assembling them in her own laboratory. Yet this system would do nothing to prevent that same bad actor from using low-cost gene-synthesis equipment in her own laboratory to build the sequence herself. In an article published early in 2009, biosecurity experts Ali Nouri and Christopher Chyba proposed building the screening system directly into the gene-synthesis equipment. Manufacturers would then program the computers that drive the machines to decline to produce sequences associated with certain dangerous agents unless the user was registered to work with them. The software, in this proposal, could automatically update its list of prohibited sequences in much the same way that antivirus software updates the list of malware it identifies and purges.[31]

One could imagine further developments of the technology that would make it far more robust as a prevention tool. What if gene-synthesis equipment alerted authorities whenever an unauthorized person tried to create a proscribed sequence? More intrusively, what if the equipment reported constantly on its own activities, so that authorities would have an ongoing audit trail that enabled them to monitor who was creating what gene sequences? Such approaches may or may not have promise as prevention methods, but as with Goldsmith's intrusion-detection system, we should not preclude them out of hand in the name of privacy.

THE SNOWDEN DISCLOSURES

In the summer of 2013, the Snowden disclosures about the NSA's surveillance activities put programmatic surveillance of platforms squarely on the public agenda. The surveillance that Snowden revealed was only partly platform surveillance of the type we are concerned with here. After all, the documents he released did not chiefly describe surveillance directed at the security of the telecommunications and Internet platforms themselves—like the scenario described in Goldsmith's hypothetical. They described, rather, surveillance on those platforms that was either directed at individuals overseas or involved the bulk collection of addressing data for telephone calls domestically—that is, so-called metadata identifying which telephone numbers are calling which other numbers and the duration of the calls. This surveillance, in the case of the bulk metadata program, takes place for counterterrorism purposes; in other cases, it takes place for broader intelligence-gathering purposes. At the same time, aspects of the programs Snowden revealed certainly have features in common with the sort of platform surveillance we are concerned with here. And they offer an interesting window into the vitality of the principles we describe.

Consider the bulk collection of domestic telephony metadata, for example. It turns out, as Snowden revealed, that the NSA was receiving, in bulk and in real time, metadata from the telecommunications carriers both domestically and with one end of the conversation happening in the United States. The agency was retaining this information in large databases for a period of five years, during which time—when it had indications that a particular phone number was associated with terrorist activity—it could query the database to find out what phone numbers had been in contact with the suspicious one and who else those numbers might be calling.[32]

President Barack Obama has called on Congress to end government bulk collection of metadata and rely instead on the private sector to retain it; legislation is still pending. But when we hold this program up against the principles we describe, it actually satisfies a number of them, though not all. It is conducted in a nondiscriminatory fashion: the government seeks to collect all telephony metadata, and although its coverage is not complete, the bulk collection does not target individuals or disfavored groups. It is plausibly calibrated to respond to a genuine threat—though questions have certainly arisen about whether it offers a useful tool to combat that threat. At the same time, the program does not focus on the security of the platform, and it is fundamentally investigative in nature. In other words, while the metadata program enjoys some of the same features that lend legitimacy to platform surveillance programs, it does not enjoy all of them.

Consider also the *New York Times*'s account of the NSA's monitoring of certain traffic into and out of the United States:

> To conduct the surveillance, the N.S.A. is temporarily copying and then sifting through the contents of what is apparently most e-mails and other text-based communications that cross the border. The senior intelligence official, who, like other former and current government officials, spoke on condition of anonymity because of the sensitivity of the topic, said the N.S.A. makes a "clone of selected communication links" to gather the communications, but declined to specify details, like the volume of the data that passes through them.
>
> . . .
>
> The official said that a computer searches the data for the identifying keywords or other "selectors" and stores those that match so that human analysts could later examine them. The remaining communications,

the official said, are deleted; the entire process takes "a small number of seconds," and the system has no ability to perform "retrospective searching."[33]

This looks a fair bit like the anthrax screening done by the postal service. As with the anthrax screening of physical mail, the NSA here is examining a very large volume of e-mail and text communications transiting particular servers. It appears to do so not on the basis of who sends the communications but instead looks at them for criteria selected for a propensity to pose a presumably genuine threat. Moreover, the NSA here conducts no search of the communications unless that initial screen triggers a warning. Thus, the privacy intrusion to the person not discussing keywords is almost entirely hypothetical.

There are key differences too, of course—differences that make the NSA surveillance more aggressive. The anthrax screening looks for ambient spores exuded by the mail; it does not look inside it. The *Times*, by contrast, is describing an initial scan of contents internal to the communications. Moreover, the program the *Times* describes is only as good as the keywords and selectors used are indicative of real threats. If these keywords are highly targeted to identify genuine threats, the program is far more defensible than if it sweeps in large volumes of perfectly innocent communications. So one would have to know a great deal of detail about the specific program to evaluate it rigorously. The point is that to whatever extent such programs find legitimacy and acceptance in the eyes of legislators, courts, and the public (a matter that remains very much in play), that legitimacy will rest on much the same foundation as we have described here with respect to measures designed to ensure the security of platforms.

The Snowden affair raises another issue that often arises with surveillance programs and will certainly arise with many serious efforts at platform surveillance over the coming years: secrecy and accountability. The broad societal discussion in the United States over the merits of these programs, it bears noting, did not result from congressional oversight or from judicial decision making. It resulted instead from a criminal act: a set of leaks. It is possible in theory to accept all the principles we have laid out for legitimate platform surveillance but also to believe that government is incapable of following those principles in actual fact. One might object that we will once again someday learn from a leaker that government has gone much further than we thought we had permitted, whether in the type and scope of the information it collected or in the uses it made of it. Better, the argument goes, to eschew such programs entirely or restrict them greatly, even though one can identify theoretical circumstances in which aggressive platform surveillance might in the aggregate enhance human freedom.

The trouble with this approach, in our view, is that it leaves the many Little Brothers too powerful. Shackling the Leviathan too tightly on grounds that we cannot allow it to grow too strong and that it will violate whatever principles we define to constrain it ignores the many other fish whose power, individually and in combination, will grow to fill the vacuum left by the Leviathan's disempowerment. For they will never be completely shackled, even if it is. And they will pose myriad threats from which we have few other protections. Far better to accept that surveillance has a legitimate role and struggle always to ensure that we tolerate only that surveillance that makes us freer. This struggle will be a constant push-pull of letting the Leviathan push against its net and then yanking on the net when it goes farther than we wished. In the world of many-to-many threats, we cannot avoid the struggle.

Surveillance is a key feature of any security regime because of both the intelligence it generates and the deterrence it creates. It will be a key feature of long-term governance of new platforms, just as guards patrolled the Roman roads and the railroads hired Pinkertons both to hunt down and to deter train robbers. Surveillance is not, however, the answer to every security problem—and it represents a complete answer to very few. There is always space between the sentries along the roads, thieves tend to know where the sentries are, and security too reliant on surveillance measures becomes brittle and shallow as bad actors learn how to evade detection. In a globalized world, surveillance is necessarily limited in its capacity and efficacy. To have high confidence that one will catch bad actors in a surveillance screen, that screen has to be very fine indeed, even as it is also very wide. Surveillance always has capacity for abuse—and the finer and wider the surveillance screen, the more it will tend to invite misuse. Patrolling platforms, therefore, offers a necessary but insufficient condition for security on those platforms. Rather, security requires deeper, more multilayered efforts not just to watch but also to influence design, architecture, and routine behavior. We turn to these efforts now.

8

OPTIONS FOR DOMESTIC GOVERNANCE

ON OCTOBER 1, 2001, then president George W. Bush spoke to employees of the Federal Emergency Management Agency about the national response to the September 11 attacks, which had taken place barely three weeks earlier. He described the war he was gearing up to fight, but he discussed—as he did in many of his speeches in that period—other dimensions of the coming battle against terrorism as well. It would be, he stressed, "a different kind of campaign than Americans [were] used to," one that "must be fought on many fronts." It would involve cutting off "these evil people's money": tracing and freezing assets, prosecuting donors, and using diplomatic leverage to get other countries to do the same. It would, of course, involve military force. "We've deployed 29,000 military personnel and two carrier battle groups, as well as an amphibious-ready group and several hundred military aircraft," Bush said. "We've called about 17,000 members of the Reserve to active duty, as well as several thousand National Guard operating under state authority." But Bush also involved diplomacy as a feature of the war, noting that the United Nations had unanimously enacted a resolution requiring member states to block terrorist funding and deny safe harbor. He also talked about law enforcement, declaring that the FBI had "conducted hundreds of interviews and searches, issued hundreds of subpoenas, and arrested or detained more than 400 people as it investigates the attacks." Bush also noted that "about 150 terrorists and their supporters [had] been arrested or detained in 25 different countries."[1]

In this speech and others the president dramatically understated the degree to which the American campaign against Al-Qaeda and its affiliates was being, as he put it, "fought on many fronts." While he described using a range of government resources to "slowly, but surely, [bring Al-Qaeda] to justice," it is worth breaking this range down and itemizing the many different types of power the Leviathan, under both Bush and his successor, has brought to bear on the problem of global jihadist terrorism.

- It went on offense militarily against enemy groups. As Bush's remarks reflect, it often did so in concert with allies, enhancing international cooperation to go after those it wished to target and deny them safe harbor.

- It also sometimes went after targets unilaterally, taking military and covert actions on the territory of countries that did not always consent to such actions—most famously, in the operation to kill Osama bin Laden in Pakistan.

- It used its investigative powers to take a variety of actions against individuals, from arrests and prosecutions to military detention and coercive interrogation, to—particularly later on—drone strikes and Special Forces raids.

- It directly regulated individuals in new ways, using both criminal and civil law to impose rules governing what individuals can and cannot do.

- It also indirectly regulated individuals—and spied on them— by regulating the intermediaries through which people have to interact in order to conduct the business of everyday life. This is what Bush was doing when he froze bank accounts associated with terrorist groups, for example, and it was what Barack Obama's administration was aiming for, years later, with the National Security Agency collection programs that Edward Snowden revealed.

- It invested substantial resources in new architectures for resilience—everything from training first responders to stockpiling vaccines and developing surge capacity in hospitals. The payoff on this investment was very much on display in the response to the 2013 Boston Marathon bombing, when emergency responders proved enormously effective, and emergency room doctors handled large numbers of seriously injured patients.

The Leviathan also helped develop a significant market for private-sector innovations that aid counterterrorism efforts—everything from backscatter machines in airports to data-analytics software of the sort developed by private companies like Palantir.

What is more, the citizenry itself mobilized to a considerable degree. Attempts to bomb airplanes were foiled by other passengers on those flights, supplementing the Leviathan's power with the uncoordinated energy of civilian eyes and ears—and muscles. Two groups of airline passengers subdued two separate terrorists—Omar Farouk Abdulmutallab and Richard Reid—who attempted to detonate bombs on transatlantic flights. An alert street vendor in New York prevented a disaster in Times Square when Faizal Shazhad attempted to detonate a car bomb there. On a day-to-day basis, the Leviathan had a lot of self-appointed help.

Given this broad spectrum of efforts, the words "war" and "campaign" are somehow inapt to describe the American effort to enhance security after the September 11 attacks. The power to make war was only one of many powers the government invoked in what was really a broad-based effort to force, urge, incentivize, and nudge a great many different actors into postures that, cumulatively, would create a global environment more secure from terrorists.

A certain amount of surveillance, as we have discussed, can be a key feature of creating a secure and free environment; that said, surveillance is not security, and enhancing surveillance alone will not produce security. Indeed, an overreliance on surveillance can be profoundly disruptive to the hostile symbiosis between liberty and security, in the sense that it can leave the individual far less free and far less secure from government power, while contributing little to his or her safety from other threats.

Enhanced security in response to complex, multifaceted threats—as the post-9/11 efforts illustrate—comes, rather, from effectuating broader-based shifts in the environment. For all of its dramatic threat of violence, Al-Qaeda and ISIS actually present comparatively simple cases for a governmental response. They have relatively few members (in the tens of thousands), after all, and while globally dispersed, they are networked together—making them at least theoretically easier to identify and track—and most of them are concentrated in certain specific geographic areas.

The world of many-to-many threats and defenses, by contrast, is more complex. It is a world in which the successful Leviathan must act world-wide to influence the behavior of literally billions of people and entities—investigating, deterring and punishing a bewildering array of potential bad actors, incentivizing individuals and corporations to make marginal decisions about their behavior that will increase, rather than decrease, the security of the everyday platforms they use, maintain, and help build. Yet the essential means available to policy makers include, broadly speaking, the same tools that the United States has used in the post-9/11 era. Let us start, therefore, by considering the domestic nonsurveillance tools available to a political community that wishes to create more secure environments in the face of a many-to-many threat environment.

Direct Regulation:
The Leviathan Orders You Around

The magnitude of the problem posed by a world of many-to-many threats, when one faces it squarely, is so overwhelming that it is tempting to simply ignore the most direct and simple tool governments have in influencing their citizens: the ability to compel people to do things and forbid them from doing other things through what one might call direct regulation. People tend to overlook direct regulation because it seems like such a nineteenth- and twentieth-century approach that is hopelessly inadequate to the challenge of terrifying new twenty-first-century realities.

But, although inadequate, it is certainly not useless. And direct regulation will continue to be an important tool in the arsenal of governments. The Leviathan may be weakened, but he is still a pretty fierce beast when he breaches the surface with his teeth bared.

These fangs include the power not only to forbid and require conduct but also to investigate conduct that might not comply with rules, to define the conditions under which conduct is tolerated, to license people to engage in certain behaviors, and to punish noncompliance with the rules. These powers may be used in a heavy-handed or highly calibrated fashion, or anywhere in between. They remain, and will remain, among the most powerful ways of influencing the behaviors of large numbers of people.

All sorts of direct regulations are already in effect with respect to technologies of mass empowerment. In the cyber arena, for example, a great many intrusions and online attacks have long been subject to criminal prohibition. Prohibited conduct that can land an individual in prison includes—to cite only some of the major statutes discussed in the Department of Justice's computer crimes prosecution manual—accessing a computer and obtaining information without authorization, trespassing upon a government computer, accessing a computer to defraud, malicious damaging of a computer or information, trafficking in passwords, intercepting communications, gaining unlawful access to stored communications, and identity theft. In robotics, on the civil side of things, the Federal Aviation Administration (FAA) has been engaged in extensive rulemaking process to regulate the integration of unmanned aerial systems into the domestic airspace of the United States. These rules will cover who is permitted to fly what sorts of drones, for what purposes, and under what circumstances. In the biological arena, to note an example in which criminal penalties back up civil regulation, the law requires people who want to work with "select agents"—particularly dangerous toxins, bacteria, and viruses—to submit to an FBI "security risk assessment," and it imposes criminal liability both for possession of select agents by those not registered to have them and for transferring select agents to unregistered persons. The law also slaps strict controls on the export of technologies with military application or of a dual-use nature. These are only some of a wide array of legal controls on individuals in their handling, acquisition, transfer, and use of technologies of mass empowerment. We mention these examples merely to emphasize that if government wants to prevent certain dangerous or malicious behaviors, telling people they cannot engage in them—and creating legal consequences if they do—is one place to start.[2]

The promise of direct regulation is twofold. First, criminal and civil regulations can establish strong behavioral norms—far stronger than government's power actually to enforce those norms. Consider a radically empowering twentieth-century technology, the automobile, which put in individual hands the power to travel quickly between cities and also to kill pedestrians and crash into other vehicles at high speeds. A series of direct regulations governs our use of motor vehicles. You need a state-issued license to operate a car, a norm that is widely respected even though nobody checks your license before you get into your vehicle. Most drivers, most of the time, display a sufficiently rudimentary respect for traffic laws that the roads are relatively safe (though far less so than are the airways or the railways)—even though drivers also know that they are likely to get away with any number of violations. People tend to drive inspected and registered vehicles with insurance, as required—though they could almost certainly get away with driving without either on any given day. And they drive cars with license plates; every car is registered in a visible sense to its owner.

The system of direct regulation of our use of this technology works because of a combination of self-interest (people do not want to hurt themselves or their vehicles or to harm others), social pressures from other drivers, occasional random enforcement—the cop with the speed gun or the officer who happens to see you run a red light—and the threat of enforcement if you get into an accident. The result is that laws that are unenforceable if widely ignored receive enough respect that the platform they are designed to secure operates in a relatively orderly fashion. Even with tens of millions of people using a lethal technology on a daily basis, direct regulation wields a sufficient influence on mass behavior that people—amazingly, really—retain confidence in a platform on which relatively untrained people are operating high-powered and very dangerous equipment at high speeds. While some of this influence flows from the threat of enforcement and the fact that compliance with the law here tends to correspond with safe (and thus self-interested) behavior on the part of the driver, some of it also simply reflects the power of law itself. In rule-of-law societies, at least, the law carries some moral force, and people tend to default in the direction of compliance.

Second, direct regulations create the legal basis for investigation and enforcement action that can play an important role in deterring abuse of highly empowering technologies, stopping and incapacitating those who misuse them, and letting potential bad actors know that authorities are watching. While enforcement by no means keeps pace with cybercrime, for instance, direct regulations allow federal authorities to initiate a lot of computer crime prosecutions every year. In fiscal year 2012 alone, for example, the Justice Department reports that federal prosecutors filed 169 computer fraud cases against 266 defendants, 401 identity theft cases against 567 defendants, and any number of other cases that may have had a hacking dimension. The public knows about Luis Mijangos, the sextortion hacker we discussed earlier, because of such federal enforcement. And it is notable that Mijangos today is not free to exploit other women and girls online; as of this writing, he is inmate number 59209-112 in the federal prison system, serving his sentence at the federal correctional facility in Greenville, Illinois.[3]

Direct regulation plays a similar role with other highly empowering technologies. Back in 2002, a scientist at Texas Tech named Thomas Butler reported that samples of bubonic plague had gone missing from his lab. The FBI descended in force on the campus to investigate, suspecting a bioterrorism incident. When it later turned out that the samples had not been stolen and that Butler may have destroyed them himself, the bureau turned its sights on him. It also turned out, as the investigation progressed, that Butler had mishandled plague samples and exported them illegally. The Justice Department prosecuted him for mishandling the highly dangerous agent, for allegedly lying about it to investigators, and for financial irregularities with respect to his university. Butler became a cause célèbre among many scientists, who saw his case as one of gross government overreaching against a distinguished scientist who was certainly no kind of terrorist. For present purposes, however, the point is that having a complex set of civil and criminal regulations governing the handling of biological materials provided a hook on which investigators could hang an investigation of someone they clearly regarded as a malicious actor. A jury ultimately convicted Butler on some charges but acquitted him on others; he served a two-year prison sentence.[4]

In the world of many-to-many threats and defenses, the power of direct regulation will continue to serve as a frontline lever for deterring, punishing, and smoking out abuses—and policy makers should not underestimate it. As technologies become more powerful and ever more widely available, we need to be imaginative about the ways people might use them maliciously or recklessly and how their routine uses might create opportunities for others to behave abusively or recklessly. We also need to create the kinds of working regulatory schemes that, as with automobiles, allow huge numbers of people to wield lethal power in relative safety.

The good news here is that we already do this instinctively. As the technologies associated with flying robots become more widely available, we have a regulatory process associated with integrating drones into the national airspace. As we have seen, regulations and criminal laws have developed around cyber- and biotechnology as those platforms have emerged as potential facilitators of deadly acts. The trick here is to regulate well, mindfully of the realistic benefits of new rules, of their costs for innovation and benign use, and of their likely effectiveness. Debates over the desirability and efficacy of regulation are endemic in almost every regulatory sphere, from environmental protection to gun control, and that will be no less true here. We must also consider the possible costs of regulation for those working to prevent bad acts; rules encumbering access to select biological agents, for example, make it harder to do defensive research.

Of course, no regulation will deter the truly evil, motivated person, whether her weapon of choice is an AR-47 rifle, a miniaturized drone, or fleas carrying the bubonic plague. Moreover, at least two features of technologies of mass empowerment make them a greater challenge for regulation than the threats posed by most other technologies. First, unlike automobiles—for which a certain number of accidents, drunk drivers, and even malicious murders presents a socially tolerable cost—true technologies of mass empowerment potentially involve actions that, even in very small numbers, do not present a tolerable cost. A single major biosecurity event could kill thousands if not millions of people. This feature makes regulation to prevent such actions more urgent. In addition, however, because technologies of mass empowerment transcend national boundaries in ways that the threats posed by conventional technologies generally do not, it is just impossible to guard against all potential threats posed by technologically empowered people around the globe. Just as it may help to think of national security as coming to resemble health and safety regulation, as we described earlier, this aspect of the problem bears a certain similarity to climate change in that it requires coordinated international action from major countries worldwide to be truly effective. Even if the United States were to get its carbon emissions under control, China and India would need to as well for emissions globally to diminish, and even if the United States were to adopt optimal security policies, other countries still might tolerate behavior that menaces Americans both abroad and at home. This globalized feature of the threat makes domestic regulation, however urgent, simultaneously less effective.

INTERMEDIARY REGULATION:
THE LEVIATHAN CONSCRIPTS PARTNERS

We looked earlier at the ways in which the law has begun requiring that telecommunications carriers and Internet companies accommodate government surveillance needs in their technological architecture. These cases offer a window into one of the most promising areas of potential government intervention as technologies of mass empowerment develop. To synthesize a biological virus requires equipment and materials that have to be manufactured and sold. To build and deploy a dangerous robot requires chips, parts, and software that likewise require development, manufacturing, and sale. Every piece of malware someone writes has to be stored on a server somewhere; to attack remotely, the malware has to transit between other servers and routers and over fiber optic cables or other data transmission pipes.

In other words, even the lone wolf is not really all that lone anymore. He is, to paraphrase Isaac Newton, standing on the shoulders of giant companies and relying on them for a huge percentage of the heavy lifting for his bad acts. Even if the state cannot directly regulate him, it often can regulate those giants, the intermediaries with whom he needs to transact his business, and conscript them as allies in detecting, investigating, and preventing his plans from coming to fruition.

The idea of intermediary regulation is not new, and it can take a number of forms. As law professor Daryl J. Levinson writes, many laws "extend liability from a primary wrongdoer to some other party—a 'gatekeeper' or an 'enabler'—who is in a position to disrupt the wrongdoing by withholding her services or cooperation, or by taking some preventive measure." Levinson lists a number of examples: fraudulent securities transactions can be blamed on lawyers or accountants who performed audits or gave legal opinions; the law in some states places "liability on bartenders and social hosts for alcohol-related damages caused by their intoxicated customers and guests"; therapists can face liability if they do not warn potential victims about likely acts of violence by their patients. And there is always the question of gun-maker liability for injuries of shooting victims.[5]

Levinson applies this idea explicitly to one type of technology of mass empowerment, the Internet, noting that "all . . . primary wrongdoers must go through an [Internet service provider], which is comparatively easy to identify and often in a better position than an outside sanctioning agent to monitor and control the activity of users and subscribers." Such gatekeeper liability, he points out, "might encourage ISPs to develop hardware and software technologies, such as filters, which would reduce the cost of screening out illegal users and increase efficiency gains relative to a direct liability regime."[6]

Indirect regulation, of course, need not necessarily impose liability on gatekeepers after the fact when something has gone wrong. As we have seen with telecommunications companies with respect to wiretapping and with color printer manufacturers with respect to counterfeiting, government sometimes proactively requires or requests certain behaviors of intermediaries. And scholars have examined in depth the modes of gatekeeper regulation and liability with respect to the Internet. Cyberlaw scholar Lawrence Lessig observed that code itself can operate as a form of law, meaning that if one can control the manner in which software is written, one can control behavior. And Jonathan Zittrain, another Internet legal scholar, traced admiringly the history of relatively light-handed regulation and gatekeeper liability, especially in the defamation and copyright infringement arenas, and argued that regulatory efforts through online intermediaries had "so far failed to provoke a significant intrusion." He worried, however, that future regulatory efforts might come to focus on "a new and less palatable set of intermediaries: software authors."[7]

Law professors Jack Goldsmith and Tim Wu, in *Who Controls the Internet? Illusions of a Borderless World*, focus on intermediary regulation as a principal explanation for why the early dreams of an Internet beyond sovereign authority turned out to be illusory: "The rise of networking did not eliminate intermediaries, the most important of which (for our purposes) are ISPs . . . , search engines, browsers, the physical network, and financial intermediaries. In short, the Internet has made the network itself the intermediary for much conduct that we might have thought had no intermediary at all prior to the Internet." Each component of the network, Goldsmith and Wu argue, is subject to regulation: the transporters of traffic, the information intermediaries, the groups that manage domains, the companies that allow us to transfer money, and others. By regulating these actors, they contend, government exerts outsized power over widespread use of a technology of mass empowerment not only at home but also beyond its own shores, making it "harder for local users to obtain content from, or transact with, the law-evading content providers abroad." China can keep huge quantities of politically undesirable data out of the public's hands, for example; Google routinely chooses to remove pages from its search results that are alleged to violate intellectual property laws; government enforcement operations can prevent some illegal online sales of contraband by compelling credit card companies to stop facilitating the transactions, and authorities can go after other illegal actors by revoking their domain registrations—effectively kicking them off the Internet.[8]

Used improperly, these powers represent terrifying tools of potential tyranny precisely because they leverage the intermediaries to reach the countless individuals who rely on them. But that is exactly what makes intermediary regulation a promising strategy for creating a safer environment with respect to technologies of mass empowerment. The promise lies in several mutually reinforcing features. Regulating intermediaries involves government interaction with far fewer actors than does direct regulation. Instead of, or in addition to, trying to regulate directly the behavior of hundreds of millions of drivers, for example, regulators were able to improve road safety by requiring a few companies to make cars safer. These companies are far more likely to comply with regulations than individual drivers are to avoid speeding or drunk driving. And because there are fewer of them, it is far easier to contemplate accountability for violations.

What is more, as Goldsmith and Wu's examples illustrate, intermediary regulation can have the important effect of muting, though not eliminating, the jurisdictional problems inherent in the regulation of widely dispersed technologies. The graduate student who wants to fabricate smallpox may be at a foreign university, but someone still has to make the gene-synthesis equipment he uses, and someone has to fill the orders for those parts of the genome he chooses to buy. A hacker may be overseas, but if she wants to attack a computer in the United States, she has to interact with US servers, providers, and manufactured goods—all subject to regulation. Some government has jurisdiction over those intermediaries, and it might well not be the government that has jurisdiction over the person who would misuse them. Even the attack spider has to be manufactured, and the airwaves over which it communicates with its controllers are subject to regulation too.

None of this is radically new. As we have seen, the Leviathan has long sought the help of those private entities with the means, capacity, and technology to contribute to larger security objectives. And outside security issues, intermediary regulation is one of the principal tools we use to protect health and safety. It entails not just regulating the manufacture of cars so as to improve road safety; it can also involve more local action: We want to reduce lung cancer, heart disease, and emphysema, so jurisdictions ban workplace smoking to reduce secondhand smoke. We want to improve health and reduce obesity, so New York City bans artificial trans fats in restaurant food and forces chain restaurants to list the calorie count of every dish they serve. We regulate drug commerce to make sure the drugs our doctors prescribe actually work—and do not poison us. Authorities regulate all sorts of intermediaries to make products and foods safer. It is one of the main tools by which government influences mass behavior.[9]

The only real difference here is that we have not traditionally thought about protecting national security in terms of influencing mass behavior. We tend to think about national security as a matter of state-to-state relationships or, more recently, of controlling certain major nonstate actors, like Al-Qaeda, ISIS, and other terrorist groups. But in the world of many-to-many threats, we are going to have to learn to think about national security as an area not all that different from the many others in which government seeks to push all people toward a safer, healthier environment. So just as we have long accepted, even demanded, that government regulate drug manufacturers to ensure that our pharmaceuticals are safe and efficacious, we are going to have to get used to thinking about national and even global security as tied to the products and services we individually receive. And we will increasingly see regulation of those products and services to ensure that they incorporate security in their manufacture and delivery.

Setting Rules for Allocating Risk

Ultimately, however, regulation can get us only so far. The Leviathan, after all, is only so big, and as powerful as it may be, the ocean is so much bigger. So even as the Leviathan regulates directly and conscripts intermediaries as allies in preventing the defiance of little fish, it also needs somehow to incentivize all those little fish not merely to behave themselves but to swim as it desires. That is, it needs to persuade them to make incremental decisions that make for a more—rather than a less—secure environment. This task may sound impossible, but we actually do it every day with respect to health and safety. When we think about security in those terms, the world of many-to-many threats and defenses starts to look at least a little bit like the broader world of risk allocation. Your house might burn down tomorrow, so you insure it. You might slip and fall in a store because of water left on the floor, and we have a liability system both to compensate you if that happens because of the storekeeper's negligence and to incentivize the store owner to keep that floor dry—and to have insurance of her own. If we want to influence the literally countless decisions that people and companies make and nudge each incremental decision toward the creation of secure platforms, it is critical to allocate risk and liability sensibly.

One of the best ways to create insecure environments is to allocate risk badly, making the wrong actors bear the risks associated with bad outcomes—actors who actually cannot prevent those outcomes. One of the best ways to improve the security of those environments is to reallocate risk so that those actors capable of preventing the bad outcomes bear more of the risks associated with them.

Consider for a moment the complex relationship among private tort liability, public regulation, and insurance with respect to building residential housing. Building codes have been around for a long time. The ancient legal Code of Hammurabi prescribes death for the negligent homebuilder who builds a house that collapses and kills its owner—and death for the homebuilder's son if the collapse kills the owner's son. But the modern system of risk allocation is far more complicated than a simple set of rules enforced by the occasional inspection. The landlord knows she is potentially liable for damages should something go wrong. She has insurance to hedge against that financial risk. The insurance company, in turn, probably has reinsurance and requires as a condition of offering her the policy that she maintain the property in compliance with the local building code—and it reserves the right to inspect the property, thus becoming, in effect, a private enforcement arm of the government. In a large city, countless actors make decisions every day to make the aggregate environment more secure because, broadly speaking, the incentives are aligned properly.[10]

One measure of how well this system works—and it actually works remarkably well—is the low death toll in the 1989 Loma Prieta earthquake that hit the San Francisco Bay Area. Although the quake did extensive damage in a major urban area and registered 6.9 on the Richter scale, it killed only sixty-three people—most of them in road and bridge collapses, not in building collapses. Contrast that with the death toll in the comparably strong 2010 earthquake in Haiti, a country without a functioning system of building codes, liability, or insurance. Estimates of deaths from that quake vary, but some are upward of three hundred thousand people—with hundreds of thousands of homes and tens of thousands of businesses collapsing on the people inside them. This eclipses by an order of magnitude the death toll in the great east Japan earthquake of 2011, despite the fact that the Japanese quake was one hundred times stronger than the Haitian quake, and most of those killed in the Japanese quake died as a result of the tsunami it unleashed. Yes, endemic poverty plays a big role in explaining these differences, but the two points are interrelated: countries with endemic poverty tend to skimp on allocating risk fairly and rationally. A builder in Haiti does not fear Hammurabi. And he does not fear a lawsuit either.[11]

In the world of many-to-many threats and defenses, in critical respects security more resembles earthquake readiness than conventional threat management. And in facing this challenge, we want to be California, not Haiti. We want our legal system to distribute risk so as to incentivize the expenditure of resources—however marginal they may turn out to be—so as to encourage the design and implementation of safer systems and to discourage the headlong technological drift toward enhanced vulnerability. At the most fundamental level, this means ensuring that parties who negligently or recklessly introduce vulnerabilities into platforms will be liable for the damages those actions inflict on others.

Stated simply and in the abstract, this point seems so obvious as to require no defense. Who, after all, would argue in principle for impunity for those who design, market, and sell systems and products without regard for the risks that using them might entail for others? Who would argue for a regime that incentivizes recklessness—that, say, encourages people not to vaccinate their kids against communicable diseases or encourages the manufacture and distribution of products that enhance people's exposure to infectious agents? Indeed, ignore this principle in the biosecurity arena, and the foolishness of policy stands out as nakedly as it would in a regime that immunized builders against housing collapses. A company or laboratory that inadvertently released a pathogen—or failed to prevent an employee from doing so maliciously—would face ruinous liability in tort from those the pathogen harmed.

But rational risk-allocation systems do not always develop organically. For the first few decades of the auto industry, for example, carmakers were largely protected in tort against liability when car crashes killed or injured passengers—even when the injuries and deaths were caused by clear defects of which the companies were aware. Only as this liability rule changed in the 1970s did cars become dramatically safer.[12]

Similarly, today, the most developed of the mass empowerment platforms, the Internet, lacks any kind of sensible allocation of risk. Specifically, software vendors and Internet service providers are the modern age's equivalent of the car companies before Ralph Nader began his crusade for auto safety. In general, liability law for software vendors who sell insecure products is astonishingly protective. As law professor Michael D. Scott has summarized, "Software vendors have traditionally refused to take responsibility for the security of their software, and have used various risk allocation provisions of the Uniform Commercial Code (U.C.C.) to shift the risk of insecure software to the licensee [the consumer]. There were a few early cases in which licensees sought to have courts hold vendors liable for distributing defective software. These cases were unsuccessful."[13] The result, in the words of Internet security expert Bruce Schneier, is that "today there are no real consequences for having bad security, or having low-quality software of any kind. In fact, the marketplace rewards low quality. More precisely, it rewards early releases [of software] at the expense of almost all quality."[14]

How have software vendors managed to maintain this highly favorable litigation environment—one that provides incentives for innovation in all areas except security? Several key roadblocks have stood between plaintiffs and liability for software manufacturers. For one thing, the damages that software vulnerabilities cause tend to be economic, not physical, in nature and are thus barred in tort by the rule against recovery for solely economic harms. It is conceivable, of course, that software vulnerabilities could cause physical injuries—for example, if software failed in a hospital system and someone died as a result. But mostly, it leads to more pedestrian harms: identity thefts, lost intellectual property, damage to data, and the like.

Even where the harms are more physical in nature, there is some question as to whether software is an actual product or instead a service that the user licenses from the provider. This makes the application of product liability rules something of a misfit. And perhaps most fundamentally, the contracts to which users agree as a condition of licensing the software in the first place generally contain broad liability shields. Those terms of service you click through without reading often release the software provider from any responsibility if its product causes you harm. And that is true even if you are a large organization. Helen Mohrmann, the head of information technology at the Brookings Institution, describes how the software vendors on which she relies often delay patching known vulnerabilities in their products. What incentive do they have to do so, she asks? Brookings, after all, bears all the risk of using the product and has no recourse against the vendor if the company's delay results in compromised data or a significant and damaging intrusion.[15]

The case for liability standards for software goes back a long way. Schneier has been talking about the subject for a more than a decade. And as long ago as 2002, an expert panel of the National Research Council urged the consideration of "legislative responses to the failure of existing incentives to cause the market to respond adequately to the security challenge" of vulnerable software. "Possible options include steps that would increase the exposure of software and system vendors and system operators to liability for system breaches and mandated reporting of security breaches that could threaten critical societal functions."[16]

More recently, a paper by Heritage Foundation scholars Steven Bucci, Paul Rosenzweig, and David Inserra argued that liability rules erode cybersecurity both because companies face potential liability if they disclose information about breaches of their systems and also because "the full costs of any breach are not incorporated in the manufacturing costs of the product that is causally tied to the breach." The authors call for Congress "to reverse the system of incentives so that costs are borne by those who [cause] them, not by innocent consumers." The creation of a liability system, they argue, will likely "[lead] to the development of an insurance system against liability. The insurance function allows a further spreading of risk in a way that fosters broad private-sector responsiveness."[17]

The details of what a legislative scheme for liability standards in software would look like are enormously complicated and vexing, and the creation of such a system is by no means cost free. What level of security does a software product need to have for its manufacturer to survive a lawsuit? Given that perfect security is impossible, what separates mere imperfection from negligence? What degree of protection should vendors be allowed to arrange for themselves contractually through license agreements, particularly when they are effectively giving licenses away for free? Such a scheme, at least in the short term, would likely have the effect of delaying substantially the time it takes to bring new products to market. It would probably also make software less rich with features—each of which adds complexity and therefore vulnerability to the overall package. In addition, as with any other liability scheme, the costs of compliance are ultimately rolled over from the manufacturer or service provider onto consumers; in the software world, that could mean higher costs of software and inhibition of crowdsourcing and other types of free software. And the jurisdictional problems do not go away with sound rules in any one country. If the United States imposes liability standards and other countries do not, might this merely encourage innovation elsewhere and discourage it domestically?

Without venturing to resolve all these questions here, we merely point out that in the world of many-to-many threats, the user of a platform cannot bear all the risk associated with that platform; those who introduce new vulnerabilities to a shared global system on which we all depend need to bear some of the risk too. And policy makers need to make sure, as these platforms develop, that they are allocating risk in a fashion that incentivizes the platform's secure flourishing, not its propagation of danger and vulnerability.

Defining the Rules of Private Interactions

Government has another power in this project, one that goes beyond forbidding and requiring conduct directly, regulating the intermediaries through whom we conduct business, and defining the proper liability and risk-allocation rules. This power overlaps in significant respects with all of these functions, but it also has distinct qualities of its own. It is also subtler than these very overt powers: government plays an important role in mediating disputes related to the empowerment and vulnerability that new technologies spread among the governed. The exercise of this power will almost always take the form of some type of regulation, whether direct or indirect. But the mediating function takes place on a different plane than does the regulation itself and at a somewhat antecedent stage of policy making. Before government can decide how to protect you from a particular threat, it has to decide whether to protect you from that threat. It has to decide whether even to define the conduct at issue as a threat at all. These are values questions, and they do not answer themselves.

Invent the firearm, for example, and some citizens will feel protected by it; others will find the empowerment of their fellow citizens threatening. Ultimately, the government—as the political expression of our collective will—must resolve such controversies by defining which perceived threats it will protect against and which the citizen must simply live with. The mode by which it does so might be regulation, but it might also be the absence of regulation. Or it might be affirmative protection of the use of the technology. In the case of firearms, in the United States anyway, the Constitution comes down decisively on the side of those who wish to own and use firearms, and the law protects those who feel threatened by this only in limited senses: by keeping guns out of certain places, for instance, and out of the hands of certain people, as well as by offering legal protections against the use of firearms in ways that menace or injure individuals. Governments in other countries have mediated those tensions very differently. Authorities in the United States also drew the lines very differently with respect to automobiles: driving is not a right but a privilege that has to be affirmatively granted by a state government before it can be exercised. These policies are not inevitable; rather, they are choices, and they go a long way toward defining what society thinks of as accepted risk in day-to-day life. Americans risk mass shootings in a way that societies with more restrictive access to guns do not; on the other hand, Americans today would not tolerate the levels of traffic fatalities endured daily in countries with laxer attitudes toward driving.

In the case of technologies of mass empowerment, disputes over uses have often arisen as privacy issues—at least so far. The most visible of these issues involve our mosaics and, more broadly, anxieties about "Big Data." But the problem arises also in the case of robotics, for example, in the fairly widespread concerns about domestic nonmilitary uses of often very small drones. The FAA's mandate from Congress to open the domestic US airspace to unmanned aerial systems has run into a wall of political concerns over the implications for individual privacy of domestic drones in the hands of both law enforcement and private parties. Privacy groups have asked the FAA to act affirmatively to protect privacy in the context of regulating drones—though that is not part of its statutory mandate—and the agency has agreed that it needs to do so. In addition, a number of state legislatures have taken up legislation to restrict the use of drones within their borders in the name of privacy. There are nonprivacy questions as well. Consider, for example, the debates over genetically modified food, where new technology has allowed the manipulation of the genomes of many crops in a fashion that some people find threatening and thus wish to restrict or stop entirely.[18]

The basic problem is inescapable. Any time a technology radically enhances what people can do and thus gives people the ability to exert power over one another—by enabling them to kill one another at a distance in the case of guns, to glean an enormous amount of information about one another in the case of the mosaic, to watch others remotely in the case of domestic drones, and to manipulate the basic genetic structures of the foods we eat in the case of genetically modified crops—there will be disputes over that technology's use. And government at some level has to mediate those disputes if the conflicts do not resolve on their own in a fashion that wins widespread acceptance.

In the world of many-to-many threats and defenses, government mediation takes on particular importance for a number of reasons. For one thing, as we have seen, technologies of mass empowerment leave the lines between national security, corporate security, and individual security pretty fuzzy. A Saudi hacker like OxOmar who wants to attack Israel does so by hacking the national airline's website and also compromising the credit card numbers of thousands of individual Israelis. A great many attacks on companies and government agencies, including by state actors, take place by means of phishing attacks on individuals within those companies. In other words, there is a relationship between the degree of our individual vulnerability and the security and vulnerability of our larger institutions. And thus, there is necessarily also a relationship between the manner in which we mediate disputes over our individual vulnerability and the security outcomes we can expect over time for much larger institutions. It is hard to build secure institutions out of individuals who are not themselves secure.

More fundamentally, these disputes have a way of defining, at least at the margins, what government is going to protect us from—that is, what we will define as an attack in the first place and what we will view as just part of modern life. In a society that accepts that everyone is watching everyone, having your neighbor's drone fly onto your property and watch you through your window might not be considered an attack. In our society, the prospect still seems pretty horrifying. On the other hand, we routinely tolerate privacy intrusions that more prudish societies would consider the grossest forms of assault on personal dignity and seclusion. The seminal 1890 *Harvard Law Review* article that first proposed "the right to privacy," remember, was occasioned by Louis Brandeis's horror at the use of cameras by the press to take pictures of society figures. An inherent part of creating a safer general environment is defining which private engagements are sufficiently threatening to warrant legal protection and which are not. What constitutes an attack against which the Leviathan is going to promise protection? With respect to what sort of vulnerability are you on your own? And for what sort of vulnerability should we turn for protection to some other actor—to privateers or hired-gun bodyguards?[19]

These questions answer themselves with respect to the employment of new technologies to bring about old harms—a murder by means of anthrax is still a murder, and sextortion by means of malware is still sexual extortion. But they are not self-answering with respect to perceived harms that are organic to the new technologies themselves. You could not drive drunk—something we now regard as a crime because of the vulnerability it creates for others—until cars allowed us to drive. And it was not inevitable that we would define the lines of protection against drunk driving in the way we did. We could have taken a far less protective position roughly analogous to the one we take with guns—that, say, people have a right to drink and a right to drive and that the state only has an interest when their use of those rights actually causes someone else harm. Similarly, only the advent of genetically modified crops compels us to consider whether to define them as beneficial or threatening or both. And only the advent of the mosaic makes us think about how we want to benefit and protect ourselves from the aggregation of huge quantities of individually trivial pieces of personal data in the hands of parties who may not have our best interests at heart.

There are no generalizable answers to these questions. They are technology specific—and different governments will handle them differently. European and American authorities have taken divergent positions toward genetically modified organisms, for example, with the European Union adopting a restrictive posture that considers them harmful to health and the environment, whereas the US government regards them as safe, economically efficient, and poverty reducing. At a more nascent level, as we have seen, different authorities within the United States are taking quite different approaches to domestic drones—with Congress pushing the FAA to open the skies to a wide array of actors, and state governments trying to apply the brakes in the name of broader privacy protections.[20]

The European Union and the United States have also taken very different, and both very complicated, positions with respect to the privacy issues surrounding mosaic data as well. Indeed, privacy issues involving mosaic data are perhaps the most developed example of the challenge of mediating private interactions in the world of technologies of mass empowerment. The Internet, after all, is the one mass-empowerment platform with which we all engage constantly. The sheer volume of private interactions on and around the Internet—both those that make us safer and those that expose us to greater vulnerability—would suggest an urgent need to define the category of interactions we seek to protect individuals from. Yet, so far, we have failed miserably to do so. The rhetoric of privacy is part of the problem here, a vocabulary we use because we do not have a better word for the value—or values—that we instinctively wish to protect.

The details of a regulatory scheme for mosaic data lie well beyond the scope of this book. And no such scheme—to the extent one could conjure it—would be generalizable to other technologies of mass empowerment anyway. That said, certain common strategies for thinking about the government's mediating function may have application across technologies. One of the most basic guiding principles will be the need to transcend current conceptions of the protections we expect from government and to develop new vocabularies to distinguish the harms against which we expect government to defend us from and the exposures with which we expect people to learn to live. The issues we debate in the language of privacy are, in some respects, the leading edge of that conversation.

We need, to put it simply, both to describe our behavior with respect to the mosaic more accurately and to adopt principles that offer more useful guidance than does the hopelessly broad and amorphous concept of privacy as to what activities we should and should not tolerate. The relevant concept, we suspect, lies not in protecting some elusive positive right to user privacy but, rather, in protecting a negative right—a right against the unjustified use of user data in a fashion adverse to the user's interests. This conception of the user's interests in the mosaic is more modest than privacy. It does not ask to be "left alone." It accepts, rather, that when you give hundreds of companies thousands of facts about yourself in an ongoing fashion, you are not going to be left alone. It asks, instead, for a certain degree of protection against tangible harms as a result of a user having entrusted elements of his or her mosaic to a third party.

Sometimes, to be sure, these tangible harms will implicate privacy as it is traditionally understood, but sometimes they will not. In our view, government should seek to protect us against the malicious, reckless, negligent, or unjustified handling, collection, or use of a person's data in a fashion adverse to that person's interests and in the absence of that person's knowing consent. This is in some respects closer to the non-self-incrimination value of the Fifth Amendment than to the privacy value of the Fourth Amendment. It asks only that we not be forced to be the agents of our own injury when we entrust our data to others—asking not necessarily that our data remain private but that they not be used as a sword against us without good reason.[21]

BUILDING RESILIENT ARCHITECTURES

If we accept—as we certainly should—that preventing all attacks is impossible, one critical aspect of creating safer environments is graceful failure. A bombing will always be a horrible event. But it is dramatically more horrible when first responders are untrained, when hospitals cannot handle a sudden surge of trauma patients, or when investigative capacity is not good enough to track the bombers down before they strike a second time. Technologies of mass empowerment force us to think about how many defenses we want to build into our systems and where and how to allow them to fail.

In any discussion of this subject, a deep tension develops quickly between those who think in terms of top-down, regulatory actions of various sorts and those who think in terms of highly distributed, bottom-up changes to system design, technical architecture, individual behavior, and culture. That is, a tension develops between those who ask what government can do and those who ask what the users and developers of platforms can do on their own, either individually or collectively. In our view, both of these general intellectual perspectives have an essential place in the creation of more secure environments, and the relationship between them should be iterative and mutually reinforcing, not preclusive and antagonistic.

At a societal level, the problem of resilience forces government to think about disaster planning. How much stored antibiotic do we want on hand for the day when the drone flying over the stadium really is packed with aerosolized anthrax? How many people—and which ones—do we want to vaccinate preemptively against smallpox, a virus extinct in the wild, when the vaccination itself will cause serious illness, even death, in a small number of people? More diffusely, how much do we want to invest in reducing the time from the first presentation of a new illness to a viable treatment for it? Reducing the time from bug to drug could prove crucial when a new pathogen appears on the scene, either by design or naturally. On the other hand, developing such treatments requires a massive—and very costly—research effort. Meanwhile, malaria, an infectious disease still endemic in many parts of the world, kills millions of people every year. So the marginal dollar spent on preparedness for a smallpox outbreak—not to mention the unknown pathogen—in a world of limited resources may well come at the cost of dealing with real, nonspeculative public health problems that exist today and already inflict mass casualties worldwide.

Still, a big part of running a safe neighborhood is a measure of certainty about what will happen when things go wrong. These investments are reminiscent of questions about how much one should spend on insurance policies. But another side of the question of resilience is less about hedging one's bets in the event of disaster and more about the design of systems to handle failures. This point has less application to biotechnology platforms than to networked computers—since humans have, by and large, not built and designed the former systems but have inherited them from nature. That is changing, of course, and there may come a day when genetic code is so engineered—and perhaps even so networked—that we have to think pervasively about how well or badly our coding errors will fail us in the interactions between our creations and the world. But for now at least, the resilience of the systems we design is largely a question for the world of human-built machines.

While this issue presents a set of top-down regulatory questions (what fail-safes do we require or encourage?), it also presents a set of bottom-up opportunities. Most hardware and software systems, after all, are designed not with regulatory mandates in mind but to please consumers. They are designed to comply with industry standards defined ultimately by standard-setting entities, many of them nongovernmental. These standards, in turn, are intended mainly to create technological compatibility across brands and products. An environment secure against both accident and attack requires a great deal of thought on the part of product developers and standard-setting bodies as to what will happen when things go wrong.

For an example of how much more secure environments are when these decisions are made well, consider Microsoft Word. Readers above a certain age—and that age is not all that great—will probably remember a time when using Word (or any other word-processing program) to compose a document carried real risks. If your computer crashed and you had not saved the document recently, you were out of luck. The crash probably meant that your entire computer had stopped functioning and needed to be restarted. And the failure to save meant that all your work would be lost; saving a document was a manual affair—disk space and speed being at a premium. The costs of failure, in other words, were very high.

Now, by contrast, the costs of failure have been dramatically reduced. For one thing, crashes tend to be more localized—to individual programs or sometimes even individual windows. More importantly, the program automatically saves files frequently and, in the event of a crash, reverts to the last intact version it can access—often saved only minutes or seconds before the malfunction. The result is that a system failure is much less likely to be debilitating. You might lose your last few sentences or paragraphs, but you are unlikely to lose the great American novel in its entirety.

The tasks of making systems more robust in the face of failure, in other words, belong not just to the Leviathan (which needs to train and fund first responders, store vaccines, write all kinds of rules, and sometimes convene standard-setting bodies) but also to intermediaries (who produce the systems we use) and to end users (who use those systems in ways that make failures more or less damaging). Zittrain has argued that there is enormous cybersecurity potential in focusing on the latter two groups rather than on the policy layer. He suggests that intermediaries should tweak systems so as to allow individual users to protect one another, analogizing the relationships between Internet users to mutual-aid treaties between countries. "The principle of distribution rather than centralization is really one of mutual aid, and it can be extended to the cybersecurity problem," he writes. Zittrain describes a simple system based on the mutual-aid concept to keep websites available even when cyberattacks have taken them down. "It is time for a metaphorical NATO for the Internet, not among states but among Internet participants, something built into its fabric through Web servers and clients. There is strength in numbers, and we can draw upon those principles of mutual aid that built the Internet to begin with in order to gather otherwise powerless individual entities together into a stronger force." At the core of the proposal is what Zittrain calls "mirror as you link." Under this system, a given website would not only display the links a user requested but actually download the linked-to pages. "The website stores not just its own information but everything it links to as well. If one site later fails or is blocked, the user can request a copy of it from the server that linked him there." As Zittrain notes, "Each participating site embodies the principle of mutual aid: if one site goes down, others will duplicate and disseminate its information. In exchange, that one site promises to do the same for those sites to whom it links."[22]

People will surely argue about the merits of Zittrain's specific proposal, but it gives texture to the idea that resilience is designed and engineered, not necessarily inherent. And it need not—indeed, cannot—be designed exclusively by the Leviathan. Zittrain offers many other examples, some of them granular and some of them more conceptual and aspirational, in his book *The Future of the Internet and How to Stop It*.[23]

In a world in which we mean to govern mass access to radically empowering technologies, there will be building codes, but there will also be cooperative arrangements between entities for mutual defense and support. The latter will play an enormous role in the environment's aggregate security.

Radically Empowered Citizen Defenses

Finally, a secure environment depends on an engaged and mobilized citizenry—a true bottom-up awareness and willingness to act in the interests of security that are not driven or directed by the Leviathan in any meaningful sense. On September 11, one hijacked plane, United Flight 93, did not slam into its intended target in Washington, DC, but crashed into a field in Pennsylvania instead. The result, the deaths of forty innocent people onboard, was a tragedy, but one with a body count of a different order of magnitude than if the plane had hit the Capitol or White House. The simple explanation for what happened on Flight 93 that day was that the passengers, aware of what had happened on the other hijacked flights, heroically took matters into their own hands, stormed the cockpit, and forced the plane down.

A mobilized, aware citizenry is an extremely powerful security instrument that helps investigators when bad things happen. It also generates tips to law enforcement of a sort that can prevent bad things from happening in the first place. It both drives markets for security goods—products and services that make the broader environment safer—and directs human and financial resources toward the innovations that feed those markets. Flight 93 is not the only example of an alert citizenry, in the absence of law enforcement, taking matters into its own hands to stop bad actors in real time. As noted above, two separate efforts to bring down airliners by individuals who had smuggled bombs onto transatlantic flights failed when passengers subdued the would-be bombers. On a more mundane level, alert, watchful citizens are key to keeping crime down; muggers and rapists tend to prefer dark alleys for a reason.

Conversely, a complacent citizenry excessively reliant on the Leviathan for its security is nearly impossible to protect. Government alone can protect against external military threats and do a certain amount of policing, but without the force multiplier of people willing to assist and take certain basic matters into their own hands, creating a secure general environment is a fool's errand. Imagine a city in which nobody bothers to lock their doors, most crime goes unreported, and people harbor a diverse array of ideological objections to participating in any sort of mass efforts at communal security. That is a rather close analogy to a populace that harbors ideological objections to immunizing its children against infectious diseases and cannot muster the will to use strong passwords or to keep software up to date.

Indeed, in the world of many-to-many threats, an aware, engaged, self-actuated citizenry is particularly critical. With the key infrastructure in private hands and the ability to innovate—for good or for ill—dispersed widely among private individuals, we have to conceptualize the task of securing the environment as dispersed as well. And while many of

our tools for ensuring security will rely on regulatory mandates and economic incentives, we should not ignore the role of ideology and public-
spiritedness either. Nor should we ignore the basic human instinct of
simple self-defense, which can drive the development of whole industries
devoted to offering protections the Leviathan cannot provide. The cybersecurity industry, after all, is largely a function of companies' and individuals' need to protect themselves. Self-preservation is a powerful motivator.
We should not underestimate either the power of large groups of connected individuals, companies, and organizations all pulling in the same
direction to improve the security of the environment.

For the Leviathan, some aspects of the engaged citizenry are unambiguously positive—for example, the eyes-and-ears dimensions, the innovations, and the development of industries designed to furnish security
goods. The Leviathan wants more cybersecurity powerhouses like Mandiant—now part of a company called FireEye—and more online bodyguards
hirable by its citizens, and it wants the cadre of highly trained people who
are all, or mostly, working in the interests of its own security policies.

But other aspects of intense citizen engagement also present governance challenges. A fine line, after all, separates an engaged citizenry from
a mob or from a group of vigilantes. Indeed, the word "vigilante" comes
from the so-called vigilance committees—citizen groups that kept a rough
sort of extralegal justice on the frontier in the pre–Civil War era.[24]

The online world is full of modern-day vigilantes. "We could not stay
silent after the pompous boasting of the Saudi hacker," an Israeli hacker
told a newspaper after OxOmar surfaced, adding that "a few Israeli hackers came together and decided on various responses for each cyber activity
that would be carried out against Israel, including responses beyond the
cyber world." The hacker added that, in case of a terrorist attack, "we will
make every effort to publish the terrorist's personal details and those of his
family. . . . Sadly, the State of Israel does not support an offensive policy
so we are forced to maintain a great deal of secrecy. If we are caught we're
facing a harsh punishment."[25]

Internet vigilantism has actively targeted pedophiles, animal abusers,
scammers, hackers, identity thieves, and intellectual property violators. Vigilantes have resorted to tactics as diverse as public shaming, taking down
websites, online harassment, private investigation, collaboration with law
enforcement agencies, and, according to some claims, even physical violence. In one famous case, a group of American hackers led a Nigerian
spammer on a weeks-long wild goose chase into a dangerous region of

Chad. In another, in the hopes of spurring law enforcement to act on the information, Anonymous published the Internet protocol addresses of 190 persons it claimed had been viewing child pornography online. It is also possible that Anonymous forced the drug gang Los Zetas to release a kidnapped hacker by threatening to publicize identifying information about Zetas members that could have led to their assassinations or arrests. Many of the tactics involved in such operations likely violated the law.[26]

Sometimes vigilantism is synonymous with patriotic hacking: during the 2012 war in Gaza, pro-Palestinian hackers attacked several Israeli websites, while several pro-Israeli hackers responded in kind; many of these people, we can presume, are nationals of the combatant sides. Often, however, the vigilantes share not national allegiances but rather an ideology that transcends borders and nationality. In sympathy with the Palestinians, Anonymous launched "OpIsrael," in which its members—most presumably not Palestinian—claimed to have knocked dozens of Israeli sites offline. In continuation of that campaign, Anonymous and the Turkish hacking group Red Hack claimed to have infiltrated the computers of Israel's Mossad intelligence service in March 2013 and posted the names of alleged Mossad employees supposedly obtained through the hacking (an allegation that the Israeli government has denied and on which media commentaries have cast doubt).[27]

The great majority of these hacking activities, despite bringing a little fame and glory to the hackers, resulted in relatively minor harm to the hacked, especially when the victim was an institution rather than an individual. The practice is sufficiently new that it attracts media attention, and there is a growing culture of ideological hacking, one that replaces protest marches and the brute force of guns with the more sophisticated use of a keyboard. But for the most part, vigilantism has yet to cause serious damage.

Yet it is not at all clear that the costs inflicted by vigilantism will remain low. A diffused world of threats and defenses, coupled with the growing empowerment of individuals and groups, is likely to breed more of a frontier self-help mentality and more privately initiated attacks and counterattacks. The challenges of state policing of threats and defenses will have to include managing vigilantism and making sure that the state's monopoly over the administration of justice is maintained.

The key point, of which Anonymous offers a daily reminder, is that while hackers will sometimes be patriotic—and thus act as a force multiplier for state policy—the engaged citizenry will not always pull in the same direction as government security policies. Indeed, the conception of security that the engaged citizenry embraces may differ considerably from the conception envisioned by the Leviathan, and even when the goals are the same, the citizenry's means will not always comport with the Leviathan's rules. Consider, for better or worse, Edward Snowden's leaks and the disparity between his citizen fans and governmental would-be prosecutors. The question of how engaged we want citizens to be is therefore not an easy one. The government can immunize the conduct of the intermediaries it enlists to help it in its own security tasks, just as it once immunized privateers for conduct otherwise indistinguishable from piracy. But it generally does not immunize the provision of the protection you seek from companies. Nor does it immunize the collective or individual self-defense actions that private citizens might take. Those have to comply with the law—and the most effective ones may not.

To take a perhaps trivial example, in 2012 a group of animal rights activists in Pennsylvania tried to use a drone to film a hunting club's pigeon shoot. The use of drones by animal rights and environmental investigators to film and expose actions they oppose has unsurprisingly gained ground as the technology has developed and become more affordable. In one case, a Texas man filmed from the air an apparent river of pigs' blood leaking from a meatpacking plant into a creek. But such surveillance, in turn, raises a question for its targets: what can one do to protect oneself from unwanted drone snooping? The members of the Wing Pointe hunting club in Pennsylvania developed a novel, if crude, approach to this problem when a group called Showing Animals Respect and Kindness (SHARK) started flying an octocopter drone over their pigeon hunt: they shot it down. That, in turn, triggered a state police investigation and, according to SHARK, caused $4,000 in damage to its drone. How does society want to think about such conflicts? If you try to spy on a commercial hunting ground, do you simply run the risk that someone will turn his shotgun on your drone? Do we want to insist that people submit to paparazzi when they are engaged in legal activities? What about when they are engaged in environmental infractions—or worse? What sort of right of self-defense do we believe in for these sorts of infringements?[28]

This question is already playing out in the less trivial domain of cybersecurity, where an active debate has erupted over the legality of so-called hacking back—the practice of going on the offensive against hackers as a form of cyberdefense. Hackbacks fall along a spectrum of aggressiveness. On the more defensive side, they can simply involve placing on one's system honeypot-type files that a hacker would want to steal; once stolen, the files phone home with information about the computers on which they are being stored, thereby outing their thieves. Think of them as the equivalent of the antitheft systems consumers place in cars, which identify a stolen vehicle's location. On the more aggressive end, hackbacks can also involve active intrusions into an attacker's computer. As former Homeland Security policy chief Stewart Baker has written in defense of hacking back, "The tools attackers use to control compromised computers are full of security holes. . . . This is great news for cybersecurity."

That is actually a contested point, and as Baker acknowledges, also contested is whether—great news or not—hacking back is legal. Indeed, the weight of opinion, from which Baker dissents, is that the same Computer Fraud and Abuse Act that prevents unauthorized intrusions by hackers also prevents unauthorized intrusions on hackers—even in real-time, self-defense situations. As Fourth Amendment scholar Orin Kerr writes, the computer-intrusion law is a trespassing statute, and "you don't have a right to break into someone else's house to retrieve your stuff" just because he stole it from your house. "That's a trespass." Paul Rosenzweig raises other issues: international law, he warns, is likely to frown on private-sector "self-help outside the framework of state-sponsored action," and hackbacks by American private-sector actors against actors in other countries will "almost certainly . . . violate the domestic law of the country where a non-US computer or server is located."[29]

We do not mean here to delve deeply into the details of these disputes. We offer only the modest suggestion that in a healthy environment, particularly one in which the government's own ability to protect people is well short of total, the law should not too readily impair the right of self-defense. In a world of aggressive hacking, there has to be some room for raising the price of bad acts for those who would attack us. In a world in which someone flies a drone over your house, there has to be some latitude to defend against the drone. The robotic spider should not receive greater legal protection against the stomping boot than does the natural spider. Put differently, it simply has to be the case that in a world of diminished government protection, the individual has greater latitude to take matters into her own hands—as well as to hire bodyguards who will help her do so.

The mobilized citizenry, in sum, presents at once a huge force multiplier to the Leviathan in security terms, an independent and uncoordinated security force of its own, and a deep challenge whose power and potential, like those of the Leviathan itself, always threaten lawlessness and danger as well as greater security. Power to the people, after all, exists in a hostile symbiosis of its own with liberty, security, privacy, and the rule of law.

Conclusion

This is only a rough outline of the domestic tools available to manage security in the world we are entering. Each element of this typology could support a book of its own. None of them offers a magic bullet. In a world with technologies of mass empowerment, most people will use this power to do great or ordinary things, and some will use it to do horrible things. Policy cannot and should not aspire to eliminate this risk—and neither individually nor collectively will these strategies achieve that. Particularly in combination with one another—and in combination with a healthy degree of platform surveillance—they offer, rather, a way to think about organizing society so as to minimize the risks of a grossly empowered citizenry: to allow the vast majority of people to enjoy the great benefits of technology while maximizing society's ability to deter, detect, and bounce back from efforts to use new technologies to perpetrate violence and other abuse.

The key point here is to counsel against despair at the enormity of the governance problem. While there is no magic policy solution to the security problems of the world we are entering, neither is society without power—in the form of government, in the form of industry, and in the form of loose collections of individuals—to make the environment safer. There are a lot of levers, and cumulatively they are highly significant.

The trouble, of course, is that the world of many-to-many threats is a world, not simply a domestic environment. And while some of these tools do extend the Leviathan's reach beyond its own domain, one cannot hope to make the world safer from radically empowering technologies without resorting to foreign policy tools—of extraterritorial reach, of diplomacy and international agreements, and of warfare—which inevitably play a big role in managing global security. We consider these next.

9

OPTIONS FOR
INTERNATIONAL GOVERNANCE

IN 2000, MORE THAN A DECADE before the controversy erupted over the publication of research on the H5N1 bird flu virus, Australian scientists sought to engineer a mousepox variant that would cause infertility in mice. Their purpose was not biological warfare or biodefense but pest control. In the course of the project, which we mentioned briefly in Chapter 1, the researchers accidentally created a virus of greater virulence than the parent strain. More worryingly in terms of potential biothreats, the new virus killed even mice that were genetically resistant to or had been vaccinated against the parent virus. As former Department of Homeland Security policy chief Stewart Baker later described it, "As a contraceptive, it turned out, the new virus was an overachiever. Dead mice don't have sex, and dead mice were what the virus produced. The new gene turned the formerly mild mousepox virus into a killer, overriding the genetic resistance of every unvaccinated mouse. And then it turned on the vaccinated mice, killing half of them for good measure."[1]

In January 2001, the researchers published their findings in the *Journal of Virology*, and their article has drawn considerable attention ever since. The experiment has been widely cited as heralding a new age in which small teams of scientists can use widely available tools and know-how to engineer highly contagious and deadly biological agents, although, as businessman and former Microsoft technology chief Nathan Myhrvold put it in 2013, "this case is just one example. Many more are pouring out of scientific journals and conferences every year."[2]

The decision to publish the mousepox article was highly controversial. Some critics worried that the paper might serve as a partial instruction manual for evildoers wishing to increase the virulence of smallpox and make it resistant to vaccination. Both the *Journal of Virology* and the so-called Fink Report, a 2004 National Research Council report titled *Biotechnology Research in an Age of Terrorism*, concluded that the benefits outweighed the marginal risk of publishing an article founded on an already extensive available literature. But whether one is inclined to defend the publication or criticize it, there is no denying that researchers made a virus closely related to human smallpox deadlier than it originally was, that the virus now tends to overcome immunization, that even the intended use of the virus—contagious infertility—would be catastrophic in humans, and that the recipe for building the mouse version of this doomsday virus is now in the public domain.[3]

For present purposes, however, we wish to focus on one aspect of the mousepox research that renders any effort to imagine its governance particularly difficult: the fact that the research was conducted, at least in part, in Australia, beyond the jurisdiction of the American government. The more recent H5N1 research was similarly undertaken overseas by Norwegian scientists in collaboration with American counterparts. The Fink Report noted not only the benefits of publishing the results of the 2000 mousepox experiments but also the futility of trying to prevent their publication; even had the US government successfully prevented publication here—an idea that raises deep First Amendment issues—the researchers could simply have published their results in a foreign publication. The Fink Report came out back in 2004—practically the Stone Age in terms of the dissemination of information that governments wish to keep under wraps. Today we know that scientists who wish to work around inconvenient governmental restraints on contraband knowledge have easy recourse to websites like WikiLeaks and any number of file-sharing systems. Put simply, today no government alone can prevent publication of recipes for even the deadliest pathogens.[4]

The limits of governmental power to regulate technologies of mass empowerment were again made vivid when the US Directorate of Defense Trade Controls Compliance, a part of the State Department, attempted in 2013 to stop the dissemination of blueprints for guns made with 3D printers. The American website that hosted the blueprints heeded the government's cease-and-desist letter to remove the files from public access; yet the files became immediately available for download, both in the United States and abroad, on several different websites, with download links posted on various social media websites. In the discussion thread on one such website, Reddit, commentators made flippant remarks regarding the impossibility of removing information from the Internet; one declared defiantly that he would download the files just "because the man said I couldn't have [them]." As a result, anyone anywhere with a 3D printer could download the files and print firearms. Indeed, that is exactly what two British journalists did in May 2013, using a £1,700 3D printer purchased off the Internet to make a plastic pistol called the "Liberator," which they then snuck onto a Eurostar train from London to Paris without being stopped. To get it through the checkpoints, they split the gun into three separate pieces, hid the pieces in their clothes, and walked through the metal detector without tripping it. Citing "safety and legal reasons," the journalists did not carry bullets or the gun's metal firing pin, but they claimed that these objects could easily be concealed to get past security. As powerful as the US Department of State may be, it cannot ultimately control what British journalists do—or make—with information available on the Internet. In fact, the book you are now reading itself contains citations to—and thus rebroadcasts—dangerous information.[5]

What might be the consequences of these developments for the state in its primary role as defender of the security of its people? As technologies of mass empowerment give foreign states, groups, and individuals the ability to strike from great distances, possibly without attribution, no state will have the singlehanded power to meet the threats posed to itself and its citizens, no matter how effective its domestic governance structures are. As in the case of other global threats that defy borders—climate change, asteroid impacts, or transnational crime—states will have to coordinate, cooperate, and sometimes act against each other, in a complex web of mixed-motive interaction. All of this will require a renegotiation of what sovereignty and independence stand for in the modern age.

In some ways, there is nothing new about this present situation. States and other political communities have always had to confront both domestic and foreign threats and adjust their relations with each other. What is new, as we have seen, is the potentially catastrophic scale of the danger and the need on the part of states to consider as strategic threats even individual actors operating from great physical distance and with little or no accountability. Protecting a state from other states, along with the occasional pirate, spy, or saboteur, is a markedly different project from protecting the state and its citizens against potential attacks from nearly two hundred other countries, countless nonstate organizations, and billions of people around the globe. While most countries, organizations, and individuals will pose no threat at all, and even those that try to will often not manage to do so effectively, the numbers of potential bad actors are still big—and they are growing. And critically, states do not know which of the myriad actors that could pose a threat actually do. Negotiating the boundaries of state power has thus become more urgent and more complex than ever before.

Advocates of greater global governance will require no further proof of its immediate necessity. A world of many-to-many threats, they reason, requires a coordinated global response, much as combating climate change does. If scientists in Australia, China, India, the United Kingdom, and the United States are to be held to uniform standards of responsible conduct in biological research, there must be a global rule-making authority, along with monitoring and enforcement bodies that can reach across borders. While no regulatory scheme can offer a complete security guarantee, anything short of a global arrangement is bound to leave dangerous gaps that, in the extreme, could put millions of people at risk.

There is much to this argument, and states will thus likely find it in their interest to enhance international cooperation with other states over the governance of technologies of mass empowerment, weaving additional threads into the existing web of multilateral agreements and institutions that govern the global space. They certainly should. But true global government is another thing entirely. Indeed, it is as fantastical today as it ever has been: there are too many political, cultural, religious, strategic, and logistical barriers in its way and too many uncertainties about its ultimate functioning even if it were to come into being. Any enhanced cooperation over the governance of technologies of mass empowerment will therefore likely develop on a regional or select-group basis rather than in a truly global fashion.

Enhanced global cooperation, even in its limited form, we suspect, will prompt a paradoxical countertrend of enhanced state unilateralism in dealing with the threats posed by technologies of mass empowerment. Without the ability to rely consistently on other sovereigns to police their territories and citizens effectively, some states will find it necessary to pursue their own security interests in defiance of other states' sovereignty, boundaries, or political independence. Indeed, both trends—greater cooperation and increased unilateralism—are already taking place alongside one another.

In this sense, the world of many-to-many threats and defenses is unlikely to bring about a dramatic transformation of international relations, which always consist of mixed cooperation and competition. States have many interests in cooperating with one another, but they also have competing interests that lead them to defect from cooperation and extract gains at the expense of other states. Yet a world of distributed threats, we predict, will exacerbate this tension between cooperation and competition. And driving both enhanced cooperation and unilateralism will be the same underlying force: the growing interests that states do and should have in what transpires in other states. Beyond a benevolent care for the well-being of people in other countries, any state's security is now dependent on security elsewhere. The success or failure of the regulatory and enforcement regimes throughout the globe now bears directly on the safety and security of one's own country and fellow citizens. Strong Leviathans are therefore likely to invest, whether unilaterally or in concert with others, in enhancing the capacity of weaker or failed countries to govern their own territories effectively. That is happening in Iraq now.

Of course, not all states are similarly situated with respect to cooperation, unilateralism, or governance enhancement. The United States is in a position to engage in unilateral actions far more than most other states in the international system, for example. It is also, however, a more likely target for attacks than are many other countries. Being on perpetual, simultaneous offense and defense means that the United States has a heightened interest both in increased multilateral cooperation and in ensuring its free hand for unilateral action. It is also uniquely positioned to invest in building other states' enforcement capacities. The self-interest calculation will, no doubt, be different for Venezuela or Nigeria. Being mindful of such variations among states, let us take a closer look at how states are already cooperating or going it alone and how these options are likely to play out in the future.

INTERNATIONAL COOPERATION AND ITS LIMITS

"If crime crosses borders, so must law enforcement. If the rule of law is undermined not only in one country, but in many, then those who defend it cannot limit themselves to purely national means," wrote Kofi Annan, then UN secretary-general, in describing the adoption of the United Nations Convention Against Transnational Organized Crime back in 2000. He added, "If the enemies of progress and human rights seek to exploit the openness and opportunities of globalization for their purposes, then we must exploit those very same factors to defend human rights and defeat the forces of crime, corruption and trafficking in human beings."[6]

On a conceptual level, it is hard to argue with Annan's point. The most straightforward means of combating transnational crimes—the way that ideally resolves the most jurisdictional clashes and is most conducive to peaceful international relations—would seem to be through international agreements that proscribe certain activities and require coordination among states in responding to them. Such agreements should seek to harmonize laws between states and provide for collaborative enforcement of those corresponding laws. Once laws blend better and successful coordination exists, it becomes much harder for individuals and groups to exploit gaps in domestic legislation and escape jurisdiction, even if some inevitable variations in actual enforcement practices persist.

The good news is that international enforcement cooperation and harmonization of law is already becoming a reality, at least to some extent. At present, several multilateral conventions coordinate the definition and scope of certain categories of crime, particularly what are commonly thought of as international crimes—genocide, crimes against humanity, war crimes, and certain acts of terrorism, such as airplane hijacking. Drug trafficking is the subject of another multilateral convention, and the 2000 Convention Against Transnational Organized Crime, about which Annan was commenting, is now supplemented by three protocols dealing with the trafficking of persons and small arms. Other multilateral conventions deal with arms control: prohibiting the stockpiling, trade, and use of certain weapons, including biological and chemical weapons. These treaties are not without consequence. For example, the Protocol to Prevent, Suppress, and Punish Trafficking in Persons, Especially Women and Children has been lauded as an effective, significant law enforcement accomplishment in reducing human trafficking. It brought trafficking into the public consciousness and drove several states to enact specific legislation to target it. This legislation proved far more effective for prosecuting traffickers than did the tangentially related criminal statutes that were previously the only weapon certain states had.[7]

The bad news is that current multilateral arrangements are far from optimal. For one thing, joining a treaty is optional for any state, and some countries have persistently refrained from ratifying these conventions. The Chemical Weapons Convention (CWC), for instance, has 190 parties, representing approximately 98 percent of the global population. Yet, only in September 2013, under enormous international pressure and facing the possibility of US military action, did Syria also accede to the CWC and pledge to abandon its chemical weapons program. Israel has signed the convention but has yet to ratify it. And the United States has still not fulfilled its own obligation under the CWC to destroy all of its chemical weapons stockpiles. Nor has it ratified other weapons conventions, such as those banning antipersonnel landmines and cluster munitions.[8]

Even when countries do ratify multilateral treaties, they often do so with reservations that free them from key substantive obligations. Several parties to the United Nations Convention Against Illicit Traffic in Narcotic Drugs and Psychotropic Substances issued such reservations, taking exception to certain obligations under the treaty, including international cooperation in enforcement. Belize, for one, announced, "The courts of Belize have no extra-territorial jurisdiction, with the result that they will have no jurisdiction to prosecute offences committed abroad unless such offences are committed partly within and partly without the jurisdiction, by a person who is within the jurisdiction." A number of countries also took exception to the full force of the convention with regard to indigenous populations, with Bolivia declaring that its "legal system recognizes the ancestral nature of the licit use of the coca leaf which, for much of Bolivia's population, dates back over centuries."[9]

In the antiterrorism context, many of fifty-eight signatories entered reservations, declarations, or understandings to the International Convention for the Suppression of Terrorist Bombings, limiting the application of some provisions or conditioning their operation in certain contexts. Pakistan, for instance, issued a declaration stating that "nothing in this Convention shall be applicable to struggles, including armed struggle, for the realization of the right of self-determination launched against any alien or foreign occupation or domination, in accordance with the rules of international law"—presumably intending to prevent the convention from applying to anti-India militants in Kashmir. In a similar vein, upon ratifying the Convention Against the Taking of Hostages, Iran declared that "fighting terrorism should not affect the legitimate struggle of peoples under colonial domination and foreign occupation in the exercise of their right of self-determination."[10]

Meaningful international controls, moreover, generally require coordination not only on the prescriptive front—that is, in deeming a particular action illegal—but also in actual detection, apprehension, and prosecution of offenders. And even when treaties achieve widespread ratification, significant gaps in compliance tend to remain. Unsurprisingly, most treaties of this sort lack any real enforcement measures. The recently adopted Arms Trade Treaty is a case in point. It aims to limit the sale of arms on the black market, to stem the tide of arms flowing to conflict regions—such as Russian arms to Syria—and, more generally, to limit the availability of weapons and thereby their capacity to fuel conflict. It obliges each state to comply with its directives within its own territory, but—and there is the rub—includes no international enforcement measures; rather, it merely "encourages" states to cooperate with each other. Such encouragement does not help much where treaty members have neither the capacity nor the will to enforce their international obligations with vigilance—much less to cooperate with one another on enforcement measures.[11]

Some treaty regimes do contemplate transnational monitoring, if not direct enforcement, as a mechanism for promoting compliance. The 1993 Chemical Weapons Convention, for instance, established the Organization for the Prohibition of Chemical Weapons, whose mandate includes inspections and verification activities in military and industrial sites worldwide. Such activities include "challenge inspections," which any state party to the convention has the right to request on short notice regarding any location under the jurisdiction or control of any other state party. The Nuclear Non-Proliferation treaty, which seeks to secure a monopoly over nuclear weapons for the five permanent members of the UN Security Council, offers another example, requiring non–nuclear weapons states to accept International Atomic Energy Agency safeguards, including inspections, to ensure their compliance with obligations not to acquire nuclear weapons.[12]

Yet, transnational monitoring is far from a perfect guarantee of compliance. Some relevant regimes—most disturbingly, the 1972 Biological Weapons Convention—do not include any mandated monitoring. Even where mandated, monitoring is not always put in practice; no state has invoked the option to demand a challenge inspection in another state under the Chemical Weapons Convention. Moreover, some states have consistently evaded or impeded international monitors—think of the Iraqi and Iranian evasions of international weapons inspectors. And nonstate actors are likely to benefit from the lack of effective international cooperation even where international monitoring does take place and indicates noncompliance.

Individual states can address some of these compliance deficits by agreeing to assist each other's enforcement efforts through extradition of suspects, evidence sharing, joint investigations, and the like. Such arrangements, however, for the most part operate as features of bilateral or, at most, regional agreements. They do not operate globally and thus leave many countries outside any mandatory cooperative framework. In some areas, like computer crime, the gaps are very large indeed. Moreover, extradition and legal assistance are almost always discretionary. Many states will not agree to extradite their own citizens, even when they have no intention of holding those citizens accountable domestically for conduct for which they are wanted overseas. Moreover, even a state that is party to an extradition agreement might not feel obligated to heed a particular extradition request. Such refusals are not always nefarious. They sometimes reflect substantive differences in values. The tension in the summer of 2013 between the United States, Russia, and China over the extradition of Edward Snowden, the wanted National Security Agency (NSA) leaker, is a case in point. The United States expected Hong Kong to extradite Snowden for compromising NSA secrets and sought his return from Russia too. But would it really extradite to China someone whom the People's Liberation Army suspected of disclosing operational details of, say, how to circumvent the Great Firewall, the mass surveillance and censorship operation run by the Chinese Ministry of Public Security and officially known as the Golden Shield Project? And would it really send back to Russia someone whom President Vladimir Putin accused of compromising secrets of the Federal Security Service of the Russian Federation? Many Americans would regard such a person as meriting political asylum precisely for having violated Chinese or Russian criminal laws. When does free speech justify violating the law? The lack of any domestic consensus around this question suggests little hope for building an international one.

Even if an agreement on extradition could be secured, extradition itself depends on the ability to detect and apprehend the suspect. And this too requires cooperation. States can and sometimes do share intelligence and expertise and even render actual physical assistance in the detection, apprehension, and prosecution of suspects. But not all states are similarly capable in investigative matters; nor do all states have real sovereign control over their entire territory.

At present, we do not have a world police force, and we are unlikely to see one in the near future. The UN Charter's vision of a standing UN army was never fulfilled. And while the UN Security Council may sometimes authorize on an ad hoc basis international peacekeeping operations or military actions—each carried out by national army contingents—such authorizations only materialize in cases of large-scale conflict or postconflict situations, never as means of policing in its traditional sense. The organized international community in its present condition can act to expel Iraq from Kuwait, but it cannot prevent a lone individual or a small terrorist cell from refining and spreading a virus.

The world's largest international police organization, Interpol, does include 190 member countries. But Interpol functions mostly as a liaison and as an information-sharing rather than an operational body. It keeps databases of criminals, maintains channels of communication and intelligence sharing, and assists member states in training personnel and developing best practices. But Interpol agents do not make arrests, and there is no Interpol jail for criminals. Even in its limited capacity, the organization faces the challenges of differences in language, culture, bureaucratic structures, and professional expertise. The fact is that even developed and highly capable states remain dependent on other states' domestic enforcement capacity and are thus, in effect, hostages to these other states' abilities and interests.

As we have noted, obstacles to cooperation among states are as old as states themselves. Yet the nature of modern security threats renders them particularly resistant to cooperative solutions. Part of the problem involves deep disagreement among states and societies as to which sorts of activities to suppress, permit, or encourage. Unlike with trafficking in women and children, say, or the hijacking of airplanes, many states regard the Internet, biotechnology, and robotics as facilitating desirable activities, even when those activities might violate the domestic laws of some countries. Consider the popular organization of the Arab Spring through social media or the use of drones by humanitarian watch groups to monitor refugees fleeing Darfur. International cooperation over regulation of these platforms would require agreement about the value and propriety of regulation. Given that different countries face different threats and stand to reap different benefits from new technologies, agreements will be hard to secure—just as it is hard, for example, to secure agreement on environmentally harmful carbon emissions from countries like China and India, which require economic growth to fight persistent and dire poverty.

Cyber-based crime, espionage, and warfare, in particular, remain underregulated domains that have so far resisted attempts at global agreement. The Council of Europe's cybercrime convention, which was open to accession by all countries, has only forty-two state parties at the moment, including the United States but not Russia and China. The mere definition of what constitutes a cyberattack is itself a point of contention, as are limitations on attacking civilian targets, the status of state-sponsored exploitations, protections for intellectual property, and Internet freedom. Here, too, profoundly divergent state interests and societal values prevent any real harmonization. When conflicting state interests inhibit cooperation over prescription or enforcement, any individual country's regulation of access to new technologies is bound to have limited practical effects. For instance, the US International Traffic in Arms Regulations, which impose restrictions on exports of certain materials and technologies from the United States, may end up having the unfortunate consequence of imposing costs on American companies without having any discernible effects on the proliferation of these technologies in and from other countries. After all, the ability to access, produce, and employ new technologies independently is what makes them mass empowering—potentially as weapons. Put restrictions on the ability to export certain robotic platforms from any one country, and you might create a negative incentive to develop them in that country but not materially diminish their availability anywhere else.[13]

Even where the world community largely subscribes to common values, coordination and enforcement with respect to technologies of mass empowerment present profound difficulties. Consider the Biological Weapons Convention, which prohibits, in Article 1, the development, production, stockpiling, and acquisition of "microbial or other biological agents, or toxins . . . of types and in quantities that have no justification for prophylactic, protective or other peaceful purposes." The convention, of course, was intended to regulate state biological weapons programs, not individual tinkering. Imagine what an international agreement would have to do to harmonize regulation of the benign or beneficial uses of agents or toxins, which in the hands of a bad actor might serve as a biological weapon. Harmonization would necessitate worldwide agreement on the conduct of scientific study and the operation of laboratories, pharmaceutical companies, and academic research facilities. It would require worldwide medical, veterinary, and agricultural standards for the use of biological agents and toxins. In any sort of strong form, such an agreement is almost inconceivable. In some ways it would be like attempting to regulate the worldwide use, stockpiling, and acquisition of knives: even if countries could agree on how to define a harmful use of knives, the prospects for effective monitoring and enforcement are too slim to justify the endeavor.[14]

NEW FORMS OF COOPERATION AND PRIVATIZATION

As unattainable as the ideal of true global governance is, that does not alter the modern reality that governance of a world of many-to-many threats will require, if it is to be effective at all, much deeper cooperation among states in policing and enforcement activities. States are generally loath to rely on one another to protect themselves and their citizens from significant threats emanating from other states' territories. But they will have no choice. Given the trajectory we are describing, it will become a matter of mutual necessity to concede some measure of domestic sovereignty and submit to transnational determinations of right and wrong, as well as to some intrusive enforcement mechanisms.

No pressure in this direction is greater than in the sphere of national security, including in meeting threats from terrorism and traditional warfare. So it is no surprise that some of the most effective and advanced models of international enforcement cooperation have developed in this field. Considering their various kinds and shapes gives us a window into the possibilities for transnational cooperation in the future regulation of new technologies.

One interesting model, which aspires to universal scope and reach, yet bypasses the domestic constraints of various countries, is the UN Counter-Terrorism Committee (CTC). This committee did not originate in a treaty, which would have required negotiation by all of the world's nations. It was formed instead through the powers of the Security Council under Chapter VII of the UN Charter to bypass the need to secure individual state consent for the definitions of crimes and their modes of enforcement. Prior to the establishment of the CTC, in 1999, Security Council Resolution 1267 simply ordered all states to impose air-travel restrictions, financial sanctions, and an arms embargo on Al-Qaeda. To monitor implementation of these measures, the resolution further established the so-called Sanctions Committee, which added Osama bin Laden and associated entities and persons, including financiers and facilitators, to its Consolidated List of designated targets in January 2001. Subsequent Security Council resolutions required all member states to enforce the sanctions regime against any person or entity so designated under the list. While the United States and a handful of other countries maintain their own national blacklists of alleged terrorists, many countries rely solely on the Consolidated List as the legal authority to impose sanctions against individuals and entities.[15]

The CTC and the Sanctions Committee, of course, reflect the interests of the most powerful states, including the five permanent members of the Security Council. Their actions have invited criticisms over legitimacy, accountability, and compatibility with human rights protections. Particularly controversial was the Sanctions Committee's order to freeze the assets of two Saudi businessmen on suspicion of involvement in terrorism—a directive that the European Court of Justice ordered European Union members to ignore because, in the court's opinion, it failed to provide the businessmen with due process. Still, notwithstanding these objections, antiterrorism sanctions have shown some signs of success and have the potential to be a valuable tool in the fight against transnational terrorism.[16]

On the regional level, states have shown some willingness to entrust greater powers to regional bodies for intervention in security matters. In the European Union, for example, domestic law enforcement units specialized in crisis responses (known as special intervention units) may be called to assist in internal crisis situations by request from any other member state. In Africa, the African Standby Force is a multinational pan-African military force with both civilian and police components. The details and functions of these various systems differ; the African Standby Force is controlled by the African Union, whereas the European special intervention units are commanded by their respective domestic governments and can only carry out operations in another European country at the request of that government. Still, these arrangements do have in common their provisions for the deployment of soldiers from regional allies who are ready to operate on another country's soil independently of that country's command-and-control structure. While all of these forces are designed for military-like operations, they form a possible model for a multinational police force tasked with a broader swath of law enforcement activities.[17]

Another model of international enforcement cooperation, one that can be defined as a form of collaboration with strong unilateral undertones, is the American-led Proliferation Security Initiative (PSI). The PSI is intended to interdict and seize weapons of mass destruction (WMD) materials on the high seas—security measures that international law presumably does not allow absent agreement between the interdicting state and the vessel's flag state. The PSI began in 2003 as a series of bilateral treaties entered into by the United States with countries that have registered maritime vessels. Designed to avoid the negotiation of a single multilateral regime, PSI now encompasses 102 countries. Because it deals with WMDs, it has particular relevance to technologies of mass empowerment and may prove an especially useful model for future international cooperation—even in the absence of universal agreement on definitions, prohibitions, or lawful practices.[18]

Most of the PSI's work is done outside the public view. However, in 2006 the then undersecretary of state for arms control and international security said that "between April 2005 and April 2006, the United States worked successfully with multiple PSI partners in Europe, Asia and the Middle East on roughly two dozen separate occasions to prevent transfers of equipment and materials to WMD and missile programs in countries of concern." The undersecretary specifically mentioned that one PSI partner had ceased assisting the development of Iran's nuclear program. But perhaps the best-known PSI success was the interdiction of the *BBC China*, a German-owned ship that was carrying centrifuge parts to Muammar al-Qaddafi's Libya. That incident is thought to have been a factor in Qaddafi's decision to give up his nuclear ambitions.[19]

Some major powers, including China, Iran, and North Korea, still contest the legality and legitimacy of the PSI program, and North Korea has asserted that the interdiction of ships flying its flag could be considered an act of war. Moreover, though officially bilateral and reciprocal, the reciprocity is—at least with respect to some states—a bit of a fiction. These partnering states are highly unlikely to interdict an American ship on the high seas. Mongolia, for instance, is a PSI partner, but it is a landlocked country without a navy. In addition, about half the world's shipping (and 68 percent of Asia's shipping) moves through ports that are not located in PSI countries. So the arrangement is far from airtight. Despite that, the PSI is generally considered a successful international regime.[20]

Naturally, anything short of effective universal cooperation will fall short of optimal security. What is more, partial cooperation between states may serve in some instances merely to divert harmful behaviors to safe havens where agreements are not respected and restrictions thus do not exist. This phenomenon has exacerbated other global problems, such as climate change, where domestic limits on carbons emissions serve to drive emitters to jurisdictions without such limits. That said, as the security risks associated with mass-empowering technologies emerge, existing models of cooperation, limited and partial though they may be, are likely to serve as blueprints for expanded cooperation. Liberty and security, it turns out, are not always in tension for states either; sometimes the best way to maximize freedom is to embrace constraint.

Just as in the domestic domain, international security will not be the province of states alone. For all the reasons for which governments rely on the private sector domestically—and other reasons peculiar to the international area—the private sector has been playing a steadily increasing role in providing security around the globe. In fact, private companies have become such a mainstay of international security that the United Nations has produced guidelines outlining their use for the protection of UN personnel. The remarkable thing about these guidelines is their forthright acknowledgment that private companies will sometimes be the only source of security in nations that are "unwilling or unable" to provide it and when no other UN member state can or will. In recognition of the importance of private actors to the provision of security, the Swiss government has convened a multiparty initiative to regulate the conduct of private security contractors, with more than seven hundred participating companies from around the world. The guidelines and initiatives are designed to allow for the use of private security contractors in circumstances in which states are incapable of providing security in a manner that is consistent with the moral conduct expected of the United Nations and other state actors. Increased international cooperation, in other words, is now a matter not simply of increased cooperation between states but also of growing cooperation between states and nonstate actors.[21]

One area where states come together in multilateral arrangements with nonstate actors to govern areas with profound security implications is technical standard setting. How do all of those cell phones talk to each other across different brands and borders? What encryption systems should companies use to secure commercial Internet transactions? These questions are decided by more than just the invisible hand of the market. Industry standards are often developed deliberately, and governments and international organizations frequently serve as conveners of the various stakeholders, who have to jointly thrash out common practices. The more globally integrated technologies of mass empowerment become, the more importance these standard-setting exercises will have for security at all levels. More broadly, the more nonstate actors take the lead in developing and operating technologies of mass empowerment, the more indispensible they will become in the international dialogue about technology governance.

Unilateral Action

While international cooperation is essential and is happening, for the foreseeable future it will not lead to true global governance. States do not share a common view of either the threats or the appropriate responses to them. This is not unique to the world of many-to-many threats or to new technologies. It is also just plain old politics. The Qatari government does not believe it should stop the Hamas leadership from plotting attacks on Israel, and Hugo Chávez–led Venezuela seemed all too happy to support the Revolutionary Armed Forces of Colombia in the group's effort to destabilize the government of Colombian president Alvaro Uribe, Chávez's regional archrival. The fact that all states now have to fear new attackers does not alter the reality that their interests diverge—sometimes sharply. Chinese economic espionage and exploitation of American companies will not stop until the Chinese government has an interest in stopping it; nor are Russian hackers likely to face any serious constraint on their operation absent a decision by the Russian government to crack down on their activities. Nor will US espionage against Chinese or Russian targets cease absent changed interests on the part of the United States.

Even when states do have a shared vision of the new threats and their new remedies, they often lack the capacity to act on that vision. The Mexican government has made great efforts to get rid of the country's drug-exporting cartels, but despite years of intense fighting that has left tens of thousands dead, it has been unable to do so. The Nigerian government presumably has an interest in stopping the NaijaCyberHactivists, a group responsible for hacking Nigerian governmental and other websites, but apparently lacks the capacity to shut it down.[22]

The limited prospects for effective international cooperation, the inability of many governments to police their own territories, and the huge stakes posed by the world of many-to-many threats cumulatively conspire to give some states strong incentives to secure their interests unilaterally. This is true even if it means that a state must violate the sovereignty of another state or act without the requisite consent of the international community. And this increased unilateralism takes place, somewhat paradoxically, alongside the increased cooperation.

Today, we tend to think of unilateralism in terms of drone strikes and the invasion of Iraq or Crimea, but unilateralism can operate more subtly. Sometimes it can take the form of expansive domestic legislation that, by its terms, regulates overseas activity on the basis of thin jurisdictional reeds. One good regulatory example is the American law on foreign corruption, specifically bribes paid out by companies to foreign officials in exchange for business concessions. In the aftermath of the Watergate scandal, Congress passed the Foreign Corrupt Practices Act of 1977 (FCPA), the first legislation in any country to prohibit domestic parties from making payments to foreign officials in return for business. At the time, most other countries prohibited only domestic bribery; some even allowed the deduction of foreign bribes as a business expense on domestic tax returns. Given other countries' tolerance of foreign bribery, the FCPA had the effect of putting American companies at a distinct disadvantage in countries where bribes routinely operate as grease for the wheels of business. American companies could be prosecuted at home for giving such kickbacks. Foreign companies got a tax deduction.

To rectify the adverse effects on American companies, with the passage of the FCPA President Jimmy Carter urged other countries to collaborate on negotiating a multilateral anticorruption treaty as a means of coordinating an international response to the problem and leveling the playing field for American companies. It took twenty-one years for the Organisation for Economic Co-operation and Development (OECD) to heed the American plea and adopt the 1998 Anti-Bribery Convention, instructing its member states to forbid the bribery of a foreign official. Even then, the convention was limited to OECD countries and was consistently underenforced.[23]

So the United States again acted on its own. Building on the OECD treaty, the United States amended the FCPA to expand its reach, so that its provisions now apply to any foreign bribery—whether by US corporations or foreign ones—if any act in furtherance of the prohibited act is committed in the United States. The term "act in furtherance" has been interpreted so broadly by the United States that, as one attorney put it, a "telephone call to the United States, a letter mailed to the United States, the use of air or road travel, or the clearing of a check or wire transfer of funds through a financial institution in the United States" is sufficient to establish a nexus with the United States. This far exceeds what the OECD countries have recognized as granting domestic jurisdiction over a foreign bribe. Given that much of the world's Internet and phone traffic is routed through the United States, a vast number of international transactions actually fall within the FCPA's reach, with the effect that non-US corporations have in recent years accounted for a large percentage of total penalties paid by corporations for FCPA violations.[24]

The FCPA is thus a unilateral American legislative act that has triggered enhanced international cooperation over time and has had significant effects on foreign bribery practices far beyond what we ordinarily regard as the reach of domestic regulation. That it builds on a multilateral treaty diminishes its unilateralism only to a degree. Fundamentally, the FCPA offers a potential model for future US legislation that would reach beyond America's borders to regulate cyber- and bioactivities that have at most an attenuated connection to the United States.

Another example of the new unilateralism arises in the context of terrorism. In the aftermath of the attacks of September 11, 2001, the United States aggressively expanded its laws that make it a crime to offer material support to an organization designated as terrorist by the secretary of state. "Material support" is now defined in the criminal code—as broadened by the Congress in both 2001 and 2004—to include almost any kind of support for designated organizations, including humanitarian aid, training, expert advice, and services in almost any form.

While the US Supreme Court has upheld the statute and domestic human rights advocates have complained about it, for present purposes the statute is especially striking in its extraterritorial reach. Following the Intelligence Reform Act, it now even covers material support given by a foreign citizen, outside the United States, to a group that is also outside the United States, even if there is no showing that the assistance to or activities of the group in question were meant to harm Americans. In one such case, an Eritrean citizen who was a lawful resident of Sweden was arrested in Nigeria in 2009 and transferred to the United States, where he was convicted and sentenced to 111 months in prison for conspiring to provide material support to al-Shabaab, a designated terrorist organization based in Somalia.[25]

Another significant form of unilateral state action involves the blatant abduction of suspects residing outside the state for purposes of subjecting them to domestic legal proceedings. As noted earlier, extradition is the conventional means of bringing a suspect from another country before a domestic court. Where extradition proves impossible, countries have sometimes resorted to abduction, without the consent of the territorial state. These cases tend to implicate the most sensitive national interests of the abducting states. In 1960, for example, Israeli agents famously kidnapped Adolf Eichmann, a Nazi war criminal and one of the architects of the "Final Solution," from Argentina and flew him to Israel, where he was convicted and executed. In 1963, French agents kidnapped Antoine

Argoud, a leader of a military revolt against President Charles de Gaulle, in West Germany and brought him to trial in France. In 1978, Lilian Celiberti de Casariego, a Uruguayan-Italian citizen, was forcibly abducted with her two children from an apartment in Brazil by Uruguayan agents on suspicion of "subversive association" and taken into Uruguay, where she was kept in preventive detention pending a military trial. In 1990, former Mexican police officers abducted Humberto Alvarez-Machain, a Mexican physician they believed to have participated in the torture and killing of a US Drug Enforcement Agency agent, from Mexico and delivered him for trial in the United States. Alvarez-Machain, incidentally, was later acquitted and moved unsuccessfully to sue his abductors.[26]

From an international legal perspective, without authorization from the territorial state in question, any abduction by foreign agents is a clear violation of that state's sovereignty, as well as a violation of the human rights of the person abducted. Yet, notwithstanding the political fallout and condemnation by international human rights–monitoring bodies that abductions generate, most domestic courts have ignored any international law violations implicated by transborder kidnapping and have enforced the law against the persons brought before them through abductions. As the Ninth Circuit Court of Appeals noted in the case of Alvarez-Machain, "In the midst of contemporary anxiety about the struggle against global terrorism, there is a natural concern about the reach and limitations of our political branches in bringing international criminals to justice." The US Supreme Court has gone even further, holding that the existence of a US-Mexican extradition treaty did not "[support] the proposition that it prohibits abductions outside of its terms." In the world of many-to-many threats, abduction may become an attractive option, at least in extreme cases. The student making smallpox in his garage may not be extraditable, and the smallpox—once released—cannot be put back in the vial. But the student can be snatched up by agents of a foreign state if he can be identified and located. And for a state facing the unthinkable, this will present at least as appealing an option as it does for a state wishing to kidnap the allegedly murderous doctor or the war criminal.[27]

The unilateral seizure of individuals has, in recent years, taken an extreme form in the context of US overseas counterterrorism operations. Since September 11, the United States has not merely captured terrorists and rendered them to law enforcement in the United States; it has also captured terrorist suspects all over the world and held them in secret prisons, transferred them to Iraq, Afghanistan, or Guantánamo Bay in Cuba, or rendered them for interrogation and detention in other countries, some of them infamous for their lack of due process and treatment of detainees. This aggressive unilateralism became part and parcel of the American view of its war on terrorism as a global noninternational armed conflict that knows no geographical boundaries and goes to the terrorist wherever he is.

In some cases, local courts condemned covert domestic cooperation or acquiescence by the state in which the suspect was captured. For example, in a 2003 CIA operation, an Egyptian cleric was grabbed off the street in Milan, where he was seeking asylum, driven to Aviano Air Base, and flown out of the country, first to Germany and then to Egypt, where he claims he was tortured by his interrogators. An Italian court convicted in absentia twenty-three Americans, twenty-two of whom were CIA employees, for the kidnapping. In 2013, Italy's intelligence chief was also convicted for his alleged cooperation in the rendition. It is unclear how much influence these lower courts' decisions have had or will have on foreign governments' cooperation with the United States in such matters in the future, and there have been no similar cases in recent years.[28]

A still more aggressive form of unilateral action is the use of lethal military force against those perceived to pose a national security threat. Short of an all-out war, military strikes against armed groups, terrorist groups, and even national leaders have taken place on occasions too numerous to list in full. Examples include repeated Israeli air strikes on militant camps in Syria and Lebanon, American strikes on Libyan leader Muammar al-Qaddafi in 1986, Russia's military strikes in Chechnya, Colombia's bombing of a guerrilla rebel base in Ecuador, North Korea's targeting of South Korean military leaders in Rangoon, and the Democratic Republic of Congo's cross-border operations against its neighbors and vice versa.

More recently, one form of aggressive unilateral military action has garnered a great deal of public attention in the United States and abroad: targeted killing. Targeted killing, the intentional killing of a specific, suspected militant or terrorist outside the targeting state's territory, has risen to prominence in recent years as drone strikes became a hallmark of the Obama administration's counterterrorism strategy. But the United States is certainly not alone in relying on this practice. Israel has been engaged in the covert killing of designated enemies since the 1950s, in places as remote as Germany, Norway, Belgium, Uruguay, the Canary Islands, Dubai, and throughout the Middle East. Since 2000, it has publicly acknowledged a policy of targeted killing of Palestinian militants in Gaza. It has also likely been behind the assassinations of nuclear scientists in Iran. Russia has performed targeted killings of militants in Chechnya, and in 2004 two Russian agents were convicted in Qatar of the car-bomb assassination of a Chechen militant in Doha.[29]

Authorities on international law disagree on the right of states to use force against threatening individuals and groups situated in another country. The International Court of Justice (ICJ), in a case concerning military operations by Uganda against rebels operating from the territory of the Democratic Republic of Congo, rejected the claim by Uganda that it had a right to use force extraterritorially in self-defense against nonstate actors where the latter were operating independently of the territorial state's government. In another case, in which the ICJ was offering an advisory opinion on the legality of the Israeli-built wall along and within the West Bank, the court further found that a state has no right to defend itself with force against threats emanating from a territory that the state occupies. At the same time, the UN Security Council in its resolutions following the attacks of September 11 declared that states did have a right to self-defense against terrorists, without demanding that a link be demonstrated between the terrorists and any particular state.[30]

The legality of targeted killings specifically, as opposed to general military action, has not yet been deliberated by any international tribunal. The United States has taken the position that it has a legal right to kill any terrorist suspect who is meaningfully part of enemy forces in its noninternational armed conflict against Al-Qaeda, the Taliban, and associated forces—though it has also adopted the more restrictive policy of limiting such killings to targets of relatively high value. Where targeting is conducted outside Afghanistan or areas in Pakistan that cumulatively constitute the zone of active hostilities of the conflict and instead takes place in the territories of other sovereign states, the United States claims the right to use force when the states in which terrorists are operating either consent to the use of force or are unwilling or unable to control terrorist activity—provided that the terrorist being targeted poses an imminent threat (a term that the United States defines broadly) to Americans and capture is not feasible. In this view, force, in such cases, is directed not against the state but only against the terrorists themselves. Under this paradigm, the United States has engaged in targeted killings of suspected terrorists in large areas of Pakistan, Yemen, Somalia, and elsewhere. In one case, a targeted killing was carried out against a suspected terrorist who was a US citizen. Several other US nationals have been killed in attacks in which they were not the specific targets.[31]

The American practice of targeted killings outside theaters of war has met with vociferous domestic and international criticism. Critics accuse the United States of bellicose policies that ignore the sovereignty of other states, inflict harm on innocent civilians, and invite other strong powers to use similar measures against their own real or perceived enemies around the globe. The UN Human Rights Council has appointed a special rapporteur to look into the American practice (as well as the British and Israeli use of drones for targeted killings in Afghanistan and Gaza, respectively).[32]

The distribution of power to actors around the globe who are now capable of inflicting remote strikes with difficult-to-trace means is almost sure to invite more of this sort of practice in places where international cooperation fails or is impossible. After all, the circumstance of an imminent threat emanating from the territory of a state that is unable or unwilling to stop attacks is not inherently limited to contemporary overseas counterterrorism. Nor is it necessarily limited to Al-Qaeda or its associated forces. It could just as easily apply to the lone terrorist or even, in theory, to criminals if the magnitude of threat they pose is great enough and the prospect of lethal attack is sufficiently imminent and not preventable by other feasible means. Already the United States has reportedly extended its "hit list" for targeted killings in Afghanistan to drug traffickers allegedly connected to the Taliban. In 2009, the Pentagon reported fifty "nexus" targets on the "kill or capture" list that linked the drug trade to the insurgency.[33]

Of course, unilateral actions are more attractive to those undertaking them than to those against whom they are planned. And the precedents now set by the most powerful nations are, as the saying goes, sauce for the gander too—at least in theory. Yet here the sovereign equality of states has a way of breaking down. Imagine that in the context of Syria's civil war, the Assad regime were to target Free Syrian Army members who were planning their future actions while in the United States, on the theory that the United States had shown no willingness to detain them. It seems inconceivable that American leaders would concede the legality of such targeting, even if it rested on the same legal theory of a noninternational armed conflict that the United States relies on for its targeted killings in the war on terrorism.[34]

Indeed, unilateralism risks exacerbating international friction and might easily spiral into broader conflict, however "surgical" or contained it is. As the United States seeks to develop international rules that will serve its security interests, especially as strategic realities change, it must also consistently consider the utilization of these rules by others—states and nonstate actors alike. This is not to say that the United States should or will eschew unilateral actions. In a world of highly empowered and highly lethal people, imperfect international cooperation will sometimes require states to take matters into their own hands. Still, the urge to respond to immediate, known threats must be countered by consideration of the broader and longer-term uses and abuses of similar responses by others.

THE SPECIAL CHALLENGE OF FAILED STATES

In its 2014 Annual Fragile States Index, the US Fund for Peace, a Washington, DC–based think tank, listed 34 out of 178 ranked countries as on "alert," with 16 of them on "high alert" or "very high alert," for state failure. It listed a total of 126 countries as showing meaningful signs of instability.[35]

Failed or fragile states are natural havens for perpetrators of crime and violence, indeed for anyone who can exploit the incapacity of the government to impose law and order. They are thus spaces of particular concern in a world of many-to-many threats. The Somali government, even if it wanted to, has no real hope of stopping the practice of piracy emanating from its shores. Mali needs heavy foreign assistance from France and the African Union to battle effectively the extreme Islamist elements fighting in its territory. The more powerful and dispersed technology grows, the more dangerous these de facto ungoverned spaces will become. As the threat level rises, even the most reticent members of the developed world will no longer be able to afford striking isolationist poses. No Leviathan, however powerful, can police the entire globe on its own; it must instead rely on other Leviathans to do their share.

Failed states are not the effective Leviathans that Thomas Hobbes envisioned, and they cannot be relied upon to perform their share of governance and effective policing. The problem of what to do about ungoverned states confounds policy makers, academics, and practitioners. Failed states generate what international relations expert Stephen Krasner has termed "an inescapable paradox" of sovereignty: the external face of sovereignty—the legal shield from external intervention in a state's internal affairs—assumes a functioning state that can rule itself; yet failed states have a legal claim to external sovereignty even as their internal sovereignty, their effective self-rule, is scant or nonexistent, threatening their own inhabitants as well as others around the globe.[36]

International law currently offers no real remedy for this paradox. A functional government is a prerequisite for international recognition of a new state to begin with (as is having territory, population, and independence). Once a state is recognized, however, the prevailing view among international law scholars seems to be that it cannot be unrecognized barring extraordinary events, such as its disintegration into smaller units or unification with—or absorption by—another state. In these extraordinary cases, the state is essentially replaced by another smaller or larger political entity. There is no standard process, however, for losing sovereignty, independence, or territorial integrity simply because the government of a state is no longer functional, and no other state gains the right to invade the failed state or otherwise impinge on its sovereignty.[37]

We are unlikely to revive the old system of placing new, weak, or ungoverned territories under a mandate (as ordered by the League of Nations) or a trust (under the United Nations) of a powerful country, as was done with much of the Middle East, Africa, and the Pacific after World War I and World War II. Indeed, with the evolution and codification of the principle of the right of peoples to self-determination, any resurrection of a mandate or trust system over failed or failing states will be politically and legally specious, absent the consent of those states themselves. Even if local consent could be obtained, questions would remain about who has a right to give such consent on behalf of the local population, especially when many fragile states have ineffective or contested governments.

Clearly, as a legal matter, the UN Security Council could, under its powers as the guarantor of international peace and security, authorize international assistance forces or other nation-building efforts in failed states, thereby overriding any objection by the local state. But local peoples will likely view international intervention that they have not invited as a modern form of imperialism and colonialism—as the imposition by the developed world of its forces, values, and interests on the developing world. Moreover, the political will and resources for such investment, mired in conflict, will be hard to find.

Nor does historical practice suggest that external intervention has beneficial effects where the local population does not embrace it. International intervention in Kosovo, for instance, has been effective in bringing the former federal unit of Serbia to its own independence, in part because of vast local support for these international efforts. Effective international involvement has taken place elsewhere—through the United Nations, the World Bank, or so-called friends of international conferences of donor countries and humanitarian groups. But all of these efforts took place at the request and with the welcome of the local authorities. In contrast, US and allied nation-building efforts in Afghanistan and Iraq, where the local populations did not fully embrace foreign involvement, are hardly ringing endorsements of the nation-building process.

Yet the state of affairs in which vast parts of the world enjoy sovereignty and immunity from external intervention, even while local authorities cannot prevent local actors from using their territories to export harm to others, is unsustainable. In all probability, once the threat becomes sufficiently great, the greater powers will simply ignore the principles of sovereignty and territorial integrity when they feel threatened and are in a position to act coercively. Over time, the international community may have to reconsider its stance on how the principles of self-determination are to be realized while still guaranteeing the safety and security of other states.

The problems do not stop with consent by the struggling state. Even were such consent freely given with no qualifications, it is not at all clear that the developed world knows how to engage in effective nation building. The chief challenge here entails not international law, but political will, resources, and know-how with respect to getting nonfunctioning states to function. As Krasner notes, "The current menu of policy instruments available for state building in badly governed or occupied countries is limited, consisting primarily of foreign assistance to improve governance and transitional administration, both of which assume that in more or less short order, targeted states can function effectively on their own. For many countries, this assumption is little more than wishful thinking." To complement these efforts, Krasner has proposed a model of shared sovereignty, in which outside actors receive official roles within the domestic governmental structures of the target state and play those roles for an indefinite period.[38]

Several states in the international system already cede some of their external defense and foreign relations powers to stronger regional actors: Liechtenstein relies on Switzerland for its external defense, and the United States has full authority and responsibility for the defense of the Federal States of Micronesia. These are models of shared external sovereignty (albeit not with failed states). It may very well be that the future security environment will prompt additional similar arrangements by which strong regional powers take over the security functions of smaller countries.

Ceding control over domestic authority is another matter, possibly a more delicate one, although we have also seen experiments in this regard in various places around the world: hybrid courts in Sierra Leone, where domestic courts were bolstered with international judges; the involvement of the World Bank in transnational infrastructure projects such as the Chad-Cameron oil pipeline and the India-Pakistan Indus waters regime; and European countries' role in the institutions overseeing the protection of human rights in Bosnia and Herzegovina.

As Krasner himself acknowledges, shared sovereignty depends on the consent of the domestic state. And while nothing in principle prevents a domestic country from giving external actors some measure of control over its policing or military power, this is not a common occurrence, especially if we exclude from our analysis places that are under transitional administration, such as Kosovo, East Timor, Afghanistan, or Iraq a few years ago. Effective shared sovereignty also depends, of course, on the willingness of the external actors to expend the resources necessary to exercise it. And none of this resolves the question of what to do when the local government does not embrace international involvement and does a poor job of policing its own territory.

The question of when nation-building efforts prove successful deserves much greater attention than we can give it here. Our point is simply to emphasize that with the spread of empowering technologies, the need for effective policing of territories around the world becomes a crucial global security interest. Many states already recognize this. According to a June 2013 *New York Times* article describing international assistance to African countries struggling with domestic counterterrorism efforts,

> This fall, the United States and Niger will bring together in that West African nation police officers, customs inspectors and other authorities from a half-dozen countries in the region to hone their collective skills in securing lightly guarded borders against heavily armed traffickers and terrorists.
>
> Denmark has already forged a partnership with Burkina Faso to combat violent extremism, and backed it up with a war chest of $22 million over five years aimed at stifling the root causes of terrorism before they can bloom.
>
> Swiss experts in a meeting in Nigeria last fall offered techniques for countries in West and North Africa to use in tackling the money-laundering schemes and illicit financing networks that are the lifeblood of Islamist militant groups.

And now, international efforts to bolster the region against terrorism are focusing on Algeria and its neighbors . . . including Mali, Mauritania and Niger.[39]

It is a sad reality that international assistance in building effective governance structures materializes with greater alacrity when the threat of terrorism is at stake, rather than when the day-to-day human security and well-being of the many millions who live in these volatile regions are at issue. The world has shown repeatedly that it is not moved to systematic action when ineffective governance entails a lack of safety, security, access to essential infrastructure, food, education, and health services for millions. Perhaps ironically, it is easier to justify transnational coercive activities on the basis of a claim that another state is "unable or unwilling" to police security threats emanating from its territory when that state is altogether ungoverned (like Somalia) than when it is governed imperfectly (like, say, Honduras) or is governed effectively but has divergent security interests (like China or Russia). In some ways, therefore, as between an altogether ungoverned state and a weakly governed one, strong powers with interventionist inclinations might actually prefer the former, in which they have a better argument for taking a freer hand.

Where no Leviathan can go it alone, each Leviathan has a clear interest in making other Leviathans effective and secure. When even residents of (or visitors to) ungoverned territories have access to technologies that allow them to attack people in the wealthier parts of the world, both humanitarian interests and self-preservation generate an interest in building more effective states. Perhaps the new threat environment will be the impetus for a greater cosmopolitan concern for the well-being of others, a concern that will increasingly overlap with a self-interested national security agenda. Perhaps this is where the world of many-to-many threats invites a world of many-to-many assistance.

CONCLUSION

By the time you read this book, much of it may be out of date. Some of the examples we have given of exciting new technologies may seem pedestrian. Some may even seem quaint. A few, like the spider drone, may still strike readers as implausibly futuristic. Then again, they may not. Technology hurtles forward at such a pace that today's surreal is next week's old news. When we began writing and talking to colleagues and audiences about the spider drone, most people reacted to it as sheer fantasy. Today, we are already seeing prototypes of mini-drones in operation. The agility and autonomy of the spider are still fantastical, as is its ability to steal and process DNA evidence from an unwilling target and match it against instantly available data about that target's DNA profile—and the mechanism of its delivery of a lethal payload remains, at a minimum, a ways off. But the idea of a lethal mini-drone in private hands seems less far-fetched today than it did only a few years back.

Indeed, by the time you read this book, new technologies that enable attacks of some sort will have emerged—if only in the form of incremental developments over technologies we possessed yesterday. New technologies of defense will develop in lagging response. There will be new ways to kill people, to steal from people, and to spy on people—and these new ways of doing these very old things will be available to more and more of us. Meanwhile, each passing year also brings new ways to exploit the vulnerabilities embedded in the mosaics of people and institutions. And each passing day sees the market for those exploitations growing, along with the number of people participating in that market.

In such a world, the idea of security, national and personal, changes radically. True, the human aspiration for security has not changed. People still seek protection from states, organizations, and individuals who would harm them. And they seek assurance that their governments will stop these entities and people if they try to do harm and punish them if they succeed. It was the wish to preserve security that led people to seek and adopt legal codes in the first place. In that sense, nothing has changed.

Yet when we speak of security today, we invoke threats that are more ubiquitous and omnidirectional than in the past—and with greater potential to cause catastrophe. At some point, these differences become far more significant than the theoretical similarity between past and future threats. In a world in which you have to worry about the vicious strain of flu accidentally released from a lab in Missouri, the virus that a chicken farmer is synthesizing in Indonesia to kill the birds of his competitors in China, the unmanned aerial vehicles your neighbors are flying over your house, surveillance equipment and cameras popping up everywhere, the 3D printers of the local animal rights activists, and the disruption of the street lamps on your block thanks to a fourteen-year-old having fun in another hemisphere, the concept of security is so broad as to seem almost hopeless. All of humanity, inasmuch as it has access to empowering technologies, now touches both our national security and our personal safety, which in turn are becoming hard to separate from one another. And, of course, you too are part of the problem—a potential threat to the security of countless people and entities around the world—or at least many people have to act as though you could be.

Not all of the threats involve malice. In the weeks that we were completing this manuscript, a series of dramatic biosecurity events took place—all involving accidents or naturally occurring outbreaks. Ebola began ravaging large swaths of West Africa. The Centers for Disease Control and Prevention (CDC) reported that no fewer than seventy-five of its workers there had been potentially exposed to anthrax. Shortly thereafter, it emerged that vials of smallpox had been sitting around a National Institutes of Health laboratory unnoticed for the past fifty years. A CDC lab also mingled a lethal bird flu strain with a comparatively benign strain and then shipped it all to another government lab. We live in a worldwide polity of superempowered governments, citizens, and subjects—some of them evil, many more of them careless or not very bright—and that is a pretty hard place to govern.[1]

Indeed, some people believe it is an impossible place to govern. The former British Astronomer Royal, astrophysicist and cosmologist Martin Rees, in a provocative book titled *Our Final Hour*, boldly states, "I think the odds are no better than fifty-fifty that our present civilisation on Earth will survive to the end of the present century. Our choices and actions could ensure the perpetual future of life (not just on Earth, but perhaps far beyond it, too). Or in contrast, through malign intent, or through misadventure, twenty-first century technology could jeopardise life's potential, foreclosing its human and posthuman future."[2] Is our situation really as dire as Rees believes? Perhaps. Civilizations do end, after all. The ancient Egyptians and Mayans built the great pyramids; the Greeks gave birth to philosophy and much of mathematics; and the Spanish invaders stood in awe of the Aztec city of Tenochtitlán when they came to conquer it. Yet nobody today thinks of native Mexico or Greece or Egypt as drivers of innovation or great creators of wealth. The roads the Romans built all led to Rome, but over the past fifteen centuries or so, the most important roads have led elsewhere. It is a plausible hypothesis that our modern state system of governance is just not up to the task of preventing a globally supercharged state of nature.

Species end too. The brontosaurus, the giant ground sloth, the saber-tooth cat, and the megalodon all cut quite a swath in their days. Modern humans have been around only thirty-five thousand years or so—which is to say about 0.000008 percent of the Earth's history.

It is therefore perhaps tempting to respond to the task of governing the world of many-to-many threats with knee-jerk despair. In Woody Allen's *Annie Hall*, the child Alvy Singer goes into a depression because he learns that "the universe is expanding." As Alvy sullenly explains to the family doctor to whom his mother drags him, "Well, the universe is everything, and if it's expanding, then some day it will break apart, and that will be the end of everything." His mother interjects, "What is that your business?" She barks at the doctor, "He's stopped doing his homework!" Alvy asks, "What's the point?"

Every generation proclaims "the end of everything." And so far, every generation has been wrong, at least with regard to the "everything" part. Most likely, the current generation's apocalyptic anxiety is also wrong. In any event, the project of governance cannot proceed on the assumption of its own futility. Just as Alvy has to keep doing his homework knowing that the expanding universe might some day break apart, we have to try to govern on the theory that the threat environment is manageable.

We are also not ready to give up on the state as the major instrument for governing such a world of heightened risk either. For all the reasons we have discussed, it is not a perfect instrument. The Leviathan is missing some teeth. It is getting older now. And it may be that ultimately some other beast will come along and supplant it as king of the deep. Maybe this will be some larger superstate structure or some more local one that gets all the little fish to swim together—or maybe both at the same time. But for now, at least, the Leviathan is still the best friend we've got. We still need it even with full awareness of its flaws and decrepitude.

There is a converse risk, one just as counterproductive as despair: overreaction. Any attack and any threat environment becomes much more devastating if it leads to a hysterical or disproportionate response that exacerbates conflict and magnifies the secondary effects of the initial attack. Neither resilience nor maturity is a given; both are taught and learned. Our focus in this book has been on threats, but the net consequences of new technologies have so far been wildly positive for human health and prosperity. Political leadership has a responsibility to encourage and cultivate the benefits of technology even while discouraging—and preparing the public for—terrible abuses.

Unlike the end of the human species, which always remains a theoretical possibility, governmental overreaction, or misdirected reaction, to threats is much more than a possibility; it is omnipresent, and its consequences are often grave. In the name of national security, governments curtail human rights, trade away important freedoms, and can be quick to sacrifice human welfare, especially of those people with lesser political power. The greater the real or perceived threat of Armageddon, the greater the justification—or sometimes just the excuse—for elevating security above all other values. This is why John Locke's refinement of Thomas Hobbes is so important: Locke more accurately assessed risk than Hobbes did. He understood that the Leviathan, even in protecting you, might turn out to be just as big a threat as any of the harms it is meant to keep us from. In other words, while we need the Leviathan, we need to keep it in chains.

In this book, we have tried to deepen our understanding of the relationship between technology, security, and violence—beyond the intuitive but simplistic association of robots with drone strikes in Pakistan, of biosecurity with state biological weapons programs, of cyberattacks with Stuxnet. We have looked at these technologies, commonly examined in isolation, for the synergies among them and the common opportunities they present for regulation and control. We have explored the extent to which our political organization, strategic planning, and legal architecture are premised on assumptions that empowering technologies increasingly challenge. And we have argued that these assumptions should be tested in an effort to examine which ones hold true regardless of what technology brings with it and which ones require change and adaptation.

We have tried to be candid and sober about the magnitude of the challenge that technologies of mass empowerment pose today. We have tried to show that we do generally possess tools for governing these technologies. We have also tried to be clear-eyed about the challenges these governance tools themselves pose to cherished and long-standing notions of how civilized peoples allocate power within states—and how states allocate power among themselves. We have tried to imagine how one would have to deploy and alter these tools in order to have a chance at governance, that is, to think broadly about how the superempowered state might try to govern the superempowered citizen—both its own citizen and that of other states.

Some of the ideas we have put forth will seem, to some readers, too extreme. Others may seem too mild. Some ideas, we suspect, will at once strike some critics as draconian and others as insufficient. Some readers will dismiss our perception of the threats before us as exaggerated, while others might accuse us of having a limited imagination regarding horrors to come. Both types of critics may well be right. We may turn out to have understated or misidentified the problem, which may end up looking nothing whatsoever like a spider drone or a recreated hyperlethal smallpox virus. The one thing of which we are confident is that the world has not exhausted the trend toward universal technological empowerment, a trend that carries with it enhanced capacity for attack, enhanced vulnerability to attack, and enhanced capacity for defense for countless people and entities on the planet. This trend necessitates serious, sustained, and careful thinking about how we organize nations and how the nations of the world move to organize the larger international system—whether one believes that our approaches to those questions are sensible or not.

In the first few pages of the Book of Genesis, God faces two bold challenges to his rule from superempowered individuals. The first is Adam and Eve's defiance of his instruction not to eat from the Tree of Knowledge. God is content for his creation to eat from the Tree of Life, as long as Adam and Eve lack access to the knowledge of good and evil. But the moment they eat from the Tree of Knowledge, God can no longer afford to have them eating from the Tree of Life too.[3] "Behold," he says, "the man is become as one of us, to know good and evil: and now, lest he put forth his hand, and take also of the tree of life, and eat, and live for ever. Therefore the Lord God sent him forth from the garden of Eden, to till the ground from whence he was taken."[4] The expulsion from Eden, in other words, flows directly from the sovereign's need to preserve his capacity to govern. Man can be immortal or he can be wise, but he cannot be both without threatening God's relative power.

A few leafs of parchment later, man once again threatens God's power to rule, this time by building the Tower of Babel. "Behold," God worries, "the people is one, and they have all one language; and this they begin to do: and now nothing will be restrained from them, which they have imagined to do."[5] By imposing different languages on mankind, God once again retains his own sovereign power, making subservient the would-be superempowered individual, who now cannot live forever and cannot communicate with all of his fellow men to plot to attain the power of gods.

Like Adam and Eve, we have now eaten from the Tree of Knowledge, and we have also built a tower of dazzling height unmolested by any higher power. As democratic societies, we are—in a political sense at least—our own sovereign power. And so, somewhat like God in Genesis, we must ask ourselves, What new rules do we now impose? And what powers do we, in our capacity as sovereigns, exercise against ourselves as upstart pretenders to the godly powers we each now wield?

ACKNOWLEDGMENTS

A large number of our friends and colleagues have read this manuscript in whole or in part, have argued with us about aspects of it, and have given us invaluable comments and suggestions. We are especially indebted to David Barron, Yochai Benkler, Peter Berkowitz, Roger Brent, William Burke-White, John Goldberg, Jack Goldsmith, Rita Hauser, Susan Landau, Nathaniel Laor, Daryl Levinson, Herb Lin, Andrew McAfee, Benjamin Sachs, Adrian Vermeule, and Jonathan Zittrain, as well as to many others at the Brookings Institution and Harvard Law School (HLS). The manuscript has also benefited from conversations with and the work of Kenneth Anderson, Philip Bobbitt, Matthew Waxman, Yitzhak Ben-Israel, Philip Heymann, Steve Krasner, Shane Harris, and Joel Brenner.

We learned a great deal from a diverse group of American and Israeli experts who participated in a two-day roundtable, titled "Technology and the Future of Violence," held at Harvard Law School in February 2013 under the aegis of the HLS-Brookings Project on Law and Security. We are thankful for the generous support of Mitch Julis, Nachum Braverman and Academic Exchange, and Dalia Rabin and the Rabin Center, who made the workshop possible. We have also benefited from a yearlong student workshop at Harvard Law School, "National and International Security: New Threats." Guest speakers and students alike have furthered our knowledge and thinking about these topics.

We both drew on prior work and publications in formulating the thesis we advance in these pages. In particular, Benjamin Wittes's articles "Against a Crude Balance: Platform Security and the Hostile Symbiosis Between Liberty and Security" (Brookings Institution, September 2011) and "Databuse: Digital Privacy and the Mosaic" (Brookings Institution, April 2011) constitute the core of Chapter 5. And Gabriella Blum's essay "Invisible Threats" (Koret-Taube Task Force on National Security and Law, Hoover Institution, 2012) informs both Chapters 1 and 2, as did a paper on global security that Benjamin Wittes wrote for *Megatrends in Global Interaction* (Bertelsmann Foundation, 2012).

The Hoover Institution's Task Force on National Security and Law, of which Benjamin Wittes is a member, provided generous support for this project.

We benefited from invaluable research assistance. We are especially grateful to Matthew Ivey, Eric Rice, Yishai Schwartz, and Ritika Singh for their research, thoughts, and advice, as well as to Zoe Bedell, Morgan Cohen, Jessica Harris, Susan Hennessey, Lucas Issacharoff, Brian Itami, Sonia McNeil, Joshua Roselman, Elizabeth Tuttle, and Martha Vega-Gonzales.

A special word of thanks to our agents, Anna Sproul-Latimer and Gail Ross, to our editor, Lara Heimert, and to Roger Labrie and Jen Kelland, whose editing greatly improved the manuscript.

If there are any errors in this book, they are ours and ours alone.

NOTES

Notes to Introduction

1. See US Department of Justice, *Amerithrax Investigative Summary* (Washington, DC: US Government Printing Office, 2010), http://www.justice.gov/archive/amerithrax /docs/amx-investigative-summary.pdf (accessed July 4, 2014). We find the Justice Department's report persuasive as to Ivins's sole responsibility, but others clearly do not. See, for example, National Research Council, *Review of the Scientific Approaches Used during the FBI's Investigation of the 2001 Anthrax Letters* (Washington, DC: National Academies Press, 2011); editorial, "Who Mailed the Anthrax Letters?" *New York Times*, October 18, 2011, A26. For a list of those injured or killed in the anthrax case, see "Anthrax: Full List of Cases," *Guardian*, November 23, 2001, http://www.guardian.co.uk /world/2001/nov/23/anthrax.uk (accessed July 4, 2014).

2. Chris Anderson, "The DIY Drone Mission (aka the Five Rules)," DIY Drones, January 4, 2008, http://diydrones.com/profiles/blog/show?id=705844:BlogPost:17789 (accessed July 4, 2014).

3. "Massachusetts Man Charged with Plotting Attack on Pentagon and US Capitol and Attempting to Provide Material Support to a Foreign Terrorist Organization," FBI, press release, September 28, 2011, http://www.fbi.gov/boston/press-releases/2011 /massachusetts-man-charged-with-plotting-attack-on-pentagon-and-u.s.-capitol-and -attempting-to-provide-material-support-to-a-foreign-terrorist-organization (accessed July 4, 2014).

4. Government's Objections to the PSR and Sentencing Position at 1, *United States v. Mijangos*, No. 10-743-GHK (C.D. Cal. July 20, 2011). For a journalistic account of the Mijangos case, see David Kushner, "The Hacker Is Watching," *GQ*, January 2012, http://www.gq.com/news-politics/newsmakers/201201/luis-mijangos-hacker-webcam -virus-internet (accessed July 4, 2014).

5. For Mijangos's modus operandi, see Government's Objections to the PSR at 3. For the number of victims, see Complaint at 10, *United States v. Mijangos*, No. 10-743-GHK (C.D. Cal. June 17, 2010), and Government's Objections to the PSR at 21.

6. Affidavit for Search Warrant, *United States v. The Premises Known As: 2326 W. Monica Lane, Santa Ana, CA 92706-1246*, March 2010.

7. Litvinenko's books include Alexander Litvinenko, *Blowing Up Russia: The Secret Plot to Bring Back KGB Terror* (New York: Encounter Books, 2007), and Alexander Litvinenko, *Lubyanka Criminal Group* (Moscow: Bookvika, 2002). The quotation from

the medical journal comes from Andrew J. Patterson, "Ushering in the Era of Nuclear Terrorism," *Critical Care Medicine* 35, no. 3 (March 2007): 953.

8. F. Cunliffe-Owen, "Death of Francis Ferdinand Makes for Peace of Europe," *New York Sun*, June 29, 1914.

9. David Starr Jordan, "The Impossible War," *Independent*, February 27, 1913.

10. President's Review Group on Intelligence and Communications Technologies, "Liberty and Security in a Changing World: Report and Recommendation of the President's Review Group on Intelligence and Communications Technologies," White House, 177–178, http://www.whitehouse.gov/sites/default/files/docs/2013-12-12_rg_final _report.pdf (accessed July 4, 2014).

11. See, in particular, Philip Bobbitt, *Terror and Consent: The Wars for the Twenty-First Century* (New York: Knopf, 2008). See also John Robb, *Brave New War: The Next Stage of Terrorism and the End of Globalization* (New York: Wiley, 2007).

12. Compare, for example, the arguments made about cybersecurity in Joel Brenner, *America the Vulnerable* (New York: Penguin Press, 2011), and in Richard A. Clarke and Robert K. Knake, *Cyber War: The Next Threat to National Security* (New York: Harper Collins, 2010), to the arguments made about biosecurity in, for example, David Fidler and Lawrence Ogalthorpe, *Biosecurity in the Global Age: Biological Weapons, Public Health, and the Rule of Law* (Stanford, CA: Stanford University Press, 2008).

Notes to Chapter 1

1. National Science Advisory Board for Biosecurity, "Addressing Biosecurity Concerns Related to the Synthesis of Select Agents," Office of Science Policy, December 2006, http://osp.od.nih.gov/sites/default/files/resources/Final_NSABB_Report_on _Synthetic_Genomics.pdf (accessed July 1, 2014).

2. For the ratio of guns to people in the United States, see Simon Rogers, "Gun Homicides and Gun Ownership Listed by Country," *Guardian*, July 22, 2012, http://www.guardian.co.uk/news/datablog/2012/jul/22/gun-homicides-ownership-world -list (accessed July 1, 2014). For the total number of firearms worldwide, see "Small Arms Survey 2007: Guns and the City," Small Arms Survey, 39, http://www.smallarmssurvey .org/publications/by-type/yearbook/small-arms-survey-2007.html (accessed July 1, 2014). For the number of gun-related homicides in the United States, see FBI Criminal Justice Information Services Division, *Crime in the United States 2012*, FBI, http://www.fbi.gov /about-us/cjis/ucr/crime-in-the-u.s/2012/crime-in-the-u.s.-2012/offenses-known-to-law -enforcement/expanded-homicide/expanded_homicide_data_table_8_murder_victims _by_weapon_2008–2012.xls (accessed July 1, 2014).

3. Andrew Krepinevich, "Cavalry to Computer: The Pattern of Military Revolutions," *National Interest* 30, no. 37 (fall 1994): 33–42.

4. Nathan Myhrvold, "Strategic Terrorism: A Call to Action" (Working Paper 2-2013, Lawfare Research Paper Series 1, no. 2, July 2013), http://www.lawfareblog.com /wp-content/uploads/2013/07/Strategic-Terrorism-Myhrvold-7-3-2013.pdf (accessed July 1, 2014).

5. See Steven Pinker, *The Better Angels of Our Nature: Why Violence Has Declined* (New York: Viking, 2011).

6. See Philip Bobbitt, *Terror and Consent: The Wars for the Twenty-First Century* (New York: Knopf, 2008). See also John Robb, *Brave New War: The Next Stage of Terrorism and the End of Globalization* (New York: Wiley, 2007).

7. Thomas Friedman, *The World Is Flat: A Brief History of the Twenty-First Century* (New York: Farrar, Straus and Giroux, 2005), 8.

8. Lawrence Lessig, "Insanely Destructive Devices," *Wired*, April 2004, http://www .wired.com/wired/archive/12.04/view.html (accessed July 1, 2014).

9. For data on global Internet access, see "Latest Global Technology Development Figures," International Telecommunication Union, press release, February 27, 2013, http://www.itu.int/net/pressoffice/press_releases/2013/05.aspx#.UuhFgGAo6AI (accessed July 1, 2014).

10. For information on the Mona Jaud Awana case, see Tania Hershman, "Israel's 'First Internet Murder,'" *Wired*, January 19, 2001, http://archive.wired.com/politics/law /news/2001/01/41300 (accessed July 1, 2014).

11. On the likelihood of a catastrophic cyberattack, see Seymour E. Goodman and Herbert S. Lin, eds., *Toward a Safer and More Secure Cyberspace* (Washington, DC: National Academies Press, 2007), 49, http://books.nap.edu/catalog.php?record_id=11925 (accessed July 1, 2014). This National Research Council panel concluded that "high-level threats—spawned by motivated, sophisticated, and well-resourced adversaries— could increase very quickly on a very short time-scale, potentially leading to what some dub a 'digital Pearl Harbor' (that is, a catastrophic event whose occurrence can be unambiguously traced to flaws in cybersecurity)—and that the nation's IT vendors and users (both individual and corporate) would have to respond very quickly when such threats emerge." Similarly, former defense secretary Leon Panetta has warned of an electronic Pearl Harbor potentially involving the financial sector—as have other senior officials. See Amy Lee, "CIA Chief Leon Panetta: Cyberattack Could Be 'Next Pearl Harbor,'" *Huffington Post*, June 13, 2011, http://www.huffingtonpost.com/2011/06/13 /panetta-cyberattack-next-pearl-harbor_n_875889.html (accessed July 1, 2014). For an account of the 2007 Department of Homeland Security test, see Jeanne Meserve, "Staged Cyber Attack Reveals Vulnerability in Power Grid," CNN.com, September 26, 2007, http://www.cnn.com/2007/US/09/26/power.at.risk/index.html (accessed July 1, 2014). For information on the Stuxnet and Olympic Games attacks, see David E. Sanger, "Obama Order Sped Up Wave of Cyber Attacks Against Iran," *New York Times*, June 1, 2012, http://www.nytimes.com/2012/06/01/world/middleeast/obama-ordered-wave-of -cyberattacks-against-iran.html (accessed July 1, 2014). See also David E. Sanger, *Confront and Conceal: Obama's Secret Wars and Surprising Use of American Power* (New York: Broadway Books, 2013).

12. For an account of the Syrian Electronic Army's attack on the *New York Times* and *Washington Post*, see Leslie Kaufman, "Washington Post Site Hacked by Syrian Group," *New York Times*, August 15, 2013, http://www.nytimes.com/2013/08/16/business /media/washington-post-says-site-breached-by-syrian-group.html (accessed July 1, 2014); Christine Haughney and Nicole Perlroth, "Times Site Is Disrupted in Attack by Hackers," *New York Times*, August 27, 2013, http://www.nytimes.com/2013/08/28 /business/media/hacking-attack-is-suspected-on-times-web-site.html (accessed July 1,

2014). For information on the attack on the Chinese Internet, see Michael Kan, "Major DDoS Attacks .cn domain; Disrupts Internet in China," *Computerworld*, August 26, 2013, http://www.computerworld.com/s/article/9241899/Major_DDoS_attacks_.cn _domain_disrupts_Internet_in_China (accessed July 1, 2014); Paul Rosenzweig, "The Big Hack This Week," *Lawfare*, August 28, 2013, http://www.lawfareblog.com/2013/08 /the-big-hack-this-week (accessed July 1, 2014). For information on the attacks on US banks, see Jeremy Kirk, "Deep Cyberattacks Cost U.S. Banks Millions," *PCWorld*, August 23, 2013, http://www.pcworld.com/article/2047299/deep-cyberattacks-cause -millions-in-losses-for-us-banks.html (accessed July 1, 2014). For information on the attacks on Israeli websites, see Ryan W. Neal, "Israeli Websites Hacked: Pakistani Hacker Claims Responsibility, Says Cyber Attack Was in Support of Palestine," *International Business Times,* August 14, 2013, http://www.ibtimes.com/israeli-websites-hacked -pakistani-hacker-claims-responsibility-says-cyber-attack-was-support-1385557 (accessed July 1, 2014). For information on the Afghan hacker attacks on Pakistani websites, see Heath Druzin, "Hackistan: Afghan Cyber Guerrillas Step Up Attacks on Pakistani Websites," *Stars and Stripes*, August 12, 2013, http://www.stripes.com/news/hackistan -afghan-cyber-guerrillas-step-up-attacks-on-pakistani-websites-1.234947 (accessed July 1, 2014).

13. Myhrvold, "Strategic Terrorism," 13.

14. On the 1984 attacks in Oregon, see C. F. Chyba, "Toward Biosecurity," *Foreign Affairs* 81, no. 3 (May/June 2002): 129. On the West Nile outbreak in New York, see Annie Fine and Marcelle Layto, "Lessons from the West Nile Viral Encephalitis Outbreak in New York City, 1999: Implications for Bioterrorism Preparedness," *Clinical Infectious Diseases* 32 (2001): 277–282. See also C. F. Chyba, "Biological Terrorism and Public Health," *Survival* 43, no. 1 (2001): 96–97.

15. For an assessment of the threat of biological terrorism by nonstate actors, see Counterproliferation Program Review Committee, *Report on Activities and Programs for Countering Proliferation and NBC Terrorism* (Washington, DC: Counterproliferation Program Review Committee, 2009), 32.

16. C. F. Chyba, "Biotechnology and the Challenge to Arms Control," *Arms Control Today* 30, no. 8 (October 2008): 12.

17. Ali Nouri and C. F. Chyba, "Proliferation-Resistant Biotechnology: An Approach to Improve Biosecurity," *Nature Biotechnology* 27, no. 3 (March 2009): 234. See also Chyba, "Biotechnology and the Challenge," 12, citing Hamilton Smith et al., "Generating a Synthetic Genome by Whole Genome Assembly: Phi-X174 Bacteriophage from Synthetic Oligonucleotides," *Proceedings of the National Academy of Sciences USA* 100, no. 26 (December 23, 2003): 15440–15445.

18. The mousepox study is available at R. J. Jackson et al., "Expression of a Mouse Interleukin-4 by a Recombinant Ectromelia Virus Represses Cytolytic Lymphocyte Responses and Overcomes Genetic Resistance to Mousepox," *Journal of Virology* 75, no. 3 (February 2001): 1205–1210. For a layman's account of it, see Stewart A. Baker, *Skating on Stilts: Why We Aren't Stopping Tomorrow's Terrorism* (Stanford, CA: Hoover Institution Press, 2010), 295–296. For the synthesis of Ebola, see V. E. Volchkov et al., "Recovery of Infectious Ebola Virus from Complementary DNA: RNA Editing of the GP Gene and

Viral Cytotoxicity," *Science*, no. 291 (March 2001): 1965–1969. For de novo synthesis of polio, see J. Cello, A. V. Paul, and E. Willmer, "Chemical Synthesis of Poliovirus cDNA: Generation of Infectious Virus in the Absence of Natural Template," *Science*, no. 297 (August 9, 2002): 1016–1018. For encephalomyocarditis virus synthesis, see Y. V. Svitkin and N. Sonenberg, "Cell-Free Synthesis of Encephalomyocarditis Virus," *Journal of Virology* 77, no. 11 (2003): 6551–6555. For the reconstruction of Spanish flu, see T. M. Tumpey et al., "Characterization of the Reconstructed 1918 Spanish Influenza Pandemic Virus," *Science*, no. 310 (October 7, 2005): 77–80. See also Tokiko Watanabe et al., "Circulating Avian Influenza Viruses Closely Related to the 1918 Virus Have Pandemic Potential," *Cell Host and Microbe* 16, no. 6 (June 11, 2014): 692–705. For a summary of the impact of the Spanish flu pandemic, see Jeffery K. Taubenberger and David M. Morens, "1918 Influenza: The Mother of All Pandemics," Centers for Disease Control, http://wwwnc.cdc.gov/eid/article/12/1/05-0979_article (accessed July 1, 2014).

19. On the difficulties of synthesizing smallpox, see A. Rabodzey, "Biosecurity Implications of the Synthesis of Pathogenic Viruses," *Politics and Life Sciences* 22, no. 2 (2003): 44–49.

20. For information on the Harris case, see Barry Kellman, "Biological Terrorism: Legal Measures for Preventing Catastrophe," *Harvard Journal of Law and Public Policy* 24, no. 2 (2000–2001): 418–488. The relevant discussion appears on 449–450. See also Jessica Stern, *The Ultimate Terrorists* (Cambridge, MA: Harvard University Press, 2001), 155.

21. The Office of Technology Assessment gave this grim assessment in *Proliferation of Weapons of Mass Destruction: Assessing the Risk*, OTA-ISC-559 (Washington, DC: US Government Printing Office, August 1993), 53–54, http://www.au.af.mil/au/awc/awcgate /ota/9341.pdf (accessed July 1, 2014).

22. See, generally, Erik Brynjolfsson and Andrew McAfee, *Race Against the Machine* (Lexington, MA: Digital Frontier Press, 2012).

23. Bill Gates, "A Robot in Every Home," *Scientific American*, January 1, 2007, 58–65.

24. Mindstorms promises "the versatility of the LEGO building system with all-new technologies, an intelligent microcomputer brick and intuitive drag-and-drop programming software. The new 2.0 toolkit features everything you need to create your first robot in 30 minutes and then thousands of other robotics inventions that do what you want!" See "Lego Mindstorms," Lego.com, http://mindstorms.lego.com/en-us /products/default.aspx (accessed March 4, 2013). A nonprofit organization called FIRST, an acronym for "For Inspiration and Recognition of Science and Technology," hosts three separate annual high school robotics competitions. "FIRST Progression of Programs," FIRST, http://www.usfirst.org/roboticsprograms (accessed March 4, 2013). For robotic gladiators, see *BattleBots*, a television program that ran on the Comedy Central cable network between 2000 and 2002. For off-road distance-travel robotic competitions, see Steve Russell, "DARPA Grand Challenge Winner: Stanley the Robot!" *Popular Mechanics*, January 9, 2006, http://www.popularmechanics.com/technology /engineering/robots/2169012 (accessed July 1, 2014). Information about the Lawfare Drone Smackdown is available at "Category Archives: Lawfare Drone Smackdown," *Lawfare*, http://www.lawfareblog.com/category/domestic-drones/lawfare-drone -smackdown (accessed July 1, 2013).

25. Department of Defense, Defense Science Board, *The Role of Autonomy in DoD Systems* (Washington, DC: Office of the Secretary of Defense, 2012), http://www.fas.org /irp/agency/dod/dsb/autonomy.pdf (accessed July 1, 2014).

26. Spencer Ackerman, "U.S. Troops Will Soon Get Tiny Kamikaze Drone," *Wired Danger Room*, October 18, 2011, http://www.wired.com/dangerroom/2011/10/tiny -kamikaze-drone (accessed July 1, 2014).

27. P. W. Singer, *Wired for War: The Robotics Revolution and Conflict in the Twenty- First Century* (New York: Penguin Press, 2009), 83.

28. "Unmanned Systems/Robotics Platforms," Metal Storm, http://www.metalstorm .com/content/view/39/107 (accessed October 23, 2012).

29. Singer, *Wired for War*, 264–265. See also Lisa Myers, "Hezbollah Drone Threatens Israel," NBCNews.com, April 4, 2005, http://www.nbcnews.com/id/7477528/ns/nbc _nightly_news_with_brian_williams/t/hezbollah-drone-threatens-israel/#.UlR2kxaPvG4 (accessed July 1, 2014). On the Israeli shoot-down of a Palestinian drone, see Peter Beaumont and Orlando Crowcroft, "Israel Says It Has Shot Down Drone Launched from Gaza," *Guardian*, July 14, 2014, http://www.theguardian.com/world/2014/jul/14 /israel-drone-launched-gaza-ashdod (accessed July 24, 2014).

30. The quotations from Peter Singer can be found at Singer, *Wired for War*, 126–128. For a more detailed treatment of autonomy in drones, see William C. Marra and Sonia K. McNeil, "Understanding 'the Loop': Humans and the Next Drone Generations," in *Issues in Governance Studies*, Brookings, August 2012, http://www.brookings.edu/~/media /research/files/papers/2012/8/27%20humans%20drones%20marra%20mcneil/27%20 humans%20drones%20marra%20mcneil.pdf (accessed July 1, 2014). The quotations from Shane Legg can be found in Bianca Bosker, "Google's New A.I. Ethics Board Might Save Humanity from Extinction," *HuffPost Tech*, January 20, 2014, http://www.huffingtonpost .com/2014/01/29/google-ai_n_4683343.html (accessed July 1, 2014).

31. For insect-like drones, see Judy Dutton, "Drones' Future: Supersonic Swarms of Robot Bugs," *Wired Danger Room*, June 22, 2012, http://www.wired.com/dangerroom /2012/06/ff_futuredrones (accessed July 1, 2014). For bird-like drones, see Rick Kubetz, "First-Ever Demonstration of Autonomous Bird-Like Robot Perching on a Human Hand," University of Illinois, Urbana-Champaign, May 1, 2012, http://engineering .illinois.edu/news/2012/04/27/first-ever-demonstration-autonomous-bird-robot-perching -a-human-hand (accessed July 1, 2014). For fish-like drones, see Mark Brown, "Meet Mantabot, the Underwater Ray-Shaped Robot," *Wired*, July 25, 2012, http://www .wired.co.uk/news/archive/2012-07/25/mantabot (accessed July 1, 2014). For worm-like drones, see Jennifer Chu, "Soft Autonomous Robot Inches Along like an Earthworm," *Massachusetts Institute of Technology News*, August 9, 2012, http://web.mit.edu/news office/2012/autonomous-earthworm-robot-0810.html (accessed July 1, 2014). On tiny batteries, see Signe Brewster, "The First 3D-Printed Battery Is as Tiny as a Grain of Sand," *Gigaom*, June 18, 2013, http://gigaom.com/2013/06/18/the-first-3d-printed -battery-is-as-tiny-as-a-grain-of-sand (accessed July 1, 2014). For information on "high- performance aerial and ambulatory microrobots," see Seth Fiegerman, "Tiny Robots Act like Bugs," *Mashable*, June 23, 2013, http://mashable.com/2013/06/23/robot-bugs (accessed July 1, 2014). The "micro aerial vehicles" video is available at "US Air Force

Flapping Wing Micro Air Vehicle," YouTube video, posted by "theworacle," July 16, 2009, http://www.youtube.com/watch?v=_5YkQ9w3PJ4 (accessed July 1, 2014).

32. Information on the Nano Hummingbird is available at "Nano Hummingbird," AeroVironment, http://www.avinc.com/nano (accessed March 4, 2013). Information on the Black Hornet is available at "Products: PD-100 PRS," Prox Dynamics, http://www .proxdynamics.com/products/pd-100-black-hornet (accessed June 6, 2014). Information on the Dragonfly is available at Evan Ackerman, "Somehow, an Incredible Robotic Dragonfly Is Now on Indiegogo," *IEEE Spectrum*, November 8, 2012, http://spectrum .ieee.org/automaton/robotics/robotics-hardware/somehow-an-incredible-robotic -dragonfly-is-now-on-indiegogo (accessed July 1, 2014). For information on the drone created at Cornell with a 3D printer, see Gabriella Blum, "Technology and the Future of Violence," *Defining Ideas*, August 17, 2012, http://www.hoover.org/publications /defining-ideas/article/125736 (accessed July 1, 2014). See also "3D Printed Hovering Ornithopters," Cornell Creative Machines Lab, http://creativemachines.cornell.edu /ornithopter (accessed June 5, 2014).

33. For a general treatment of 3D printing, see Hod Lipson and Melba Kurda, *Fabricated: The New World of 3D Printing* (Indianapolis: Wiley & Sons, 2012). Obama's comments on the subject can be found at Barack Obama, "State of the Union Address," White House, February 12, 2013, http://www.whitehouse.gov/the-press-office/2013/02 /12/remarks-president-state-union-address (accessed July 1, 2014). For information on 3D-printed firearms, see Robert Beckhusen, "Watch the New and Improved Printable Gun Spew Hundreds of Bullets," *Wired Danger Room*, February 28, 2013, http://www .wired.com/dangerroom/2013/02/printable-receiver (accessed July 1, 2014).

34. Henry Fountain, "Tools of Modern Gunmaking: Plastic and a 3-D Printer," *New York Times*, January 29, 2013, http://www.nytimes.com/2013/01/30/science/surprising -tools-of-modern-gunmaking-plastic-and-a-3-d-printer.html (accessed July 1, 2014). See also Ricardo Bilton, "3D-Printing Gun Site DEFCAD Now Attracting 3K Visitors an Hour, 250K Downloads Since Launch," *Venture Beat*, February 19, 2013, http:// venturebeat.com/2013/02/19/defcad-gun-traffic-growing (accessed July 1, 2014).

35. Fritz Allhoff, Patrick Lin, and Daniel Moore, *What Is Nanotechnology and Why Does It Matter? From Science to Ethics* (Oxford: Wiley-Blackwell, 2010), 13–14.

36. For an example of microrobotics, see Brian Handwerk, "New Microscopic Robot's Tiny Step Is a Huge Leap," *National Geographic*, October 26, 2005, http:// news.nationalgeographic.com/news/2005/10/1026_051026_tiny_robot.html (accessed July 1, 2014). On self-assembling microrobots, see Henry Kenyon, "Energy Lab's Microscopic Robots Assemble Selves, Can Move Large Objects," *GCN*, August 30, 2011, http://gcn. com/articles/2011/08/30/argonne-lab-microscopic-robots.aspx (accessed July 1, 2014). On surgical applications in the eye, see Olivia Solon, "How to Drive a Microscopic Robot Around the Inside of Your Eye," *Wired*, April 27, 2011, http://www.wired.co.uk/news /archive/2011-04/27/eye-robot (accessed July 1, 2014).

37. For information on the use in humans of tracking chips, known as radio-frequency identification (RFID) chips, which are still comparatively large, and the numerous ethical and privacy concerns they raise, see David Kravets, "Tracking School Children with RFID Tags? It's All About the Benjamins," *Wired*, September 7, 2012,

http://www.wired.com/threatlevel/2012/09/rfid-chip-student-monitoring (accessed July 1, 2014). See also Daniel Sieberg, "Is RFID Tracking You?" CNN, October 23, 2006, http://www.cnn.com/2006/TECH/07/10/rfid (accessed July 1, 2014). For information on the MIT Institute for Soldier Nanotechnologies, see "The Mission" in "About ISN," Institute for Nanotechnologies: Enhancing Solider Survivability, http://web.mit.edu/isn/aboutisn/index.html (accessed July 1, 2014). For information on the Air Force's nanoparticle sprays, see David Hambling, "Drones Tag and Track Quarry Using Nanoparticle Sprays," *New Scientist*, August 21, 2013, http://www.newscientist.com/article/mg21929315.100-drones-tag-and-track-quarry-using-nanoparticle-sprays.html#.Uh-mXydQXzx (accessed July 1, 2014). The quotation from the nanotechnology text comes from Allhoff, Lin, and Moore, *What Is Nanotechnology and Why Does It Matter?* 173–174, 224.

38. On ANTS generally, see "Autonomous Nanotechnology Swarm (ANTS)," Goddard Space Flight Center, http://attic.gsfc.nasa.gov/ants/ArchandAI.html (accessed July 1, 2014). On the TET warfighter, see "TET Warfighter," YouTube video, posted by "Redazione YouTech," August 8, 2012, http://www.youtube.com/watch?v=i9MPBPj-KsM (accessed July 1, 2014).

39. For example, the Parrot AR Drone can be controlled with an iPhone, iPad, or Android device. See "Parrot ARDrone 2.0," Parrot USA, http://ardrone2.parrot.com/usa (accessed March 5, 2013). Information on the BioBricks Foundation can be found at http://biobricks.org (accessed March 5, 2013).

40. Concerning the influence of biology in robotics: The US Air Force has built a "micro-aviary" at Wright Patterson Air Force Base for testing drones that resemble the size and behavior of bugs and birds. See John Horgan, "The Drones Come Home," *National Geographic*, March 2013, http://ngm.nationalgeographic.com/2013/03/unmanned-flight/horgan-text (accessed July 1, 2014). Researchers have borrowed from birds and insects to develop drones and robots with bug eyes, bat ears, bird wings, and even honeybee-like hairs that can be used to detect chemical, biological, and nuclear weapons. Ms. Smith, "The Future of Drone Surveillance: Swarms of Cyborg Insect Drones," *Network World*, June 18, 2012, http://www.networkworld.com/community/blog/future-drone-surveillance-swarms-cyborg-insect-drones (accessed July 1, 2014). DARPA (the Defense Advanced Research Projects Agency) has taken inspiration from the aviary and entomological worlds to the extreme. Its Hybrid Insect Micro-Electro-Mechanical Systems (HI-MEMS) program endeavors to "provide control over insect locomotion." In 2008, one DARPA researcher inserted a mechanized system into a larva's thorax; tissue actually developed around the machine as the insect grew into a moth. See Spencer Ackerman, "Air Force Keeps 'Micro-Aviary' of Tiny, Bird-Like 'Bots,'" *Wired Danger Room*, November 2, 2011, http://www.wired.com/dangerroom/2011/11/air-force-micro-aviary-drones (accessed July 1, 2014). On the creation of cyborg insects, see Ewen Callaway, "Free-Flying Cyborg Insects Steered from a Distance," *New Scientist*, October 1, 2009, http://www.newscientist.com/article/dn17895-freeflying-cyborg-insects-steered-from-a-distance.html (accessed July 1, 2014). See also Noah Shactman, "Pentagon's Cyborg Insects All Grown Up," *Wired Danger Room*, March 19, 2008, http://www.wired.com/dangerroom/2008/03/for-years-now-p (accessed March 5, 2013). The quotation from the National Research Council report can be found at Committee on Advances

in Technology and the Prevention of Their Application to Next Generation Biowarfare Threats, National Research Council, *Globalization, Biosecurity, and the Future of the Life Sciences* (Washington, DC: National Academy Press, 2006), 17.

41. Ray Kurzweil, *The Singularity Is Near* (New York: Viking, 2005).

42. James D. Fearon, "Catastrophic Terrorism and Civil Liberties in the Short and Long Run" (paper presented during Columbia University's 250th anniversary celebrations, October 17, 2003), www.stanford.edu/~jfearon/papers/civlibs.doc (accessed March 4, 2013).

43. See John Webster, *The Duchess of Malfi*, act 4, scene 2, line 262. On viewership of YouTube videos of targeted killings, see Dora Apel, *War Culture and the Contest of Images* (New Brunswick, NJ: Rutgers University Press, 2012), 182. For concerns about the "PlayStation mentality," see Jane Mayer, "The Predator War: What Are the Risks of the C.I.A.'s Covert Drone Program?" *New Yorker*, October 26, 2009, http://www.newyorker .com/reporting/2009/10/26/091026fa_fact_mayer (accessed July 1, 2014). See also Philip Alston and Hina Shamsi, "A Killer Above the Law?" *Guardian*, August 2, 2010, http:// www.theguardian.com/commentisfree/2010/feb/08/afghanistan-drones-defence-killing (accessed July 1, 2014).

Notes to Chapter 2

1. Kenneth Cukier and Viktor Mayer-Schönberger, *Big Data: A Revolution That Will Transform How We Live, Work, and Think* (New York: Houghton Mifflin Harcourt, 2013), 8–9.

2. For an account of the time a fly really did land on President Obama's forehead, see Jason Howerton, "The Latest in the Obama vs. Fly Saga: Large Fly Lands Defiantly on President's Forehead," *Blaze*, January 24, 2013, http://www.theblaze.com/stories/2013/01 /24/the-latest-in-the-obama-vs-fly-saga-large-fly-lands-defiantly-on-presidents-forehead (accessed July 4, 2014). The quotations from Joel Brenner can be found in Joel Brenner, *America the Vulnerable* (New York: Penguin, 2011), 1, 32.

3. See David Brin, *The Transparent Society* (Cambridge, MA: Perseus Books, 1998); Jeffrey Rosen, *The Naked Crowd* (New York: Random House, 2004); Robert O'Harrow Jr., *No Place to Hide: Behind the Scenes of Our Emerging Surveillance Society* (New York: Simon and Schuster, 2005); Jeffrey Rosen, *The Unwanted Gaze: The Destruction of Privacy in America* (New York: Random House, 2001). For information on the Target incident, see Charles Duhigg, "How Companies Learn Your Secrets," *New York Times*, February 16, 2012, http://www.nytimes.com/2012/02/19/magazine/shopping-habits.html (accessed July 4, 2014).

4. Ynet reporters, "Journalist Accused of Leaking Secret IDF Documents," YnetNews.com, August 4, 2010, http://www.ynetnews.com/articles/0,7340,L-3871981 ,00.html (accessed July 4, 2014).

5. Edward Wyatt, "F.T.C. Says Webcam's Flaw Put Users' Lives on Display," *New York Times*, September 4, 2013, http://www.nytimes.com/2013/09/05/technology/ftc -says-webcams-flaw-put-users-lives-on-display.html (accessed July 4, 2014). See also "Agreement Containing Consent Order in the Matter of Trendnet, Inc.," FTC.gov, September 4, 2013, http://www.ftc.gov/sites/default/files/documents/cases/2013 /09/130903trendnetorder.pdf (accessed July 4, 2014).

6. For the quotations from Baker, see Stewart A. Baker, *Skating on Stilts: Why We Aren't Stopping Tomorrow's Terrorism* (Stanford, CA: Hoover Institution Press, 2010), 12.

7. Brenner, *America the Vulnerable*, 54.

8. Ibid, 11.

9. Vida M. Antolin-Jenkins, "Defining the Parameters of Cyberwar Operations: Looking for Law in All the Wrong Places?" *Naval Law Review* 51 (2005): 133. The same figure is used in Gregory F. Intoccia and Joe Wesley Moore, "Communications Technology, Warfare, and the Law: Is the Network a Weapon System?" *Houston Journal of International Law* 28 (2006): 473, quoting Lawrence T. Greenberg et al., *Information Warfare and International Law* (Washington, DC: National Defense University Press, 1998), 12, http://www.dodccrp.org/files/Greenberg_Law.pdf (accessed July 4, 2014). Paul Rosenzweig offers a slightly lower figure, maintaining that between 85 and 90 percent of US government Internet traffic occurs on nongovernment networks. See Paul Rosenzweig, *Cyber Warfare: How Conflicts in Cyberspace Are Challenging America and Changing the World* (Santa Barbara, CA: Praeger, 2013), 226.

10. For Brenner's account of the Israeli operation and the data exhaust it left, see Brenner, *America the Vulnerable*, 161.

11. On the costs of cybercrime, see Peter Maass and Megha Rajagopalan, "Does Cybercrime Really Cost $1 Trillion?" *ProPublica*, August 2, 2012, http://www.propublica .org/article/does-cybercrime-really-cost-1-trillion/single (accessed July 4, 2014). See also Ross Anderson et al., "Measuring the Cost of Cybercrime" (paper presented at the Workshop on the Economics of Information Security, Berlin, Germany, June 25–26, 2012), 25, http://weis2012.econinfosec.org/papers/Anderson_WEIS2012.pdf (accessed July 4, 2014).

12. See US Department of Justice, *Victims of Identity Theft, 2012* (Washington, DC: Bureau of Justice Statistics, 2013), 1, http://www.bjs.gov/content/pub/pdf/vit12.pdf (accessed July 4, 2014); Lynn Langton and Michael Planty, *Victims of Identity Theft, 2008* (Washington, DC: Bureau of Justice Statistics, 2010), 1, http://www.bjs.gov/content/pub /pdf/vit08.pdf (accessed July 4, 2014).

13. Personal theft declined by 26.6 percent between 2001 and 2010, although it rose by almost 3 percent between 2009 and 2010. US Department of Justice, *Criminal Victimization, 2010* (Washington, DC: Bureau of Justice Statistics, 2011), 2, http://bjs .ojp.usdoj.gov/content/pub/pdf/cv10.pdf (accessed July 4, 2014).

14. On the Indiana case, see M. Alex Johnson, "Indiana ISP Owner Charged with 'Sextortion' of Minors," MSNBC.com, April 9, 2012, http://usnews.nbcnews.com/_news /2012/04/09/11103049-indiana-isp-owner-charged-with-sextortion-of-minors-hundreds -of-victims-might-have-been-targeted?lite (accessed July 4, 2014). US Attorney's Office, "Indiana Man Charged with Coercing a Minor to Produce Child Pornography," US Department of Justice, press release, April 13, 2012, http://www.justice.gov/usao /mie/news/2012/2012_4_13_rfinkbiner.html (accessed July 4, 2014). On the Florida case, see US Attorney's Office, Northern District of Florida, "Federal 'Sextortion' and Cyberstalking Charges Filed," FBI, May 15, 2012, http://www.fbi.gov/jacksonville /press-releases/2012/florida-man-indicted-by-federal-grand-jury-for-sextortion-and -cyberstalking (accessed July 4, 2014). On the California case, see "FBI Charges

Californian for 'Sextorting' 17-Year-Old Irish Girl, Getting Her to Strip," *IrishCentral*, September 27, 2013, http://www.irishcentral.com/news/fbi-charge-californian-for -sextorting-17-year-old-irish-girl-getting-her-to-strip-video-225552492-237780091.html (accessed July 4, 2014). The Israeli court decision can be found at Crim. App. 2656/13, *Plony (John Doe) v. The State of Israel*, delivered on January 21, 2014.

15. "New Wave of Cyber Blackmail Identified," Nett.com, August 24, 2010, http://nett.com.au/technology/new-wave-of-cyber-blackmail-identified-2 (accessed July 4, 2014).

16. U.S. Department of Education and U.S. Department of Justice, Office of Justice Programs, *Indicators of School Crime and Safety: 2012*, Bureau of Justice Statistics, June 2013, 44, http://www.bjs.gov/content/pub/pdf/iscs12.pdf (accessed July 4, 2014). See also Harvey Morris, "Fighting Cyberbullies with Laws and Laughter," *New York Times*, June 9, 2012, http://rendezvous.blogs.nytimes.com/2012/06/09/fighting-cyberbullies-with -laws-and-laughter (accessed July 4, 2014).

17. Department for Business Innovation and Skills, "2013 Information Security Breaches Survey," gov.uk, 2, https://www.gov.uk/government/uploads/system/uploads /attachment_data/file/200455/bis-13-p184-2013-information-security-breaches-survey -technical-report.pdf (accessed July 4, 2014).

18. For the Russian case, see Jart Armin, "Cyber-Blackmail Threatens Enterprises," *Internet Evolution*, May 20, 2010, http://jartarmin.com/index.php?option=com_content &view=article&id=350:cyber-blackmail-threatens-enterprises (accessed July 4, 2014). For the Indian case, see Shilpa Kannan, "India Steps Up Battle Against Rising Cyber Crime Wave," BBC.com, May 7, 2012, http://www.bbc.co.uk/news/business-17950502 (accessed July 4, 2014).

19. Charles Wilson, "Man Guilty of 'Sextortion' of Teens," *Boston Globe*, February 1, 2013, http://www.bostonglobe.com/news/nation/2013/02/01/indiana-man-plead-guilty -sextortion/uybAf1BdrvMpbuWpiEO7xL/story.html (accessed July 4, 2014).

20. SecDev Group and Munk Centre for International Studies, *Tracking GhostNet: Investigating a Cyber Espionage Network* (Toronto: Information Warfare Monitor, 2009), 14–15, http://www.scribd.com/doc/13731776/Tracking-GhostNet-Investigating-a-Cyber -Espionage-Network (accessed July 4, 2014).

21. For information on Anonymous, see Gabriella Coleman, *Hacker, Hoaxer, Whistleblower, Spy: The Story of Anonymous* (Brooklyn, NY: Verso, 2014). See also Parmy Olson, *We Are Anonymous: Inside the Hacker World of LulzSec, Anonymous, and the Global Cyber Insurgency* (New York: Little, Brown and Company, 2012).

22. Jana Winter, "Unmasking the World's Most Wanted Hacker," FoxNews.com, March 6, 2012, http://www.foxnews.com/scitech/2012/03/06/exclusive-unmasking-worlds -most-wanted-hacker (accessed July 4, 2014).

23. For the announcement of the Anonymous arrests, see US Department of Justice, "Sixteen Individuals Arrested in the United States for Alleged Roles in Cyber Attacks," July 19, 2011, http://www.justice.gov/criminal/cybercrime/press-releases/2011/cooper Arrested.pdf (accessed July 4, 2014). The criminal information against Monsegur can be found at *U.S. v. Monsegur*, 11-Cr.-666 (SDNY). The LulzSec indictment, along with a variety of others, can be found at "Court Documents," freeAnons, http://freeanons

.org/resources/court-documents (accessed July 4, 2014). For information on Monsegur's assistance to law enforcement and his sentencing, see Benjamin Weiser and Mark Mazetti, "Hacker Helped Disrupt 300 Web Attacks, Prosecutors Say," *New York Times*, May 24, 2014, http://www.nytimes.com/2014/05/25/nyregion/hacker-helped-disrupt -attacks-prosecutors-say.html (accessed July 4, 2014); see also Benjamin Weiser, "Hacker Who Helped Disrupt Cyberattacks Is Allowed to Walk Free," *New York Times*, May 27, 2014, http://www.nytimes.com/2014/05/28/nyregion/hacker-who-helped-disrupt -cyberattacks-is-allowed-to-walk-free.html (accessed July 4, 2014).

24. The editor of *Science* said that he would withhold some details from publication on the condition that the missing information would be made available to legitimate scientists worldwide. Denise Grady and William J. Broad, "Seeing Terror Risk, U.S. Asks Journals to Cut Flu Study Facts," *New York Times*, December 20, 2011, http://www .nytimes.com/2011/12/21/health/fearing-terrorism-us-asks-journals-to-censor-articles-on -virus.html (accessed July 4, 2014).

25. National Science Advisory Board for Biosecurity, *Findings and Recommendations*, NIH, March 29–30, 2012, 4, http://www.nih.gov/about/director/03302012_NSABB _Recommendations.pdf (accessed July 4, 2014).

26. The publication itself can be found at Sander Herfst et al., "Airborne Transmission of Influenza A/H5N1 Virus Between Ferrets," *Science* 336, no. 6088 (June 21, 2012): 1534–1541, http://www.sciencemag.org/content/336/6088/1534.full (accessed July 4, 2014). On the moratorium, see Nell Greenfieldboyce, "Scientists Take Cautious Tack on Bird Flu Research," National Public Radio, February 13, 2012, http://www.npr .org/2012/02/13/146784264/scientists-take-cautious-tack-on-bird-flu-research (accessed July 4, 2014). On its end and for Fouchier's and the other researcher's comments, see Nell Greenfieldboyce, "Scientists Put End to Moratorium on Bird Flu Research," National Public Radio, January 23, 2013, http://www.npr.org/blogs/health/2013/01/23/170072436 /scientists-put-an-end-to-moratorium-on-bird-flu-research (accessed July 4, 2014).

27. On the hack of the drone feeds, see Siobhan Gorman et al., "Insurgents Hack U.S. Drones," *Wall Street Journal*, December 17, 2009, http://online.wsj.com/article /SB126102247889095011.html (accessed July 4, 2014). On the virus that hit the drone fleet, see Noah Shachtman, "Exclusive: Computer Virus Hits U.S. Drone Fleet," *Wired Danger Room*, October 7, 2011, http://www.wired.com/dangerroom/2011/10/virus-hits -drone-fleet (accessed July 4, 2014).

Notes to Chapter 3

1. SecDev Group and Munk Centre for International Studies, *Tracking GhostNet: Investigating a Cyber Espionage Network* (Toronto: Information Warfare Monitor, 2009), http://www.scribd.com/doc/13731776/Tracking-GhostNet-Investigating-a-Cyber -Espionage-Network (accessed July 11, 2014). The quotation appears on p. 47 (emphasis in the original).

2. See "APT1: Exposing One of China's Cyber Espionage Units," Mandiant, February 19, 2013, http://intelreport.mandiant.com/Mandiant_APT1_Report.pdf (accessed July 11, 2014). See also Paul Rosenzweig, "DoD Says Earth Is Round . . . ," *Lawfare*, May 6, 2013, http://www.lawfareblog.com/2013/05/dod-says-earth-is-round (accessed July 11,

2014), citing Associated Press, "Pentagon: Chinese Government Waging Cyberattacks," FoxNews.com, May 6, 2013, http://www.foxnews.com/politics/2013/05/06/pentagon -chinese-government-waging-cyberattacks (accessed July 11, 2014). The indictment against five Chinese military officers was announced on May 19, 2014. See Indictment, *U.S. v. Wang Dong et al.*, 14-cr.118 (West Dist. Pa. May 1, 2014), http://www.justice .gov/iso/opa/resources/512201451913235846I949.pdf (accessed July 11, 2014). The Justice Department's announcement of the charges can be found at "U.S. Charges Five Chinese Military Hackers for Cyber Espionage Against U.S. Corporations and a Labor Organization for Commercial Advantage," Department of Justice, May 19, 2014, http://www.justice.gov/opa/pr/2014/May/14-ag-528.html (accessed July 11, 2014).

3. The quotations from the Palantir website can be found at "Mission Focus," Palantir, http://www.palantir.com/mission-focus (accessed July 5, 2013), and "About," Palantir, http://www.palantir.com/about (accessed July 5, 2013). The quotation from the Harris article can be found at Shane Harris, "Killer App," *Washingtonian*, January 31, 2012, http://www.washingtonian.com/articles/people/killer-app (accessed July 11, 2014). Harris's book on this history of data mining is Shane Harris, *The Watchers: The Rise of America's Surveillance State* (New York: Penguin Press, 2010).

4. See Erica Goode, "Shots Fired, Pinpointed and Argued Over," *New York Times*, May 28, 2012, http://www.nytimes.com/2012/05/29/us/shots-heard-pinpointed-and-argued -over.html (accessed July 11, 2014). See also ShotSpotter, "SST: World Leader in Gunshot Detection," Shotspotter.com, http://www.shotspotter.com (accessed November 30, 2012).

5. Dana Priest and William M. Arkin, *Top Secret America: The Rise of the New American Security State* (New York: Little, Brown and Company, 2011), 181–183. P. W. Singer, *Wired for War: The Robotics Revolution and Conflict in the Twenty-First Centtury,* (New York: Penguin Press, 2009), 370–373.

6. The leak on the NSA call records program can be found at Glenn Greenwald, "NSA Collecting Phone Records of Millions of Verizon Customers Daily," *Guardian*, June 5, 2013, http://www.theguardian.com/world/2013/jun/06/nsa-phone-records-verizon -court-order (accessed July 11, 2014). For leak of PRISM targeting of Internet and telephone communications worldwide, see Barton Gellmann and Laura Poitras, "U.S., British Intelligence Mining Data from Nine U.S. Internet Companies in Broad Secret Program," *Washington Post*, June 7, 2013, http://www.washingtonpost.com/investigations /us-intelligence-mining-data-from-nine-us-internet-companies-in-broad-secret-program /2013/06/06/3a0coda8-cebf-11e2-8845-d970ccb04497_story.html (accessed July 11, 2014). On the volume of e-mails NSA collected, see Jennifer Valentino-Devries and Siobhan Gorman, "What You Need to Know on New Details on NSA Spying," *Wall Street Journal*, August 20, 2013, http://online.wsj.com/news/articles/SB10001424127887324108 204579025222244858490 (accessed July 11, 2014). On the NSA's breaking of encryption systems, see Jeff Larson, Nicole Perlroth, and Scott Shane, "N.S.A. Able to Foil Basic Safeguards of Privacy on Web," *New York Times*, September 5, 2013, http://www.nytimes .com/2013/09/06/us/nsa-foils-much-internet-encryption.html (accessed July 11, 2014).

7. For an overview of the first two major Snowden leaks and the substance of what they revealed, see Robert Chesney and Benjamin Wittes, "A Tale of Two NSA Leaks: One Is Unsurprising, and Damaging; the Other Is Worth Debating," *New Republic*, June 10,

2013, http://www.newrepublic.com/article/113427/nsa-spying-scandal-one-leak-more -damaging-other (accessed July 11, 2014).

8. David H. Petraeus, remarks presented at In-Q-Tel CEO Summit, Arlington, Virginia, CIA, March 1, 2012, https://www.cia.gov/news-information/speeches -testimony/2012-speeches-testimony/in-q-tel-summit-remarks.html (accessed July 11, 2014).

9. For information on Kaspersky Lab, see "About Kaspersky Lab," Kaspersky .com, http://www.kaspersky.com/about (accessed December 2, 2012). For an account of Kaspersky Lab's revealing of the Flame virus, see Chloe Albanesius, "Massive 'Flame' Malware Stealing Data Across Middle East," *PC World*, May 28, 2012, http://www.pcmag .com/article2/0,2817,2404951,00.asp (accessed July 11, 2014). The ITU's account of Flame can be found at "ITU Cybersecurity Activities," International Telecommunication Union, http://www.itu.int/cybersecurity/Articles/FAQs_on_FLAME.pdf (accessed July 11, 2014).

10. The text of CALEA can be found at 47 U.S.C. §§ 1001–1010. On the controversy surrounding it, see Larry Thompson, "CALEA: The Challenge of New Technologies," in *Protecting What Matters: Technology Security and Liberty Since 9/11*, ed. Clayton Northouse (Washington, DC: Brookings Institution Press, 2006), 93–94.

11. See CALEA at §§ 1002(a)(1), 1008(a).

12. For CALEA's growth to include Internet traffic and VOIP, see "Joint Petition of United States Department of Justice, Federal Bureau of Investigation and Drug Enforcement Administration, for Rulemaking to Resolve Various Outstanding Issues Concerning the Implementation of the Communications Assistance for Law Enforcement Act," FCC, March 10, 2004. The commission's ruling can be found at Second Report and Order and Memorandum Opinion and Order, FCC, May 12, 2006, https://apps.fcc.gov/edocs_public/attachmatch/FCC-06-56A1.pdf (accessed July 11, 2014).

13. On the Clipper Chip debate, see Peter H. Lewis, "Of Privacy and Security: The Clipper Chip Debate," *New York Times*, April 24, 1994, http://www.nytimes. com/1994/04/24/business/of-privacy-and-security-the-clipper-chip-debate.html (accessed July 11, 2014). The Clipper Chip, writes Lewis, "aimed to make it easier for law enforcement officials to conduct legal wiretaps on new generations of devices that send information over the telephone system, including wireless phones, computers and facsimile machine." On the NSA's post-Clipper efforts to circumvent encryption systems, see Larson, Perlroth, and Shane, "N.S.A. Able to Foil Basic Safeguards of Privacy on Web."

14. The FISA Amendments Act of 2008 is Pub. L. 110-261. The Protect America Act of 2007 is Pub. L. 110-55. The FISA Amendments Reauthorization Act of 2012 is Pub. L. 112-238.

15. United States Senate, "Foreign and Military Intelligence: Final Report of the Senate Committee to Study Governmental Operations with Respect to Intelligence Activities," Report No. 94-755, 94th Cong., 2d Sess., April 26, 1976, Book III, 740.

16. The requirement to report wire transactions in excess of $10,000 stems from the Bank Secrecy Act, which is codified at 31 U.S.C. § 5313 (1988). The criminal prohibition against structuring transactions to evade reporting requirements appears at 31 U.S.C.

§ 5324. The suspicious transaction reporting requirements are in § 351 of the USA PATRIOT Act of 2001, Pub. L. 107-56. The suspicious activity reporting forms can be found at IRS Cat. No. 22285L, box 35, http://www.ofi.la.gov/sarform-fincen.pdf (accessed July 11, 2014).

17. The Oil Pollution Act is codified at 33 U.S.C. § 2701 (1990).

18. Jason Tuohey, "Government Uses Color Laser Printer Technology to Track Documents," *PC World*, November 22, 2004, http://www.pcworld.com/article/118664 /government_uses_color_laser_printer_technology_to_track_documents.html (accessed July 11, 2014). See also Melissa Riofrio, "Why You Can't Print Counterfeit Money on Your Color Laser," *PC World*, June 7, 2011, http://www.pcworld.com/article/229647 /why_you_cant_print_counterfeit_money_on_your_color_laser.html (accessed July 11, 2014).

19. Jon Michaels, "Deputizing Homeland Security," *Texas Law Review* 88, no. 7 (2010): 1440.

20. The Nuclear Waste Policy Act, codified at 42 USC §§ 10151–10157, regulates the handling of spent nuclear fuels, including the responsibilities of the operators of nuclear energy plants. The Invention Secrecy Act is codified at 35 U.S.C. §§ 181–188 (1951).

21. Although modern interpretations view the Second Amendment as expressing an individual's right to bear arms, many scholars have maintained that the Framers originally crafted it to express a preference for state-run citizen militias over large, federal standing armies. See, for example, Akhil Reed Amar, *America's Constitution: A Biography* (New York: Random House, 2005), 318–322. After the colonies declared their independence, the Continental Navy comprised very few ships. Lacking the funds to build a navy sufficient to defend against the British, the Continental Congress issued letters of marque and reprisal, giving privately owned, armed merchant ships permission to attack enemy merchant ships. See Robert H. Patton, *Patriot Pirates: The Privateer War for Freedom and Fortune in the American Revolution* (New York: Pantheon Books, 2008).

22. Alexander Hamilton, "Federalist No. 23," in *The Federalist Papers: A Collection of Essays Written in Support of the Constitution of the United States*, ed. Roy P. Fairfield (Baltimore: Johns Hopkins University Press, 1981).

23. The quotation is from Alexander Hamilton, "Federalist No. 70," in *The Federalist Papers*, Library of Congress, http://thomas.loc.gov/home/fedpapers/fed_70.html (accessed December 3, 2012).

24. For examples of restrictions on bars, see Christina Ng, "Alaska Cops Arresting Drunks in Bars," ABCNews.com, January 10, 2012, http://abcnews.go.com/US/illegal -drunk-alaska-bars-law/story?id=15330748 (accessed July 11, 2014); Texas Alcoholic Beverage Commission (TABC) Rule § 45.103, January 2013, TABC, https://www.tabc .state.tx.us/laws/other/TABCRules.pdf (accessed July 11, 2014); Title IV Alcoholic Beverage Control, Rule 73.1, Delaware General Assembly, May 17, 1997, http:// regulations.delaware.gov/AdminCode/title4/regulations-81.shtml (accessed July 11, 2014).

25. The John Adams quotation can be found in C. Kevin Marshall, "Putting Privateers in Their Place: The Applicability of the Marque and Reprisal Clause to Undeclared Wars," *University of Chicago Law Review* 64, no. 3 (1997): 960. The Thomas

Jefferson quotation can be found in Gomer Williams, *History of the Liverpool Privateers and Letters of Marque* (New York: Augustus M. Kelley, 1966 [1897]), 459, quoted in Robert P. DeWitte, "Let Privateers Marque Terrorism: A Proposal for a Reawakening," *Indiana Law Journal* 82, no. 1 (2007): 134. The authority to grant letters of marque and reprisal can be found in US Const. art. I, § 8, cl. 11.

26. Stephen Budiansky, *Perilous Fight: America's Intrepid War with Britain on the High Seas, 1812–1815* (New York: Alfred A Knopf, 2010), 247–248, 286.

27. The banning of privateering in international law took place in the Paris Declaration Respecting Maritime Law, April 16, 1856, published in Natalino Ronzitti, *The Law of Naval Warfare: A Collection of Agreements and Documents with Commentaries* (Dordrecht: Martinus Nijhoff, 1988), 61.

28. For an example of a proposal to use privateering in the context of counterterrorism policy, see DeWitte, "Let Privateers Marque Terrorism," 130–158.

29. For the use of zero-days in Stuxnet, see Dan Goodin, "Discovery of New 'Zero-Day' Exploit Links Developers of Stuxnet, Flame," *Ars Technica*, June 11, 2012, http://arstechnica.com/security/2012/06/zero-day-exploit-links-stuxnet-flame (accessed July 11, 2014). For the use of zero-days in the attacks on Google, see Kim Zetter, "Sleuths Trace New Zero-Day Attacks to Hackers Who Hit Google," *Wired Threat Level*, September 7, 2012, http://www.wired.com/threatlevel/2012/09/google-hacker-gang -returns/all (accessed July 11, 2014).

30. For information on the commercial trade in zero-days, see Nicole Perlroth and David Sanger, "Nations Buying as Hackers Sell Flaws in Computer Code," *New York Times*, July 13, 2013, http://www.nytimes.com/2013/07/14/world/europe/nations-buying -as-hackers-sell-computer-flaws.html (accessed July 11, 2014). For an example of the US government's conflicting interests with respect to zero-day vulnerabilities, consider the controversy that erupted over the so-called Heartbleed flaw in the OpenSSL cryptography system. Bloomberg News reported that the NSA had exploited the flaw—a charge the NSA quickly denied. See "Statement on Bloomberg News Story That NSA Knew About the 'Heartbleed Bug' Flaw and Regularly Used It to Gather Critical Intelligence," April 11, 2014, http://icontherecord.tumblr.com/post/82416436703/statement-on-bloomberg -news-story-that-nsa-knew (accessed July 11, 2014). The statement declared, "When Federal agencies discover a new vulnerability in commercial and open source software— a so-called 'Zero day' vulnerability because the developers of the vulnerable software have had zero days to fix it—it is in the national interest to responsibly disclose the vulnerability rather than to hold it for an investigative or intelligence purpose." The statement described a process used to determine whether to exploit or reveal a discovered zero-day and concluded, "Unless there is a clear national security or law enforcement need, this process is biased toward responsibly disclosing such vulnerabilities."

31. Eric S. Raymond, "The Cathedral and the Bazaar," catb.org, http://www.catb.org /esr/writings/homesteading/cathedral-bazaar (accessed July 11, 2014).

Notes to Chapter 4

1. Neal Purvis, Robert Wade, and John Logan, *Skyfall,* dir. Sam Mendes (Los Angeles: Metro-Goldwyn-Mayer Studios and Columbia Pictures, 2012).

2. Alfred Lord Tennyson, "Ulysses," in *The Complete Poetical Works of Tennyson*, ed. W. J. Rolfe (Boston: Houghton Mifflin, 1898), 89.

3. Maximilian Weber, "The Profession and Vocation of Politics," in *Political Writings*, ed. Peter Lassman and Ronald Speirs (Cambridge: Cambridge University Press, 2010), 310–313 (emphasis in the original).

4. See Janice E. Thomson, *Mercenaries, Pirates, and Sovereigns: State-Building and Extraterritorial Violence in Early Modern Europe* (Princeton, NJ: Princeton University Press, 1996), 42–43, 59–68. See also Gary M. Anderson and Adam Gifford Jr., "Privateering and the Private Production of Naval Power," *Cato Journal* 11 (1991): 99, 118; Alexander Tabarok, "The Rise, Fall, and Rise Again of Privateers," *Independent Review* 4 (spring 2007): 565, 573–574.

5. For Marx's speculations about technology and the decline of the state, see Karl Marx, "Manifesto of the Communist Party," in *The Marx-Engels Reader*, ed. Robert C. Tucker (New York: W. W. Norton & Co., 1978), 475–483, 488–489. For speculation that globalization will lead to the decline of the state, see Martin Wolf, "Will the Nation-State Survive Globalization," *Foreign Affairs* 80 (January/February 2001): 178. For discussion of the belief that the Internet will spark the decline of the state, see Jack Goldsmith and Tim Wu, *Who Controls the Internet? Illusions of a Borderless World* (New York: Oxford University Press, 2006), 179.

6. See Steven Pinker, *The Better Angels of Our Nature: Why Violence Has Declined* (New York: Viking, 2011). The first quotation can be found on p. 680; the second can be found on p. 313. Pinker doubts that even the world wars of the twentieth century were unprecedented in their death toll compared to earlier conflicts, especially when controlling for relative population sizes. Note that the emergence of the state is only one, however important, factor among those that led, per Pinker's analysis, to the decline of violence in our present age.

7. Plato, "Crito," in *Plato: Six Great Dialogues*, trans. Benjamin Jowett (Mineola, NY: Dover, 2007), 23–33.

8. Carl Stephenson, *Mediaeval Feudalism* (Ithaca, NY: Cornell University Press, 1942), 45.

9. Charles Tilly, "Reflections on the History of European State-Making," in *The Formation of National States in Western Europe*, ed. Charles Tilly (Princeton, NJ: Princeton University Press, 1975), 42. See also B. D. Porter, *War and the Rise of the State: The Military Foundations of Modern Politics* (New York: Free Press, 1994), 31; Clifford J. Rogers, "The Military Revolutions of the Hundred Years War," in *The Military Revolution Debate: Readings on the Military Transformation of Early Modern Europe*, ed. Clifford J. Rogers (Boulder, CO: Westview Press, 1995), 75; Hendrick Spruyt, "The Origins, Development, and Possible Demise of the Modern State," *Annual Review of Political Science* 5 (2002): 127, 135–136.

10. Hugo Grotius, *The Rights of War and Peace*, trans. A. C. Campbell (London: M. W. Dunne, 1901), 63–72 (book 1, parts 8–11).

11. Thomas Hobbes, *Leviathan*, ed. Ian Shapiro (New Haven, CT: Yale University Press, 2010), 77–78.

12. Ibid., 104–105.

13. Ibid., 106–110.

14. Ibid., 132–134.

15. John Locke, "Second Treatise on Government," in *Two Treatises on Government*, ed. Mark Goldie (Rutland, VT: Everyman, 1993), 158, 225–226, 232.

16. The first quotation can be found in Jean-Jacques Rousseau, *On the Origin of Inequality*, trans. G. D. H. Cole (New York: Cosimo, 2005), 52–53. The second is from Jean-Jacques Rousseau, "Of the Social Contract—Essay on the Form of the Republic (Geneva Manuscript)," in *The Social Contract and Other Later Political Writings*, trans. and ed. Victor Gourevitch (Cambridge: Cambridge University Press, 1997), 153. For Rousseau's vision of the purpose of government, see Jean-Jacques Rousseau, "Of the Social Contract or Principles of Political Right," in Gourevitch, *The Social Contract and Other Later Political Writings*, 50.

17. For Rawls's vision of the social contract, see John Rawls, *A Theory of Justice* (Cambridge: Belknap Press of Harvard University, 1971). For Nozick's vision, see Robert Nozick, *Anarchy, State, and Utopia* (New York: Basic Books, 1974).

18. See Nozick, *Anarchy, State, and Utopia*, 26–28.

19. Locke, "Second Treatise on Government," 121.

20. Dante's use of the phrase "many-headed beast" appears in Dante Alighieri, *Monarchy*, ed. and trans. Prue Shaw (Cambridge: Cambridge University Press, 2003), 28. The second quotation comes from Dante Alighieri, "The Banquet [Convivio]," in *Reading in Medieval Political Theory: 1100–1400*, ed. Cary J. Nederman and Kate Langdon Forhan, trans. Kate Forhan (Indianapolis: Hackett, 2000), 169. His endorsement of a restoration of the Holy Roman Empire to its former glory appears in Alighieri, *Monarchy*, xvi.

21. Castel's proposal can be found in Abbé de Saint-Pierre, *Projet pour render la paix perpétuelle en Europe* (Paris: Fayard, 1986). Rousseau's account of the project can be found in Jean-Jacques Rousseau, *A Lasting Peace Through the Federation of Europe and the State of War*, trans. C. E. Vaughan (London: Constable & Co. Ltd., 1917), 63. Kant's proposal can be found in Immanuel Kant, "The Metaphysics of Morals," in *Political Writings*, ed. Hans Reiss, trans. H. B. Nisbert (New York: Cambridge University Press, 1991), 102–105. Kant's contemporary Anacharsis Cloots (Jean-Baptiste du Val-de-Grace, baron de Cloots) similarly relied on social contract theory to advocate a universal republic in lieu of a system of sovereign states. See Pauline Kleingeld, *Kant and Cosmopolitanism: The Philosophical Ideal of World Citizenship* (Cambridge: Cambridge University Press, 2012), 40–42.

22. Alfred Lord Tennyson, "Locksley Hall," in *The Complete Poetical Works of Tennyson*, ed. W. J. Rolfe (Boston: Houghton Mifflin, 1898), 93. On Truman's keeping the poem in his wallet, see Paul Kennedy, *The Parliament of Man: The Past, Present, and Future of the United Nations* (New York: Harper Collins, 2007), xi. The quotation from Einstein can be found at Albert Einstein, "Towards a World Government (1946)," in *Out of My Later Years: The Scientist, Philosopher and Man Portrayed Through His Own Words* (New York: Wings Books, 1956), 138.

23. See Philip Beidler, "Remembering Wendell Willkie's One World," *Canadian Review of American Studies* 24 (1994): 87. See also Emery Reves, *The Anatomy of Peace* (New York: Pocket Books, 1946).

24. Vladimir Lenin, "The Communist Manifesto and the State," in *The Communist Manifesto*, ed. Fredric Bender (New York: W. W. Norton, 1988), 135.

25. The Maastricht Treaty can be found at Treaty on European Union, 1992 O.J. (C 191) 1; 31 I.L.M. 253, Eur-Lex, http://eur-lex.europa.eu/en/treaties/dat /11992M/htm/11992M.html (accessed August 15, 2013); on European consolidation, see also Kimmo Kiljunen, *The European Constitution in the Making* (Brussels: Center for European Policy Studies, 2004), 21. The Rome Statute can be found at UN General Assembly, Rome Statute of the International Criminal Court, July 17, 1998, 2187 U.N.T.S. 90, United Nations Official Legal Affairs, http://untreaty.un.org/cod/icc /statute/romefra.htm (accessed August 15, 2013).

26. On United Nations dysfunction, see Kenneth Anderson, *Living with the UN: American Responsibilities and International Order* (Stanford, CA: Hoover Institution Press, 2012).

27. Hobbes, *Leviathan*, 79.

28. For the assets of HSBC and JP Morgan Chase, see "HSBC Holdings PLC," *CNN Money*, http://money.cnn.com/quote/financials/financials.html?symb =HBC&dataSet=BS (accessed July 6, 2013); "JP Morgan Chase," *CNN Money*, http://money.cnn.com/quote/financials/financials.html?symb=JPM&dataSet=BS (accessed July 6, 2013). On Hezbollah's fighting strength, some analysts estimate that Hezbollah has five thousand active fighters with another fifteen thousand in reserve. See Anne Bernard, "Hezbollah Takes Risks by Fighting Rebels in Syria," *New York Times*, May 8, 2013, A6, http://www.nytimes.com/2013/05/08/world/middleeast/hezbollah-takes -risks-by-fighting-rebels-in-syria.html (accessed July 6, 2013). The US State Department estimates Hezbollah to have "several thousand supporters and members." See "Country Reports on Terrorism," US Department of State, http://www.state.gov/j/ct/rls/crt/2011 /195553.htm# (accessed July 6, 2013). Hamas, meanwhile, has been estimated to have about twenty-five hundred military personnel, in addition to about fourteen thousand police and intelligence personnel. See Jim Zanotti, "Hamas: Background and Issues for Congress," Congressional Research Service Report for Congress, Federation of American Scientists, December 2, 2010, 9, https://www.fas.org/sgp/crs/mideast/R41514.pdf (accessed July 16, 2014). The US State Department estimates that Hamas has "several thousand Gaza-based operatives," in addition to the police and intelligence apparatus, estimated to number about nine thousand personnel. See "Country Reports on Terrorism," US Department of State. FARC is estimated to have eight to nine thousand fighters. See "Country Reports on Terrorism," US Department of State. For an account of ISIS funding, see Martin Chulov, "How an Arrest in Iraq Revealed ISIS's $2bn Jihadist Network," *Guardian*, June 15, 2014, http://www.theguardian.com/world/2014/jun/15 /iraq-isis-arrest-jihadists-wealth-power (accessed July 16, 2014).

29. Philip Bobbitt, *The Shield of Achilles: War, Peace, and the Course of History* (New York: Knopf, 2002), 304.

30. Barack Obama, "Remarks by the President on Review of Signals Intelligence," January 17, 2014, http://www.whitehouse.gov/the-press-office/2014/01/17/remarks -president-review-signals-intelligence (accessed July 15, 2014).

Notes to Chapter 5

1. The letter itself can be found in Benjamin Franklin, "Pennsylvania Assembly: Reply to the Governor, November 11, 1755," in *The Papers of Benjamin Franklin*, ed. Helene H. Fineman and Leonard W. Labaree (New Haven, CT: Yale University Press, 1963), 6:242. For background on the politics of the confrontation between the government and the assembly, see H. W. Brands, *The First American: The Life and Times of Benjamin Franklin* (New York: Anchor Books, 2002), ch. 11. See also Walter Issacson, *Benjamin Franklin: An American Life* (New York: Simon & Schuster, 2003), ch. 7.

2. *United States v. Kincade*, 379 F.3d 813 (9th Cir. 2004).

3. *United States v. Amerson*, 483 F.3d 73, 86 (2d Cir. 2005).

4. The Supreme Court in 2013 upheld the collection of DNA samples from individuals merely charged with a crime. Notably, even the dissenting justices acknowledged that "it would have been entirely permissible as far as the Fourth Amendment is concerned . . . to take a sample of . . . DNA as a consequence of . . . conviction." See *Maryland v. King*, 133 S. Ct. 1958 (2013).

5. William H. Rehnquist, *All the Laws but One: Civil Liberties in Wartime* (New York: Alfred A. Knopf, 1998), 222.

6. Eric A. Posner and Adrian Vermeule, *Terror in the Balance: Security, Liberty, and the Courts* (New York: Oxford University Press, 2007), 12.

7. Ibid., 26.

8. See, for example, President Barack Obama, "Remarks by the President on National Security," White House, May 21, 2009, http://www.whitehouse.gov/the-press -office/remarks-president-national-security-5-21-09 (accessed July 18, 2014).

9. See "Worst of the Worst," Freedom House, http://www.freedomhouse.org/sites /default/files/WorstOfTheWorst2011.pdf (accessed October 2, 2013).

10. Thomas Hobbes, *Leviathan*, ed. Ian Shapiro (New Haven, CT: Yale University Press, 2010), 104.

11. Charles de Montesquieu, *The Spirit of the Laws*, ed. Anne Cohler et al. (Cambridge: Cambridge University Press, 1989), 157.

12. John Locke, *Political Writings: John Locke*, ed. David Wootton (Indianapolis: Hackett, 2003), 306.

13. George Orwell, *1984* (New York: Signet Classic, 1950), 103.

14. See Alexander Hamilton, "The Federalist No. 1: Introduction," in *The Federalist Papers: A Collection of Essays Written in Support of the Constitution of the United States*, ed. Roy P. Fairfield (Baltimore: Johns Hopkins University Press, 1981). See also Alexander Hamilton, "The Federalist No. 8: The Consequences of Hostilities Between the States," in Fairfield, *The Federalist Papers*.

15. James Madison, "The Federalist No. 51: The Structure of the Government Must Furnish the Proper Checks and Balances Between the Different Departments," in Fairfield, *The Federalist Papers*.

16. Alexander Hamilton, "The Federalist No. 70: The Executive Department Further Considered," in Fairfield, *The Federalist Papers*.

17. Philip Bobbitt, *Terror and Consent: The Wars for the Twenty-First Century* (New York: Knopf, 2008), 241. Writes Bobbitt, while "there is something to . . . these intensely

and sometimes unthinkingly held assumptions, . . . the spectrum view [of liberty and security] and its corollaries are . . . radically incomplete " (242).

18. Samuel D. Warren and Louis D. Brandeis, "The Right to Privacy," *Harvard Law Review* 4 (1890): 193, 195. We focus here on informational privacy, as distinct from decisional or "constitutional" privacy; the latter protects certain substantive rights, such as the right to access to contraception or to decide to have an abortion, and is a distinct doctrine in US courts' jurisprudence.

19. See Judith Jarvis Thomson, "The Right to Privacy," *Philosophy and Public Affairs* 4 (summer 1975): 295. See also Daniel J. Solove, *The Digital Person: Technology and Privacy in the Information Age* (New York: New York University Press, 2004), 38.

20. Federal Trade Commission (FTC), *Protecting Consumer Privacy in the Information Age: A Proposed Framework for Businesses and Policymakers* (Washington, DC: FTC, 2010), 20, http://www.ftc.gov/os/2010/12/101201privacyreport.pdf (accessed July 18, 2014).

21. For an overview of the subject from the perspective of the US government, see Stewart A. Baker, *Skating on Stilts: Why We Aren't Stopping Tomorrow's Terrorism* (Stanford, CA: Hoover Institution Press, 2010), 89–105.

22. FTC, *Protecting Consumer Privacy in the Information Age*, vii.

23. Rosen's article can be found at Jeffrey Rosen, "The Web Means the End of Forgetting," *New York Times Magazine*, July 21, 2010, http://www.nytimes.com/2010/07/25/magazine/25privacy-t2.html (accessed July 18, 2014). The quotation from Solove's book can be found at Daniel Solove, *The Future of Reputation: Gossip, Rumor, and Privacy on the Internet* (New Haven, CT: Yale University Press, 2007), 11. For an account of Anonymous's threat to out cyberbullies, see Emily Bazelon, "What Do Anonymous and MTV Have in Common?" *Slate*, November 20, 2012, http://www.slate.com/articles/news_and_politics/bulle/2012/11/anonymous_and_mtv_trying_to_protect_kids_online.html (accessed July 18, 2014). See also Cavan Sieczkowski, "Amanda Todd's Alleged Bully Named by Anonymous After Teen's Tragic Suicide," *Huffington Post*, October 16, 2012, http://www.huffingtonpost.com/2012/10/16/amanda-todd-bully-anonymous-suicide_n_1969792.html (accessed July 18, 2014). The dismissed teacher-in-training sought recourse in federal court but was denied relief. See *Snyder v. Millersville Univ.*, 2008 WL 5093140, No. 07-1660 (E.D. Pa. Dec. 3, 2008).

24. Herbert George Wells et al., *The Science of Life* (New York: Doubleday, Doran & Co., 1939), 932.

25. For a useful discussion of the moral dimensions of this sort of distribution of protection for liberty and security, see Jeremy Waldron, *Torture, Terror, and Trade-Offs* (Oxford: Oxford University Press, 2010), 33–39.

26. *Terminiello v. Chicago*, 337 U.S. 1, 37 (1949).

27. Ibid., 35 (internal citations omitted).

Notes to Chapter 6

1. See Aviel Magnezi, "Saudi Hacker Strikes Again," YnetNews.com, January 11, 2012, http://www.ynetnews.com/articles/0,7340,L-4174603,00.html (accessed July 21, 2014). See also Amy Teibel, "Hackers Disclose Israelis' Credit Card Information," *Daily Caller*,

January 3, 2012, http://dailycaller.com/2012/01/03/hackers-disclose-israelis-credit-card
-information (accessed July 21, 2014).

2. Al Arabiya, "Israel Vows to Hit Back After Saudi Hacker Exposed Its Citizens'
Credit Cards," Al Arabiya News, January 7, 2012, http://www.alarabiya.net/articles/2012
/01/07/186957.html (accessed October 21, 2013).

3. On the ILOVEYOU bug, see Susan W. Brenner, *Cybercrime: Criminal Threats from
Cyberspace* (Santa Barbara, CA: Praeger, 2010), 33. On the scope of the damage, see Mark
D. Goodman and Susan W. Brenner, "The Emerging Consensus on Criminal Conduct
in Cyberspace," *International Journal of Law and Information Technology* 10 (2002): 139,
141; see also Mark Landler, "A Filipino Linked to 'Love-Bug' Talks About His License to
Hack," *New York Times*, October 21, 2000, http://www.nytimes.com/2000/10/21
/business/a-filipino-linked-to-love-bug-talks-about-his-license-to-hack.html (accessed
July 21, 2014).

4. On the de Guzman investigation, see Wayne Arnold, "Philippines to Drop
Charges on E-Mail Virus," *New York Times*, August 22, 2000, http://www.nytimes
.com/2000/08/22/business/technology-philippines-to-drop-charges-on-e-mail-virus
.html (accessed July 21, 2014). On the failure of the US extradition request, see Goodman
and Brenner, "The Emerging Consensus on Criminal Conduct in Cyberspace," 141. De
Guzman was listed as number eight among the top ten hackers in the world, according
to the *World Top 10* blog; see Kamal Goyal, "Top Ten Hackers of the World," *World Top
Ten*, January 25, 2012, http://worldtop10.net/top-10-hackers-of-the-world (accessed July
21, 2014).

5. Philip Bobbitt, *Terror and Consent: The Wars for the Twenty-First Century* (New
York: Knopf, 2008), 290.

6. On British impressment of American seamen and the different conceptions of
citizenship and nationality that drove it, see Stephen Budiansky, *Perilous Fight: America's
Intrepid War with Britain on the High Seas, 1812–1815* (New York: Alfred A Knopf, 2010),
54.

7. *S.S. Lotus (Fr. v. Turk.)*, 1927 P.C.I.J. (ser. A) No. 10, at 18, WorldCourts, http://
www.worldcourts.com/pcij/eng/decisions/1927.09.07_lotus.htm (accessed July 21,
2014).

8. Restatement (Third) of Foreign Relations Law §§ 402, 421, 431 (American Law
Institute, 1987).

9. *Blackmer v. United States*, 284 U.S. 421 (1932).

10. *Joyce. v. Director of Public Prosecutions* [1946] AC 347, 372 House of Lords.

11. Noriega was convicted of eight of the ten counts and sentenced to forty years'
imprisonment, later reduced to thirty. *United States v. Noriega*, 746 F.Supp. 1506, 1514
(S.D. Fla. 1990) aff'd, 117 F.3d 1206 (11th Cir. 1997). Under the Foreign Trade Antitrust
Improvements Act of 1982 (FTAIA), the Sherman Act "shall not apply to conduct
involving trade or commerce . . . with foreign nations." 15 U.S.C.A. § 6a. However, the
FTAIA excepted from this general bar conduct that directly, substantially, and reasonably
foreseeably affected domestic trade or commerce, imports, and American exports. *Id.*;
see *F. Hoffmann-La Roche Ltd. v. Empagran S.A.*, 542 U.S. 155, 165, (2004). Note that
the substantial effects theory could have justified Turkey's claim of jurisdiction over the

French ship, since the actions of Monsieur Demons ended up causing great damage to a Turkish vessel, which, under international law, is an extension of Turkish territory. The same theory could have also justified the criminal trial of de Guzman in the United States for the harms he ended up causing to American computers.

12. Erica M. Davila, "International E-Discovery: Navigating the Maze," *University of Pittsburgh Journal of Technology Law and Policy* 8 (2008): 5; Restatement (Third) of Foreign Relations Law § 442. See also *Vanity Fair Mills, Inc. v. T. Eaton Co.*, 133 F.Supp. 522, 529 n.2 (S.D.N.Y. 1955) modified, 234 F.2d 633 (2d Cir. 1956).

13. For an example of domestic courts rejecting claims of extraterritorial jurisdiction, see *United States v. Ali*, 885 F.Supp. 2d 55 (D.D.C. 2012), in which a US district court refused to enforce an American hostage-taking statute extraterritorially because of due process concerns. The case was reversed by an appeals court. See 718 F.3d 929, 943 (D.C. Cir. 2013).

14. For instance, the United States refrained from ratifying the 1977 Additional Protocols to the Geneva Convention (both I and II). See Derek Jinks and David Sloss, "Is the President Bound by the Geneva Conventions?" *Cornell Law Review* 90 (2004): 97, 111. Those protocols expanded the protections given to nonstate actors, forbade almost all forms of belligerent reprisals (reciprocal violations of the laws of war), and added special protections to particular types of objects (for example, the environment). See Protocol I, June 8, 1977, 1125 U.N.T.S. 3, United Nations Treaty Collection, http://treaties.un.org /doc/Publication/U.N.T.S./Volume%201125/volume-1125-I-17512-English.pdf (accessed October 21, 2013); Protocol II, June 8, 1977, 1125 U.N.T.S. 609, United Nations Treaty Collection, http://treaties.un.org/doc/Publication/U.N.T.S./Volume%201125/volume -1125-I-17513-English.pdf (accessed October 21, 2013).

15. For a discussion of the convergence of criminal and military law in counterterrorism, see Robert Chesney and Jack Goldsmith, "Terrorism and the Convergence of Criminal and Military Detention Models," *Stanford Law Review* 60 (2008): 1079.

16. See, for example, Universal Declaration of Human Rights, G.A. Res. 217 (III) A U.N. Doc. A/RES?217(III) (Dec. 10, 1948). Article X requires that criminal defendants have the right to a public hearing on the charges against them. Article XI provides all criminal defendants with the rights to be considered innocent until proven guilty, to a public trial, and to "all the guarantees necessary for [their] defense"; it also bans the retroactive application of laws. Another example is the International Covenant on Civil and Political Rights, art. 14, December 19, 1966, 999 U.N.T.S. 175, which provides for the rights to, among other things, a public trial, presumption of innocence, knowledge of charges, adequate time and facilities to prepare a defense, counsel, examination of witnesses, and appeal, as well as the right to avoid self-incrimination.

17. See Theodor Meron, "The Humanization of Humanitarian Law," *American Journal of International Law* 94 (2000): 239, 245.

18. See letter from Lt. Gen. Dana K. Chipman to Rep. Thomas J. Rooney, ABCNews.com, May 16, 2013, http://abcnews.go.com/images/Blotter/Army Response_052213.pdf (accessed July 21, 2014).

19. For an example of an argument for greater state responsibility for terrorist acts emanating from the state in question, see Tal Becker, *Terrorism and the State: Rethinking the Rules of State Responsibility* (Oxford: Hart Publishing, 2006).

20. The principles governing state responsibility are enumerated in the Draft Articles on State Responsibility, a document produced by the International Law Commission and largely seen as reflecting customary international law, even if some issues are still under debate. See Draft Articles on State Responsibility (2001), International Law Students Association, http://www.ilsa.org/jessup/jessup06/basicmats2/DASR.pdf (accessed October 21, 2013).

21. Compare International Court of Justice (ICJ), *Case Concerning Military and Paramilitary Activities in and against Nicaragua* (Merits), judgment of June 27, 1986, at ¶¶ 105–115, and ICJ, *Case Concerning the Application of the Convention on the Prevention and Punishment of the Crime of Genocide*, judgment of February 26, 2007, ¶¶ 385–420 (both demanding effective control), with *Prosecutor v. Tadić*, International Criminal Tribunal for the Former Yugoslavia, Case No. IT-94-I-A, July 15, 1999, at 39–75 (requiring a weaker test of overall control); see also Antonio Cassese, "The *Nicaragua* and *Tadić* Tests Revisited in Light of the ICJ Judgment on Genocide in Bosnia," *European Journal of International Law* 18 (2007): 649.

22. Jack Goldsmith, "Cybersecurity Treaties: A Skeptical View," in *Future Challenges in National Security and Law*, ed. Peter Berkowitz (Palo Alto, CA: Hoover, 2001), http://www.hoover.org/research-teams/national-security-law-task-force/essay-series /future-challenges (accessed July 21, 2014).

23. Jason Healey, "Beyond Attribution: Seeking National Responsibility for Cyber Attacks," Atlantic Council Issue Brief, Financial and Banking Information Infrastructure Committee, January 2012, https://www.fbiic.gov/public/2012/mar/National _Responsibility_for_CyberAttacks,_2012.pdf (accessed October 21, 2013).

24. See Goldsmith, "Cybersecurity Treaties," 9. Even threatening states with the milder punishment of burden shifting is likely to be ineffective in many cases. The burden shifting would have the advantage of forcing the state to share any information it might have about the source of an attack, but to the extent that a state is unable to trace an attack, the burden-shifting proposal would be no different in practice from the more punitive proposal.

25. Ibid. For a developed criticism of these proposals, see also Jack Goldsmith, "How Cyber Changes the Laws of War," *European Journal of International Law* 24 (2013): 129, 135; James A. Lewis, "Multilateral Agreements to Constrain Cyberconflict," *Arms Control Today*, June 2010, http://www.armscontrol.org/act/2010_06/Lewis (accessed October 21, 2013); Kim Zetter, "Former NSA Director: Countries Spewing Cyber Attacks Should Be Held Responsible," *Wired*, July 29, 2010, http://www.wired.com/threatlevel/2010/07 /hayden-at-blackhat (accessed October 21, 2013); Healey, "Beyond Attribution," 6–7.

26. Amos Lerah, "Saudi Hacker OxOmar Killed by a Sandstorm. Or the Mossad," *JSS News*, April 30, 2012, http://jssnews.com/2012/04/30/le-hacker-saoudien-oxomar-tue -par-une-tempete-de-sable-ou-par-le-mossad (accessed October 21, 2013). There were also reports that a different Saudi hacker, who went by the creative nom de guerre "Cyber Terrorist," had died from an asthma attack. See Al Arabiya, "Saudi Hacker Dies of

Asthma Attack," Al Arabiya News, April 22, 2012, http://www.alarabiya.net/articles /2012/04/22/209470.html (accessed October 21, 2013).

Notes to Chapter 7

1. Benjamin W. Wells, "Trade and Travel in the Roman Empire," *Classical Journal* 19 (1923): 7–16. See also Romolo Augusto Staccioli, *The Roads of the Romans* (Los Angeles: Getty Publications, 2003), 10.

2. Staccioli, *The Roads of the Romans*, 5.

3. We are indebted to Jack Goldsmith for the parallels between Roman roads and modern cybersecurity issues.

4. Ray Laurence, *The Roads of Roman Italy* (New York: Routledge, 1999), 178–185.

5. Sam Moorhead and David Stuttard, *AD 410: The Year That Shook Rome* (Los Angeles: J. Paul Getty Museum, 2010), 94–95. See also Arther Ferrill, *The Fall of the Roman Empire: The Military Explanation* (London: Thames & Hudson, 1986), 103.

6. On the relationship between railroads and standardized time, see Duncan Steel, *Marking Time: The Epic Quest to Invent the Perfect Calendar* (New York: John Wiley & Sons, 2000), 261–266.

7. See William A. Pinkerton, "Highwaymen of the Railroad," *North American Review* 157 (1893): 530–540.

8. On the history of railroad law enforcement, see Dorothy M. Schulz, "Holdups, Hobos, and the Homeless: A Brief History of Railroad Police in North America," *Police Studies* 10 (1987): 90–95. On the other measures taken by railroads to counter the train robbers, see Richard Patterson, "Train Robbery: The Birth, Flowering, and Decline of a Notorious Western Enterprise," *American West* 14 (1977): 48–53.

9. For an example of the use of "platform" by engineers in robotics, consider the iRobot company, which makes both military and consumer robots and describes one of its educational robots as an "affordable programmable, mobile-platform robot." "FAQs," iRobot.com, http://www.irobot.com/hrd_right_rail/create_rr/create_fam/createFam_rr _faqs.html (accessed May 18, 2013). It also describes its Ranger robot, a torpedo-shaped underwater robot, as "an A-sized [unmanned underwater vehicle] platform that weighs less than 20 kilograms [and] supports technology development for a variety of military and commercial applications." See "Advanced Platforms," iRobot, http://www.irobot .com/us/cool_stuff/Research/Advanced_Platforms.aspx (accessed May 18, 2013). For an example of military drones as an intelligence collection platform, see US Army, *Field Manual Interim 3-04.155: Army Unmanned Aircraft System Operations* (Washington, DC: Department of the Army, 2006), 1–2.

10. See Bhavya Sehgal and Pronab Gorai, "Platform Strategy Will Shape Future of OEMs," Evalueserve white paper, Sand Hill, January 2012, http://sandhill.com/wp-content /files_mf/evalueservewhitepaperplatformstrategywillshapefutureofoems.pdf (accessed July 21, 2014). As an example of an automotive platform, consider Toyota's use of its MC platform not only for its popular Camry sedan but also for several of its luxury Lexus models, its Highlander SUV, and a number of other models across its various brands.

11. For an explanation of computing platforms, see June Jamrich Parsons and Dan Oja, *Computer Concepts* (Boston: Cenage Learning, 2010), 64. For a discussion of vaccine

platforms, see Rick A. Bright, "Review of New Vaccine Platforms and Influenza Vaccine Pipeline," presentation slides, World Health Organization, http://www.who.int /influenza_vaccines_plan/resources/bright.pdf (accessed July 21, 2014).

12. See "About," BioBricks Foundation, http://biobricks.org/about-foundation (accessed July 21, 2014); "About," iGem, http://igem.org/About (accessed July 21, 2014).

13. Arduino's makers describe it as:

> an open-source electronics prototyping platform based on flexible, easy-to-use hardware and software. It's intended for artists, designers, hobbyists, and anyone interested in creating interactive objects or environments.
>
> *What Arduino Can Do*
> Arduino can sense the environment by receiving input from a variety of sensors and can affect its surroundings by controlling lights, motors, and other actuators. The microcontroller on the board is programmed using the Arduino programming language . . . and the Arduino development environment. . . . Arduino projects can be stand-alone or they can communicate with software running on a computer.

14. On the insecurity of the rails and the Roman roads inhibiting travel, see Pinkerton, "Highwaymen of the Railroad," 530–540; Laurence, *The Roads of Roman Italy*, 177–179, 185. On the drop-off in use of the mail after the anthrax attacks, see *Postal Facts 2011* (US Postal Service, 2011), 6, http://about.usps.com/future-postal-service/postalfacts-2011.pdf (accessed July 21, 2014). See also *Transformation Plan: April 2002* (US Postal Service, 2002), 4, http:// about.usps.com/strategic-planning/2002transformationplan.pdf (accessed July 21, 2014).

15. On the prevalence of surveillance cameras in Britain, see "Britain Is 'Surveillance Society,'" BBC News, November 2, 2006, http://news.bbc.co.uk/2/hi/uk_news/6108496 .stm (accessed July 21, 2014). On its wide acceptance, see Mark Landler, "Where Little Is Left Outside the Camera's Eye," *New York Times*, July 8, 2007, http://www.nytimes .com/2007/07/08/weekinreview/08landler.html (accessed July 21, 2014). On the use of cameras in the Boston Marathon bombing investigation, see Shelley Murphy, Andrew Ryan, and Martin Finucane, "Suspect Seen Carrying, and Perhaps Dropping, Black Bag," *Boston Globe*, April 17, 2013, http://www.bostonglobe.com/2013/04/17/boston -medical-center-reports-five-year-old-boy-critical-condition-victims-treated-from -boston-marathon-bombings/UiktKly6oy4m8UVHeNu8NP/story.html (accessed July 21, 2014). On changing American attitudes in the wake of the bombing, see John Swaine, "Americans in Favour of CCTV Cameras in Public Places," *Telegraph*, May 1, 2013, http://www.telegraph.co.uk/news/worldnews/northamerica/usa/10031439/Americans -in-favour-of-CCTV-cameras-in-public-places.html (accessed July 21, 2014). For Cathy Lanier's remarks, see "Intelligence and Counterterrorism Policy, Anti-defamation League Centennial Summit," CSPAN, April 30, 2013, http://www.c-spanvideo.org/program /IntelligenceandC (accessed July 21, 2014).

16. Somini Sengupta, "Privacy Fears Grow as Cities Increase Surveillance," *New York Times*, October 13, 2013, http://www.nytimes.com/2013/10/14/technology/privacy-fears -as-surveillance-grows-in-cities.html (accessed July 21, 2014).

17. Ibid.

18. Stewart A. Baker, "The Regulation of Disclosure of Information Held by Private Parties," in *Protecting America's Freedom in the Information Age*, ed. Zoe Baird (New York: Markle Foundation, 2002), 161.

19. For example, the problem that led to the Foreign Intelligence Surveillance Act (FISA) Amendments Act in 2008 was that a large volume of overseas communications had become subject, in a fashion Congress never intended, to the FISA warrant requirement because these communications happened to pass through US-based servers, which swept them within warrant requirements designed to protect domestic communications. See David Kris, "Modernizing the Foreign Intelligence Surveillance Act: Progress to Date and Work Still to Come," in *Legislating the War on Terror: An Agenda for Reform* (Washington, DC: Brookings Institution Press, 2009), 217–251.

20. On the special-needs doctrine generally, see *New Jersey v. T.L.O.*, 469 U.S. 325, 351 (1985) (Blackmun, J., concurring). The Supreme Court has upheld sobriety checkpoints on roads and drug testing of railway employees—both essentially exercises in platform surveillance—as special-needs searches. See *Michigan Dept. of State Police v. Sitz*, 496 U.S. 444 (1990); *Skinner v. Railway Labor Executives' Association*, 489 U.S. 602 (1989). The special-needs doctrine, however, has also been used to justify supervising probationers and searches of students in schools, the latter of which the Court justified less on the basis of the security of the school as some kind of platform for learning than on the need for order and discipline in educational settings. As to supervising probationers, see *Griffin v. Wisconsin*, 483 U.S. 868, 875–877 (1987). As to searches in schools, see *New Jersey v. T.L.O.*, 469 U.S. 325, 351 (1985).

21. See 18 U.S.C. § 2703(a) and (b), which require the government to obtain a warrant before collecting the contents of unaccessed stored electronic communications less than 180 days old but allow for the contents of older communications and of accessed communications stored in remote computing services to be collected with a subpoena.

22. *United States v. Jones*, 132 S. Ct. 945 (2012).

23. See Lois M. Davis et al., *The Role of the United States Postal Service in Public Safety and Security: Implications of Relaxing the Mailbox Monopoly* (Santa Monica, CA: Rand Corporation, 2008), 51–52, http://about.usps.com/universal-postal-service/rand-report .pdf (accessed July 21, 2014).

24. *City of Indianapolis v. Edmond*, 531 U.S. 32 (2000).

25. The stop-and-frisk decision can be found at *Floyd v. City of New York*, 959 F.Supp.2d 540 (S.D.N.Y. 2013).

26. The ACLU's views on body-imaging technologies in airports can be found at "ACLU Backgrounder on Body Scanners and 'Virtual Strip Searches,'" ACLU.org, January 8, 2010, http://www.aclu.org/technology-and-liberty/aclu-backgrounder-body -scanners-and-virtual-strip-searches (accessed July 21, 2014).

27. See, for example, Siobhan Gorman, "U.S. Plans Cyber Shield for Utilities, Companies," *Wall Street Journal*, July 8, 2010, http://online.wsj.com/article/SB10001424052748704545004575352983850463108.html (accessed July 21, 2014).

28. On the requirement for reasonable suspicion before a police officer can conduct a cursory search of someone in the interests of self-protection, see *Terry v. Ohio*, 392

U.S. 1 (1968); *Floyd v. City of New York*, 813 F.Supp.2d 457 (2011). On the requirement for cause before one's letters can be opened, see *Ex Parte Jackson*, 96 U.S. 727 (1876).

29. Jack Goldsmith, "Cyberthreat, Government Network Operations, and the Fourth Amendment," in *Constitution 3.0: Freedom and Technological Change*, ed. Jeffrey Rosen and Benjamin Wittes (Washington, DC: Brookings Institution, 2011), 47–68.

30. For a discussion of the existing intrusion detection systems and their legality, see Steven G. Bradbury, "The Developing Legal Framework for Defensive and Offensive Cyber Operations" (keynote address at the *Harvard National Security Journal*'s "Cybersecurity: Law, Privacy, and Warfare in a Digital World" symposium, Cambridge, Massachusetts, March 4, 2011), http://harvardnsj.org/wp-content/uploads/2011/04 /Vol.-2_Bradbury_Final.pdf (accessed July 21, 2014). See also Office of Legal Counsel, "Legal Issues Relating to the Testing, Use, and Deployment of an Intrusion-Detection System (Einstein 2.0) to Protect Unclassified Computer Networks in the Executive Branch," memorandum, US Department of Justice, January 9, 2009, http://www.justice .gov/olc/opiniondocs/e2-issues.pdf (accessed July 21, 2014); Office of Legal Counsel, "Legality of Intrusion-Detection System to Protect Unclassified Computer Networks in the Executive Branch," memorandum, US Department of Justice, August 14, 2009, http://www.justice.gov/olc/opiniondocs/legality-of-e2.pdf (accessed July 21, 2014). For the effect of the Snowden disclosures on NSA plans for cyberdefense, see David Sanger, "N.S.A. Leaks Make Plan for Cyberdefense Unlikely," *New York Times*, August 12, 2013, http://www.nytimes.com/2013/08/13/us/nsa-leaks-make-plan-for-cyberdefense-unlikely .html (accessed July 21, 2014).

31. On existing practices of gene-synthesis companies, see H. Bügl et al., "DNA Synthesis and Biological Security," *Nature Biotechnology* 25 (2007): 627–629. See also Jeremy Minshull and Ralf Wagner, "Preventing the Misuse of Gene Synthesis," *Nature Biotechnology* 27 (2009): 800–801. On the Nouri-Chyba proposal, see Ali Nouri and C. F. Chyba, "Proliferation-Resistant Biotechnology: An Approach to Improve Biosecurity," *Nature Biotechnology* 27 (2009): 234.

32. Robert Litt, "NSA Data Collection and Surveillance Oversight" (testimony before the House Committee on the Judiciary, July 19, 2013), http://www.c-spanvideo .org/program/GovernmentInte (accessed July 21, 2014).

33. Charlie Savage, "N.S.A. Said to Search Content of Messages to and from U.S.," *New York Times*, August 8, 2013, http://www.nytimes.com/2013/08/08/us/broader-sifting -of-data-abroad-is-seen-by-nsa.html (accessed July 21, 2014). For analysis, see Benjamin Wittes, "Thoughts on Yesterday's NYT NSA Story," *Lawfare*, August 9, 2013, http://www .lawfareblog.com/2013/08/thoughts-on-yesterdays-nyt-nsa-story (accessed July 21, 2014).

Notes to Chapter 8

1. George W. Bush, "We're Making Progress," White House: George W. Bush, October 1, 2001, http://georgewbush-whitehouse.archives.gov/news/releases/2001 /10/20011001-6.html (accessed October 23, 2013).

2. For a list of federal computer crimes, see Office of Legal Education, Executive Office of the United States Attorneys, "Prosecuting Computer Crimes," Department of Justice, http://www.justice.gov/criminal/cybercrime/docs/ccmanual.pdf (accessed

October 23, 2013). For information on the regulation of domestic drones and the FAA, see Federal Aviation Administration Modernization and Reform Act of 2012, Pub. L. 112-95 § 332; Wells C. Bennett, "Unmanned at Any Speed," *Issues in Governance Studies* 55 (December 2012), http://www.brookings.edu/~/media/Research/Files/Papers/2012/12 /14%20drones%20bennett/1214_drones_bennett.pdf (accessed October 25, 2013). For the requirement of the "security risk assessment" for people who work with select agents, see 42 C.F.R. § 73.7. For criminal prohibitions against transferring select agents both to those unregistered to receive them and persons who are restricted from handling them, see 18 U.S.C. § 175b(b) (c). For export controls on dual-use technologies, see 22 U.S.C. § 2778; 15 C.F.R. § 730.3.

3. For statistics on cybercrime prosecutions, see US Department of Justice, "Fiscal Year 2012: United States Attorneys' Annual Statistical Report," Department of Justice, 36–37, http://www.justice.gov/usao/reading_room/reports/asr2012/12statrpt.pdf (accessed April 15, 2014). Luis Mijangos's status was last checked on June 29, 2014, on the US Bureau of Prisons Inmate Locator (http://www.bop.gov/inmateloc).

4. Kenneth Chang, "Split Verdicts in Texas Trial of Professor and the Plague," *New York Times,* December 2, 2003, http://www.nytimes.com/2003/12/02/us/split-verdicts -in-texas-trial-of-professor-and-the-plague.html (accessed October 25, 2013); Katherine S. Mangan, "Researcher Who Was Convicted in Plague Case is Sentenced to 2 Years in Prison," *Chronicle of Higher Education,* March 11, 2004, http://chronicle.com/article /Researcher-Who-Was-Convicte/101776 (accessed October 25, 2013). For further documents and news stories on Butler, see http://www.fas.org/butler/index.html.

5. Daryl J. Levinson, "Collective Sanctions," *Stanford Law Review* 56 (2003): 365.

6. Ibid., 366–368. For earlier work on gatekeeper liability, see Reinier H. Kraakman, "Gatekeepers: The Anatomy of a Third-Party Enforcement Strategy," *Journal of Law, Economics, and Organization* 2 (1986): 53.

7. See Lawrence Lessig, "The Limits in Open Code: Regulatory Standards and the Future of the Net," *Berkeley Technology Law Journal* 14 (1999): 759; Jonathan Zittrain, "A History of Online Gatekeeping," *Harvard Journal of Law and Technology* 19 (2006): 254.

8. Jack Goldsmith and Tim Wu, *Who Controls the Internet? Illusions of a Borderless World* (New York: Oxford University Press, 2006), 68–79.

9. On workplace smoking bans, see Howard K. Koh, Luk X. Joossens, and Gregory N. Connolly, "Making Smoking History Worldwide," *New England Journal of Medicine* 356 (2007): 1496–1498. The New York trans-fat and food labeling rules can be found at New York City Health Code §§ 81.08, 81.50. The law giving federal regulators the power to ensure that drugs are safe and efficacious can be found at 21 U.S.C. § 355.

10. The Hammurabi's Code of Laws can be found at http://eawc.evansville.edu /anthology/hammurabi.htm (accessed June 29, 2014). See laws 229–230.

11. On the Loma Prieta earthquake, see US Geological Survey, "Historic Earthquakes: Santa Cruz Mountains (Loma Prieta), California," http://earthquake. usgs.gov/earthquakes/states/events/1989_10_18.php (accessed October 28, 2013). On the Haiti earthquake, see US Geological Survey, "Earthquake Information for 2010," http:// earthquake.usgs.gov/earthquakes/eqarchives/year/2010 (accessed October 28, 2013). On the 2011 Japan earthquake, see US Geological Survey, "Deaths from Earthquakes in 2011,"

http://earthquake.usgs.gov/earthquakes/eqarchives/year/2011/2011_deaths.php (accessed October 28, 2013); Encyclopedia Britannica, "Japan Earthquake and Tsunami of 2011," http://www.britannica.com/EBchecked/topic/1761942/Japan-earthquake-and -tsunami-of-2011 (accessed October 28, 2013).

12. John D. Graham, "Product Liability and Motor Vehicle Safety," in *The Liability Maze: The Impact of Liability Law on Safety and Innovation,* eds. Peter William Huber and Robert E. Litan (Washington, DC: The Brookings Institution, 1991).

13. Michael D. Scott, "Tort Liability for Vendors of Insecure Software: Has the Time Finally Come?" *Maryland Law Review* 67 (2008): 427. On the Nader campaign for auto safety, see Ralph Nader, *Unsafe at Any Speed: The Designed-In Dangers of the American Automobile* (New York: Grossman, 1965).

14. Bruce Schneier, "Liability and Security," *Crypto-Gram Newsletter,* April 15, 2002, http://www.schneier.com/crypto-gram-0204.html#6 (accessed October 28, 2013).

15. Helen Mohrmann, e-mail to Benjamin Wittes, October 15, 2013.

16. National Research Council, *Cybersecurity Today and Tomorrow: Pay Now or Pay Later* (Washington, DC: National Academies Press, 2002), 14.

17. Steven P. Bucci, Paul Rosenzweig, and David Inserra, "A Congressional Guide: Seven Steps to U.S. Security, Prosperity, and Freedom in Cyberspace," http://www .heritage.org/research/reports/2013/04/a-congressional-guide-seven-steps-to-us-security -prosperity-and-freedom-in-cyberspace (accessed October 28, 2013). On software liability standards in cybersecurity, see also Jane Chong, "Bad Code: Should Software Makers Pay? (Part I)," *New Republic,* October 3, 2013, http://www.newrepublic.com/article /114973/bad-code-should-software-makers-pay-part-1 (accessed October 28, 2013); Jane Chong, "Why Is Our Cybersecurity so Insecure?" *New Republic,* October 11, 2013, http:// www.newrepublic.com/article/115145/us-cybersecurity-why-software-so-insecure (accessed October 28, 2013).

18. On the FAA's recognition that it must address privacy issues, see Bennett, "Unmanned at Any Speed." See also Federal Aviation Administration, "Unmanned Aircraft Systems Test Site Program," *Federal Register* 78 (February 22, 2013): 12259. For examples of state-level legislation on drones, see Alaska HCR 6 (2013), Idaho SB 1134 (2013), Montana SB 196 (2013), Tennessee SB 796 (2013), Texas HB 912 (2013), and Virginia SB 1331 (2013).

19. For an example of neighbors spying on neighbors using drones, see Rebecca J. Rosen, "So This Is Where It Begins: Guy Refuses to Stop Drone Spying on Seattle Woman," *Atlantic,* May 13, 2013, http://www.theatlantic.com/technology/archive /2013/05/so-this-is-how-it-begins-guy-refuses-to-stop-drone-spying-on-seattle -woman/275769 (accessed October 28, 2013). The famous Warren-Brandeis article on privacy can be found at Samuel D. Warren and Louis D. Brandeis, "The Right to Privacy," *Harvard Law Review* 4 (1890): 195.

20. On differing US and EU approaches to GMO foods, see Diahanna Lynch and David Vogel, "The Regulation of GMOs in Europe and the United States: A Case-Study of Contemporary European Regulatory Politics," Council on Foreign Relations, April 5, 2001, http://www.cfr.org/agricultural-policy/regulation-gmos-europe-united-states-case -study-contemporary-european-regulatory-politics/p8688 (accessed September 14, 2014).

21. For a fuller treatment of this concept, see Benjamin Wittes, "Databuse: Digital Privacy and the Mosaic," Brookings Institution, April 1, 2011, http://www.brookings .edu/research/papers/2011/04/01-databuse-wittes (accessed October 28, 2013). See also Benjamin Wittes and Wells Bennett, "Databuse and a Trusteeship Model of Consumer Protection in the Big Data Era," Brookings Institution, June 4, 2014, http://www .brookings.edu/research/papers/2014/06/04-databuse-trusteeship-consumer-protection -big-data-era-privacy (accessed September 13, 2014).

22. Jonathan Zittrain, "The Fourth Quadrant," *Fordham Law Review* 78 (2010): 2779; Jonathan Zittrain, "A Mutual Aid Treaty for the Internet," in *Constitution 3.0: Freedom and Technological Change*, ed. Jeffrey Rosen and Benjamin Wittes (Washington, DC: Brookings Institution, 2011), 100–129.

23. Jonathan Zittrain, *The Future of the Internet and How to Stop It* (New Haven, CT: Yale University Press, 2008). See, in particular, chapters 7 to 9.

24. David A. Johnson, "Vigilance and the Law: The Moral Authority of Popular Justice in the Far West," *American Quarterly* 33 (1981): 558–586.

25. Aviel Magnezi, "Israeli Hackers: We've Obtained Saudi Credit Card Info," YNetNews.com, January 9, 2012, http://www.ynetnews.com/articles/0,7340,L-4173264, 00.html (accessed October 28, 2013).

26. For examples of online pursuit of a variety of different offenders, see Nancy Gohring, "Digital Vigilantes: Hacking for a Good Cause," *PCWorld*, December 25, 2007, http://www.pcworld.com/article/140731/article.html (accessed October 28, 2013). See also John Leyden, "FBI Condemns Vigilante Hacking," *Register*, September 17, 2001, http:// www.theregister.co.uk/2001/09/17/fbi_condemns_vigilante_hacking (accessed July 22, 2014); Kim Zetter, "Vigilantes Hack Criminal Carding Forum and Expose Underground Dealings," *Wired*, May 19, 2010, http://www.wired.com/threatlevel/2010/05/carderscc (accessed October 28, 2013); Christina Mendonsa, "Hacktivist Anonymous Turns Online Hacking into Vigilantism," News10.net, June 9, 2011, http://www.news10.net /news/specialreports/138048/47/Hacktivist-Anonymous-turns-hacking-into-vigilantism (accessed October 28, 2013). For the case of hackers chasing Nigerian spammers into a war zone in Chad, see "Enforcers," *This American Life*, September 12, 2008, http:// www.thisamericanlife.org/radio-archives/episode/363/transcript (accessed October 28, 2013). On Anonymous's outing of alleged child-pornography viewers, see Gerry Smith, "Anonymous Reveals IP Addresses of Alleged Child Porn Viewers in Latest Sting," *Huffington Post*, November 2, 2011, http://www.huffingtonpost.com/2011/11/02 /anonymous-ip-addresses-child-porn-viewers_n_1072134.html (accessed October 28, 2013). On its involvement against Los Zetas, see Paul Rexton Kan, "Cyberwar in the Underworld: Anonymous Versus Los Zetas in Mexico," *Yale Journal of International Affairs* (winter 2013), 40–51, http://yalejournal.org/wp-content/uploads/2013/03/Kan.pdf (accessed July 22, 2014).

27. On Palestinian hacks of Israeli government websites, see Steven Scheer, "Israeli Government Websites Under Mass Hacking Attack," Reuters, November 18, 2012, http:// www.reuters.com/article/2012/11/18/us-palestinians-israel-hacking-idUSBRE8AH0DL 20121118 (accessed October 28, 2013). On the response of Israeli hackers, see Sean Gallagher, "Israeli and Palestinian Hackers Trade DDOS Attacks in Rising Cyber-Gang

War," *Ars Technica*, January 17, 2012, http://arstechnica.com /business/2012/01/israeli-and-palestinian-hackers-trade-ddos-attacks-in-rising-cyber -gang-war (accessed October 28, 2013).

28. On the drone spying on a meatpacking plant, see Meghan Keneally, "Drone Plane Spots a River of Blood Flowing from the Back of a Dallas Meat Packing Plant," *Daily Mail*, January 24, 2012, http://www.dailymail.co.uk/news/article-2091159/A-drone -plane-spots-river-of-blood-flowing-Dallas-meat-packing-plant.html (accessed October 28, 2013). For the incident between the pigeon shooters and the drone-wielding activists, see Amy Worden, "Activist Group's Drone Shot While Filming PA Pigeon Shoot," *Philadelphia Inquirer*, November 21, 2012, http://www.philly.com/philly/blogs/pets /Activist-groups-drone-shot-while-filming-PA-pigeon-shoot.html (accessed October 28, 2013).

29. The Baker and Kerr quotations can be found in Stewart Baker, "The Hackback Debate," *Steptoe Cyberblog*, November 2, 2012, http://www.steptoecyberblog.com/2012 /11/02/the-hackback-debate (accessed October 28, 2013). The Rosenzweig quotation can be found in Paul Rosenzweig, "International Law and Private Actor Active Cyber Defensive Measures," *Stanford Journal of International Law* 47 (2013): 3, http://papers .ssrn.com/sol3/papers.cfm?abstract_id=2270673 (accessed October 28, 2013).

Notes to Chapter 9

1. For an account of this incident, see Committee on Research Standards and Practices to Prevent the Destructive Application of Biotechnology, National Research Council, *Biotechnology Research in an Age of Terrorism* (hereafter "Fink Report") (Washington, DC: National Academies Press, 2004), 26, http://www.nap.edu/openbook .php?record_id=10827 (accessed July 23, 2014). See also Stewart A. Baker, *Skating on Stilts: Why We Aren't Stopping Tomorrow's Terrorism* (Stanford, CA: Hoover Institution Press, 2010), 295–296.

2. The mousepox study can be found at R. J. Jackson et al., "Expression of a Mouse Interleukin-4 by a Recombinant Ectromelia Virus Represses Cytolytic Lymphocyte Responses and Overcomes Genetic Resistance to Mousepox," *Journal of Virology* 75, no. 3 (February 2001): 1205–1210. For an example of the study's resonance, see Rachel Nowak, "Killer Mousepox Virus Raises Bioterror Fears," *New Scientist,* January 10, 2001, http:// www.newscientist.com/article/dn311-killer-mousepox-virus-raises-bioterror-fears.html (accessed August 20, 2014); Lawrence Lessig, "Insanely Destructive Devices," *Wired*, April 2004, http://www.wired.com/wired/archive/12.04/view_pr.html (accessed July 23, 2014). The Myhrvold quotation can be found in Nathan Myhrvold, "Strategic Terrorism: A Call to Action" (Working Paper 2-2013, Lawfare Research Paper Series 1, no. 2, July 2013), 13, http://www.lawfareblog.com/wp-content/uploads/2013/07/Strategic-Terrorism -Myhrvold-7-3-2013.pdf (accessed July 23, 2014).

3. On the reaction to and defense of the decision to publish the paper, see the Fink Report, 25–28. See also interview of Ronald Jackson and Ian Ramshaw by Michael J. Selgelid and Lorna Weir, "The Mousepox Experience," *EMBO Reports*, December 11, 2009, http://embor.embopress.org/content/11/1/18 (accessed September 14, 2014).

4. Fink Report, 27.

5. On the State Department's efforts to stop the dissemination of 3D-printable gun blueprints, see Andy Greenberg, "State Department Demands Takedown of 3D-Printable Gun Files for Possible Export Control Violations," *Forbes*, May 9, 2013, http://www .forbes.com/sites/andygreenberg/2013/05/09/state-department-demands-takedown-of-3d -printable-gun-for-possible-export-control-violation (accessed July 23, 2014). On the site's reaction, see Todd Sperry, "U.S. Requires Group to Remove 3-D Gun Instructions from Its Website," CNN.com, May 9, 2013, http://www.cnn.com/2013/05/09/politics /3-d-guns (accessed July 23, 2014). The site itself was DEFCAD (http://defcad.org, accessed September 11, 2013). The site bore a notice reading, "DEFCAD Files Are Being Removed at the Request of the US Department of Defense Trade Controls. Until Further Notice the United States Government Claims Control of the Information." The Reddit thread is available at http://www.reddit.com/r/technology/comments/1eoybl/3d_gun _blueprints_taken_down_defcad_files_are (accessed July 22, 2013). On the building of the "Liberator" by journalists and its smuggling onto a Eurostar train, see Simon Murphy and Russell Myers, "How Mail on Sunday Printed First Plastic Gun in UK Using a 3D Printer," *Daily Mail*, May 11, 2013, http://www.dailymail.co.uk/news/article-2323158 /How-Mail-On-Sunday-printed-plastic-gun-UK—took-board-Eurostar-stopped-security -scandal.html (accessed July 23, 2014).

6. Foreword to United Nations Convention Against Transnational Organized Crime and the Protocols Thereto, United Nations Office on Drugs and Crime, November 15, 2000, http://www.unodc.org/documents/treaties/UNTOC/Publications/TOC%20 Convention/TOCebook-e.pdf (accessed July 23, 2014).

7. On the definition of international crime, see Convention on the Prevention and Punishment of the Crime of Genocide, December 9, 1948, 78 U.N.T.S. 277; Rome Statute of the International Criminal Court, July 17, 1998, 2187 U.N.T.S. 90; International Convention for the Suppression of the Financing of Terrorism, December 9, 1999, 2178 U.N.T.S. 197; International Convention for the Suppression of Acts of Nuclear Terrorism, April 13, 2005, 2445 U.N.T.S. 89; Convention for the Suppression of the Unlawful Seizure of Aircraft, October 14, 1971, 860 U.N.T.S 105. On drug trafficking, see Convention Against Illicit Traffic in Narcotic Drugs and Psychotropic Substances, December 20, 1988, 1582 U.N.T.S. 95. On trafficking in persons, see Protocol to Prevent, Suppress, and Punish Trafficking in Persons, Especially Women and Children, November 15, 2000, 2237 U.N.T.S. 319; Protocol Against the Smuggling of Migrants by Land, Sea, and Air, November 15, 2000, 2241 U.N.T.S. 507; Protocol Against the Illicit Manufacturing of and Trafficking in Firearms, Their Parts and Components and Ammunition, May 31, 2001, 2326 U.N.T.S. 208. On the banning of chemical and biological weapons, see Protocol for the Prohibition of the Use in War of Asphyxiating, Poisonous or Other Gases, and of Bacteriological Methods of Warfare, June 17, 1925, 26 U.S.T. 571, T.I.A.S. No. 8061, 94 L.N.T.S. 65; Treaty on the Non-Proliferation of Nuclear Weapons, July 1, 1968, 726 U.N.T.S. 161; Convention on the Prohibition of the Development, Production and Stockpiling of Bacteriological (Biological) and Toxin Weapons and on Their Destruction, April 10, 1972, 1015 U.N.T.S. 163; Convention on the Prohibition of the Development, Production, Stockpiling, and Use of Chemical Weapons and on Their Destruction, September 3, 1992, 1974 U.N.T.S. 45. For

commentary on the human trafficking treaties, see Kelly E. Hyland, "The Impact of the Protocol to Prevent, Suppress and Punish Trafficking in Persons, Especially Women and Children," *Human Rights Briefs* 8 (2001): 30–31, 38. See also LeRoy G. Potts Jr., "Global Trafficking in Human Beings: Assessing the Success of the United Nations Protocol to Prevent Trafficking in Persons," *George Washington International Law Review* 35 (2003): 227, 228.

8. On the number of states that are signatories to the convention, see Richard H. Carmona, "Sarin Gas: Too Heinous Even for War," *Huffington Post*, September 9, 2013, http://www.huffingtonpost.com/richard-h-carmona-md/sarin-gas-too-heinous -eve_b_3883515.html (accessed July 23, 2014). Syria, shortly after the publication of this article, became the 190th state to sign the treaty. See statement of UN Secretary-General Ban Ki-moon, "Secretary-General Receives Letter from Syrian Government Informing Him President Has Signed Legislative Decree for Accession to Chemical Weapons Convention," United Nations, September 12, 2013, http://www.un.org/News /Press/docs/2013/sgsm15274.doc.htm (accessed July 23, 2014). On the United States' struggles to eliminate its own chemical weapons, see Paul Lewis, "US Struggles Show Hazards of Chemical Weapons Destruction," *Guardian*, September 11, 2013, http://www .theguardian.com/world/2013/sep/11/us-syria-chemical-weapons-destruction (accessed July 23, 2014). For arms treaties the United States has not signed, see Convention on the Prohibition of the Use, Stockpiling, Production and Transfer of Anti-personnel Mines and on Their Destruction, September 18, 1997, 2056 U.N.T.S. 211; Convention on Cluster Munitions, opened for signature on December 3, 2008, 48 I.L.M. 357.

9. United Nations Convention Against Illicit Traffic in Narcotic Drugs and Psychotropic Substances, December 20, 1988, 1582 U.N.T.S. 95, reservations of Belize and Bolivia.

10. For Pakistan's declaration in connection with the bombing treaty, see International Convention for the Suppression of Terrorist Bombings, December 15, 1997, 2149 U.N.T.S. 256. For Iran's declaration in connection with the hostage-taking treaty, see International Convention Against the Taking of Hostages, December 17, 1979, 1316 U.N.T.S. 205 (1983), declaration of Islamic Republic of Iran.

11. Arms Trade Treaty, March 27, 2013, A/CONF.217/2013/L.3, United Nations, https://www.un.org/disarmament/ATT/docs/ATT_text_(As_adopted_by_the_GA)-E .pdf (accessed July 23, 2014).

12. For inspections regimes for chemical weapons, see Convention on the Prohibition of the Development, Production, Stockpiling, and Use of Chemical Weapons and on Their Destruction, January 13, 1993, S. Treaty Doc. No. 103-219, 1974 U.N.T.S. 317. For nuclear inspections regimes, see Treaty on the Non-Proliferation of Nuclear Weapons, March 5, 1970, 729 U.N.T.S. 161, at art. 3(1); see also International Atomic Energy Agency (IAEA), "IAEA Safeguards Overview: Comprehensive Safeguards Agreements and Additional Protocols," IAEA, http://www.iaea.org/Publications/Factsheets/English /sg_overview.html (accessed July 23, 2014).

13. The Council of Europe's Convention on Cybercrime can be found at http:// conventions.coe.int/Treaty/Commun/ChercheSig.asp?NT=185&CM=&DF=&CL=ENG (accessed July 23, 2014). On the contested nature of the definition of cybercrime, see

Jack Goldsmith, *Cybersecurity Treaties: A Skeptical View* (Washington, DC: Hoover Institution, 2011), 6–7, http://media.hoover.org/sites/default/files/documents /FutureChallenges_Goldsmith.pdf (accessed April 16, 2013). The Department of State's responsibility for the control of the permanent and temporary export and temporary import of defense articles and services is governed primarily by 22 U.S.C. § 2778 of the Arms Export Control Act (AECA) and Executive Order 11958, as amended. The AECA, among these other requirements and authorities, provides for the promulgation of implementing regulations, the International Traffic in Arms Regulations (22 C.F.R. § 120–130).

14. There are some discrete attempts at international regulation of hazardous materials, which are limited by subject matter and region; see, for example, Basel Convention on the Control of Transboundary Movements of Hazardous Wastes and Their Disposal, March 22, 1989, 1673 U.N.T.S. 126; 28 I.L.M. 657 (1989); International Plant Protection Convention, December 6, 1951, 150 U.N.T.S. 67; North American Free Trade Agreement, 32 I.L.M. 289, 605 (1993), art. 724, which regulates pesticide production and trade among the parties to the North Atlantic Free Trade Agreement.

15. See "Security Council Committee Pursuant to Resolutions 1267 (1999) and 1989 (2011) Concerning Al-Qaida and Associated Individuals and Entities," United Nations, http://www.un.org/sc/committees/1267/aq_sanctions_list.shtml (accessed July 23, 2014). On bin Laden's designation, see "Osama bin Laden Removed from UN Sanctions List," *Telegraph*, February 26, 2013, http://www.telegraph.co.uk/news/worldnews/al-qaeda /9894262/Osama-bin-Laden-removed-from-UN-sanctions-list-two-years-after-death .html (accessed July 23, 2014).

16. See joined cases C-402/05 P and C-415/05 P, *Kadi & Al Barakaat v. Council of the European Union*, 3 C.M.L.R. 41 (2008), for commentary on the effectiveness of the tool.

17. For the EU Council decision permitting special intervention units, see Council Decision 2008/617/JHA, 2008 O.J. (L 210) 73, Eur-Lex, http://eur-lex.europa.eu/Lex UriServ/LexUriServ.do?uri=OJ:L:2008:210:0073:0075:EN:PDF#zoom=100 (accessed July 23, 2014). On the African Standby Force, see Solomon A. Dersso, "The Role and Place of the African Standby Force Within the African Peace and Security Architecture," Institute for Security Studies Paper 209, January 2010, http://www.issafrica.org/publications/papers/the-role-and-place-of-the-african-standby -force-within-the-african-peace-and-security-architecture (accessed September 14, 2014).

18. Emma Belcher, "The Proliferation Security Initiative: Lessons for Using Nonbinding Agreements," Council on Foreign Relations, July 2011, http://i.cfr.org /content/publications/attachments/IIGG_WorkingPaper6_PSI.pdf (accessed July 23, 2014).

19. See Robert G. Joseph, US Undersecretary of State for Arms Control and International Security, "Broadening and Deepening Our Proliferation Security Initiative Cooperation" (speech in Warsaw, Poland, June 23, 2006), http://2001-2009.state.gov/t /us/rm/68269.htm (accessed April 24, 2013). See also Belcher, "The Proliferation Security Initiative."

20. On North Korea's assertion that interdiction would constitute an act of war, see John Yoo and Glen Sulmasy, "The Proliferation Security Initiative: A Model for

International Cooperation," *Hofstra Law Review* 35 (2006): 414–416, http://scholarship
.law.berkeley.edu/cgi/viewcontent.cgi?article=1837&context=facpubs (accessed July
23, 2014). For states participating in the PSI, see "Proliferation Security Initiative 10th
Anniversary: Joint Statement on Ensuring a Robust Initiative," US Department of
State, http://www.state.gov/t/isn/jtstmts/211497.htm (accessed July 23, 2014); see also
"Mongolia," CIA World Factbook, https://www.cia.gov/library/publications/the-world
-factbook/geos/mg.html (accessed March 6, 2014). On the percentage of shipping going
through non-PSI ports, see Jonah Friedman, "The Proliferation Security Initiative: A
Model for Future Nonproliferation Efforts," Center for Strategic and International
Studies, August 1, 2011, http://csis.org/blog/proliferation-security-initiative-model-future
-nonproliferation-efforts (accessed July 23, 2014), citing Jeffrey Lewis and Philip Maxon,
"The Proliferation Security Initiative," *Maritime Security* 2 (2010): 38–39, http://www
.peacepalacelibrary.nl/ebooks/files/UNIDIR_pdf-art2962.pdf (accessed July 23, 2014).

21. For the UN guidelines on private security companies, see United Nations
Department of Safety and Security, "Guidelines on the Use of Armed Security Services
from Private Security Companies," University of Denver Private Security Monitor,
November 8, 2012, http://psm.du.edu/media/documents/international_regulation
/united_nations/internal_controls/un_unsms-operation-manual_guidance-on-using
-pmsc_2012.PDF (accessed April 24, 2013). For the Swiss multi-stakeholder initiative,
see International Code of Conduct for Private Security Service Providers (http://www
.icoc-psp.org, accessed July 23, 2014).

22. For information on the NaijaCyberHactivists, see Richard Essien,
"NaijaCyberHactivists Hacks Army Website," *Daily Times* (Nigeria), January 16, 2012,
http://www.dailytimes.com.ng/article/naijacyberhactivists-hacks-army-website (accessed
July 23, 2014).

23. OECD Anti-Bribery Convention, art. 4, 37 I.L.M. at 5.

24. The relevant US law, the Foreign Corrupt Practices Act, is codified at 15 U.S.C.
§ 78dd-3(a). On the breadth of the term "act in furtherance," see H. Lowell Brown,
"Extraterritorial Jurisdiction Under the 1998 Amendments to the Foreign Corrupt
Practices Act: Does the Government's Reach Now Exceed Its Grasp?" *North Carolina
Journal of International Law and Commercial Regulation* 26 (2001): 359. On patterns of
FCPA enforcement, see "FCPA Digest: Recent Trends and Patterns in the Enforcement
of the Foreign Corrupt Practices Act," Shearman and Sterling, January 2012, http://www
.shearman.com/files/Publication/bb1a7bff-ad52-4cf9-88b9-9d99e001dd5f/Presentation
/PublicationAttachment/6ec0766a-25aa-41ec-8731-041a672267a6/FCPA-Digest-Trends
-and-Patterns-Jan2012.pdf (accessed July 23, 2014).

25. Benjamin Weiser, "Man Offers Guilty Plea, Upending Terror Case," *New York
Times*, June 13, 2012, A28, http://www.nytimes.com/2012/06/14/nyregion/man-who
-trained-with-somalis-offers-guilty-plea-ending-pivotal-case.html (accessed July 23, 2014).
See also "Al Shabaab Operative Sentenced in Manhattan Federal Court to 111 Months
in Prison for Conspiring to Support and Receive Military-Type Training from a Foreign
Terrorist Organization," FBI, press release, March 27, 2013, http://www.fbi.gov/newyork
/press-releases/2013/al-shabaab-operative-sentenced-in-manhattan-federal-court-to-111

-months-in-prison-for-conspiring-to-support-and-receive-military-type-training-from
-a-foreign-terrorist-organization (accessed July 23, 2014).

26. *Sosa v. Alvarez-Machain*, 542 U.S. 692 (2004).

27. The Security Council has acknowledged that "abductions are offenses of grave concern to the international community, having severe adverse consequences for the rights of the victims and for the promotion of friendly relations and cooperation among States" and has condemned "unequivocally all acts of . . . abduction." S.C. Res. 579, U.N. Doc. S/RES/579 (1985), reprinted in 25 I.L.M. 243 (1986). For an example of a domestic court ignoring this principle, see *Attorney General of the Government of Israel v. Adolf Eichmann*, 36 I.L.R. 277 (1962) (Sup. Ct. Israel). An exception to this point is the South African Supreme Court, which held that the courts of South Africa lacked jurisdiction to try a person kidnapped from Swaziland, with whom South Africa had an extradition treaty. The Court reasoned that "the bounds of jurisdiction must not be exceeded, sovereignty must be respected, the legal process must be fair to those affected and abuse of law must be avoided in order to protect and promote the integrity of the administration of justice." See *State v. Ebrahim*, 1991 (2) 553 (CC) (S. Afr.). The quotation from the Ninth Circuit Court of Appeals comes from *Alvarez-Machain v. United States*, 331 F.3d 604, 608 (9th Cir. 2003) rev'd sub nom. *Sosa v. Alvarez-Machain*, 542 U.S. 692 (2004) and vacated, 374 F.3d 1384 (9th Cir. 2004). The quotation from the US Supreme Court is from *Alvarez-Machain v. United States*, 504 U.S. 655, 666–669 (1992).

28. See Associated Press, "Italy: Pardon Granted in Rendition Case," *New York Times*, April 5, 2013, http://www.nytimes.com/2013/04/06/world/europe/italys-president-grants -pardon-in-rendition-case.html?ref=extraordinaryrendition (accessed July 23, 2014); "Italy's Ex–Spy Chief Convicted over 2003 CIA Rendition," BBC News, February 12, 2013, http://www.bbc.co.uk/news/world-europe-21435632 (accessed July 23, 2014).

29. For an account of some of Israel's targeted killing operations, see Ian Black and Benny Morris, *Israel's Secret Wars: A History of Israeli Intelligence* (New York: Grove Press, 1991). On its post-2000 policy, see Heather Sharp, "Long History of Israel's 'Covert Killing'" BBC News, January 29, 2010, http://news.bbc.co.uk/2/hi/middle_east/8488249 .stm (accessed July 23, 2014). On Russian targeted killing of a Chechen militant in Doha, see Nick Paton Walsh, "Top Chechen Separatist Dies in Qatar Bomb Blast," *Guardian*, February 14, 2004, http://www.guardian.co.uk/world/2004/feb/14/chechnya.nickpaton walsh (accessed April 25, 2013); Steven Lee Myers, "Qatar Court Convicts 2 Russians in Top Chechen's Death," *New York Times*, July 1, 2004, http://www.nytimes.com/2004 /07/01/world/qatar-court-convicts-2-russians-in-top-chechen-s-death.html (accessed July 23, 2014).

30. For the Uganda-Congo case, see *Case Concerning Armed Activities on the Territory of the Congo* (*Democratic Republic of the Congo v. Uganda*), Judgment, I.C.J. Reports 2005 168, ¶¶ 146–147 (December 19, 2005). For the case on the Israeli security barrier, see *Legal Consequences of the Construction of a Wall in the Occupied Palestinian Territory*, Advisory Opinion, I.C.J. Reports 2004 136, ¶ 139 (July 9, 2004) (noting that "as Israel itself states, the threat which it regards as justifying the construction of the wall originates within, and not outside, that territory . . . [and consequently] Article 51 of the Charter has no relevance in this case"). For the Security Council's declaration, see S.C. Res. 1368, U.N.

Doc. S/RES/1368 (September 12, 2001) (recognizing "the inherent right of individual or collective self-defence" in the context of terrorism).

31. For the US position regarding when it will use drone strikes and other targeted killings, see "Remarks by the President at the National Defense University," White House, May 23, 2013, http://www.whitehouse.gov/the-press-office/2013/05/23/remarks -president-national-defense-university (accessed July 23, 2014); "Remarks of John O. Brennan, 'Strengthening Our Security by Adhering to Our Values and Laws,'" White House, September 16, 2011, http://www.whitehouse.gov/the-press-office/2011/09/16 /remarks-john-o-brennan-strengthening-our-security-adhering-our-values-an (accessed July 23, 2014). President Obama said in his May 2013 speech, "Where foreign governments cannot or will not effectively stop terrorism in their territory, the primary alternative to targeted lethal action would be the use of conventional military options." For an explication of the "unwilling or unable" test, see Ashley S. Deeks, "'Unwilling or Unable': Toward a Normative Framework for Extraterritorial Self-Defense," *Virginia Journal of International Law* 52 (2012): 483. For the US position when the target is a US citizen, see "Remarks by the President," May 2013. See also letter from Attorney General Eric H. Holder Jr. to members of Congress acknowledging the deaths of four US citizens in counterterrorism strikes outside the zone of active hostilities, May 22, 2013, available on the Department of Justice website at http://www.justice.gov/slideshow/AG-letter -5-22-13.pdf (accessed July 23, 2014).

32. Ben Emmerson, "Statement Concerning the Launch of an Inquiry into the Civilian Impact, and Human Rights Implications of the Use [of] Drones and Other Forms of Targeted Killing for the Purpose of Counter-Terrorism and Counter-Insurgency," Office of the United Nations High Commissioner for Human Rights, January 2012, http://www.ohchr.org/Documents/Issues/Terrorism/SRCTBenEmmerson QC.24January12.pdf (accessed April 26, 2013).

33. "Afghanistan's Narco War: Breaking the Link Between Drug Traffickers and Insurgents," Report to the Committee on Foreign Relations, US Senate, Government Printing Office, August 10, 2009, http://www.gpo.gov/fdsys/pkg/CPRT-111SPRT51521 /html/CPRT-111SPRT51521.htm (accessed July 23, 2014). See also James Risen, "U.S. to Hunt Down Afghan Drug Lords Tied to Taliban," *New York Times*, August 9, 2009, http://www.nytimes.com/2009/08/10/world/asia/10afghan.html (accessed July 23, 2014).

34. Jonathan Horowitz and Naz Modirzadeh, "How International Law Could Work in Transnational Non-international Armed Conflicts: Part I of a Two-Part Series," *Opinio Juris*, April 11, 2013, http://opiniojuris.org/2013/04/11/guest-post-how-international -law-could-work-in-transnational-non-international-armed-conflicts-part-i-of-a-two -part-series (accessed July 23, 2014).

35. "The Fragile States Index 2014 Interactive Grid," Fund for Peace, http://ffp .statesindex.org/rankings-2014 (accessed July 23, 2014).

36. See Stephen D. Krasner, "The Hole in the Whole: Sovereignty, Shared Sovereignty, and International Law," *Michigan Journal of International Law* 25 (2003– 2004): 1081, 1099.

37. On government being a prerequisite for recognition, see Article 1 of the Convention on the Rights and Duties of States (Montevideo Convention), December

26, 1933, 165 L.N.T.S. 19 (the independence requirement is read from the more formal condition of "capacity to enter into international relations").

38. Krasner, "The Hole in the Whole," 1089, 1091–1100.

39. Eric Schmitt, "International Effort Seeks to Counter Jihadists in Africa," *New York Times*, June 26, 2013, http://www.nytimes.com/2013/06/27/world/africa/nations -focus-antiterrorism-efforts-on-west-and-north-africa.html (accessed July 23, 2014).

Notes to Conclusion

1. Denise Grady, "Pathogen Mishaps Rise as Regulators Stay Clear," *New York Times*, July 19, 2014, http://www.nytimes.com/2014/07/20/science/pathogen-mishaps-rise-as -labs-proliferate-with-scant-regulation.html (accessed July 24, 2014); Laurie Garrett, "It's 10 O'clock—Do You Know Where Your Bubonic Plague Is?" *Foreign Policy*, July 11, 2014, http://www.foreignpolicy.com/articles/2014/07/10/it_s_10_o_clock_do_you_know _where_your_bubonic_plague_is_smallpox (accessed July 24, 2014).

2. Martin Rees, *Our Final Hour: A Scientist's Warning* (New York: Basic Books, 2004), 8.

3. Genesis, 2:16–17.

4. Genesis, 3:22–23.

5. Genesis, 11:6.

INDEX